THEOLOGICAL
INVESTIGATIONS

Volume VI

THEOLOGICAL INVESTIGATIONS

VOLUME VI
CONCERNING VATICAN COUNCIL II

by
KARL RAHNER

Translated by
KARL-H. and BONIFACE KRUGER

CROSSROAD · NEW YORK

1982

The Crossroad Publishing Company
575 Lexington Avenue, New York, N.Y. 10022

A translation of
SCHRIFTEN ZUR THEOLOGIE, VI
published by Verlagsanstalt Benziger & Co. A. G., Einsiedeln

Printed in the United States of America

Library of Congress Catalog Card Number: 82-071546
ISBN: 0-8245-0382-1

Nihil obstat: Nicholas Tranter, S.T.L., Censor.
Imprimatur: ✠ Patrick Casey, Vic. Gen. Westminster, 5th May, 1969.

CONTENTS

Presuppositions: The pluralism of sciences in general and of
theological sciences as such in particular – The existential
situation of the young theologian – The level of intelligence
of the theological student – Orientation towards practical
pastoral care.

The basic Theological Discipline.

The basic Theological Discipline in the Framework of the
whole of Theology: The position of philosophy – 'Old' and
'New' Fundamental theology – 'Mystery of Christ' – Unity
of formation – Further practical considerations – Basic
discipline and other subjects – Theology and the spiritual life
– Lay theologians.

PART THREE *Theological Anthropology*

I Freedom in the theological sense is freedom received from
and directed towards God. II Freedom as total and finalising
self-mastery of the subject. III Freedom regarded as a dialogic
capacity of love. IV The mystery of freedom. V Created freedom in an unavoidable situation of guilt. VI Freedom as
liberated freedom.

I The Reformation formula. II The Catholic rejection of the
Reformation formula *Simul justus et peccator*. III The properly
understood Catholic 'yes' to the formula *Simul justus et
peccator:* (a) Uncertainty of salvation. (b) The sinfulness of
man through 'venial' sins. (c) Man the pilgrim is just and
sinner at the same time.

Active love as the illuminating situation of modern man's
existence – Love of neighbour understood as love of God: the
declarations of scripture – The teaching of theology – Love
as a reflected and explicit mode of action and as an unconceptualised transcendental horizon of action – The anonymous
'Christianity' of every positively moral activity – Love of
neighbour as the basic moral activity of man – Love of
neighbour as man's manifestation of his wholeness and
essence – The encounter of the world and of man as the
medium of the original, unobjectified experience of God –
Love of neighbour as the primary act of love of God – The
topical significance of the love of neighbour for modern man's
knowledge of God.

PART FOUR *Contributions to a Theology of the Church*

A. THE PILGRIM CHURCH

B. THE BISHOP IN THE CHURCH

Foreword. I. II:1 The College of Cardinals. 2 Titular Bishops.
3 'Relative' and 'Absolute' Ordination. 4 The Essential Nature
of the Diocese. 5 The Bishop and his Priests. 6 The Unity of
Offices and Powers in the Church. 7 Exemption. 8 The duties
of the Bishop. 9 The Idea of the Patriarchate. 10 A Consultative Board of Bishops around the Pope.

ABBREVIATIONS

AAS   Acta Apostolicae Sedis
AKKR Archiv für Katholisches Kirchenrecht
CIC   Codex Iuris Canonici
DDC   Dictionnaire de Droit Canonique
DS   Denzinger-Schönmetzer, Enchiridion Symbolorum
GuL   Geist und Leben
LTK   Lexikon für Theologie und Kirche (3rd ed.
       unless otherwise indicated)
PG   Patrologiae graecae, ed. J. P. Migne (Paris 1844 –)
PL   Patrologiae latinae, ed. J. P. Migne (Paris 1857–)
RGG   Die Religion in Geschichte und Gegenwart
ThPQ Theologische Praktische Quartalschrift
Tüb.Th Quartalschrift. Tübinger Theologische Quartalschrift
TWNT Theologisches Wörterbuch zum Neuen Testament (Kittel)
ZKT   Zeitschrift für Katholische Theologie

Note. The author rarely quotes scripture directly in German, and when he does so he appears to make his own translations. In the present translation, accordingly, the author's renderings are retained, though of course the standard English versions have been consulted.

PREFACE

In due course, there now follows here a sixth volume of my *Theological Investigations*. Among these essays there are several until now unpublished. For this publication the essays printed here have been looked over once more to correct mistakes and stylistic and suchlike imperfections. As compared with their original form, the essays 'The Episcopal Office', 'The sinful Church in the decrees of Vatican II, and 'Anonymous Christians' have been enlarged by the addition of longer preliminary remarks, supplements or other insertions. Detailed notes of where the various items first appeared will be found at the end of the book.

Karl Rahner, S.J.

TRANSLATORS' NOTE

As in previous volumes, I wish to record once more with sincere gratitude and appreciation my indebtedness to Fr A. Monaghan for his invaluable help in reading the manuscript and for his valuable suggestions. As before, he has also been responsible for the composition of the two Indexes. I am also very grateful to Mr F. Kerr for his help in reading the proofs and to many other friends who have helped in various indirect ways.

St Andrew's College,   Karl-H. Kruger
Drygrange

I wish to add my expression of sincere gratitude to Fr Michael Mitchell O.F.M., M.A., and to Br Kenelm McShane, O.F.M., for their great assistance in reading the manuscript of my part of the translation and making their own most valuable comments and suggestions. I am also most grateful to Fr Ignatius Kelly, O.F.M., D.D., for his valued advice on certain points, and to Brs Isidore Faloona, Paul Roberts, Kenelm McShane and Antony Thouard, O.F.M., for their ready assistance in the typing of the final script.

St Mary's Friary,   Boniface Kruger, O.F.M.
East Bergholt

PART ONE

Christianity in the Present Age

I

THE MAN OF TODAY AND RELIGION

B Y giving these reflections the title 'the man of today and religion', immediate reference is made to a much wider question than can be dealt with really objectively in a short essay. The critical but sympathetic reader of what follows should therefore keep in mind that *in magnis voluisse sat est*.

The first and rather more introductory point we would like to make is that the man of today is never *merely* a man of today. This is indeed something he must not be. The quality – however elusive – which characterises contemporary man, is not and must not be thought or lived as the whole of his humanity, no matter how much it does give its own particular stamp to everything in it. You may say that this is a platitude, and yet it is more than that. Man has an infinitely profound yearning for unity. And rightly so. This is why he is always in danger of oversimplifying, in danger of wanting to design everything in his life from one *single* angle and of wanting to determine everything as a function of one single, definite entity which is familiar to him and controllable by him. This is true not only in the theoretical sphere but also in the realm of practical action. Thus contemporary man is in danger of wanting to be nothing but a man of today. What, for instance, we call the 'manager type', is not from a more profound point of view the person who works himself to death, for there has always been this type of person either of necessity or by choice. At a closer look, one will find the 'manager' in an existentially ontological and really ethical sense wherever someone can no longer think of anything in his life except as a derived function of his enterprises, whenever he simply identifies his life and his enterprises. This must inevitably lead to a perversion of the remaining realisations of his life, even when they are still present in a material sense and even when there still remains everything belonging to the life of man. Thus, for example, marriage, art, even religion, friendship and everything else in the life of

man can become the means of the representational forms of an enter-
priser's existence; they can be lived, consciously or not, as the continuation
of business life as such; the person can become quite blind to the meaning
of these other realities of human existence and all these other realisations
can come to bear no more pregnant and justifying meaning in themselves
than the limits of what they signify for business and its undertakings.
When this happens and when it is really true that an individual 'lived
completely for his business' – as is often stated in death notices in this or
some such stupid phrase – then there occurs a narrowing, a disappearance
of the meaning of human life which becomes fatal for man. To be sure life
today, constructed as it is through and through in a technological and
scientific way, can presumably provide more in terms of total human
fulfilment of existence than was possible in many occupations in the past;
for it demands more in total human realisation – in other words, more in
the creative, artistic and political fields, wider horizons, more understanding for new research – than most previous occupations. Yet it remains
true that man precisely as he is today and man as such cannot be simply
equated. The courage necessary to put up with this pluralism and to
accept it quite naturally, the courage not to think (in the words of an
old mystic) that one can attain everything 'in one go' – this belongs to the
basic conditions of an authentic and healthy human existence. Since the
part always lives by the whole and yet never is the whole, the modernity
of a man always exists by reason of the total human fulfilment of life. In
this way, the will or the desire to be nothing but precisely a man of today
and tomorrow, is not only truly inhuman but actually – whatever may
be the judgement of shortsighted experience – harms a man's authentic
'being-a-man-of-today'. It is simply a characteristic of the mysteries of
a finite existence that every part of it is different from every other and yet
cannot exist without the other and remains dependent on it.

Thus, when in what follows we inquire into the relationships between
religion and the specific 'todayness' of man, there is from the outset no
intention of suggesting that this particular quality alone could provide a
sufficient and acceptable basis for a man's religion. If man were no longer
authentically and fully a man – a poet, a lover, a man who faces up to the
ultimate mysteries of existence which are called finiteness, dread, the
beatitude of beauty, death and whatever other name may be given to all
the powers of a full human existence – he could neither in the long run be
a real man or a true *homo religiosus*. Religion in particular – this authentic

relationship to God the absolute, all-supporting and all-saving mystery of existence – is not just a particular area of human existence but rather at once its original and once more all-unifying unity, and hence draws its life also out of the totality, out of this one, still-to-be-unified existence. In every case where a man of today, in this his peculiar situation, is tortured by the impression gained from his experience of life that his being a man of today turns him, consciously or unconsciously, into an a-religious person, he should be asked to begin by asking himself whether he is not already more basically too little of a human being and too much merely a 'manager' (in the existentially ontological sense indicated above), someone who no longer wants to do more than one thing and yet seeks this one thing within the context of what is available, can be done and planned in this world instead of looking for it in the unspeakable mystery of God, the silent and unmanageable, who disposes over us.

1. These preliminary remarks had to be made so that what follows would not be misunderstood. We will now ask (from a very general theological point of view) in what exactly this 'modernity' consists, so that we can then consider what relationship to religion is given thereby in the man of today himself. To answer this question, let us state and then explain the following perfectly simple proposition: man today has clearly and definitively entered in his historical development into the phase of a peculiar creativeness and has become the rationally planning master of action and power both with regard to himself and with regard to his environment. This proposition is not meant to express the deepest and most original characteristic of the man of today, nor is it meant to imply that there was no creativeness in art, word and spirit, previous to this which might have realised this concept in an even more radical sense than is meant here. It suffices for our purposes if from this new type of creativeness referred to here we attain a generally comprehensible understanding of the religious situation of the man of today.

What, then, is meant *here* by the creativeness of the man of today? Man lives in an environment, he is always a being referred to the other – to the other with which he associates, which he accepts, on which he depends. Up till now, this reality surrounding him and sensibly supporting him was called 'nature'. Of course, man has always intervened in this nature. He did not stand still in the course of his history at the 'collector stage'; he very soon came to live no longer merely off what nature offered him but tamed the beasts, cultivated the land in a certain systematic way, invented, built houses and constructed tools for himself. Yet until very recently everything he thus created remained as it were implanted in the always still open realm of nature which man always encountered directly, to which he felt himself exposed and entrusted, with regards to which he felt himself near to its being though it remained quite independent of him. *Nature*, therefore, was for him something majestic which held sway and was powerful, something clothed directly with the simultaneously repelling and attracting splendour of the *numinous*, that which according to its own law nourishes, preserves, is wrathful and destructive. This meant also, however, that the rule of God (i.e. the real God) and the rule of nature were experienced and undergone in a peculiar unity. In it, He spoke; in it and through it both His grace and anger became in themselves tangible. The weather, the plague, lightning, the newly appearing springs, earthquakes, such and a thousand other happenings – in the very uncontrollableness and unforseeableness of their appearance and disappearance – were almost directly experienced as expressions of God's action on man itself. For such a man, in the sphere of open and uncontrollable nature, natural history and the divine history of salvation and damnation were really *one* or were at least fused into one another practically without any clearly distinguishable boundaries. Of course, even in this world of open, near and uncontrollable nature there was the commonplace and familiar, the predictable; already in the Old Testament we find here and there events which show that man recognised differences and degrees in his world of numinous nature conceived as the presence of direct divine rule, and that he did not experience everything with absolutely *equal* urgency as God's insurmountable power. Yet there really was no concept of a nature whose strict laws, to which one knew it was bound itself, could be ingeniously derived so that, armed as it were with this law stolen from nature, one could attack nature itself, force it, and emancipate oneself from the brutally unyielding character of these laws when directed against man, and thus in effect subjugate nature. Even for a religion which did not mistake nature for God – a religion which recognized the sun, the moon and the stars and even more so the elements of this earth as God's creatures, and did not simply experience them as appearances of God . . . even for such a religion, nature was nevertheless the viceroy of God and man had no choice but to show humble and silent obedience or to use prayer to beseech the Lord of this nature, he who reigned over all.

Today all this has changed enormously. Whether one wants to characterise this change as an essential one or merely as one of degree depends on the conception intended by such words and on the viewpoint from which one regards this change; this is not something, however, we wish to treat of here. This change, which in its essentials is connected with modern natural science and with this science's turning in towards the subject in philosophy at the beginning of the modern period, is certainly much greater than is commonly realised by Christians; furthermore, it will go on developing immensely in the coming ages of technology on the plane of microphysics and with the help of automation and cybernetics, and it will go on changing man's consciousness very much more. Of course, even today, there is still an open and uncontrolled nature in the existential sense of which we have just spoken. But in the attitudes of contemporary man, this nature has already become something like a residue, an island of folklore from past ages. I do not maintain that it is really this, but it is felt like this. Even the objectively justified change in man's relation to nature is without doubt immense. There is still the weather which we cannot control, but we no longer starve when the harvest is destroyed by bad weather in some particular region. We still fall ill, yet we now have exact conceptions of diseases and their laws; we can fight against them and have at least doubled the average life-expectancy of man. We no longer live *in* nature; we are *changing* it. We are no longer just thinking subjects distinguished intellectually and in a religious sense from sub-human nature, creatures who feel themselves superior to it in the awareness of a direct relationship to God, the Lord and creator of nature; this nature has been 'degraded' to being the matter and tool of man's creative activity even in its physical reality and even down to the brutal reality of everyday life. Wherever we turn in our sphere of existence, we encounter first of all for long stretches a nature made by ourselves and not the objects made by God. We encounter *our* light, our new materials, the means of locomotion invented by *us,* the plants and animals bred by *us,* and this today no longer as lucky coincidences of almost playful experiments but as the result of rational planning which coldly and almost arbitrarily determines its own goal and then commands that this goal be achieved. The tirades which one reads everywhere today on the subject of space-flight may in many cases be inspired by a childish imagination; they may often depict a still very Utopian and perhaps for all times unrealisable future. Yet it remains nevertheless a terrifying thing that one can today shoot a lump of earth formed by human hands at the goddess

Selene of the Greeks – the moon which, according to scripture, God set in his heavens as the light of the night. It remains something terrifying that one now simply experiences this moon as a lifeless ball made up of the same materials as are found on this earth, whereas previously (and this is still the case in the world-picture of the New Testament) the moon belonged to a sphere whose inhabitants were not subject to any temporal corruption or change and in which bodies moved fatelessly along their celestial orbits in an unchangeable, soft harmony with themselves. For contemporary man, nature is no longer the lofty viceroy of God, one which lies beyond man's control, but instead has become the material which he needs so as to experience himself in his *own role of free creator* and so as to build *his* own world for himself according to his own laws. Of course, it is true that this material of human creativeness has laws proper to itself which still weigh heavily on man. It is true that this human creativeness consequently subjects itself, whether it likes it or not, to what is alien and given to it; it is not pure creativeness as we acknowledge it of God; it does not come completely from within and it is not simply a law unto itself; it does not evoke matter and form out of nothing, and hence this creativeness of man, which has to deal with the laws of matter, is naturally also in every case a growth in obedience and 'servitude' in the face of an alien law ... but it is creation in a knowing, willing and mastering sense, a creativeness which forces nature into its own service.

This fact, however, means that man is delivered in a real and not merely figurative sense into his own hands; the world surrounding him is of his own making, and what he encounters first of all in this environment is himself. We cannot enter further here into this change, this subjectification of man within the real, directly experienced world. We do not dispute the fact either that different men arrive in very different measures at this experience of the peculiarity of the man of today – of his rationality, his technology and cybernetics, his active creativeness – according to differences in occupation, age, breadth of immediate surroundings and culture and according to the different degrees of courage with which they allow or, on the contrary, suppress this experience. We do not dispute the fact that clerics in all denominations make this experience slowest and most reluctantly of all, a fact that follows from the blessings and dangers of such a 'spiritual, religious life'. But, on the whole, it is inevitably true in an ever increasing measure that the man of today and tomorrow is the man who has really become a subject: a man who is responsible for himself not merely in a theoretical, contemplative sense but in real practice; a man who has carried through the Copernican revolution from 'cosmocentrism' to 'anthropocentrism', not merely as a thinker and not merely in his religious attitude but in practical life itself. He plans, he is in direct contact with that form of science which is not content merely to contemplate the world aesthetically and philosophically but reflects (even in its theoretical branches) on how one can master and overpower nature and force it to give up into our possession the secret and law of action. He determines new goals and tasks, he freely invents new needs which he himself creates and promises to fulfil. If we look at the art of the so-called manipulation of man, at advertising and at propaganda, he is in danger of regarding even *man* himself simply as material which he forms according to his own intentions and self-chosen ends. In practice and experience, he really stands in the realm of nature as in a quarry or on a building site on which must first be constructed the world in which man wants to live as in his own world, the world in which he encounters once more his own reflection: he is *almost* like his own creator and God.

2. Before we go on to ask what this experience of creativeness and hominisation of the world of man involves for a relationship to God and hence religion in general, it is necessary to make a further observation on the twofold level of the history of the spirit and of theology, viz. that the development described above is something inevitable and, in the last analysis, such a development corresponds to the nature of Christianity itself. Any romantic yearning for pure nature, for its numinous rule, its pristine beauty and fruitfulness, is and remains romanticism. For even where we protect nature – where we establish national parks and lay out lawns, guard against river-pollution and try to prevent the extermination of whales – the nature which thus survives is once more a nature *we* have freely chosen not to destroy, one laid out by us, our garden and not nature in the raw. Even this nature, therefore, is no longer the one in which the ancients lived as part of the whole, but a nature made by us, artificial nature, a nature which is a refined art and which once more reflects the image of man. This development is inevitable. There is no need to ascribe to this development the meaning given by the Marxist ideology, nor does one need to have very triumphal and happy sentiments about it. It exists and will continue to exist. Man, having once discovered this possibility, will never now give up being the master: a master and creator of his own world, who has to fight furiously, suffer a thousand defeats, and yet wins

more and more new intoxicating victories over nature with a view to its subjugation. What is even more significant is that this development, when looked at from an ultimate viewpoint of the history of the spirit and the nature of Christianity, is not something which has arisen in spite of, contrary or parallel to Christianity, even though this truth – by a gentle irony of God – is recognised consciously last of all by the churchman. Rather, this development springs from the very nature of Christianity itself and is a necessary moment in its own history. This is not altered by the fact that we can discover this connection only once this new phase of history has already begun, and that we have not really foreseen it. It is not altered by the fact that we have often experienced this history in practice merely in fear, uneasiness and petty complaints, not wanting to understand that it was a matter of the history of Christianity's own reality, of a historical phase which this Christianity did not indeed always possess (otherwise it would not after all experience and suffer history) but which nevertheless belongs to the unfolding and realisation of its own, essentially historical life. Nowhere more than in the Christian religion is man the free partner of God, so much so that he does not passively undergo his eternal salvation but must *achieve it in freedom* (even though this achievement considered as his free act is given to man by God, his creativeness and grace). Right on the first page of God's sacred book we read: 'subdue the earth'. The Christian could not and did not need to foresee what tasks and history was hidden in these words. But man, understood in a Christian sense, is someone who is conscious of being in a most radical way a subject of freedom and directly present to God. Man in the Christian sense is someone who has really understood that nature, which means everything surrounding him, is not God but merely a creature of God which is lower than man who is a partner of God himself. The Christian is someone who knows that in man himself, and only in him, has the world become – in the incarnation – God's very own history. He knows therefore that he, man, stands over against this creature on the side of God and that he therefore cannot really regard it quite simply as God's deputy in relation to himself but rather that he himself has in the God-man become God's deputy towards nature. This man and Christian, I say, had one day to come to discover that this basic Christian relationship to the world and nature is not only realised in the interiority of faith, conscience and prayer, but also in and by means of the world itself, in an act of insight by means of worldly science and the consequent action of subjugation of nature. Thus the Christian can also see this necessity and the Christian originality of this development perfectly well as a task demanded of him by his Creator and grace-giving partner.

3. What, then, does this characteristic of the contemporary human situation mean when looked at from the point of view of its religious relevance? This is the question we must ask ourselves now; in it alone our whole reflection really reaches its decisive subject.

To begin with, it must be stated quite soberly, courageously and honestly that at first sight and when first experienced, this situation represents a great difficulty and a very far-reaching burden for the religious relationship of man to God. God – so it would seem at first sight – has actually become more distant for man since nature seems to have been 'degraded' by the action of man into becoming the material for his own creative acts. Through the discovery of its manageable and manipulable laws, the world has certainly come to be at the disposal of man, but precisely by reason of this fact it appears as a thick wall separating man from God. It seems that man only discovers in nature, and in what he makes of it, a 'world': the laws of matter and his own image. Of course, one can always say: precisely this world is the one created by God, the laws man discovers are those imposed by God and indeed what man does himself, he does by virtue of his spiritual and free nature created and called by name by the same God. But all this, however true it is and remains, in no way alters the fact that this world has become *more godless*. What happens in it, is no longer experienced – at least no longer as immediately and massively – as the action of God in and on the world. Miracles are no longer encountered every day, the extraordinary has now become almost exclusively the province of science which is asked to explain it and thus bring it down to the ordinary. The misery of this world is not felt as a challenge to prayers of entreaty to the Lord of nature but rather as a challenge to an even more determined combat with the powers of nature until these have been conquered or tamed and contained. The world remains 'demythologised', secularised and hominised even though this by no means signifies that it has been humanised since, even out of this hominised world, there can rise once more the spectre of the inhumanity of man himself in the face of the devastation of nature by ABC-weapons and similar horrors. But this concept of a *'demythologised'* and *hominised* world implies to begin with an inevitable distancing of God, a paling and incomprehension of the idea of God, an exiling of God from the world and a decategorising of God. Anyone who is unwilling to acknowledge this fact in view of his own experience, must allow himself to be asked whether his experience of God is really so strong or whether it is merely a friendly relic from earlier ages which has been passed on to him by tradition, just as even the most modern capitalist still decorates the walls of his modern villa with the pictures of his forefathers. He must allow himself to be referred to the modern, world-wide atheism and the (at least apparent) disappearance of the capacity for religious realisation which reveal in social extension and in macroscopic enlargement what he does not see or simply does not wish to see in his own individual experience, perhaps on account of its very limitations. In this respect it is also no use saying that besides and far above nature we have God's directly revealed word in the scriptures. Long before we can even begin to *hear* or *read* this Word, we are already imprisoned in this world of today, as sceptics and rationalists, people brought up on scientific and historical derivations and explanations. We experience even the scriptures at first as an echo of a long-lost world, as an expression of a world-picture no longer familiar to us. Only with great effort and much spiritual pain and heart-searching can we manage to produce a successful translation of the scriptures into our own language, that it might no longer appear to us merely as a document of a past and perished age in the history of religion.

If it is true, however, that this European profaneness of the world is an inevitable fact, itself of *Christian* origin, a fact which today – in the age of the *one* political world, of assisted development, rationalisation and technologisation of the whole world – has become the fate of all men and peoples, then this profanity of the world which seems to make the world godless and God world-less, must after all have a *positive* meaning and must be an undeniable *religious task*. This is in fact the case.

First of all, the world of men, even today, remains ultimately an uncontrollable world whose future is dark and unknowable. In making this statement, we do not mean so much that even today the material of creative man imposes laws and limits on this man, that even today he does not yet dominate this world. We do not mean to merely say that even today the material of human creativeness is still brittle and hard, that man ultimately still eats his bread by the sweat of his brow, that he cultivates earth which is full of thistles and thorns. Even though this really characterises the whole of man's creativeness right down to its very roots and to its proudest heights – a characteristic quality which discloses this *creativeness* as something belonging to the *creature* and makes it suffer under the weight of creaturehood – we do not even merely mean that today, as always, this modern titan is a poor mortal in all his Promethean pride; that as someone dying alone and miserably even in modern clinics, he still experiences as he has always done the radical and ultimate 'no' to his absolute autonomous power. Though he be banished to his lonely death, which no one may disturb, far away from his own in a clinic with all the latest comforts for dying, he always remains the individual, one whose place can be taken by no one else precisely *in such a sense* that he cannot gain comfort or satisfaction about his lot from the thought that others after him, bearing the torch of proud progress and titanic development, will carry on the course for this in each case ends in death.

Over and above all this, we mean something quite different here. We mean that the uncontrollable and fate itself arise once more out of what man controls and plans, that things are such that man experiences his own orientation as something he himself cannot control, not only in unmastered and open nature but also just as much in his own creations.

In point of fact, are not man's proudest and best thought-out plans even today always also the march into an unforeseeable, *unplanned future* full of surprises? Does not man feel himself today more than ever before exposed to an existential anguish which proves that his planned and directed action is always and even more than ever before changed into the unforeseen suffering of a dark fate? Is not his freedom, which seems to have itself under control, always the daring of an obscure futurity, the exposing of oneself to something still to come which remains unknown? Have not even the communistic planners of a rationalised future of Utopian glory ever seen no more at best than the development of the next few years? And is not this inevitable, since every act of freedom in its objective nature faces once more the obscure freedom at least of those who hold power on this earth in the succeeding age – those who understand precisely these plans and planned realisations as once more the material *for* decisions to be treated in a purely arbitrary manner – those who out of a thousand possibilities (which grow in numbers the more powerful and free man becomes) arbitrarily choose *one*?

Indeed, man continues to live in the land of the *uncontrollable*, and out of an uncontrollable nature has come a world of man which he has indeed made himself but which by this very fact becomes even more threatening, more uncontrollable and more sinister. The free man experiences himself in his very freedom as someone condemned to freedom, as someone who freely inaugurates the uncontrollable. He may still be intoxicated to some extent with the emancipation which he has won for himself *vis-à-vis* a *nature* which was impinging directly upon him and threatening him. He will soon notice, however, and experience more and more – and the wise have already had this experience even today – that his creative freedom experiences *itself* as a freedom which is disposed and dares to advance into the immeasurable darkness. Yet to whom should man confide this disposed being, from whom is he to accept it, where can he know his daring freedom to be safe, this freedom which falls into obscurity? If the secret – the absolute, silent and infinite secret – no longer comes to him so clearly and directly from his natural surroundings, it now breaks out of his own being. We call this secret *God*. The more we become what we are – the free and powerful, the masters of the world – the more we look to him in whom this disposed and never self-possessed mastery can be confided . . . and that is God. If the fear of freedom is not merely theoretical but becomes practical fear, then a certain realisation rises for the wise man of today out of the ground of freedom – slowly and quietly, but more powerfully than ever before – the realisation of the disposed nature of existence before God. This happens precisely when this disposed being is no longer mediated by the dispensation of nature but has become more directly present to God than ever before since it is experienced in that freedom itself which seems to be disposing and not disposed.

Furthermore, the more powerful man becomes and the more he subjugates nature to himself, the greater becomes his *responsibility*, the more radically he is delivered up to himself, the more his possibilities reach beyond his own individual circle into the fate of more and more people, and the more everyone becomes gradually but in very truth responsible for everyone else. It has been said often before that the moral progress of humanity has not kept up with its scientific, technological and civilising progress, that man becomes more and more the barbarian who can produce nothing out of the possibilities of existence apart from destruction, threats and superficiality. It has been said often before, but does that mean it is true? The watchful and knowing man at any rate can draw completely new experiences of the *burden* of responsibility and of the *seriousness* of life out of his situation of creativeness with regard to a subject nature and out of his real and not merely theoretical personalisa-

tion. After all, it is not really as if the man of modern science and technology must necessarily and inevitably be the less humane and the less
moral man. At a closer look, the feeling-for-life of the modern scientist
and technologist gives rise just as much if not more than ever before to
an attitude of objectivity, humility, responsibility, sobriety, of simple and
silent seriousness, which in a way are the human counterpart to the quiet,
exact objectivity of fully automated works in which, despite the absence of
human beings, there are invested immense human qualities. In fact, a
genuine relationship to God is realised, even though perhaps quite
unconsciously and reticently, precisely where new virtues arise out of
this new situation or where virtues can be or actually are newly developed;
this relationship is realised wherever man discovers that he has more
responsibility because he and the world around him are left more than
ever to his own decisions, when freedom is experienced as responsibility
(and where it otherwise punishes itself with the absurdity of self-cancella-
tion); it is realised, whenever such a responsibility is really accepted and
when this accepted responsibility is absolute (and then only is it what it
should be), as inescapable and eternally valid. This is because the last,
absolute reason for all responsible freedom and power – for that unspeakable, silent listening as to how we should act responsibly – is called
God. And when we speak of God, we mean precisely that being whom
we encounter – even when we do not name him and shyly look away
from him – when we see the power and extent of our real freedom bear
down on us as an immense burden and when we do not cowardly run
away from this truth of our existence.

A third factor should be mentioned regarding the question as to how
the contemporary creative situation of man develops and renders present
in our life the correctly understood, purified and matured religious
element. We have spoken of the secularity and 'demythologisation' of the
world. It is quite true that the man of the past was more exposed to nature
than we are. But nature was for him at the same time 'mother nature' of
whom one could expect (if we may express it this way) the caprice of
mildness, of gay surprise and of indulgence. It was easier than today to
have the courage to invoke coincidence and to trust in 'luck', the goddess
Fortuna with her cornucopia. Of course, even today chance still belongs
to the unavoidable factors of human existence and this element of chance
suddenly appears even in the midst of the most precise calculations of the
natural scientist and the technologist, like a cruel caprice or the whimsical

gamble of a goddess, bringing destruction or blessing. But on the whole, the world of man has become *sober*, *objective*, and to some extent depersonalised (one might almost say: precisely because man, the person, has subjected himself to it). The world which man has constructed for himself is hard, schematic and impoverished since it has been constructed by a very finite being who must economise because his life is so short. Yet man is sensitive to all this just the same. Whence otherwise the romantic dreams and the yearning after the old, gay fullness of a lost nature? Thus man suffers under the secularity of his world, under its hardness and impoverishment, under its rational exactness, all of which he finds it very difficult to soften. If, however, we could investigate this phenomenon of man's suffering under a self-constructed world and of the reason for this suffering in his own world more exactly, then it would become clear that the reason for it is the finite, mortal nature of man, his limited nature, his fear because of his limitations, a fear which he then impresses today also on his world and which he finds reflected in his own creations. The hard, impassive reality of this world – the new cruelty which he cannot help communicating to his own world (and even though it is his) so as to enable it to survive and not collapse – would then appear simply as just another, new and changed *form of his mortality* and of his exposure to death. It would become clear that all this is part of that *prolixitas mortis*, that continuing presence of death in the midst of life in all the dimensions of man, with which the ancient thinkers about man and his death were already familiar. It can then be said, however, with all truth that – for the Christian – this accepted, never-ending suffering of this hard, stark, exact world which man has created for himself as the objectification of his own finite freedom, is in very truth a participation in the death of Christ. It is not merely a case of our even today having still to undergo death at the end of life and of this *death* being existentially still as hard as in the old days. No, this death of man – the ever-present, secret essence in all life itself – has entered also into those possibilities of human existence which the man of today has conquered for himself for the first time. Such a death, and above all the Christian nature of such a death, may be very anonymous; the stupid and dull may merely suffer it without recognising it, when they imagine they are merely living their life and think that death does not come until afterwards, at some distant date in the future. The wise man of today knows that in life he is always dying, and also that he comes face to face with this death in the sober hardness of the world, a world which he has created for himself in order to make life easier for himself in his exposure to an inhuman nature, and which now appears itself as the pain which he must cause himself so as to be able to go on existing. If, however, he accepts this pain and the death which resides in all – even modern – human existence as such, then this existence enters into the saving death-agony of the redeemer, whether man be conscious of it or not. For this death of the Lord is precisely *the* death, i.e. the fate inescapable for man becomes a victory because it itself has been assumed by God himself.

Furthermore, we have already indicated previously that, in spite of all sinful and unbelieving distortions, the structure of our age is in its basic traits not only not unchristian but has ultimately been created by Christianity itself. Christianity demythologises the world and makes it the material of the human person: because only thus does man become completely what he should be, viz. the free, self-responsible subject before God (and this even in the realm of his 'belonging-to-the-world' and in his exposure to nature), and because only God dawns so completely on man as the one He is for the Christian. For the Christian, God cannot be regarded as the creator who realises himself first of all in his world, giving it his splendour for this purpose; rather, he is the one who lives above everything which is or can be thought to be outside him, infinitely exalted in his own but for us inaccessible, eternally promised glory. It follows from this, however, that the positive *creative relationship to the world* – in the way in which contemporary man is beginning to experience it and as it shows itself in anyone who 'undertakes' something, who 'gets to the bottom' of the world and its reasons so as to dominate it – can be experienced and accepted quite impartially in the man of today, the 'entrepreneur', as a factor in the correctly understood Christianity. Of course, Christianity is critical and sober even in this feeling-for-life. But this is so because it is sober, sceptical and watchful with regard to *everything*, since everything can become a curse and serve as an excuse and means for the pride of a man who closes himself against God. Yet Christianity has no reason for being more critical and careful about this particular feeling-for-life than it was about the good old days. The old *and* the new world belong to the 'wicked' world. But this is no more true of the new than of the old; although this is not meant to deny that, where the possibilities for man's action in the world grow enormously, sinful activity too can take on apocalyptic proportions, and that the Christian

– the only courageous and true sceptic in a world full of intramundane analgesics of existence stemming from liberal or communistic origins – must honestly take account of the actual existence of *such* sin. Yet, why should the experience of creative power, creative responsibility, creative planning almost into the realm of the immeasurable and utopian, be less becoming for a Christian than the existential understanding of previous ages? If the world is a world of becoming that originates from God; if in man and in his creative act within the world it only attains what it has always been, and it is always meant to be in its origins from God; and if this world of becoming, with all its finiteness and transitoriness and guilt, is a world which in the God-man reaches eternally into the very life of God himself and has become *his* history . . . then it is impossible to see why the Christian should face the new age as one more dangerous for him than previous ones, a situation about which he as a Christian can only be happy with a bad conscience or a situation which can only lead him away from God and not closer to him. The Christian can get tied up in this world. Yet surely he discovers God only if – radically – he walks its ways right to the end, and not at all if he does not enter these ways and instead takes refuge in a time which no longer exists or which is gradually disappearing. If it is true, as Claudel has said, that man must not be dead so that God may live, if God's glory can only ultimately grow in the world if man's glory grows in it, if our ascents and not *merely* our falls praise and confess Him, if He has created not only the heavens but also the earth . . . then, though this alone does not indeed make the mere existence of this world created by man to be as such a service of God which must be rendered to God by the spiritual creature . . . but it means it is part of it.

4. Two things must be added. Firstly, it must be stated even more clearly than we have up until now that (to use a phrase of E. Schillebeeckxs) this profane world in its undiminished profaneness is not indeed a sacralised world yet nevertheless – at least in the Catholic understanding of the world – it is a sanctified one. What we call grace – innermost divinisation of the creature from its very roots and its openness to the immediacy of God himself – does not merely begin at the same point as does the explicit message of faith, Church, sacrament, worship or the written Word of God. All these explicitly sacral elements are rather the necessary, divinely disposed, reflex realisation of that divinisation of the world freely caused by God's favour yet truly caused by him, in which God has always already accepted and sanctified the whole world in all its

dimensions. This sacralising appearance of the secret acceptance of the whole world is certainly itself a moment and a historical phase of this sanctification of the world from its very origins. But appearances and what appears, sacrament and grace, are not the same. This grace-caused sanctification of the profane world which – precisely because it is sanctified by grace – must remain profane (since the grace of God must still hide its victorious power so as to leave room for man's freedom), always remains until the end of its history in permanent opposition to guilt, and thus the world in its concrete constitution remains always the humanly inexplicable unity of God's 'yes' and man's 'no'. God has, however, given his effective yes to the whole world in its innermost depths from the very beginning, and hence – and not out of itself alone – the world falls everywhere into the abyss of the secret of his love, whenever it follows its path to the very end. The Church with her Word simply proclaims that God's grace is more powerful than man's guilt. This does not mean that the Church and the sanctified world are identical in their extent, mission and success. It may be difficult to discover the silent mystery of the absolute nearness of God in this world of today ... but it is everywhere and continues to the end.

Secondly, in her relationship to the sanctified but not sacralised world, the Church is still very much in a state of becoming. This is so theoretically because she is only beginning to learn the theological dialogue with the existential understanding of the man of this world, and because her theology – even at the Council – was, and inevitably had to be, still much more a working out of the latent possibilities of her own past than new beginnings on the soil of contemporary man. It is so also in practice, because the Church can still give up quite a lot of historically sacralised ground which she has in the past rightly cultivated but which does not belong to her for ever, and because the Church as an institution must still learn in many ways that she can no longer *directly* administer ethically and religiously all the questions and answers which arise or are looked for in the realm of the creative possibilities of this day and age. Such a reflection on the eternally old and new gospel in dialogue with the new world and such an emancipation of the world into things proper to it which cannot be administered by the Church as an institution, do not in any way signify a capitulation in the face of an autonomous understanding of existence of the man of today nor a retreat from a merely profane world into a merely sacral realm. The gospel promises its last mystery of salvation even in time to come to a world always sanctified by God, a mystery which it can forget or culpably suppress. Christians too, as distinct from the official element of the Church, are always called upon and called in grace to be both in the world and above the world. This is so because these positions are not the same and yet both reach their fulfilment only in the other, even when no one can administer the unity of both by further planning. Nevertheless the glory must be given – in the renunciation of the power over this unity – to God alone.

Hence (and in this way we take up again one of our initial reflections in a more extended form), the experience of the creative power of man, the experience of the withdrawal of the self-created world into a new sphere beyond the power of man, the experience of the staggering responsibility of creative man, the experience of the repelling hardness and sobriety of the new world and finally the just mentioned experience to the effect that the worldly creativeness of man can never adequately determine his life and that he can therefore never be a mere 'entrepreneur' . . . all these experiences and attitudes remain together for the one man in his existence in a pluralism impossible for him to administer. He experiences himself as the one who has never only one task, who can never invest his life only in one ideal, who must 'go out' to many things and who can never realise as something calculated and dominated by him the sum total of these his attitudes so as to enjoy himself in the achievement of such a synthesis. Man experiences himself in this undominated pluralism as a mere project, as a task, which recedes all the more from man into mystery the more he achieves the reality of his life. Once more man actively discovers in this experience what is really meant by 'God'. God is that mystery of infinite, unspeakable, saving fullness which has summoned forth man's beginning, holds together his uncontrollable manifoldness and guarantees it in its unity; he is that mystery which takes up that fulfilment of existence which escapes man himself, if only it has been willingly aimed at with a view to this mystery.

2

A SMALL QUESTION REGARDING THE CONTEMPORARY PLURALISM IN THE INTELLECTUAL SITUATION OF CATHOLICS AND THE CHURCH

I T is true, and indeed obvious, that it is a bad thing to be one of those people who are always merely proposing questions and then leave the answers to others. Such people, who are always simply bringing up 'problems' which they declare to be insoluble, think they are wiser than others ... yet in so far as they do not feel sufficient responsibility to contribute to the answer as much as they have the courage to pose in the question, they ultimately belong merely to the category of children and fools, one of whom can put more questions than a hundred wise men can answer. Nevertheless, it is allowable from time to time to put forward a question without immediately providing an answer to it. This can happen above all when the clear formulation of the question, one which otherwise disturbs the intellectual life of the man of today only vaguely and unconsciously, is itself already a first step towards an answer. A further point to be noted is that when one states that something is 'new', was not 'like this' before, then such a statement can be correct and indeed of the highest significance even though a metaphysician who explores man's being may maintain that this was 'really' always so. To this metaphysical statement one can then reply: yes, perhaps, but it is nevertheless 'essentially' very much a matter of the degree to which this was the same yesterday and today. The reason for saying all this will become clear to the reader in a moment.

A STATEMENT OF THE SITUATION

Many realisations, proofs, solutions of questions, etc., are basically necessary to lay the rational, apologetic foundations of the Catholic

world-view related to the Christian faith: that there is a God, that there is
more than just matter, that there is a spiritual soul, that determinism is not
right, that Jesus of Nazareth has declared himself to be the Son of God,
that he founded a Church, that he was not mistaken about the end of the
world, that St Peter was not merely a sort of 'caliph' for a time in Jerusalem and then disappeared again, that Pope Vigilius did not solemnly
approve a heretical formula, that . . . etc. The point we are trying to make
is that such and a thousand more facts, questions, problems, solutions
and difficulties are significant for a 'world-view'. But each is so in a
different way and to a different extent and yet each in some way and
indeed many to a very high degree. Not all the insights and problems of
men and their sciences are like this.

It is certainly often difficult to say whether something is significant or
not in a 'world-view' sense. Is, for example, the question of the continuous
expansion of the cosmos significant or not in a 'world-view' sense? Has
quantum physics something to do with the faith or not? Nevertheless,
there are questions which are irrelevant for a world-view. For example,
the question about the development of the fashion of wearing beards
among the Sumerians, or the fashion in Egypt under the fifteenth
dynasty. There are a great number of such questions and bits of knowledge which are irrelevant for a world-view. The development of the
modern sciences and arts during the last few hundred years tends in a
sense precisely towards the creation of a kingdom of the spirit, of truth
and culture, of the beautiful and the interesting. This kingdom, however,
is on the one hand a creation of man and, on the other hand, it is irrelevant
for a 'world-view'; it is 'profane', i.e. something which had scarcely any
existence previously because man was occupied either with 'transcendence' (as one is accustomed to say nowadays) or with the simple assertion
of biological existence, these two spheres touching directly on each other.

This brings us to the real statement: in previous ages (until roughly the
end of the nineteenth century) an educated person could *himself* have at
least an approximate over-all view of the whole field of insights and questions relevant to a world-view and given or imposed as tasks on his age; he
was thus able, as it were at first hand, to form more or less adequately *direct*
judgements about world-view questions. Nowadays, however, the number
of such questions has grown to such an extent that no individual can
personally enter into a direct contact with the *whole* mass of such questions,
methods, insights, difficulties, and so on. It should be noted right away in

this connection that in matters of a 'world-view' it is *not* possible in the very nature of things (at least not in the same sense or in the same way and to the same extent as in the 'profane' sciences) to have teamwork and simply to take over the results achieved by others. In Christian circles and in the affairs of the Church, however, there is not yet a willingness to face up fairly and squarely to this fact.

We are forming experts in the Church for everything and anything, and if possible investigating all questions significant for a world-view with the help of such experts, in the fields of the natural sciences, sociology, the political sciences, the science of statistics, cybernetics, logistics, etc. This is all very good and praiseworthy. But all these efforts do not alter the fact just stated. The world-view expert in the field of sociology has no idea and *cannot* have any idea of the problems of the investigation into the life of Jesus. The ecclesiastic who knows something today in the field of palaeontology (unless he is a genius of the dimensions of an archangel) will certainly be a greenhorn (even though he may not know or admit this) in the field of real theology and philosophy, even though he is a priest and has completed his philosophical and theological studies in the seminary. It just cannot be otherwise. Today, every science – even in what is significant for a world-view – is so many-sided and difficult, so complicated in its methods, so vast in its field of research, that at best a single person may still understand something of *one* science while being and remaining a dabbler in all others. Furthermore, if one has no illusions and does not underestimate the situation, one will realise that all these sciences are such that their 'results' apart from the research and efforts leading to these results can be communicated only in small part, or even not at all. Only in a manner bordering on the laughable can the physicist still tell a layman what has emerged from his researches. One has to travel the road oneself in order to reach the goal in any real sense . . . and it is precisely this that is impossible today, or at least is possible only to a very small extent.

All we have to do to realise this is to enter properly into genuine conversation with a scientist engaged in a subject different from our own. Depending on his temperament, he will be more or less happy to tell us something of his problems and the results of his science . . . but he will never get the impression that I, the other, could talk with him on equal terms about the relevance of his science for a world-view. The modern brain specialist will always get the impression that I, who simply have not studied the physiology of the brain for twenty years, could not possibly appreciate the real weight of his world-view problems and the real extent of his results, no matter how intelligently I try to join in the conversation by using my general, formal philosophical training. He need not even necessarily be right in this impression, but he gets this impression and cannot free himself from it. He has studied brain-physiology for twenty years, and this fact is itself simply a . . . fact, making him a man with a different outlook from mine quite independently of any objective or logical validity of his knowledge and arguments. The bare fact of his long, 'one-sided' studies, from which he can never abstract since otherwise he could not achieve what is demanded of him in his own special field, makes him a conversational partner of a type that did not exist among the educated of previous ages when they talked to each other. This mere fact makes him incapable of being a philosopher or a theologian, even though he may be interested in philosophy or theology 'on the side' and as a hobby; it makes him – even by the mere pressure of the multiplicity of his associations, complexes of feeling, etc. – quite a different sort of man from what I can ever be, and this necessarily so. In the old days everyone knew or at least was capable of knowing roughly the same sort of things, and in cases where this equality was not present right away it could at least be established in principle in a short time. Furthermore, any differences between the concrete experiences of different people which could not be overcome, were also quite unimportant for a world-view.

The example just referred to also applies, of course, in reverse. Which theologian has not at some time had the feeling in conversation with natural scientists that it is simply impossible to find the sufficiently exact 'wave-length' in the other which would be necessary if he is really to understand what one is talking about as a theologian? Who has not at some time, in conversation with the average doctor, in practice capitulated when faced with the blockage – almost inevitably brought about by medical studies – of the really and existentially necessary openness to certain aspects of moral questions in the field of medicine? The strangest experience of all, however, is to find that ecclesiastics and theologians – who are deputed as it were to be the representatives of the Faith and the Church in the camp of the other contemporary sciences, so that they are taken there as the experts and confidants of both parties – usually become just as exclusively interested in the other 'subject' as the other representatives of these sciences. They do not, of course, normally cease to be good Christians and priests but they usually become just as one-sided in the field of their science, just as method-obsessed representatives of their profane sciences as all the others.

So it happens, for example, that a Teilhard de Chardin is recognised by theologians as a natural scientist but not as a philosopher and theologian, whereas the natural scientist will think of him as a theologian who has not quite managed to keep up to date with the most recent findings of the natural sciences. Thus it happens (to give another example) that ecclesiastical explanations which are worked out by theologians and which deal with matters belonging in the first place to the profane sciences, are often felt by the representatives of the particular subject to be indeed well-intentioned yet not quite up to date. One need only think for example of the allocution of Pius XII to the astronomers or certain declarations about psycho-analysis, etc. Furthermore, all these strange relationships cut both ways. The natural scientists, too, often imagine they are 'strong' in philosophy or theology, and so make painfully insufficient contributions in these fields when they enter into questions of a world-view. Far from taking offence at this, we must even demand it, since they should be interested in such questions.

These relationships obtain not only between philosophy and theology, on the one hand, and the natural sciences on the other but they exist also, for example, between philosophy and theology themselves. Philosophy is no longer such today that it would be possible to train a young and gifted candidate for the priesthood to become a philosopher within two to three years, so that he could seriously understand the problems of the philosophy of today and be able to take part in real philosophical discussions. It cannot even be said that this is still possible at least with regard to questions in philosophy which are relevant for a world-view and for faith. It is all the more impossible if one means by this a formation on the basis of real philosophy such as it is practised today. (Whether it is possible to bring the young student of theology in contact with these questions of philosophy in some other way, and what form this process would take, is quite a different question and precisely the question we are posing here.)

The same is true of the historical sciences which deal with questions and answers relevant to a world-view. The average theologian of today cannot really be trained to be a specialist in questions of the science and history of religion, the history of the Near East, biblical criticism, the relationship of primitive Christianity to its Jewish and Greek environment, investigation into the life of Jesus, etc. etc. Whatever is true about the practical incommensurability between various sciences which can no longer be overcome directly, such as we have seen to exist between the natural sciences and theology, is equally applicable here. It is not a question here, it must be remembered, of *contradictions* between the answers obtained by theology, as well as faith, and by these sciences. Our question goes beyond such a possibility and the task of removing such apparent contradictions. Our question concerns the impossibility of even acquiring the minimum of direct acquaintance with these other sciences and their questions and findings as would seem to be necessary 'in itself' for a theologian and his problems in constructing a world-view. If I do not happen to be a specialist in exegesis, can I really take part in a discussion of even such a simple and small question as, for instance, the one regarding the meaning and range of Mt 16:18? Yet I should be able to do so even as a simple theologian and not just as an exegete, since it is after all a question of the highest significance for any world-view.

What can an average Catholic parish priest seriously say today to a biblical expert on the Protestant side? A little example like this may help to compare the situation of today with that of the sixteenth century, and help us to understand what our statement really means. We might express the assertion we are seeking in a different somewhat mathematical form, and say that the total number of possible and necessarily relevant problems and insights necessary for a world-view to be found in any sphere is so great today in contrast with previous ages, that a single person trying to acquire direct knowledge and come to terms with the matter as a whole can no longer master it all in a single lifetime and integrate it into a world-view.

As has already been said, this assertion has nothing to do yet with the question about whether and to what extent these sciences result in particular conflicting situations amongst themselves. Our assertion is significant even apart from this possibility and refers to a completely new intellectual situation for the man of today whether such apparent or real conflicts take place or not. It means, even in this more limited sense, the assertion of a pluralism in the intellectual world of today; a pluralism that can no longer be overcome by any positive and direct integration of all our knowledge and problems into a unified world picture. Unlike the case of the purely natural sciences where one can advance further and further even though no one any longer understands everything, the integration we speak of – if it were actually to take place – would be possible only in the minds of many individuals as such, for the transference of knowledge in this field into an objective scheme (e.g. into an apparatus, etc., constructed by others and then merely used by me, etc.) cannot be still admissible when used as a conveyance of knowledge.

THE QUESTION

If the individual person in spite of all this is to be capable of accepting responsibility and making decisions with regard to a world-view, then the question must be faced as to how this can be done if the above description of the situation is correct. One cannot simply say that this situation has always been the same in the last analysis, since even previously no man – being finite and having only a limited time and possibilities – has ever, on the basis of the total problems and insights relevant for this, made an absolute decision about his world-view and his faith. In the past he did not have as great a number of such problems in practice; at the most, so many problems were merely an objective possibility. Today, however, there is this great number of problems and insights relevant to a world-view but they are dispersed in many different minds without any one of them being capable of collecting them together even approximately (as was the case in the past) in his own mind; in all this the individual (and this is equally important) *knows* it as a fact for himself that he will never be able to catch up not only with all the knowledge in itself *possible* but even with what is merely actually available. Hence the question is, what is he to do in the present, no longer reversible situation? What *indirect* methods are conceivable for mastering this situation? Is there anything like a general ideological probabilism? In other words, is it possible to transfer *mutatis mutandis* what has commonly been said up till now about the indirect solution of a problem in moral theology by the moral system of probabilism to the mastering of a universal situation in this matter of a world-view which, on account of the insurmountable intellectual pluralism of today, can no longer be worked out directly or in an adequate way?

It must not be objected that these great questions of a world-view ought necessarily to be capable of a direct and certain solution, since this is implied in the teaching of the Church about the rational and certain demonstrability of the credibility of the Christian and Catholic faith and of our duty to believe. Christianity certainly can be rationally demonstrated. For God (and this is part of the Christian faith itself) has ultimately called all men to this Christian faith; he cannot and will not call them to this by overriding their rational insight and morally-based freedom; they must therefore in principle be capable of reaching certain knowledge as to the credibility of Christianity. But must this knowledge be completely direct knowledge consisting in an immediate working out of *absolutely all* pertinent questions? How could one prove this *a priori*? Even in the past (this nobody can deny) there have been quite a number of *'rudes'* (simple, uneducated people) who were or became Christians and to whom no one would seriously ascribe a direct or even merely proximately adequate knowledge of the objectively sufficient reasons of fundamental theology. Why should this state not become more general especially since in it there simply comes to light and is brought directly into consciousness what has always been part of subjective exercise of fundamental theology even among the 'educated' and well-informed individuals of the past (even though they might be unaware of it), viz. that in its *subjective* exercise it corresponded only very approximately to what it should really be objectively.

One might counter this by saying that in the past the fundamental theology of the educated nevertheless reached a sufficiently *objective* certitude based on this or that particular reason. Such reasons would be the convergence of probabilities, the moral justification for accepting the insurmountable historical conditioning of perspectives, the inescapable selection of matter for exact examination, the legitimate and justifiable fact of allowing other in themselves equally important viewpoints and problems to recede into the background, etc. But by saying this, one would already be involuntarily going on to reflections which, precisely in view of the contemporary intellectual situation of the unmasterable pluralism, would have to be developed more explicitly and exactly. These reflections could then show that one need have no worry in admitting this situation and need not dispute it at all, since it can be overcome indirectly by the very basic reflections and methods which are the subject of our present inquiry. Even the *rudis* of the old fundamental theology attained, in *his* analysis of faith and from among the apparently sufficient reasons which seemed to be all that was at his disposal, objectively valid reasons for his judgement of credibility; or at least he did have reasons which – even though it was not easy for this kind of analysis to say what they consisted in – legitimately sufficed for man's making a moral decision. This situation has now quite simply become a more generally and explicitly conscious one: it becomes necessary in this intellectually plural situation of today to develop more exactly the reasons for saying that man can have the right and duty to believe even *before* he has adequately worked out the actual problems of fundamental theology.

There is no doubt that such an objectively exact and existential exposition of these reasons would have a liberating effect for the willingness-to-believe of many Catholics. They suffer almost universally under the apparent dilemma that, on the one hand, they live in a milieu of men who have a different world-view and yet, on the other hand, they are neither in a position nor willing to deny to these men either the same intelligence or the same honesty which they ascribe to themselves. How can a Catholic in this situation reach an objectively justified judgement of credibility when he cannot regard non-Catholics as either more stupid or as having less good will than himself and when he cannot say either that they have simply and in *every* respect come less into contact with those objective reasons which support his own rational judgement of credibility? I say, simply and in every respect; for it may certainly be possible to regard this or that element of proof in his fundamental theology and in his preambles of faith as having affected the Catholic more than the non-Catholic. As against this, however, the Catholic will have to suppose that certain counter-reasons have remained more unfamiliar to him (even though he may suppose that they will not be objectively stringent), objections which are objectively and existentially more familiar to the non-Catholic or non-Christian simply on account of these historical contingencies and coincidences of his own, for him inevitable, starting-point.

One cannot say with regard to this reflection that a realised, objective reason, by its stringent evidence, destroys all counter-reasons right from the start, even when these have not yet been examined. This may be true in the case of metaphysical reflections but such an argumentation is surely very questionable in the case of historical reflections. A historical fact and the certainty based on it is after all composed of a great number of factors which can only offer a real, direct historical certainty when all these factors have been combined and thoroughly examined. If one wanted to bring forward good reasons against this conception, they would undoubtedly bring us back once more in the direction of the question posed here and the answer to it; they would almost inevitably point in the direction of the moral and ethically sufficient certainty of a converging although incomplete proof by induction, a position which Cardinal Newman was the first to develop in these questions and one which has not really been accepted yet in the schools, although the opposition to this part of his teaching is gradually dying down.

Together with the question which we have said can only be posed here without being answered, we are also faced with the question as to what method can be adopted in conversation of an apologetic and missionary kind with the contemporary 'unbelievers'. It is not true that – at least in the field in which the unbeliever feels at home scientifically speaking, and especially when the Catholic partner in conversation is not himself also a 'specialist' in the same field (and how could one manage always to get together only specialists on both sides for a conversation?) – the direct 'attack' leads to unending debates conducted with ever greater subtlety, without any final result being achieved in the limited time available for conversation? *How* can one in such conversations get round the impossibility of finding a definitive answer to the contemporary problems in the field of history, textual criticism, philology and exegesis? *Why* is this possible? How and why is it possible to appeal to an existential wholeness in man – and this in a perfectly rational way – which would make it comprehensible that one can possess the totality of faith without having synthetically built up this totality, with its rational reasons of credibility, out of all the factors involved in this totality but lying beyond our actual calculations?

Posing the question in this way in view of the after all fairly new intellectual situation of the man of today, is of course not meant to imply that the traditional fundamental theology, apologetics and apologia has not provided us with any elements for an answer. After all, we have just pointed out one such starting-point in the traditional *analysis fidei* with regard to the *'rudes'*, and no doubt there are many others. The contemporary situation does nevertheless pose the question more sharply, it does signify a more general need and demands that one sees the question more clearly and concerns oneself with finding a clearer, more comprehensive and usable answer.

3

REFLECTIONS ON DIALOGUE WITHIN
A PLURALISTIC SOCIETY

I HAVE been given the great honour today of receiving the Reuchlin Prize of the town of Pforzheim, this festivity being at the same time in memory of the great humanist, i.e. the human man, Reuchlin. In the past, this prize has been bestowed on representatives of the arts and sciences of widely different stamp and outlook, while I myself have the honour of being a theologian in a philosophical faculty. For all these reasons I am inclined to think that the very general question about dialogue in a pluralistic society must be a question within the sense of this hour.

We live in a pluralistic society. The phrase 'pluralistic society' is a rather ugly one for which I can unfortunately offer no better equivalent. The statement itself – that we live in such a society – is by now a platitude which one would rather not repeat. Nevertheless we must ponder a little on it at the beginning of our reflections for the apparently commonplace is what is truly mysterious and dangerous. If we intend here to reflect a little on pluralistic society, then our regard must not be directed towards the social institutionalisations in which the different attitudes, convictions and orientations of men living together embody themselves and thus try to make themselves felt, in which they achieve power and in which they reach their goals ... in other words, our regard must not be directed towards the churches, denominations, parties, associations of mutual self-interests, and similar institutions. It must be directed rather to what lies behind all these, what merely makes its appearance in these social institutions. In other words, we must direct our regard towards the pluralism of the attitudes, convictions and orientations of men themselves. In this pluralism of 'views' (if we may summarise everything meant here in this one phrase), a view may be in fact particular without wanting to be anything more or it may be in fact particular, i.e. not shared by all, while *wanting* to be *universal*, i.e. while making the theoretical demand and having the practical goal of wanting to win over *everyone* to its view. An essentially particular view implies only at most *theoretically* the problem as to whether such a particularism in the very nature of the view can be meaningful in certain cases, i.e. whether this moderation does not slowly kill the view itself; *in practice*, it implies the problem of a 'technical' harmonisation and compatibility of the social materialisations of such an essentially particularised view in the activities of one society. The real problem of the pluralism of views, however, arises where actually particular views must in principle claim universal validity if they do not wish to destroy their own very existence. To take an example: a Mozart- and a Hindemith-society, an association of entomologists and a society of friends of the Aquarium, each represent a particular view and do not in any way claim to desire to win the interest of everyone. On the other hand, Christianity, a Christian denomination, the ideology of the 'Humanistic Union', a party of militant dialectical materialism – if they are not to deny their own nature – feel themselves endowed with a claim to truth and called to a mission which is directed to all inasmuch as each is basically a universal view and in fact a world-view. The doctrine, however, which teaches that there cannot be any such view in principle, that such a universalist claim must from the very start be always and in every case false, would itself be precisely such a universal view with very practical consequences.

If we presuppose that there are meant to be such actually particular views which are universal by their basic self-understanding and claims, and that they are meant to live together and enter into dialogue with each other, then there arises the one, many-sided question: is such a dialogue possible, what is its nature, how must it be conducted? We will attempt to say something on this old and ever new question, and this will itself be dialogic since obviously dialogue about dialogue must be, even if not in practice yet at least in theory, the first subject of conversation among those who, holding different views themselves, regard the dialogue between different views as a vital necessity and who recognise the acknowledgement of this necessity itself as a factor in their own view.

That such a dialogue must be free, is something we will presuppose here rather than expound. It means that this dialogue must from the very start renounce any use of force in its various explicit or anonymous forms in society. By force is to be understood everything here which tries to influence a view and the internal or external attitudes of men without appealing in this to the individual insight and free consent of the other and without basically and really allowing the other person at least the inner and also external possibility of saying no to the view which one wants to mediate and transmit. When we say that the dialogue must from the very start renounce force, this is neither meant to imply the utopian thesis that every form of force is immoral in every case, nor is it meant to veil the fact that even at this stage there already appear many obscure questions which we cannot go into here: questions like the right to defend by force the freedom of one's own opinion against assaults on one's own attitude; the safeguarding, by force if necessary, of a necessary public order even against those who violate this order by appealing to the freedom of their own opinion and even when one admits that the public order itself does not possess any absolutely fixed boundaries and is subject in its concept and extension to historical evolution; the problem of force which is inevitably given together with every necessary and unavoidable institutionalisation of a particular view, no matter how tolerant it may be; the problem of force (in this basic sense) in relation to minors, those in need of education, in whose case there is always also a factor of 'breaking in' by force, and so on.

The problem on which we are reflecting does not therefore concern the renunciation of force by the different views but their dialogue itself. One might think that there is no problem left once the 'world-views' renounce force. For, given this renunciation and given that every 'world-view' wants to pass of its very nature from being an actually particular view to being also an actually universal one, there remains no other means open to it apart from the mission by talk and the attempt to convince, in short . . . dialogue. It is not however quite as simple as all that. For, is all talk which seeks to enlighten and convince the other without using force already a dialogue or is it not simply preaching and propaganda? Is not dialogue based on the renunciation of any attempt to 'convert' the other, on a renunciation therefore which is profoundly contrary to the nature of a world-view which makes absolute and universal claims (no matter which one does this)? Yet again, if this were so, would not dialogue then become a harmless exchange of opinions which right from the start does not mean to say anything essential or binding to the *other*? Does not such a dialogue become then merely a better means of conversation, making no demands on anyone, for a tea-party? Is the dialogue which is meant here merely a pedagogical aid by means of which one person leads someone else through questions to his own opinion, somewhat in the style of what is usually understood by 'socratic dialogue'? But will genuine universal views wish to conduct dialogues with each other *in this sort of way*? If the dialogue is entered with the foregone conviction that one will not 'agree' anyway, is it worth while in that case to start the dialogue at all, or can it then be anything other than the somewhat laborious means of expressing the desire that one wants to get along well with one another in spite of one's differences of opinion? Does dialogue receive its meaning and its weight only from the at least hoped for and possible final agreement, or does it – without of course simply giving up this goal – carry its meaning and dignity in itself even before this goal is reached and in a certain independence of it, as a dialogue still going on and unfinished? Is there something like an unending dialogue which is meaningful even though it never comes to a conclusion in the realm of final and yet tangible 'results' but merely has an 'eschatological' hope and therefore meaning?

Before we proceed to try to say a little directly on these knotty and obscure questions, we should reflect a little on the situation of contemporary world-view dialogue since this will make us understand a little better the radical sharpness of the contemporary question and thus see the real problem precisely. One can probably say quite rightly that the situation of universal outlooks and world-views facing each other in dialogue has really come about only today in *our* historical hour. It is not surprising, then, that the catchword 'dialogue' has only been explicitly pronounced for the first time in an official pronouncement of the Catholic Church in our days. Of course, there has always been proclamation, mission, preaching, religious conversation – even in literary form – beginning (within Christianity) with the *Dialogus cum Tryphone* of St Justin and the *Octavius* of Minucius Felix, but not until now has there ever been an age of dialogue. Up until now certain homogeneous social structures were always very quickly formed in which there reigned only *one* world-view which pushed any differences there still were out of the public social dimension or made them relatively unimportant and basically 'particular' views. Homogeneous social structures always arose which existed and lived separated from each other either by force or by a mental and cultural no-man's-land. It must also be remembered that the extent of knowledge and of problems present in such homogeneous, closed spiritual landscapes was such that the individual was still able on the whole to survey and manage it, so that the one same thing was still really communicable to others and could in fact still be possessed by many together. There simply was no really pluralistic society. In such social structures with their homogeneous world-view – whether they were States or closed cultural areas – there was then preaching and educational communication of what was universally binding, and perhaps conversation among friends about the more exact interpretation of what was binding on all, but no dialogue between *different* world-views; at the most there was missionary activity which was able to make use of the difference in cultural level between the missionary and those being evangelised and thus was able to appear as a one-way proclamation but not as a dialogue. Today all this is quite different. Peoples and cultures are no longer separated by a historical and cultural no-man's-land; what there is of different universal views and their social representations is now pushed and pressed together into the one space of the one only now really beginning world-history; and all this since the individual spaces which were up till now homogeneous in their world-views had lost their *internal* homogeneity simultaneously and by reciprocal effect with the development of this one world-history by the rational, technological world civilisation and European colonialism. For better or for worse, everyone has become everyone else's neighbour. If, therefore, one does not want to hold the absurd opinion that the existence of man can be regulated and preserved in the same living space independently of his views and opinions – in other words, that culture is not at all important for life on the biological and civilisational, social plane of human existence – then in that case dialogue between world-views becomes possible and indeed necessary for life. No world-view in this unity of the spiritual-personal *and* bodily-social existence of man can possibly renounce objectifying itself bodily and socially into that spatio-temporal, social space of human existence which is common to everyone; it cannot possibly withdraw itself any more into an 'interiority' which has nothing to do with anyone else. Today, furthermore, it is also no longer able to conquer the bodily and social sphere of existence for itself alone. The universal views confront each other in the same historical space of existence and *remain* so confronted. Dialogue then becomes the only possible mode of co-existence, a mode which did not exist before and one which will remain; for the world-views can never separate again into different historical spaces nor *may* one destroy the other by force nor does it even have any chance of doing this, nor finally is there any chance (for a reason to be touched on later) that one will dissolve all the others by pure conviction (especially since the Christian theology of history itself does not envisage the total intramundane victory of its world-view).

But is such a dialogue possible? Will it not fail by reason of intrinsic meaninglessness? A radical meaninglessness seems to annul it from within. In a real world-view dialogue, which therefore has neither an experimental scientific knowledge which exhibits the object directly and with evidence nor a basically particular view on the object, each world-view *must* try to 'convert' the other partner; it must try to get the other to accept its world-view and yet has not got any prospect of doing this – or at least can no longer begin and continue the dialogue *today* with this prospect – since perhaps a few people can be convinced but the overall state of the world-views engaging in dialogue is not thereby significantly changed; such 'conversions' are still possible but will come from each side to the other. The dialogue seems to become senseless, therefore, on account of its hopelessness at the very moment when dialogue becomes necessary in a pluralistic (and permanently pluralistic) society.

The alternative, however, that dialogue in a permanently pluralistic world becomes senseless either because it must remain without success or because it annuls the universal demands of a world-view, is not really true.

Even the essentially universal outlooks and world-views are subject to the law of history. They have a particular point of departure, a finite inherited vocabulary, a *difference* between what is really meant but merely formally anticipated – as it were abstractly presupposed without any concrete experience – on the one hand, *and*, on the other hand, what is concretely realised, i.e. what is experienced, the particular historical conception and view in which they render present what they really mean. Even an essentially universal world-view can acknowledge this its historicity, the incompleteness of the existential and historical realisation of its basic project, without denying its own principles. In fact, it is only by thus recognising its historical origin from a particular, finite past and its orientation towards a still outstanding self-realisation in the future, that it can lay claim to universal validity and does it and justifies its universality. It belongs to the nature of a universal world-view to appeal to its own future and to accept its own eschatological character which calls its own present before the tribunal of self-criticism and places it under the judgement of the future. The basic universality and openness towards its own expectantly and hopefully anticipated future do not contradict each other. Where this openness is not present, there is proof that the claim to universality is illegitimate from the very start. This lack would freeze such a world-view in its unhistorical nature so that it would then certainly be quite incapable of dialogue and would simply drag out an existence for a time carried along by the changes of history as a relic from the past. If, however, a world-view recognises itself in this sense as one which opens out into the future, then it will be capable of dialogue; a dialogue has meaning for it, even before it ends – in a utopian or asymptotic manner – and this meaning lies in its victory and in its transition from the actually particular to an *actually* universal validity. After all, the world-view itself learns from and enriches itself in this dialogue; in this never-ending dialogue, it catches up more and more on its own possibilities; it can recognise and realise itself more and more by means of and in the partner of this dialogue and in this way it learns for the first time what it had already always known. The only presupposition is that it does not simply identify its own present historical stage with its absolute being and with the *entire* historical commission of its evolution ... though it does not necessarily do this even when it posits itself basically as a truth for everyone and universally. All that has to be presupposed is that the world-view is *not* committed to the conviction (which is not demanded by its nature) that in dialogue it is met merely by a partner of conversation who is intent on nothing but a flat denial of everything that it itself maintains as its own truth. This situation of flat opposition between saying yes and no to the same proposition, which is presumed to be understood in the same sense by both sides, is of course to begin with and indeed over and over again present in the dialogue situation. Yet this opposition is not the only thing which characterises the dialogue situation, least of all in the situation of a pluralistic society. For, where the right or wrong of such apparently diametrically opposed propositions (e.g. God exists; there is no God) cannot simply be verified like an experiment of natural science by being able to produce the object, it is always a question of concepts and propositions with a long history of comprehension and interpretation which can never be made definitive; it is always a question of meanings which are always already known and yet must ever be looked for and sought after anew. What is meant by freedom, person, God, love, moral obligation, salvation and so on, is always something at the same time both well-known and unfathomed; it is always known and always questioned. It is precisely in such always known and always unfathomed matters, at which one always arrives without ever fully comprehending them, that historically and thus always particularly constituted men arrive – or perhaps do not arrive or perhaps not completely – at a conclusion in different ways and each in a way ordained for him. This is then the mystery of their ultimate personal decision which ultimately is not subject to their own reflection or the judgement of others. World-views and universal outlooks are distinguished by differences in interpretation, conceptual articulation and theoretical objectification of this envisaged, attained or existentially missed arrival at the ultimate all-comprehending but never comprehended reality, and these differences form precisely the object of their dialogue. This object remains significant and necessary, since even the conceptually reflex interpretation of the ultimate and most original experience of the whole can be absolutely significant for the existential success of this most original experience. Hence, in the first place, we must *not* say that the seemingly contradictory differences of the objectified propositions are really certain and always represent exactly the same absolute contradiction in man's existential realisation as the contradiction which appears at first sight. Someone who denies God, for instance, perhaps merely denies something which does not exist even in the opinion of the theist who really understands his theism or who – in dialogue with the atheist – comes to understand it properly for the first time or at least more properly and radically than he had done up to that moment.

Secondly, it is possible in a dialogue slowly (and perhaps merely asymptotically) to take hold of the historical, individual and collective experience which is perfectly legitimate and from which the other arrived at his 'viewpoint', even though in the judgement of his partner he has interpreted it wrongly or inadequately in the reflex interpretation of his world-view. Victory over his own narrowness is in any case promised to the one who really and truly enters into dialogue, even though he is convinced that his own proper principle, with which he must always still catch up but according to which he has started out, will be preserved and prove itself, even when he cannot hope that the dialogue will produce an agreement in his empirical sphere of life which can objectify itself in an institution. Even someone who professes an absolute viewpoint can realise that he is still 'on the way'; but he follows his path only if he enters into dialogue, opens himself out, allows himself to be attacked by others, is willing to *learn* even when he teaches and apparently is merely seeking to defend his own position and trying to make it 'come out on top'. Only once a partner in a dialogue knows for certain that through the dialogue he has completely appropriated the *whole* existential experience out of which his partner expresses his propositions and opposition, can he presume to say with certainty that not only what the other says but also what he really means to say in the world-view dialogue is false or already positively and completely included in his own view in the sense in which it is really meant.

This total inclusion of the existential experience of the other is far less completely possible, not merely in principle but also in practice, than ever before. Even in Humboldt's time it was still possible to be of the opinion – and with very good reason – that an educated person could positively and personally know all that happened and offered itself in his own existential space of existence by way of experience and knowledge relevant to a world-view. In such an age and under such a presupposition, it was easy to have dialogue if one had it at all; prescinding from the *completely* individual character of the intellectual life of the other, one was able to presuppose in a dialogue (and one did in fact presuppose) that one understood the statements of the other not only in a scientifically and socially manipulable sense but also in the sense really intended, i.e. as objective realisation of the real original exercise of existence and as the manifestation of the free truth of the person. Today things are much more difficult for us in a dialogue. The intellectual and scientific knowledge with which we are faced today is so differentiated and so impossible to survey that humanity and society as a whole have become immeasurably more knowledgeable while the individual, relative to the whole of this knowledge, has become ever more 'ignorant' since he personally can grasp less and less of this continually growing mass in his own individual consciousness. This is so precisely because the intellectual, the educated person must of necessity be more and more a specialist who only knows more and more in an ever-diminishing sector of the total field of knowledge (and thus moves towards that vanishing point where the individual knows everything . . . about nothing). Yet dialogue can be conducted only by individual consciousnesses, and it is – unfortunately or thanks be to God – not to be expected that it will ever be possible to introduce an electronic 'brain' (who would be able to programme it?) into a dialogue involving world-views, a dialogue which is always concerned with the whole of reality as such; it is not to be expected that this would ever become a possibility for overcoming the contemporary situation of dialogue in which, from the very start or in the end, no one *can completely* possess all the knowledge relevant to a world-view possessed by the other, at least not in an actual and explicit way and in its concrete, material contents. The dialogue of *today*, therefore, is not only characterised by the fact that the partners in this dialogue hold different views and represent opposite viewpoints, but even before this by the fact that no one any longer knows or *can* know everything his conversational partner knows. This makes dialogue more difficult today; but it also gives it a meaning even before any agreement is reached, viz. that one can learn an infinite amount from each other; one will never reach a point where one can learn no more, but one can also never again say that one cannot learn anything more from dialogue with the other than the mere fact that he subscribes to a view which one holds to be false oneself and which one simply accepts with a shrug of the shoulder as an incomprehensible fact. Today more than ever before, every world-view considering itself to be universal can experience and acknowledge itself as infinitely open towards the material fulfilment offering itself to it through dialogue in that knowledge and experience of the other which one cannot possess for oneself except by the knowledge of the other opening itself in dialogue.

There can and must be dialogue today. This does not mean a cowardly, relativistic dialogue in which the partners no longer take their own convictions seriously and thus cannot really talk in any true sense because they have nothing to say to each other. It means dialogue in genuine freedom and not merely in that 'toleration' and co-existence where one puts up with one's opponent merely because one does not have the power to destroy him. It must be a dialogue in which one risks oneself; an essentially universal world-view asserted absolutely must be especially capable of this and is allowed of its essence to do this. After all, it can make such a universal claim only if it opens itself to everything and also tries in this way to discover the basis of the 'no' of the opponent within itself; it can make such a universal claim only if it knows that it overcomes this basis within itself by a fuller 'yes' only by facing up to it and by thus putting itself at risk. Dialogue must be on its guard against idle talk and non-involvement. The finite man in dialogue must have the humility and courage to choose his partner since he cannot talk with everyone if his dialogue is not to degenerate into empty chatter; he may even reserve the right and indeed the duty to himself of breaking off a *particular* dialogue (but not dialogue *as such*) when, even after the strictest self-criticism and a *last* (and not just penultimate!) refusal to judge the other person, he feels himself obliged to the view that he is not being met by the goodwill on the other side which is the necessary presupposition for every dialogue. A Christian will conduct his dialogue with the seriousness of knowing the danger that his own dialogue may be marred and rendered a social lie by the guilt of his arrogance, obstinacy, false self-assurance and violent aggressiveness; he will always recognise himself also as a sinner and will therefore submit his own part in the dialogue to the judgement and mercy of God. The Christian knows that love alone is the highest light of knowledge and that what St Paul says about love must therefore also be valid of *dialogue*: 'If I have all the eloquence of men or of angels, but speak without love, I am simply a gong booming or a cymbal clashing' (1 Co 13:1). He knows that one should be able to say of one's dialogue what the Apostle says of love: in true dialogue one is patient, kind, never jealous, never boastful or overbearing, never deceitful, never seeking one's own; in true dialogue one never becomes embittered, never bears ill-will for a wrong suffered, hopes everything, suffers everything; for one knows, even in the conviction of one's own truth, that one sees as in a mirror darkly and in puzzles. Even the dialogue between world-views which consider themselves absolute can and must be based on the knowledge that there is an unbridgeable gap between the conviction objectified in propositions – which is the only plane on which one can directly conduct a dialogue – and the conviction implied in the unreflected immediate exercise of existence itself; in other words, it can and must be based on the knowledge that even the truest conviction objectified in propositions and doctrines is not yet a guarantee of one's 'being in the truth' of existence, and that behind what one judges to be the falsest theory can be hidden the 'being-in-the-truth' of the man who accepts his existence silently but nevertheless genuinely; or to use St Augustine's formula regarding the Church: some think they are 'inside' when in terms of their own truth they are really 'outside', and some consider themselves or are considered to be 'outside' when in reality they are 'inside'. Only if the dialogue of the 'head' is inspired by this respect for the *mysterium ineffabile* of the 'heart' which only God sees, is the dialogue as it should be if it is to be able to stand before conscience and God.

Such a dialogue must bear the motto of St Anselm of Canterbury:

consideratio rationabiliter comprehendit incomprehensibile esse: reflection comprehends rationally that the incomprehensible exists and holds sway. One must speak clearly and simply – in short, reasonably – in dialogue, because only in this way can one speak *with each other.* But the dialogue must remain surrounded by that silent respect for the fact that what is being spoken about transcends by far everything that is said: the man who, as Pascal says, infinitely transcends man, and his secret which is God. Thus dialogue must remain enclosed by the silence in which man puts up with himself and accepts himself in the incomprehensibility of his existence whose depth is God. Moreover, this dialogue with all its learnedness, uncompromising thought and sharp definition of standpoints, must be a dialogue of love even when one modestly keeps silent about it. It must and can be this. Why should it not be possible? If God commands us to love our enemies, then he surely has also told us by this that even the most difficult dialogue must still be supported by love. But love has then already unified. Hence every true dialogue is merely the infinite effort which tries to ensure that in the splendour of the expressed and mutually possessed truth there may also *appear* what can already be present in the depth of the heart, as long as we really desire it: the love which alone is believable.

4

IDEOLOGY AND CHRISTIANITY

THE subject of this evening's reflections is 'Ideology and Christianity'. We intend to ask first of all what is to be understood by 'ideology' in the present reflections; after all, this notion is not so clear (and is not defined in exactly the same sense by everyone) that it could be simply presupposed here as something already known. In the second part of our reflections we will then go on to ask briefly about the reasons for the opinion that thinks of Christianity as an ideology and then rejects it simply because it is an ideology. A third part will then attempt to make it clear that Christianity is not an ideology and hence cannot be rejected on that ground. In the fourth and last part of our reflections, we will draw certain conclusions from the basic thesis of our third 'movement'.

1. What is meant in these reflections by 'ideology'? This is the first question we must ask ourselves. It is not possible here to describe the origin and history of the concept of ideology. This concept indeed is used in that history in so many different and contradictory ways that nothing else is left to us but simply to give a brief definition – with an eye, no doubt, on this history – of what *we* mean here by ideology. This definition naturally is not to be understood as an arbitrary one but as an objectively philosophical definition. Ideology, it must be emphasised right away, is understood here in a negative sense. In other words, it is understood as an erroneous or false system which must be rejected in view of a right interpretation of reality. We can prescind in this from the question as to whether the false 'system' is clearly constituted by theoretical reflection or whether it represents more an unreflected attitude, in the sense of a mentality and arbitrarily and freely created mood. It remains a completely open question here, of course, as to where this sort of ideology is to found in the concrete; in other words, whether, for example, every metaphysics is to be understood as an ideology in this sense. What,

43

however, distinguishes such an ideology in its essence from simple, basically open error, is the voluntary element of closure by which the ideology understands itself as a total system. To this extent, ideology is then a fundamental closure in face of the 'wholeness' of reality, one which turns a partial aspect into an absolute. Bearing in mind common usage, one would have to complete this abstract description of the nature of ideology by pointing out that – in so far as reality as a whole can demand recognition from man – the conversion of a partial aspect of reality into an absolute takes place with a view to practical action, and thus usually takes the form of a basic determination of political activity; indeed, in its ultimate intention, it will try to determine the norm for the whole life of a society. From this point of view, ideology could also be defined with R. Lauth as a pseudo-scientific interpretation of reality in the service of a practico-social orientation which it is meant to legitimate retrospectively. This formal definition of the nature of an ideology, regarded as a definitive erection into an absolute of a partial aspect of the whole of reality, makes it *a priori* possible to recognise a threefold form of ideology. This is not meant to imply that these three forms are ever realised in a pure state and completely separated from each other but that there is in a real sense an ideology of immanence, an ideology of 'transmanence' and an ideology of transcendence. We will now give a short explanation of this division.[1]

Ideologies of immanence convert certain finite areas of our experiential world into absolutes and regard their structures as the law of reality as such. This group embraces the greater part of what is normally referred to as ideology: nationalism, the ideology of 'blood and soil', racialism, Americanism, technicism, sociologism and of course that materialism for which God, spirit, freedom and person signify just empty talk in the real sense of the term. The opposite of the ideology of immanence – an opposite we often fail to recognise immediately – is the ideology of 'transmanence', i.e. supernaturalism, quietism, and certain forms of utopianism, chiliasm, indiscreet 'brotherhood', etc. In this kind of ideology, the ultimate and infinite – that which permeates and governs all areas of reality – is turned into an absolute (or better, perhaps, is totalised) in the sense of cheating the relatively ultimate finite reality – that which is already always given and accepted – out of its relative

[1] Cf. on this J. Splett, 'Ideologie und Toleranz', *Wort und Wahrheit* XX (1965), pp. 37–49.

rights; the relatively ultimate is passed over and one tries to project and manipulate it purely from the standpoint of that absolutely ultimate reality: this is the typical danger for the philosopher and the religious person. The third form of ideology is called the ideology of transcendence. This tries to overcome the first-mentioned forms of ideology but in its turn hypostasises in itself, as the only valid thing, the actual empty formal process of surmounting what is meant by the first two forms of ideology. In this case, what is immediately given in experience is devalued negatively into historism, relativism, etc., and what is properly transcendent is experienced merely as something which refuses to communicate itself, as something unspeakable. From this stems the ideological programme of unrestrained and so-called 'openness' for everything and anything, an attitude which timidly avoids any clear engagement in anything definite, with the result that such a professedly typical Western attitude is then brought face to face with the demands of a Western ideology; in this lies the ever new attraction for Western intellectuals of that communism which demands 'engagement'.

2. The reproach is made against Christianity that it too is such a negative ideology. Before we can reflect on this claim and on the reason why this reproach is quite unjustified, it will be necessary to reflect at least briefly on the reasons which can provide apparent justification for the interpreting of Christianity as an ideology.

(a) First of all, this reproach can appear to be justified from the viewpoint of either an unreflected attitude or the explicit position of a general scepticism and relativism. There is an attitude which, for whatever reasons of a personal or scientific kind, immediately identifies experience and reality with the type of experience and reality which can be directly proved by natural science and this in a strictly technical way; it regards every other reality and experience simply as a freely exchangeable, i.e. ideological, superstructure of the true reality of so-called exact empirical science; metaphysics is experienced by it as merely a matter of personal opinion and of completely free conceptual composition, a point of view based on the indemonstrability of its objects in an experience which has been narrowed down right from the outset by the principles of natural science. Wherever we find such an attitude, it is only possible for Christianity to be experienced from the very start as merely an ideology. In the last analysis, it is quite immaterial to such a view what reasons one may give in explanation of the origin of this ideology: whether one regards it as the opium of the people or the product of a particular social structure, as a utopian over-elevation of human existence or as the effect of an unquenchable desire for a comprehensive interpretation of the meaning of existence, a desire which simply gives rise to ideologies.

(b) A further reason for interpreting Christianity as an ideology is to be found in the historical fact that Christianity has often been used – sometimes in a revolutionary manner but mostly in a conservative and reactionary way – to justify social, economic, political, cultural and scientific conditions which cannot claim permanent validity. Whenever Christianity is abused in this way – which is often hardly avoidable and which abuse in most cases can only in fact be overcome by a slow historical process – it is in fact turned into an ideology, and such a conservative ideology has very often been quite rightly attacked precisely *as* an ideology, and this in the name of Christianity. If real Christianity itself had to suffer in the process, then this was the fault or the tragic misfortune of the representatives of Christianity and the Church who provided the occasion for mistaking Christianity for an ideology such as would have to be overcome.

(c) An even greater and more subtle danger of mistaking Christianity for an ideology lies, however, in the necessity of having to objectify the real nature of Christianity – the incomprehensible mystery of the transcendent God and of his salvation in absolute, forgiving self-communication – through categories and historical, institutional, sacramental and juridical forms in the human word of revelation, in the sacramental sign and in the socially constituted condition of believers. Such a categorising objectification of God's actual divine self-communication, which takes hold of man from his transcendental origin, is necessary. Man necessarily lives his uniquely original being and his eternal destiny as a historical being in spatio-temporal history. He must live in this way and cannot find his own being either in a merely interior inwardness, mysticism or purely negative turning-away-from his historical existence. These objectifications are necessary, they are the body in which the spirit achieves and finds itself. But they also necessarily obscure the real meaning of Christianity, they make it ambiguous and render it liable to abuse and constriction. Thus, having turned immanence into an ideology, they continue always to provide the temptation and occasion for radically committed Christians to tend both towards the ideology of 'transmanence' and towards the ideology of transcendence; both then get confused with the real nature of

Christianity and thus expose Christianity itself to the reproach of merely being an ideology,

(d) A further reason for the danger of regarding Christianity as an ideology lies within the actual contemporary pluralism of world-views, which in its turn is a cause of that sceptical relativism which we referred to as the first reason for confusing Christianity and ideology. If the man of today, starting from natural science, is naturally inclined to presuppose the universal validity of real truth for all men as the obvious ideal and norm, and if, in his fundamental democratic sentiment, he is inclined to grant in principle just as much intelligence and goodwill to everybody else as to himself, then he must inevitably be surprised and disturbed by the fact that men are so completely disunited in their world-views and this even with regard to the comprehensive interpretation of the meaning of existence. He is then in danger of jumping to the conclusion that all knowledge which goes beyond the sphere of exact scientific and universally acknowledged insight is a non-binding mental fiction which at most can be granted subjective significance; and, since Christianity is contradicted in the same way, he will then be tempted to range Christianity among such world-view fictions and ideologies and to grant it at most in our lives a greater degree of subjective affinity.

3. Having thus enumerated in rough detail the reasons one might have for evaluating Christianity as an ideology, we now come to the third 'movement' of our reflections and with it to the central question as to why Christianity is not an ideology. An adequate answer to this question would of course coincide with the proof that Christianity has a legitimate claim to declare the truth about the whole of reality and to be the absolute religion or (if one shrinks from the word religion in this context) to fulfil what human religion of itself seeks for in vain. It is obvious that such a proof cannot be offered in the short space of one hour. We would have to raise too many questions and speak about too many things. We would have to speak about what in this connection is really meant by truth and absolute validity; we would have to ask how man can – in any case – find entry into God and his revealed Word; we would have to ask what is and what is not really declared by this message, what in this message is image, symbol and cypher and what intended content, reality and truth. It is obvious that these and many other necessary questions cannot be posed and answered here. It can be merely a question here of picking out a few factors within Christianity, or ideologies, which differentiate

Christianity from what is particularly characterised and stressed by the word 'ideology' in an erroneous system. Everything that follows, therefore, must be understood in the light of this preliminary qualification.

(a) First of all, one must make it clear that it is really impossible to suspect Christianity of being an ideology by the mere fact that it makes absolute declarations with the claim to truth, in the perfectly simple and ordinary sense of this word, i.e. because it makes declarations which can be called 'metaphysical': since, on the one hand, they are declared with an absolute claim to truth and, on the other hand, cannot be directly verified as valid on the empirical plane of natural science. Anyone, of course, who holds that every 'metaphysics' is false or non-demonstrable cannot consider authentic Christianity, even as understood by itself, as anything but an ideology; he may then perhaps go on to reflect – in what would be an existentially irrational way – on why this Christianity can and should nevertheless have an essential significance for his life; he would then of course be overlooking the fact that such a reflection of an irrational positing and ideologising of life would itself imply a metaphysics, even though it be a bad one. What has been said here is not, of course, meant to imply that the knowledge of faith and philosophical metaphysics are the same in their basic structures and merely differ with regard to their declared objects. It is true, all the same, that the Christian declaration of faith and metaphysics do coincide with regard to the just mentioned claim to truth, so that where the possibilities of a metaphysical declaration are denied in principle and from the outset, Christianity too can only be accorded the rank of a subjective ideology. For in this view, a subject before whom such an absolute claim to truth can be announced and to whom it can be imparted, just does not exist; in such a view, only individual men exist, individuals who try to make their existence a little more bearable and dignified by such mental fictions. Hence, in defence against the reproach that Christianity is an ideology, it must in the first place be emphasised here that metaphysics must not be suspected from the outset and in every case of being an ideology. This is shown by the very fact that the proposition stating that every metaphysics is in the last analysis a non-binding ideology, is itself a metaphysical proposition, whether it be expressed reflexedly with theoretical universal binding force or is implied in the attempt to live life free from metaphysics (by an absolutely sceptical 'epoché' regarding all matters beyond the immediate brute experience of life and natural scientific knowledge). Relativism and scepticism, whether they be theoretically formulated or non-theoretically attempted in life, are metaphysical decisions. Metaphysics is inescapably given together with man's existence. He always interprets his existence within a horizon of *a priori* pre-decisions which have already preceded this experience and embrace it. True and genuine metaphysics goes further and – precisely speaking – only consists in reflection on those transcendental, inevitably given implications which actually bear their evidence and certainty already within themselves and are necessarily posited together with every intellectual and free exercise of human existence. Metaphysics, as reflex knowledge, does not produce these implications itself but simply reflects on the implications there and so renders them systematic; it is therefore a systematisation of a transcendental experience which, as the unsystematic ground of every empirical experience and understanding of truth, essentially transcends the latter in insight and certitude. This metaphysics can therefore unashamedly admit the unfinished nature of its reflection, the necessity of always beginning it anew and its imperfection; and yet it can say quite confidently that its meaning, i.e. the transcendental experience itself, is still the common property of all men open to the truth; it shows itself as such even in the plurality of metaphysical systems, even where these systems appear totally contradictory to the superficial regard of the ordinary man and even of the bad historian of philosophy, and thus gives the impression of being merely mental fictions and arbitrary subjective assumptions. Only someone capable of utter silence and absence of any thought, i.e. someone capable of living in a purely animal immediacy to his biological existence and who therefore would not even know anything about this his metaphysical suspension of judgement (in other words, someone who would not exercise it at all), would be really free of metaphysics and could avoid the claim of being made for absolute truth. If, however, there can be a metaphysics, at least in principle, which cannot be simply disposed of as an ideology from the very start, then *a fortiori* Christianity cannot be rejected as being an ideology simply because the horizons of its declarations of faith do not coincide with primitive, factual everyday experience and the experience of the empirical natural sciences. The fact of a pluralism of world-views cannot be a legitimate reason for dismissing every world-view (in so far as one wants to subsume metaphysics and the Christian teaching of faith under this title) as being a mere ideology. Precisely this attitude would itself go beyond the objects of individual empirical experience and their functional connections and would make experience as a whole – which as such is not an object of experience – the object of a declaration which by definition would then itself be an ideology. The right relationship to the pluralism of world-views and metaphysical systems cannot consist in a flat suspicion of every world-view as mere mythology; it can only consist in an attitude which carefully and critically examines, holds itself open to further knowledge and modifications of previous knowledge, is modest, tries to discover the transcendental experience in all the 'systems' put forward, and yet has also the courage to make decisions, to commit itself with the quiet assurance that absolute truth is already reached even in an historically conditioned, finite, incomplete, still open declaration ... even though this absolute truth always ultimately remains that unspeakable, holy mystery which can no longer be confined in any system superior to it and manageable by us. When and where metaphysics understands itself in the last analysis as that rational, or better, intellectual introduction into the attitude of openness as adopted towards the absolute mystery, an attitude which always holds sway in the ground of our intellectual and freely responsible existence but for this precise reason must not remain indifferent in itself for man, then metaphysics loses its appearance of being merely an ideological fiction, even when confronted with the pluralism of world-views of our existence. This pluralism of world-views destroys in reality only the rationalistic presumption of any false metaphysic which might maintain that in it man can grasp the totality of reality right down to its last bases and so manage it in his own system, instead of – as in life – being struck dumb in reflecting on the implications of the ground of total reality by which one is seized.

(b) Proceeding from this, it can be seen under a still wider aspect that Christianity is not an ideology. We have already said that the basis of all metaphysically valid knowledge of truth is transcendental experience (even before any objective individual experience), an experience by which man is always already referred to the unembraceable totality of reality and into its very ground, that ground which is that always already present holy mystery which removes man into the distance of his finiteness and guilt ... and which we call God. This transcendental experience possessed in knowledge and responsible freedom is again unsystematically also the basis, necessary condition and horizon of everyday experience and as such is the first and proper 'place' for the reality of Christianity, and this without prejudice to its historicity and history about which we will have to speak later. Christianity cannot be an ideology because, on the one hand, this experience of transcendence, being the introduction to an absolute sacred mystery which is no longer grasped but which on the contrary lays hold of one, makes every ideology transcendent by its own transcendental necessity in so far as such an ideology turns a certain limited intramundane area of experience into an absolute. On the other hand then, in so far as Christianity is not abbreviated in any way and represents in its teaching the right interpretation of this transcendental experience as it really achieves itself in its own, unabridged being, Christianity signifies in its reality precisely this adequate transcendental experience. Thus Christianity cannot be an ideology. This is not the place to ask in what sense such a starting-point for the understanding of Christianity is to be found, and what effect it has, in Rudolf Bultmann and others. Can we not say that the reality of Christianity is what Christians are accustomed to call grace? Is grace not the self-communication of God to the finite creature, the direct presence to God, the dynamism directed towards participation in the life of God who is above every finite and mortal creature? Does not grace signify that man, in spite of his finiteness and guilt, is superior to all worldly powers and forces, even when he suffers under them to the bitter end? Is not this grace always offered to all men on account of God's universal salvific will and is it not effective in everything even when man closes himself to it in free guilt? Taking all this together, it means surely that man is someone who is borne by God himself and is driven towards direct presence to God in the very ground of his personal being. In other words, what we call grace, is the real truth and the property, freely given by God, of the transcendental experience of the openness of the personal spirit to God. If Christianity in its proper being signifies grace, and if grace is the innermost possibility and reality of the reception of God's self-communication in the very ground of human existence, then Christianity is none else but the deepest reality of the transcendental experience, the experience of the absolute and forgiving nearness of God himself who is distinct from and above all intramundane reality and yet is the one who in this very way (even in this absolute nearness) remains the holy mystery to be worshipped. If, however, this is the proper nature of Christianity, then every ideology has already been surpassed and this because every ideology is concerned with what is verifiable in intramundane experience, whether this refers to blood and soil, sociability, rational technologisation and manipulation, the enjoyment of life or the experience of man's own emptiness and absurdity, or whatever else, and it posits this as the basic condition of human existence. Christianity declares these powers and forces, the masters of unredeemed existence, not merely theoretically but absolutely basically to be worthless idols which must never become our masters; it declares that man has in the ground of his existence always already overcome these powers and forces in grace, and that the real question is whether he assents in his free actions to this his transcendental openness to the immediacy of God through grace, which is eternal life; his free action itself originating once more from the power of this grace. Since, therefore, the basic fulfilment of Christianity finds its point of insertion in the very midst of man's transcendentality, a transcendentality which always rises above any intramundane ideology (even though merely or rather precisely because it is a transcendence towards the absolute mystery of God in his absolute and forgiving nearness), Christianity is from the outset no mere ideology. At least, it is not an ideology of immanence. The transcendence referred to here, however, is not an externally superadded dimension to the realm of man's intramundane existence. Hence it cannot be regarded as a subsequent ideologisation of human existence, as if it were superfluous for the fulfilment of human existence in the world.

(c) Christianity, however, is also at the same time essentially a history, since it directs man's attention towards spatio-temporally fixed events of human history understanding them as saving events which find their unsurpassable summit, centre and historical measure in the absolute saving event of Jesus Christ. If this history itself is part of the nature of Christianity, and not just an accidental interchangeable stimulus of that transcendental, supernatural experience of the absolute and forgiving nearness of the holy mystery which overcomes all intramundane forces and powers, then Christianity appears clearly as the negation of every ideology of transmanence and transcendence. (This must not be understood as the annihilation of transcendence, but must be seen as the negation of the ideologisation of transcendence into a bare and empty formalisation of genuine transcendence.) Two things will have to be understood if we are to be able to think of this concept. Firstly, it will be necessary to make clear the inner connection between the genuine and unsurpassable historicity of Christianity in its turning to history regarded as a real event of salvation and the transcendental nature of Christianity understood as the openness by grace to the absolute God; in other words, it will have to be shown that genuine transcendentality and genuine historicity determine one another and that man by his very transcendentality is referred to real history, a real history he cannot 'annul' by *a priori* reflection. Secondly, it will have to be understood that by the genuine imposed nature of real history, man is empowered and indeed bound to take things really seriously even in his profane existence and to be really involved in the external historical reality, even where he recognises and experiences by suffering the contingency and thus the relativity of this historical reality. As regards the first question, it must be said straight away that the correctly understood history of man is not an element of mere chance imposed on man in addition to his existence as a being of transcendence but that it is precisely the history of his transcendental being as such. He does not live out his existence orientated to God in a pure or even mystical interiority, in some sort of submersion running away from history but lives it out precisely in the individual and collective-history of his very being. Hence Christianity can still be seen to consist absolutely in the grace-constituted transcendental being of man and yet still in very truth be the actual history in which this being is achieved and which confronts man himself in spatio-temporal facticity. Truly there is then a history-of-salvation of the human word in which the divine word gives itself; the Church furthermore is truly the assembly of salvation and the sacrament, even though all these historical objectifications of man's absolute depth-of-being open to God's grace only have and retain their own nature when all these historical manifestations appear as what they are, namely as instruments of mediation and signs pointing to the incomprehensibility of a God who communicates himself in all truth and reality to man through these signs so as to become directly present in an absolute and forgiving manner. If and as long as these historical mediations are really mediations to the presence and acceptance of the mystery of God, and while retaining their relative nature yet prove themselves even in this way as unavoidable for the historical being of man in this aeon before the direct vision of God is reached, history and transcendence will never be subject in Christianity to an ideology of immanence, i.e. to the idolisation of intramundane powers, or to an ideology of transmanence and transcendence, i.e. to the idolisation in empty, formal abstractions of man's transcendentality by grace. Two further points must be noted in this connection. Firstly, the historicity of man, understood as mediation of his transcendental being elevated by grace reaches its unsurpassable climax in

Jesus Christ, the God-man; in him God's promise of himself to the world, its historical mediation and its acceptance by man have become absolutely one in a union which is not fusion and yet eliminates separation; thus this represents the historically unsurpassable eschatological communication of God to man himself through the history of grace in the world (without it being thereby possible simply to identify in some monophysite sense the historical mediation of God and God himself); man can and must accept this mediation-by-immediacy to God as something quite irreplaceable, by humbly accepting it in his own transcendentality by grace as something which is historically ordained and freely contingent. Man's reference to this historical mediation of his own grace inserted in the ground of his being does not take place merely or in the first place by a theoretical, historical knowledge about these historical events of salvation, a sort of knowledge which could be suspected as an ideology; it is given in an immediate, realistic manner which, through the living unity of the history of salvation, through the Church (which is more than just the subsequent totality of the theoretical opinions of those who agree), through sacraments and worship, through what we call anamnesis, tradition, etc., bursts open any merely theoretical information. Because man is mediated to the historical event of salvation and this mediation does not take place merely by way of theoretical information – since he experiences this mediation as the event of his own transcendental and supernaturally elevated being – he has always gone beyond the three above-mentioned basic forms of ideology. Secondly, it must be stated here that the necessary historical mediation of transcendentally established grace also draws the Christian's attention to the fact that he can and must also take his 'profane' history absolutely seriously. He does this not by turning it into an ideology and by thus erecting it into an absolute, but by the fact of experiencing it as the concrete expression of the will of God who posits it in freedom: thereby he both removes it from himself as the conditioned and historically contingent and lends it the seriousness proper to the situation in which an eternal destiny is decided before God. The consequences of this for a serious approach to history which avoids erecting an ideology will have to be mentioned again later on.

(d) There is a fourth point to be stressed against the thesis that Christianity is an ideology. Ideologies mutually exclude one another in their doctrine and intention and are nothing more than the factor by which they negate and fight each other, since what is in fact common to them exists in a sense in spite of the ideological theory and not because of it. Christianity, however, includes in its teaching what we will simply call 'anonymous' Christianity. Christianity does not restrict that which constitutes its most proper reality, viz. forgiving and divinising grace, to the circle of those who explicitly acknowledge the reflex and historical, instructive objectification of this ubiquitously active grace of God, in short, the explicit Christian doctrine and its bearer, the Church. Christianity, therefore, in view of the universal salvific will of God and the possibility of justification even before reception of the sacraments, includes its doctrinal opponents in its own reality and hence cannot even regard them as opponents in the same sense as ideologies do and must do. Ideologies, if they are tolerant (which cannot be completely reconciled with the nature of an ideology) may indeed accept their opponents in so far as they are human beings or have some other neutral common basis. But no ideology can admit that what is really meant, what is specific in its own position, can be conceded to its opponents on the plane of theoretical reflection and social constitution. An ideology cannot admit a third possibility outside itself which could bring about this community of reality before and behind the differences of its reflex explicitness. An ideology can never be greater than itself, whereas Christianity is more than itself precisely in the sense that it is the movement in which man surrenders himself to the unmasterable mystery and in so far as, fixing its regard on Jesus Christ, it knows that this movement actually finds the sheltering nearness of this mystery.

4. We wish now to add some of the consequences of our basic thesis to the aforegoing fundamental reflections on why Christianity is not an ideology.

(a) Christianity is not an ideology. From its nature and reflex doctrine about this its own reality, we could certainly derive general norms about God-conformed human activity, even in the sphere of the profane world, norms whose ultimate import is to preserve the openness of man to the God of absolute and forgiving nearness, and this in all dimensions of human existence, i.e. not limiting faith to a particular human existential dimension but making it the inner, formal law of man's whole life. But these general norms, in so far as they are contained in the message of Christianity and are proclaimed in the Church by her magisterium, leave room for imperatives and programmes which are determined by situations and history. Two conclusions follow from this. On the one hand, the

Church as such cannot become the direct and, as it were, official bearer of such concrete imperatives or of such concrete, history-forming guiding ideas; she cannot tell the Christian concretely in his individual and collective history what he must do exactly here and now; she cannot relieve him of the burden of the daring historical decision and its possible failure, and she cannot preserve him from the fact that history frequently gets into impossible situations. In other words, the Church must defend herself against becoming an ideology, if this is understood in the sense of a historical guiding idea which believes that if it is to have any real historical impact it must assert itself absolutely. On the other hand, the refusal by the Church to becoming an ideology in this sense does not mean that the Christian as such has no obligation in his individual and collective decision, and by reason of his Christian responsibility, to decide on some definite concrete imperative for the here and now and to bear the burden and risk for actions subsequent on such a concrete imperative. If his transcendentally Christian being realises itself in its history, and this in all its dimensions, then, even though the Church as such cannot furnish him with them, this quite simply entails the necessity and duty of finding concrete imperatives of his historical action in the midst of Christian existence. The Christian accepts this Christian responsibility for concrete decision in his historical situation; he takes this responsibility seriously as being obedience to the absolutely binding will of the living God; yet he does not turn this decision into an ideology since, without holding everything to be relative in a quietistic or sceptical way, he always lodges his decision again within the providence of the incontrollable Lord of history, in whose grace the success and failure of this decision can be saved and become availing unto salvation, and who can expect other decisions in conformity to his will from other ages and indeed enable men to take them.

(b) If Christianity is not an ideology – if, in other words, the imperatives and concrete decisions about intramundane actions and positions which Christians may and must have, must not be turned into an ideology – then there must be tolerance among Christians as an expression of the necessary avoidance of particular ideologies in the Church. Such tolerance is necessary because it is not to be expected that this choice of concrete imperatives, this interpretation of the historical moment and the decision for a particular path of history, will always be seen to be the same for all Christians. The struggle between such different decisions will be utterly unavoidable even among Christians; it cannot be avoided by any purely theoretical debates since this would presuppose that, at least in principle, the concrete imperatives for the here and now can be derived from universal principles and from a purely statistical, neutral analysis of the particular situation; such a possibility is a rationalistic error, since every decision for a concrete action adds a non-derivative factor to the *a priori* intuition of essences, viz. the choice of concrete existence from among many possibilities. Precisely because we cannot avoid a struggle, i.e. a real competition between opposite tendencies of realisation beyond the plane of the purely theoretical, there must necessarily be among Christians and in the Church what is meant by tolerance: understanding for the other's position, fairness in battle even when it is conducted seriously, that rare unity in determination with which one fights for one's own position, and the readiness to allow oneself to be defeated and to remain in the totality of the Church which decides differently.

From what has been said above about anonymous Christianity, as being the very opposite to an understanding of Christianity as an ideology, it follows then that there must be a similar attitude of positive tolerance towards non-Christians; this tolerance distinguishes the firmness and missionary zeal of the Faith from the fanaticism which is and must be characteristic of an ideology because only by such fanaticism can an ideology safeguard its strict boundaries against the greater reality surrounding it; Christianity in contrast is of its very nature commanded to look for itself in the other and to trust that it will once more meet itself and its greater fullness in the other.

(c) Naturally, Christianity must always be on its guard against the danger of misunderstanding itself as an ideology. It comes to the same thing in the end whether this happens in an ideology of transmanence or one of transcendence, or whether a particular position and decision – which in itself may be perfectly correct for a certain temporal situation and which at this time may be accepted in practice by the whole of Christendom – comes to be turned into an absolute ideology and to harden into a particular, reactionary ideology. Christianity is not – as it were – preserved from the outset from such dangers and it also cannot say that it has never and nowhere fallen into them. Everything as such which is purely doctrinaire and institutional offers no guarantee against such ideological fossilisation, especially since the protest against it can in its turn be made absolute in the form of an empty ideology. The Christian has the quiet confidence that God's pure and gratuitous grace will always prevent the danger of Christianity being turned into an ideology. Christians may be disunited in the question as to where precisely this invisible grace of God inserts itself concretely into his Church and as to what exactly belongs to that which both preserves this grace in his Church and saves it from becoming absolute in an ideology ... but Christians are united in the actual trust which they place in this grace. In the last analysis it is also the grace of preservation from an ideology which is nothing other than man's turning himself into an absolute.

5

MARXIST UTOPIA AND THE
CHRISTIAN FUTURE OF MAN

THE subject I have been given could be formulated as 'the Christian doctrine of the future of man'. It could also be expressed more polemically as the difference between Christian eschatology and intramundane utopia. Two preliminary remarks should be made as to the treatment of this subject. Firstly, it will be impossible to deal here explicitly with the humanly Christian experience of God as such. We must presuppose this subject here. This presupposition can, of course, be made in such a way that it is shown at least implicitly that the question about man's absolute future includes at the same time the question about God; in other words, that the man who opens himself to his absolute future, experiences also what is really meant by the word of God; it remains a secondary question whether he makes use of this word or not, whether or not he explicitly reflects on this unity of the absolute future and God. Secondly, since even the description of Christian eschatology already goes far beyond the possibilities of a brief paper, we can only touch marginally on what we have just called the intramundane utopia in contrast to Christian eschatology. Hence we will not treat of the question, but leave it open to discussion, as to whether the Marxist expectation of the future is the direct contradiction of the Christian teaching about the absolute future of the individual man and of humanity as a whole; whether, in other words, they contradict one another directly *or* whether the Christian doctrine about the future basically only fills an empty space left in the nature of things by the Marxist expectation of the future, since it merely envisages a possible, genuine, intramundane, and forseeable future which can be described in categories and which can be planned; this latter would mean that the Marxist denial of the Christian future, which of course does exist, is merely an external and separable addition to the blueprint of this intramundane future. Although there is really only one thing to be said on this point, viz. that God is present for us as the absolute future, this one thing can only be said in a series of consecutive expressions. It follows from this that every expression only becomes completely comprehensible when taken in conjunction with all the others and that we must therefore ask the listener to be patient and to wait until the end.

1. Christianity is a religion of the future. It can indeed be understood only in the light of the future which it conceives as an absolute future gradually approaching the individual and humanity as a whole. Its interpretation of the past takes place in and through the progressive unveiling of an approaching future, and the meaning and significance of the present is based on the hopeful openness to the approach of the absolute future. After all, Christianity understands the world within the framework of salvation *history*; this means, however, that properly speaking and in the last analysis it is not a doctrine of a static existence of the world and of man which, remaining always the same, repeats itself in an of-itself-empty period of time, without actually progressing; rather, it is the proclamation of an absolute becoming which does not continue into emptiness but really attains the absolute future, which is indeed already moving *within* it; for, this becoming is so truly distinguished from its yet-to-come future and fulfilment (without implying pantheism, therefore) that the infinite reality of this future is nevertheless already active within it and supports it as an inner constitutive element of this becoming, even though it is independent of this becoming itself (and in this way every form of primitive deism and any merely external relationship of God and the world are eliminated from the very start, and the truth *in* pantheism is preserved). The real nature of man can therefore be defined precisely as the possibility of attaining the absolute future, i.e. not this or that state which is always embraced and thus made relative again by some other and greater future still to come and yet imposed as a task, which would then also be recognised as such a relative future. Christianity, therefore, is the religion of becoming, of history, self-transcendence, and of the future. For Christianity, everything given is something imposed as a task, and everything is understandable only by what is yet to come. The tending towards a still outstanding future has indeed its own measure and a nature behind it which projects a horizon of the possible in front of it, and also a law in accordance with which it takes up position. But since the absolute fullness of the divine reality is

the ultimate reason, and since this very God who starts everything by giving himself as the end is the ultimate goal, any understanding of being and nature conforms to reality only if it seeks to understand in the light of that future which unveils the beginning for the first time.

2. Christianity is the religion of the *absolute* future. We have really already indicated the meaning of this in the previous paragraph. Man (and humanity) is the reality which knowingly and willingly is always ahead of itself, the reality which constitutes itself by projecting its future, or better, by projecting itself (i.e. its nature) towards *it* (or, since it is a question of the projecting of the *absolute* future which *per definitionem* cannot really be planned and formed: lets this future approach him). If this is so, then the decisive question for a metaphysical anthropology will be whether the future, towards which man projects himself, is merely a categorial future, i.e. one whose single and distinct, and therefore spatio-temporally bound elements form this future in combination (possibly planned and manipulated, possibly also always more complex), so that being something finite, it is always still basically encompassed by a further empty future possibility, *or* whether the unsurpassable, infinite future as such comes towards man and hence the possible space of the future and the future in the present become identical.

With regard to this question, Christianity opts for the second possibility: the absolute future is the true and real future of man; *it* is a real possibility for him, it is offered to him, it is something coming towards him, it is the future state and its acceptance is the ultimate task of his existence. Since the only way in which man can be concerned about a feasible future which has a spatio-temporal point and which is constructed out of the partial elements of his world, is by passing beyond it into the basic totality of unbounded possibility, man's intramundane care always contains (at least implicitly, and often perhaps also deliberately pushed aside) the question about the possible encounter with this infinite totality as such; in short, with the absolute future. Christianity answers this question in the sense that this absolute future is not only the always still absent condition of the possibility of a categorised intramundane planning of, hoping for and attaining of the future, but also becomes as such the communicated, attained future of man itself.

Christianity therefore poses man the *one* question as to how he wants basically to understand himself: as a being only acting *in* the whole but having nothing to do with the whole as such, even through projection towards the whole as an asymptotic horizon is always the condition of the possibility of his knowledge and action; or as a receptively acting being *of* the whole, a being which has something to do even with this condition for his knowledge, action and hope as *such* and which allows this totality, the absolute future itself, to approach it and to become an event for it in the action by which it creates the future within the bounds of this totality. This ultimately is the only question posed by Christianity. It follows from the very nature of the totality of the absolute future that this totality cannot really become the object of a proper classification or of a technical manipulation, but remains the unspeakable mystery which precedes and surpasses all individual cognition and each individual action *on* the world.

A mere glance at the current concepts of Christian dogmatic theology in which this thesis of Christianity as the religion of the absolute future is expressed, will show us that Christianity really understands itself in this way. Absolute future is just another name for what is really meant by 'God'. For the absolute future by its very concept cannot exist as a future which is manufactured out of finite, individual material and by classifiable combination; but it cannot be a merely empty possibility in the sense of being the not-yet-real, even when seen as the end and warrant of the dynamism of the world's and man's movement into the future, or as the sustaining hope; if it is the sustaining ground of the dynamism towards the future, then it must be the absolute fullness of reality. In point of fact the absolute future understood *in this way* is precisely what we call God. Conversely, from what has been said, there follows a twofold conclusion concerning God. Firstly, it follows that he is known precisely *as* the absolute future; in other words, he is not one object among many others with which one is concerned as individual objects within the unbounded system of co-ordinates of knowledge and planning action for the future, but rather is the ground of this whole projection towards the future. Knowledge of God is therefore always included when man projects himself towards the future, especially when man gives no name to this whole but tries to leave it unspecified. Secondly, God – understood as the absolute future – is basically and necessarily the unspeakable mystery, since the original totality of the absolute future, towards which man projects himself, can never really be expressed in the precise characteristics proper to it by determinations taken from intramundane, classifiable experience; thus he is and remains essentially a mystery, i.e. he is known *as* the essentially transcendent, of whom it is of course said that, understood precisely as this mystery of infinite fullness, he is the self-communicating absolute future of man.

Both these characteristcs of the knowledge of God give rise to the possibility of atheism. Atheism is possible because, firstly, it is always possible for man's knowledge-by-categories to refuse to enter into the transcendental conditioning of its own possibility. It is possible, secondly, because the confrontation with the fundamental mystery can always be declared to be something which is destroyed in its nature when it takes place in religion, for religion necessarily makes use of categories and social forms. It is possible, finally, because man can be an atheist in so far as he denies or doubts that God himself can become man's own absolute future and hence can be of the opinion that he has at any rate nothing to do with such a God.

If the absolute future of the world and of man is thus called God in Christian terminology, the event of its happening, sent to us by God, is called the definitive immediacy of the world to the self-communicating God. In a somewhat intellectualistic terminology, it means the direct vision of God, i.e. the direct presence of the world in its highest point, viz. man, to the absolute but communicated mystery. What Christianity calls grace, is nothing other than the self-communication of God, the absolute future, at the stage in which the history of its approach and acceptance is still going on. What is called the incarnation of the divine Logos in Jesus Christ means nothing other than that in Jesus this self-communication of God, the absolute future of the world, comes into such historical presence, objectively and for us, that it becomes credible as something given, irreversible and comprehensible by the categorising experience of humanity *as such*. But God, the definitive immediate presence to him, grace and Jesus Christ, embrace the whole of the salvific reality confessed by the Christian faith. Yet since all these words declare only the one thing, viz. that the world – by the very fact of being really saved – has an absolute future and that its becoming attains its goal only in God's absoluteness, we are justified in saying that Christianity is the religion of the absolute future.

3. Being the religion of the absolute future, Christianity has no utopian ideas about a future in this world. It does indeed declare that for each individual it is decided with his *death* whether or not he has opened himself by the deed of his life to the absolute future of God. But with regard to the collective history of mankind as such, it has no indication to start with

about how long this collective history will last in this world. It also remains neutral, moreover, with regard to the material *content* of this future. It does not set up ideals for the future with any definite content; it makes no prognoses in this matter and does not oblige man to any particular goal regarding his future in this world. Any future which is planned by man and is to be produced by the intramundane means at his disposal and which is posited as an *absolute* beyond which there is nothing and there is nothing to be expected, would be rejected by Christianity as an expectation for the future which only amounts to utopian ideology.

Christianity would reject it as an ideology whose nature consists in turning a particular, individual reality of the pluralistic world of our experience into an absolute, fixed point; it would also reject it as utopian because in the long run it is individually and collectively impossible to confuse an intramundane and therefore finite future – no matter how concrete it may be – with the absolute future, or to forbid man to inquire beyond this finite future when, having recognised it to be finite, he always situates it in any case within the wider framework of infinite possibilities. Where one abstains, however, from turning an intramundane future into an absolute in such a utopian-ideological way, Christianity does not remain merely neutral with regard to any sensible planning of the future in this world but takes up a *positive* attitude towards it. The rational and actively planning construction of an intramundane future, the greatest possible liberation of man from the dominion of nature, the progressive socialisation of man for the attainment of the greatest possible scope for freedom, are regarded by Christianity as part of the task demanded of man by his divinely willed nature, a task to which man is obliged and *in* which he fulfils his real religious duty, viz. the openness of freedom in believing hope for the absolute future.

In so far as the basis for the *absolute* value of each man is provided in Christianity solely by the absolute future of every man, a conviction emerges from this which in its turn provides the firmest and deepest basis for the intramundane concern for the future, having for its aim as perfect a social order as possible. In Christianity, the love of God and the love of man signify the *one* commandment and the one accomplishment of authentic Christianity; love of God does not imply some sort of ideological extra, added to the real accomplishment of existence, but implies the accepting, hoping openness to the total meaning of human existence and to the absolute future; and this precisely where this concern no longer permits the active construction of a purely intramundane kind of future. It follows then that by this one commandment and by this one accomplishment of human existence we are given a proper statement also of the innermost dynamism of the intramundane change of man and of his social situation, without Christianity thereby becoming a contradiction of or competitive to intramundane planning of the future. Christianity itself has no intramundane utopian view of the future. It leaves all objective planning of the future free and rejects only – but radically – every ideological utopian view of the future in which the absolute future is confused with an intramundane and categorisable future and in which the ultimate future of man is seen to consist in something less than the unspeakable, sacred mystery of the absolute God who out of sheer grace communicates himself to man and who with a view to this communication has made the dynamic the ultimate meaning and motor of the history of the world and of humanity.

4. Even though it is the religion of the absolute future, a religion which remains neutral in the face of the individual and collective aims of man and leaves them free, Christianity has an inestimable significance for this movement towards genuine and meaningful earthly goals. Christianity, it is true, does not maintain that only *its* followers can serve this earthly future objectively and with the involvement of the whole man. This would be no more true than to say that it regards itself as the sole genuine bearer of such intramundane aims for the future or that it disputes the fact of having been in quite a few cases an actual obstacle to such efforts on account of the historico-ecclesiastical forms in which it has manifested itself. There are obviously men who – without being manifestly Christians – spend themselves in selfless service for the welfare and social development of man. Christianity, it is true, maintains by its very teaching about the oneness of the love of God and of neighbour that whenever someone serves man and his dignity lovingly and in *absolute* selflessness, he affirms God at least implicitly and also works out his salvation before God by his affirmation of absolute moral values and imperatives ... but it does not maintain in any sense that this is possible only in someone who is explicitly a Christian.

Nevertheless, Christianity even taken as the thematically explicit religion which sees God as the absolute future, has great significance for intramundane society and its goals. By its hope for an absolute future, Christianity defends man against the temptation of engaging in the justified intramundane efforts for the future with *such* energy that every generation is always sacrificed in favour of the next, so that the future becomes a Moloch before whom the man existing at present is butchered for the sake of some man who is never real and always still to come. Christianity makes it comprehensible why even *that* man preserves his dignity and intangible significance who can no longer make any tangible contribution to the approach to the intramundane future. Christianity lends ultimate radical significance to the work for this intramundane future: it declares in its teaching on the unity of the love of God and of neighbour that the positive relationship to man is an indispensable, essential element and the irreplaceable means for the relationship to God, the absolute future (and 'salvation'). If, however, this man who is to be loved cannot exist except as someone who makes projects with a view to his future, then this means that the love of God understood as the love of neighbour cannot exist without the will to *this* man and hence also to his intramundane future. This does not ideologise this will or estrange it from itself, but merely makes it explicit in its absolute dignity and in its radical nature as an obligation.

5. Christianity, understood as the religion of the absolute future, will always remain.

(a) It will remain. No one will be able in the long run to deter man from taking himself seriously. The more 'rational' man becomes in the history of humanity, the more he is conscious of himself and the more he experiences himself in his completely personal uniqueness, freedom and dignity. The more important and demanding society appears to him, the more the individual will grow in significance. Otherwise society itself would inevitably degenerate into a herd of insignificant beings. The dignity of society, the radical seriousness of the tasks and demands imposed by it, increases rather than diminishes the dignity and radical seriousness which the individual owes to himself and to every other individual. Even from this point of view, he will experience his absolute uniqueness more rather than less keenly in future. The freer man becomes of the fetters of nature, the more he becomes conscious of himself and free for and towards himself. No economic change and no social system will be able to prevent man from knowingly experiencing his death as a boundary and from putting himself as a whole in question.

One cannot deprive man of the question about himself as a whole and about the meaning as such of his existence which is no longer orientated towards the functional connections of the individual moments of his world and existence but towards the meaning of the *whole*. He may then declare that he has no answer to this question; he may perhaps try *for this reason* to declare this question itself to have no meaning. But the question will always pose itself again; it will always be and at least remain there as a question to be always explained *anew* as meaningless. Thus there will also always be men who have the courage to respond to this question with the answer of the religion of the absolute future. Such men do not say that they have an answer to the question about the one total meaning of human existence and the world on *that* plane on which the content of the answer could be shown to exist in this world *alongside* other realities of experience. They say rather that the one ground of the whole variety of reality – the one ground which in itself anticipates everything – always and necessarily is and remains an incomprehensible mystery when regarded from the point of view of the plurality of these empirical realities.

They believe, however, that God sends himself precisely in this way to men as the absolute future for man, and that he can and must therefore be named and expected by man. This is what they understand by religion. Religion for them is not the solution of those questions arising in this world, as it were functionally, *between* individual realities in their mutual relationships; it is the solution of the question which refers to the *whole* of these many different realities. Since this question will always remain, religion too – Christianity – will always remain, since its nature consists precisely in not confusing the question of the world with the question *in* the world.

(b) This permanent religion will always remain as an institutional religion. Since man must *also* accomplish, in a reflex way, even his transcendental relation to the one totality of his existence, his world and his future, he has to accomplish it also in conceptual categories, in concrete actions, in the social order, briefly: in a Church. He cannot do it in any other way. If, therefore, the religion of the future is to be present always, then it will always be there as a social quantity. This quantity in its historical concreteness will always depend *also* on the profane order of secular society. Since Christianity has no concretely binding view of this profane society and is also incapable of prophesying about it, it cannot make any prediction about the *concrete form* of its own socio-ecclesiological structure of the future.

Since Christianity – however much it knows itself to be the religion which in itself is meant for all men – knows in the *very* nature of things and in its *eschatology* that it will be a controversial and even rejected institution until the dawn of the absolute future itself, this reason alone suffices to prevent it from counting on ecclesiastical and secular society ever becoming even merely materially identified. It itself is after all the socially organised community of free belief in the absolute future, of a belief therefore which is necessarily based on the individual decision of each person. Hence it cannot expect in any way that all men will ever *in actual fact* belong to it. Since the earthly future of mankind, however, tends more and more towards a social organisation of mankind as one and as a whole, and not to historically and geographically limited cultures particular to each individual people, a situation is rapidly approaching when everyone will be the neighbour of everyone else. This means that in future there also will be no more *homogeneous* regional strata and societies in the Christian sense. In the historical and social unity of the one humanity, Christianity will therefore be everywhere as well as being everywhere merely a part of humanity, since presumably embracing only a minority.

It is, therefore, in the interests of Christianity itself to be able to live in freedom in a secular society which itself intends to be pluralistic in the religious field and which creates or at least permits the possibilities and presuppositions for this; this does not decide anything about the extent to which a society must presuppose or create an intramundane homogeneous 'world-view' for its own continued existence. A society of the future can support such a religious pluralism all the more easily as it will certainly not wish to aspire seriously to an absolute uniformity even as an ideal in so far as an *intramundane* ideology is concerned, since such a uniformity would mean the end of history. Every theory about a future within this world which as such does not wish to annul history must, therefore, necessarily develop a theory of legitimate intramundane and, in this sense, democratic pluralism. It must therefore inevitably make room of its own accord for there being *those* in this future who, professing themselves as such, wait hopefully for the absolute future.

PART TWO

Questions of Fundamental Theology

6

PHILOSOPHY AND THEOLOGY

THE overall theme of this symposium – even though it is historical – permits also of a systematic view. In this hour's talk, we mean simply to consider a small *part* of this total systematic view, viz. the relationship between theology and philosophy. This means more precisely that we are going to ask about how and why revelation and reflection on it (which we call theology) leave room of *themselves* for a philosophy, understood as an independent and basic science and *as* a condition of the possibility of theology. For, if the relationship between the two is not seen simply as one of peaceful co-existence or as the encounter of two sciences alien to each other by their very origins and merely having an ultimately common source in God, but is seen rather in the sense just indicated regarding the question posed, then the connection between the question about the relationship between philosophy and theology and the overall theme becomes immediately evident. If theology of its very nature presupposes philosophy as a condition of its own possibility, and presupposes it as an independent basic science, then it is quite possible that Western philosophy – in so far as it corresponds to and obeys this its basic origin – should be both the harbinger and forerunner of what the West is even now still charged to give to the world: the message of Jesus Christ, the divine Logos in the flesh of the world. It is quite possible then that it should also fulfil this commission precisely by turning to men in the world on their own ground, which is philosophy itself representing man's own understanding of himself.

It is all-important, therefore, to attain the envisaged unity and diversity of philosophy and theology, and this precisely as originating from theology itself. If this attempt is successful, then it will no longer be necessary to speak directly about the connection of this reflection with the overall theme itself, for this will then be perfectly evident.

It is not my intention to conjure up anew the controversy about the possibility and nature of a *Christian* philosophy, a controversy which – while renewing even earlier problems – has been carried on in the last few decades. In referring to this question, we are trying to come to the real point right away. Whatever may have been the results of the controversy just referred to, it will surely be impossible to deny that the opinion of a basic strangeness existing between philosophy and theology still prevails among Catholics. One stresses with the Vatican Council the duality of knowledge by natural reason and by revelation supported by grace; it is said that these two cannot contradict each other because they both have their ultimate source in God, the One Truth; it is denied that philosophy and the philosopher (if he is a Catholic) can emancipate themselves completely from the higher norm of revelation and of the Church's magisterium, but one adds immediately that it is simply a question here of a *norma negativa*. One stresses the necessity and significance of philosophy within theology itself; one also points to the in fact very varied stimuli for new themes which theology has offered to philosophy in the Christian sphere, yet these stimuli are allowed validity in most cases only as a kind of external growth-stimulant for a development which after all only philosophy can give itself. All in all, philosophy and theology are simply conceived as two basically different sciences and this conception is more or less presupposed as self-evident. Philosophy 'is simply there'; one has it, engages in it, knows what it is, and so this structure, whose difference one declares to be 'natural', comes face to face with theology; they meet one another like two people who did not previously know one another, who are unrelated and will now try to see whether – even after all this time – one could not combine together in a tolerable symbiosis.

What is then, in reality, the truth about this relationship?

This question is ultimately only part of a much greater theological question about the relationship between nature and grace. In saying this, however, we must add right away that nothing much is gained by making this statement, since the relationship between the *latter* two factors is no clearer. It is important just the same not to overlook this greater problem when dealing with the smaller.

Starting from this, it can be said to begin with that just as the concrete reality of grace includes nature as an inner moment within itself, so also in our question . . . philosophy is an inner moment of theology. Grace is not a thing, but a particular condition of a spiritual person (really of this person *himself*, even though not owed to him). As the determination of a subject, it is – as such – formally distinct from this subject, in fact in no way owed to it. But it can also exist *as* this determination of this subject, as a particular manner-of-being of this spiritual person. It can exist and be understood in this way only in the sense that through it the *person*, i.e. 'nature', exists, viz. exists *in this way* and is understood as being in this way. Fulfilment in grace is necessarily also fulfilment of the natural person. In *this* sense, therefore, the latter is an inner moment of the concreteness of grace, just as potency is the potency of *act* and act is the act of the *potency*, and both therefore mutually embody one another in the concrete so as to exist and to exist as such themselves. Grace exists by affecting a spiritual, personal substantiality, by being the divinising condition *of the latter*, and hence presupposes and incorporates into itself the whole reality of this person as the condition of its own possibility and makes it part of the factors of its own concrete being.

This is also the way in which we must understand the relationship between revelation and theology, on the one hand, and philosophy, on the other. First of all, revelation understood as something heard and believed, is necessarily also already theology. It may be only the rudimentary beginnings of theology, but it really is already theology. After all, revelation – wherever and indeed because it is taken as historical and propositional revelation – is heard by a human being who already knows other things besides this revelation, a revelation which does not occur always and everywhere but only here and now. But the hearing of a message by someone who already has other knowledge can only be possible – since it takes place in the unity of this one person – in confrontation with this other knowledge, however undefinitive this confrontation may be; it is hearing by means of categories already possessed from elsewhere, a reception within previously given horizons, however much these horizons themselves may be altered by this hearing; in other words, it is already an active effort of thought by man; in short, it is theology, however much this theology may in certain circumstances be thought of as being subject also to the direction and control of the original process of revelation. Such theology, however, being a necessary and unavoidable element of the hearing of revelation and hence of revelation itself, necessarily implies philosophy, i.e., a previous, transcendental as well as historical self-comprehension of the man who hears the historical revelation of God. Whether or not this self-understanding may already be called philosophy in the technical sense is quite immaterial in the final analysis, as long as one admits that even philosophy in the strictest sense cannot be anything other than the methodically exact, reflected and most expediently controlled representation and articulation of this original and never quite attained self-understanding. In other words, anyone who admits that in the unity of the one subject, every bit of knowledge is also the function of every other part of knowledge possessed by this subject, and who does not maintain by this that every knowledge has to do with revelation (a point to which we will have to return), must admit that revealed knowledge is also the function of philosophy, given that philosophy is understood as the basic formula of man's self-understanding in so far as the latter is not simply itself an effect of revelation.

If, however, this relationship of dependence is not to detract from the dignity and autonomy of revelation and theology, then it can be understood only in the sense that revelation is the highest entelechy and norm of this knowledge, unified in the unity of the one subject and thus presupposes this different 'philosophical' knowledge – precisely *as* a different kind of knowledge – as the condition of its own possibility. Only under this condition is it possible to avoid the dilemma of considering revelation either as being dependent on a knowledge different from it or as having to be quite independent of philosophy. This is especially true since the inner objective reconciliation and the original unity of what remains indifferent in knowledge cannot be brought about by the simple expedient of falling back on the one objective source of both kinds and powers of knowledge.

This brings us to a problem which we cannot really consider in its *formal* nature more exactly, viz. the general question as to whether and how a being can presuppose another being – precisely in so far as it is *another* – as the real condition of its own being, and thus presuppose itself, and whether and how the other – precisely as other – can be the inner condition of an existent (without reducing this to the category of the relationship of efficient causality) and how one can recognise this kind of thing. We intend to leave this problem to one side and will turn again to our own more limited question. That something like philosophy is an inner moment of theology (and therefore also of revelation), poses no difficulties in itself, since every being can be conceived as constructed of different constitutive elements and hence one moment of theology might very well be called – philosophy. The difficulty, however, is to understand the fact that, and the way in which, theology distinguishes this moment within its own being as something other than itself and at the same time introduces it into its own autonomous being; this being the only way in which it can make it a real condition of its own being. The difficulty in all this lies in the fact that the indispensable *ancilla theologiae* can be such only if it is at the same time *domina* in its own house without the role of *ancilla* being simply a part-time job alongside the principal job of being master, and that this mastery is possible only through the services to theology rendered as *ancilla*. What is the reason for this?

We can make this clear by a series of connected theological reflections. We must first of all fall back again on the relationship of nature and grace, and ask: why cannot the reality called 'nature' be conceived simply as an inner moment in the concrete relationship to God, which is known as the order of grace, in such a way that if it is not given grace, it must always be thought of as always and completely meaningless and hence simply sinful? The answer is: because grace, understood as the absolute self-communication of God himself, must always presuppose as a condition of its own possibility (in order to be itself) someone to whom it can address itself and someone to whom it is not owed; which therefore means also someone who can be thought of without contradiction even apart from this communication. Accordingly, it must be said that since revelation is a moment in this free self-opening-out by gratuitous grace, it presupposes as a condition of its own possibility the one to whom this revelation remains unowed; revelation taken as the gnosis of the child adopted gratuitously by *grace* presupposes the servant as the condition of its own possibility. God has created the servant only in order to make him his child; but he was able to create the child of grace, in distinction to his only-begotten Son, only by creating the addressee without claim to sonship, i.e. the servant. In the same way, God has willed the truth of philosophy only because he willed the truth of his own self-revelation, i.e. the absolute, beatifying truth which he is himself and which for us is the vision which is the nearness and not the distance of the absolutely Incomprehensible. He could, however, only will precisely this divine truth which is given out and away from himself, as the truth which is a gratuitous grace and is expressed in and out of love. For this reason he had to create the one from whom he could keep this truth a secret, i.e. the philosopher who, because he himself experienced God as the one who conceals himself, could accept revelation from him *as a grace*. What we call revelation, therefore, is not something added which – simply resting in itself and self-evident – is presupposed by a spiritual nature and its self-understanding. Rather, the spiritual nature is the necessary condition presupposed by revelation *itself* and set free *so that* revelation can be what it is, viz. the grace which is the personal and free self-communication of God. The statement that the covenant includes creation and that the latter does not simply precede the former in time, can be understood in a perfectly correct sense which does not destroy the real Catholic meaning of the distinction between nature and grace but rather makes it possible and indeed provides the basic reason for it. Since the self-disclosure of God in a personal revelation and as a free act of love can appear only to someone who understands himself and who thus disposes autonomously over himself, revelation presupposes a clearly distinguished, free philosophy as the space for its own possibility. This reflection could be supplemented by a glance at the fact that this revelation, since it is to be responded to by free faith, must also be able to exist in the mode of rejection, and that it itself can create *this* its own possibility only if the 'disbelief' does not thereby simply cancel itself out but still remains nature and self-consciousness which can explain itself philosopically.

The question about the *temporal* succession of philosophy and theology (revelation) must be distinguished from these essential relations between revelation and philosophy (understood as the other-than-itself pre-supposed by revelation itself). The essential relationship envisaged here can exist even though there is philosophy *before* revelation *in time*, for the temporal succession is precisely the historical manner of appearance of this essential relationship. Even what is earlier in time can be and can become precisely *because* it is the condition of the possibility of what comes later in time, for both come about because they are supported by the one God who simply wants one thing, viz. to communicate himself; hence two factors must be posited, viz. the constitution of the hearer *who is to be given the grace* of the message and the message itself. These two must be distinct if the message is to be an act of the free love of the personal self-communication of God. The autonomy of the spirit as 'nature' is the condition of the possibility of that obedience by which alone revelation can be accepted as it should be, viz. in the free acceptance of *grace*.

We cannot show here, of course, what exactly is to be understood – from the point of view of philosophy itself – by the thus postulated free-dom of that autonomous philosophy which is introduced by revelation and its theology into this freedom in order to serve them. We cannot show here how this autonomy is to be conceived more exactly, so that it can be the autonomy of a ἐπιστήμη πρώτη without endangering the ultimate originality and independence of revelation and faith and without subjecting these, contrary to their nature, to *its* law. Instead, we would simply refer the reader to J. B. Metz: 'Theologische und metaphysische Ordnung', *ZKT* LXXXIII (1961), pp. 1–14

The unity of philosophy and theology within their theological distinction is much closer than has been suggested in our reflections up to this point. To see this, we must attend to the difference between general salvation- and revelation-history, on the one hand, and the special and official revelation-history expressed in concepts and words, on the other hand, which alone is usually called revelation-history. Anyone who believes in the universal, serious and efficacious salvific will of God towards the whole of humanity and this to include even infralapsarian mankind – and anyone who believes in this salvific will as a supernatural, gratuitous order of salvation and as the basis of the one supernatural goal of man – cannot seriously dispute the fact that salvation-history (as the accepted or rejected, but real offer of God's self-communication to man) is co-existent with the whole personal history of mankind; in other words, he cannot seriously dispute that salvation-history and world-history are not indeed absolutely identical but nevertheless coincide in space and in time. But anyone who as a good thomist holds fast to the principle that the supernatural gratuitous elevation of man by the grace of salvation (whether accepted or rejected) is an elevation to a new formal object of the spirit which is unattainable by any merely natural act – i.e. an elevation to a new, even though perhaps permanently unthematic horizon, within which every spiritual existence takes place – cannot really deny that the universal salvation-history co-existent in space and time with world-history signifies also in a true sense a co-extensive universal *revelation-history*, if it is permissible to give the name of revelation even to the simple opening out of an *absolute* horizon of spiritual existence by the free act of God's self-communication. If this is so, then it follows that what we normally call revelation and revelation-history is in reality the conceptually concrete, propositional and divinely controlled '*thematisation*' of the universal gratuitous revelation and its history achieved by God through his witnesses and miracles, and not the first most original or slowly generalised revelation-history which could be contrasted only to the so-called *natural* revelation-history. If there is indeed a universal, supernatural salvific will of God, then there is a revelation-history which is co-existent with the history of mankind and hence with the whole history of religion. This general revelation does not occur directly by way of the objectivity and conceptuality constitutive of the 'thematic content' of human words, but by a change in the unthematic horizon and in the basic condition of the mind of the person, a change which necessarily takes place on account of the accepted or rejected supernatural grace. The reflection on, and thematisation and interpretation of this supernatural basic condition, in which the absolute mystery is experienced as the absolute, giving nearness, may not be possible at all up to a certain point by man's unaided powers; it may have a long history; the way in which it is directed or furthered by God, and guaranteed by prophets and miracles, may not be the same everywhere; it may often be mixed up with false interpretations, a fact which proclaims the helplessness and the guilt of unbelief or of any proud wanting-to-be-like-God by one's own powers. Yet the effects of the supernatural basic condition of man – understood as an existential signifying revelation and given by grace – are unavoidably being produced wherever man lives his life under that grace which calls him whether he is conscious of it or not and whether he listens to it or deliberately and disobediently turns a deaf ear to it. It follows from this, however, that in the present, universal order of salvation which actually concerns all men in all ages, that self-clarification of man's existence which we call philosophy, can certainly be 'pure' philosophy in a particular sense; namely in the sense that it does not take any of its material contents and norms from the official, socially constituted and hence ecclesiastical, special and thematised revelation; it is not true in the sense that the unthematic illumination of human existence, out of which it draws life and which it never adequately catches up on or can replace, *only* contains elements arising out of the *natural* being of man.

The depth of the human abyss, which in a thousand ways is *the* theme of philosophy, is already the abyss which has been opened by God's grace and which stretches into the depths of God himself; and this precisely when and where the philosophising man cannot attain this fact of his spiritual existence by exact reflection, when and where he cannot distinguish nature and grace in the accomplishment of his spiritual existence.

It follows from this, however, that where the official, explicit Christian revelation presupposes philosophy as the condition of its own possibility, and brings it into its freedom, this in no way takes the form of a positing of the *pure* possibility but inevitably takes place in the form of a philosophy already actuated to some extent by Christianity. This is so not only when men engage in philosophy who are explicitly conscious of being Christians but also when those men philosophise whom we might call anonymous Christians (and this applies in principle to all men who do not explicitly call themselves Christians). The anonymous Christians – whether they know it or not, whether they distinguish it from the light of their natural reason or not – are enlightened by the light of God's grace which God denies to no man. From this point of view, it is correct to say that in every philosophy men already engage inevitably and unthematically in theology, since no one has any choice in the matter – even when he does not know it consciously – whether he wants to be pursued by God's revealing grace or not. Only we Christians are on the whole too blind or too lazy to recognise this latent 'Christianness' in the history of human existence, of religion in general and of philosophy. Unconsciously we are often guilty of living in the selfish narrow-mindedness of those who think their knowledge is more valuable and more blessed with grace if it is possessed only by a few; we rather foolishly think that God himself only makes an impression on men with His truth when *we* have already made an impression on them with our thematic and sociologico-official and explicit form of this truth.

Before thinking this out further, it must be remembered also that the philosophy of the West has been freed to live its own life in a thousand different explicit and historically tangible ways by Christian revelation and theology. This is well known and has been stated often. Yet it is perhaps well to acknowledge that this does not happen only in patristic and medieval philosophy but also in modern philosophy right up to the present day. The philosophers themselves may often have been only lukewarm Christians or no Christians at all; their philosophy in its propositional results (which are not indeed the be all and end all of philosophy) may often have to be rejected in the name of Christianity; yet the questions, the development of themes, the opening up of new horizons in all this dialogue contain many more Christian elements than we faint-hearted Christians – if we serve more the letter than the spirit of a Christian philosophy – would be prepared to admit. One could say quite rightly that the turning from a cosmocentric objective philosophy of the Greeks to the anthropocentric transcendental philosophy of the moderns is perfectly Christian in principle and basically already begins with St Thomas; it would be quite true to say, therefore, that the ecclesiastical 'philosophy of the schools' has still much to catch up on and to save with regard to what has been developed apart from it, though without being fully conscious of itself, as a partial realisation of what in fact is possible only in the *kairos* of Christianity and yet is still genuinely independent philosophy outside the orthodoxy of the magisterium.

After these reflections, we now go on to presuppose that the Church – and secondarily, by derivation from her, the Western world – still have the historically unfulfilled and still valid mission and commission to proclaim Christ's revelation to the whole world and to the future, globally unified history. What follows then – under this presupposition – from what has been said up to this point, with regard to the philosophy of the West?

1. First of all, the West need not abandon its own synthesis of theology and philosophy in favour of an attempt to hand on the, as it were, naked message of Christianity without the so-called 'overlay' of Western philosophy. This need not happen because there can be no proclamation of revelation without theology and no theology without philosophy. One can only spread abroad what one has heard ... but whatever is to be spread abroad, is heard only in the measure of its acceptance within the whole of one's own spiritual existence. An unphilosophical theology would be a bad theology ... and a theology which is bad, cannot render its necessary service to the proclamation of revelation.

2. This does not mean, however, that the Western world should be simply allowed to extend its traditional philosophy in a traditional way into a world-philosophy, perhaps even with the tacit view that a philosophical garb which has become unfashionable with us, will still be good and modern enough for the barbarians. This philosophy is necessary and useful for the procalamation of Christianity precisely if it is adequate enough for the really sufficient hearing of revelation by *ourselves*. This is so, however, only if we attain this philosophy anew in and out of our own actual spiritual situation, which really is ours here and now, and thus when it is not merely 'the handed-down' but a creatively and newly fashioned philosophy. After historism, and in the age of microphysics and cybernetics, of a history which is becoming planetary and in an age or a more deeply structured society, etc., *our* own existential situation that is to be illumined by philosophy is different from what it was before; and hence

our philosophy too must be different. This includes even the philosophy by which, in the evening of its existence, the Western world must deliver the gospel message.

3. Furthermore, this situation which is also the *kairos* of our philosophy today, embraces also encounter with the existence and hence with the explicit or implicit philosophy of those to whom we, in the evening of our history, may and must still bring the ever-young message of the Lord. The listeners change the situation of the speakers, and this even in favour of the *Christian character* of our own situation as philosophers. As we have said already, there can be no philosophy which could be simply a-Christian. The Western message of Christianity, even by means of the philosophy which precedes and accompanies it, has also undoubtedly the task of furthering the philosophical self-understanding of the non-Western world and of helping it to become more conscious of itself and free itself both from error and the abbreviation of its self-interpretation. Yet, since the Western world, during its wanderings into strange lands while carrying Christ's message, always encounters a world in which Christ's grace has long been at work even though not called by its own name, the reverse must necessarily also happen if everything runs its proper course: the anonymous Christianity (i.e. humanity and endowment with grace) of non-Western philosophy can bring to light and eradicate abbreviations of its Christian nature in the explicitly Christian philosophy of the West; it can liberate latent possibilities of its nature which even Christian philosophy, in spite of its name and of its inherent possibilities, and even as a specifically Christian philosophy, has not caught up with. In brief, the proclaiming West can itself become more Christian and more philosophical by having to listen in order to become comprehensible. Whether and to what extent there thereby arises anything like a common Christian world-philosophy – or whether and how national and historical individual and incommensurable traits may unfold themselves in multiple philosophies which need not necessarily contradict each other and yet may be multiple – all this depends on the question (which we cannot enter into here) as to whether and how the unity and interlacement of the until now separated historical spheres will produce a homogeneous and yet still and indeed even more differentiated world-culture.

7

A SMALL FRAGMENT 'ON THE COLLECTIVE FINDING OF TRUTH'

I F a human community has no longer any common possession of truth, then both it and the individual would be destroyed, i.e. degraded to a merely biological and physical level, a level on which alone man (taken as an individual and as community) cannot exist. In man, seen as the being of inescapable reflection, reflection itself belongs also to the conditions of his material and biological existence. His 'ideology', therefore, is just as much the 'substructure' as the 'super-structure' of his human existence. A common truth (understood at least as the common basis for the validity of the 'rules of the game' of interpersonal activity) is also always present at least in an ultimate basic 'store', since this is already implied in the existence of language, without which man cannot live. Words, which are used in relation to someone else, always presuppose a common valid meaning; at the very least – in the most extreme case – in the words by which one person maintains that there is no such meaning and by which it is understood by another person, or by which the denial of someone else's proposition is communicated to him. Even someone who says that every language is related to a finite system of reference and is valid only within this system, communicates with this other person by this statement, especially if it is heard by the other and is accepted by him (and this is the intention of this statement); he communicates with the other in the permanent openness of what is unspeakable and hence present, in whose presence he achieves the know-ledge of the invincible finiteness of his system of reference and of his language and by which – without destroying this finiteness – he has nevertheless already crossed over it.

If, therefore, it is a question of the attempt at a collective finding of truth, or of a 'dialogue' which seeks agreement and unity, of discussion, debate, conflict of opinion – and ultimately all these terms mean the same thing – then this attempt does not start off from absolute zero. This beginning does not necessarily have to take place in a formulated, explicit series of propositions. Not every dialogue by which a truth is sought begins like a Catholic Council with a presupposed and explicitly formulated profession of faith which becomes lost on the wings of a hymn into the incomprehensible nature of God and which serves as the starting-point from which each and every person, together with all the others, tries to find the collective truth. It need not always be like this, and this simply because, even in the just-mentioned case, the newly sought collective truth is precisely the better understanding of that common possession of the truth; hence its starting-point and goal strangely coincide. If one were, however, simply to presuppose in any attempt at a collective finding of truth that one does not yet possess any common truth, or that the other person is simply and purely in error, then one could not even begin. At least an unadministered, not yet counted capital of common convictions is invested in every dialogue.

The question of the collective finding of truth, of course, presupposes that there is such a finding which is possible only in such a dialogue. There is no dialogue in the research laboratories of the modern exact sciences. There one merely points out certain facts to one another, facts which everyone can see for himself; the object itself does not exist in dialogue as such. Here, however, we are referring to the fact that there are truths to be found which are present only in the process of the collective finding of truth and which only thus begin to appear. There are such truths, even though too indiscreet a conception of the objectivity of truth (even that which is sought in dialogue) may give the impression that even the dialogue is merely one – basically replaceable – way of drawing attention to the intended truth, so that one may then equally well associate with it on one's own and in silence. The dialogue whose object is meant here is concerned with man himself. But man is himself only by being someone who lives, someone who cares about others, someone who opens himself, who accepts absolute responsibility for and before the other, the place in which the whole gathers together and thereby reveals itself – by rejecting and accepting at the same time – as what is different from that which simply collects together. This man, therefore, neither finds himself ultimately by specialised scientific and technological examination or by lonely self-reflection, because what is attained in these ways is either (in the first case) merely something *about* man, or because (in the second case) man is blinded or becomes dumb concerning himself since he has no longer anything to which he could contrast himself. This does not apply, of course, to the case in which he calls upon and thus turns to that incomprehensible breadth itself which he knows is always embracing him by supporting and differentiating him, since it is the very condition of the possibility of his coming to *himself* and not merely to something about himself. It is true, in other words, of all cases except in the case where man prays – whatever name he himself may give to the acceptance of this governing power of the all-embracing mystery of his existence – but this merely reinforces what we have said, viz. that the finding of the truth of man takes place in dialogue; it really *is* a collective seeking for truth and does not merely use dialogue as a help.

If our first two reflections just briefly indicated are correct, then the collective finding of truth can really and ultimately consist only in the fact that a person makes an effort in such a dialogue to recognise as his own the community which he presupposes and this in the way in which it is given in others; conversely, it means that the person lets the other recognise this community as his own just as it is given in himself and is brought before his own and the other's consciousness in the dialogue. Dialogue, therefore, presupposes and seeks unity, and lives in a genuine tension between both these attitudes.

A dialogue concerned with the collective finding of truth can create an agreement: one agrees on a formula. This formula has its own significance because a reflex (i.e. formulated) self-understanding is itself a moment in the totality of man's personal, spiritual self-possession; man lives out of its never adequately administered fullness (and history), and is all the time striving towards that silent and yet – *dum silentium tenerent omnia* – self-communicating and original fullness of reality which we call God. Yet, since man only possesses himself in his original self-understanding – which he is but cannot administer as he wills – by attributing something of it to himself and to others, the formula is important and essential for the whole (and especially the intellectual) life of man. Moreover, since man always exists only by being open to dialogue with others, the common formula – or the 'confession of society' by which it is supported – is a goal of the dialogue for the collective finding of the truth towards which one ought necessarily to strive. If we were no longer to strive for it, there would no longer be a dialogue, since a mere 'understanding' of someone else's opinion of making of one's own opinion understood, already necessarily includes a moment of approval (at least in the sphere referred to here), an approval which wants to widen and deepen itself. But this attempted and attainable formula, being embraced by an existential questionableness which can never be completely overcome, is always at the same time open also towards the future. The remaining paragraphs will explain what this means.

The formula is never the thing itself and remains inadequate in comparison with it. Even in the case of the objects of a dialogue, it is never possible to say that one is speaking about *one* thing and is leaving everything else to one side, as if one could ever express the former adequately and could thus reach complete agreement for all time about it, having 'polished it off', so to speak. It may be said quite correctly of abstraction that '*abstrahentium non est mendacium*' but the more personal a reality is, the more it is true that the reality of one thing is inextricably bound up with other things, the more proximate becomes the danger of an abstraction being substituted (even though unavoidably) for the understanding of what is abstracted, and the more is one forced by the particular into the unsurveyable whole. This also makes even the best formula all the more inadequate, precarious and provisional in view of an all-embracing insight – or of another formula which gains new insight but only at the price of a new obscurity which represents the absence or recession of a previous clarity. It follows from this that someone who thinks he possesses a clear insight (and is even quite justified in thinking this), must nevertheless ask himself whether he has not unconsciously gained it too easily and at the price of no longer seeing it in its – for us painful – surrender to the incomprehensible mystery from which an individual real truth can no more free itself than the individual existent can free himself from God. Anyone who does not understand the clear formula, or feels himself impelled to reject it as false, must ask himself whether he does not reject it because he expects too much of it, proudly and impatiently demanding that it should say everything at once. In general, any agreement on a formula, whether one adverts to it or not, is also necessarily a fixing of *terminology*, which is an act of voluntary and practical decision and not merely of seeing something to be so in theory. This decision may then be made by an official authority (for instance, a Council of the Church or a Politbureau) or may be the result of no official decision but rather simply the spirit of the age. Out of the infinite variety of realities, the word selects a certain number and summarises these in a definition. It will always be possible to summarise and define these things in a different way and to emphasise other aspects while letting others recede into the background. It will always remain possible to form concepts which would force one to turn the main clause of a formula into a marginal reference and, vice versa, to turn what was admitted incidentally and subsequently, or what was merely not denied, into the content of the explicit main statement. Such determinations of terminology will always be basically changeable, and every dialogue looking for understanding contributes consciously or unconsciously to this change. Thus, every dialogue demands a ready obedience in the speaker with regard to this kind of linguistic regulation, in so far as an in itself infinite dialogue (i.e. one which conjures up the infinite) must always be broken off again and again in time and yet is expected (at least in certain circumstances) to have reached a uniting formula by the time it is thus broken off for the time being. Understood wisely and lovingly, it never closes the openness for a more comprehensive or better future formula, nor does the dialogue – simply because the right formula has to be narrowly hedged around – cease to be a sacrament of initiation into the nameless mystery which all formulae must serve.

Furthermore, the formula seen as the result of a collective finding of truth, remains burdened with a never adequately resolved existential questionableness: when the dialogue ends – for the time being – nobody can have the absolute assurance that both sides really understand it in the same 'subjective' sense. A formula of exact science, because it is understood in the same way by all parties, can be confirmed by each 'participant in the dialogue' (if this phrase is still applicable in this case), using it in such a way that there is brought about one and the same physical effect (the machine, bridle, explosion, etc.) which faces the 'partners-in-dialogue' as one and the same 'third term'. In the case of formulae which are meant to express the whole of man, including the mystery which surrounds him, this kind of 'objectification' is not possible. The intended reality, as something possessed by everyone in common, is present only in the formula, i.e. in an inter-human manner. What is held directly in common, therefore, is the statement and not the understanding of it. That this understanding of the common statement is the same, is not absolutely guaranteed even when there is complete agreement about the formula. This is so even for the simple reason that the sum total of all the individual and historical presuppositions of the understanding of words and sentences is different, and at the same time is never so adequately reflected upon that even on this one could come to some explicit understanding. This questionableness of the agreement reached is so self-evident for the Christian understanding of the faith, for instance, that one always knows that the explicit acceptance of a common formula of belief provides no subjective and absolute person-to-person certitude as to whether the person concerned is really a believer. In addition, it must be remembered that the achieved and mutually accepted formula is never so 'clear' that it brings its own absolute understanding with it and that it cannot be given nor indeed require any further interpretation. Thus it can be said there is probably no formula of faith in Christian theology, for instance, which is not interpreted differently by the different theological 'schools', without it being thereby permissible to say that this means that there is no common understanding at all of such a formula; then, on the other hand, one cannot say either that these different interpretations by different schools are simply extrinsic additions to the formula which do not touch the formula itself. This is the case even by the mere fact of the mediate, inter-personal meaning of a formula; it is all the less possible, therefore, to know absolutely whether the subjective understanding of such formulae in its personal achievement coincides in the partners in a dialogue. Every formula receives its *total* meaning from the *total* system of reference of each speaker. These systems as a whole can no longer be adequately compared.

Yet formulae and agreement on them are necessary and meaningful. This seemingly so very precarious agreement can exist by reason of the basic intellectual confidence that man in his imposed and supporting self-understanding cannot *simply* 'fall out of' the truth. The truth shows itself to have a certainty sufficient for the continuance of intellectual existence by the mere fact that the real life-together in all dimensions, the common celebration, cult, personal love and other active fulfilments of human and *inter*-human existence – which rest on the realities meant by the formulae – actually succeed. The truth is, therefore, ultimately sufficiently sure of itself, because *these* formulae are ultimately simply initiations into the acceptance of the mystery which governs everything in unspeakable nearness, this mystery which, as it were, manages to force its way through even the chinks in the falsely, crookedly or only half understood formula, into that central core of man in which he achieves himself in freedom, where he is so much at one with himself that he posits himself but can no longer step back from himself theoretically, and where he expresses himself but does not make a statement about himself. Yet Christianity at least knows that man in his freedom can open *or* close himself to this permanent, inescapable nearness of the absolute mystery (given by the transcendence of the spirit and grace together), and that the decision on this question of eternal life or eternal death is *also* inevitably conditioned by the reflex understanding of this situation, i.e. also by the formula. Hence Christianity and, before and together with it, all wise and experienced humanity, acknowledges the significance even of the formula for 'existence' itself; it does not therefore permit the agreement of men either as an ideal to be sought for only in the biologico-technical dimension of man, i.e. in 'peace' on this plane, or as an ideal to be thought of as banished into the realm of an absolute, subjective loneliness and thus to be misinterpreted to mean a merely absolute, asymptotically envisaged ideal.

8

SCRIPTURE AND THEOLOGY

1. *The notion of scripture.* Because the entire self-disclosure of God is given in Jesus Christ in the form of the final and eschatologically victorious salvation of the whole human race, salvation-history has entered its eschatological phase. This phase can only be succeeded now by the cessation of history itself when this salvation – which has already taken place – becomes revealed in the direct vision of God and established by the irrevocable transfiguration of the world in the resurrection of the body. For this reason, and in this sense, is God's revelation closed; and all official and general salvation- and revelation-history has entered into a stage which can no longer be surpassed. Anything that happens from the time of Jesus Christ – the crucified and risen Lord in whom this final salvation took place and became manifest – must have the character of anamnesis, of being knowingly and existentially (believingly) referred back to this all-opening and already all-embracing beginning of the end which is given in Jesus Christ; and this even in spite of the length of time and the greatness and depth of the historical 'material' by means of which this final understanding of human existence at the end of time must develop, prove itself, and become conscious of itself by continual growth.

For this to be possible, it is presupposed that this beginning remains ever-present even in that same dimension (although not only in it) in which the Church herself exists (as the enduring form of the salvation of Christ in this final age), i.e. in the dimension of the explicit profession of faith, of the faith conceived in ideas, of a common norm of faith obligatory on all, of the possibility of an *inter*-humanly verifiable reference back to this permanent, normative beginning of the final age which will no longer be succeeded or surpassed by any new beginning in salvation-history. The pure objectification of this eschatological beginning of the end, i.e. the 'primitive Church' – an objectification therefore which forms an absolutely normative *norma non normata* – is called 'scripture' in the

89

just mentioned dimension. By inspiration scripture became the work of God precisely in its role of the objectification of the faith of the primitive Church understood as the permanent norm of the faith of all later Christian ages, and this as a pure norm; in the face of this norm, any really critical distinction of spirits (regarding what in this reality comes from the Spirit of God and what is merely human invention) is no longer necessary or permitted, even granted the recognition of the contingent nature of the historical and the realisation that so much in the historical is capable of, and indeed requires, developing and unfolding. It should be noted in passing that this shows us the theological meaning of the inerrancy of scripture; scripture is the *norma non normata*, and it must be *such* that it can be this: being a work of God it is absolutely inerrant. This formal statement, however, still leaves open the question as to whether the scriptural writers ever meant to make any absolutely firm, declaratory statement which does not lie within this very proclamation of the Christian salvation, though including everything which according to scripture itself belongs to this and not what is included in it according to our own standard applied to scripture in an *a priori* manner. The declaration of the Church's magisterium to the effect that one must not limit the inerrancy of scripture *a priori* to its teaching about religious truths (*DS.* 3411, 3650, 3887) is of course formally correct; but it does not tell us anything about *what* the scriptural writers really wanted to say unambiguously and in a declaratory manner in every material respect and what they did not mean to assert in such a way.

Since the primitive Church always professed herself to be the true successor to the Old Testament and always held the history of the Old Testament to be her own pre-history, knowledge about the authentic pre-history is indeed a factor of the primitive Church herself; hence this knowledge – and consequently also the pure objectification of this knowledge, which is the Old Testament understood as an inspired book – are also part of the normative elements of the later ages of the Church.

2. The nature of *theology* and what functions it performs in the consciousness of faith of the individual and of the Church, must be treated under this catchword of 'theology' itself. Here it is only important to emphasise that theology is not merely a scientifically methodic reflection on the Church's consciousness of faith but also an intrinsic element of this consciousness of faith itself. It is this in such a way (even though, of course, in a greater or lesser systematic 'scientific way') that this very

consciousness of faith itself unfolds itself with the assistance of this reflection (called 'theology'), becoming more reflexly conscious of itself and so becoming capable of leading to new explicit definitions and 'new' propositions of faith. All this is really self-evident. The Church's consciousness of faith must not be something purely abstract and unhistorical, but must constantly refer to the particular mental situation of the believers; in a word, even without prejudice to the permanent truth and closure of revelation, it must be something historical which is not merely accompanied by a history of theology but which itself forms a real history of *dogmas*. If this is so, then this history of the consciousness of faith must include all those factors which belong to the historicity of intellectual phenomena and hence must also include reflection. Hence, for a Catholic understanding of faith (which is characterised by the possibility of an evolution of irreformable 'new' dogmas), theology is ultimately not merely the non-binding human reflection – of an always reformable kind – on an unchangeable phenomenon without a history (e.g. a sacred scripture understood in this way); rather, it is the way in which an absolute history of faith takes place, a history which is irreversible and opens only into the future.

3. *Theology and scripture.* This history of faith, by reason of theological reflection as one of its moments (but not the only one, and in a Christian respect not even its most decisive one), remains nevertheless bound to its beginning, to the revelation of Jesus Christ in the apostolic age, in the pure form and as the *norma non normata* in which it has objectified itself in scripture. We may indeed even say (even though the inner Catholic theological discussion on this question has not yet come to a definite conclusion) that theology is referred to scripture as its only *material*, absolutely original and (*quoad nos*) *underived* source. Of course, scripture is known to us as such only in so far as it is handed down in the living, 'oral' tradition of the Church as something inspired and as the *norma non normata* of the Church's faith, since it is the pure objectification of the permanently authoritative conviction of faith of the apostolic Church. To this extent there is, of course, *one* dogma which the scriptures assert only in so far as they are a moment of the Church herself and not in so far as they are (also) something facing the ecclesiastical consciousness of faith. We refer, of course, to the dogma about sacred scripture itself, about its inspiration and the extent of the Canon of scripture. Yet this relationship between scripture and oral kerygma which follows in the nature of

things at least does not *need* to be universalised, since it is quite clear why it *can* be a unique relationship. Conversely, there is probably no dogma of the Church of which the Church herself has declared infallibly that it is known to her only through oral tradition (as a clearly distinct material source) *in such a way* that there is no basis at all for recognising it in scripture.

There is also no *consensus* among theologians as to whether and above all as to which dogmas of such a kind could be named. After all, such a 'tradition' should not merely be something postulated *by* the existence of the dogma (a tradition postulated by a theologian because he maintains that in his opinion this dogma cannot be derived from scripture and is not implied in it). Such a 'tradition' ought to be historically tangible for us, and this in such a way that it can be traced back to the apostolic age itself. Only in this case can the appeal to tradition do the job which belongs to it and which exists as the proper task of historical theology (even when a dogma or the definability of a proposition can be recognised without it by recourse to a unanimous consciousness of faith of any – even today's – epoch of the Church). This task of tradition and historical theology is to show *how* one of today's dogmas goes back to the consciousness of faith of the apostolic Church. It will, however, be possible to say that in practice and in fact, the extra-biblical attestations of the Church's faith – at least during the first two centuries – do not furnish any contents which, on the one hand, are clearly to be designated *as* proper convictions of faith and, on the other hand, must be described as having absolutely no basis in scripture. In other words, the postulate of a materially richer tradition as opposed to scripture, by which fact tradition could become an independent material source of faith for *us*, is of practically no use at all. If we were inclined in different cases to trace later dogmas back to the apostolic tradition by appealing to oral tradition, then such a procedure will be no more successful and no more convincing in the concrete than if we were to look for the 'ultimate foundation' of such dogmas in scripture. If exegetes do not think they are able to do this in this or that case, then it would have to be asked whether this apparent inability does not arise out of an inexact knowledge about the dogma concerned or whether it is not possibly conditioned by a biblicist positivism which is tacitly presupposed as the method to be used and which underestimates the possibilities of a legitimate unfolding of biblical data. It must be remembered in all this, of course, that there is a great difference between the degree of certitude with which an individual theologian or exegete, on the one hand, and the Church's total consciousness of faith and the ecclesiastical magisterium, on the other hand, undertake such an explication of original biblical data. We may therefore state quite confidently that for theology, scripture is in practice the only material source of faith to which it has to turn as being the absolutely original, underived source and *norma non normata*.

All this in no way excludes tradition from its role as something indispensable to theology. Tradition, if and in so far as it is an attestation to the Church's consciousness of faith and of the teaching of the magisterium, always remains an authentic norm for the individual theologian's interpretation of scripture. It is after all the living self-understanding of the Church and hence also the living, permanent understanding of the scriptures, since the self-understanding of the Church always refers back to its own past and hence to the authoritative and unsurpassable self-understanding of the primitive Church which is given in its pure objectification in scripture. Thus scripture is always (explicitly or implicitly) read together with tradition; this is not as if tradition were trying to replace scripture (because it has already read it adequately and once and for all) nor as if scripture were trying to replace tradition. Nor is the ecclesiastical magisterium even in the least extent excluded or unjustly hemmed in in its function, by our description of scripture as in practice the only material source of the Church's consciousness of faith, one which no longer requires any further norm but is in fact the norm of everything else. The Church's magisterium after all is in no way a source of the content of faith since it receives no new revelation but simply has to safeguard and expound the *depositum fidei*. It has, therefore, a conserving, distinguishing and binding function with regard to the property transmitted by scripture and tradition (tradition understood as the expounding transmission of scripture) to the belief of the later Church and presented to the individual believer with a demand for his faith, but it does not create any new contents. As far as these contents are concerned, the Church of a particular age – just like the individual believer – is dependent on scripture and the tradition which continues to attest it, even though the fulfilment of this duty of referring back to scripture is not dependent for validity on the confirmation by the individual believer as if he were thus giving it its obligation.

Seen in this light, it is possible to make clear the unique position of scripture in theology. It is indeed true that wherever the living faith of the whole Church (in whatever form) attests itself with regard to a truth understood as revealed by God and demands the individual believer's absolute acceptance of this attestation, there is also a guarantee that this demand is justified and that it is a matter of a truth really revealed by God. The actual proclamation of the Church, however, does not and cannot adequately separate ideas, propositions, etc., which it holds on to with absolute assent and obligation of faith, from those concerning which it does not demand this absolute assent of faith (*fides divina et catholica*) or does not yet demand it, or is not yet quite clear about the possibility of such a demand – and those propositions which represent merely a human, theological opinion; in other words, it does not distinguish exactly between a *traditio divina* and a *traditio mere humana*. It often does separate them and indeed very precisely ... but it would be impossible for it to distinguish always and at every point, with absolute reflex exactitude and unambiguous certitude, between the content of faith and its merely human interpretation. This is absolutely impossible. Every drawing of boundaries results again in new propositions, in more numerous and more intricately differentiated propositions. These may give the impression for the moment that 'everything is now clear', and they certainly do clear up a little further, and this for all future time, those questions which one had posed before such a defining determination of boundaries. Inevitably, however, they evoke new questions and new needs for an even more reflex or different distinction between what is really said in the new proposition and what is not really implied by it; although it was reflexly clear to the actual authority to what extent its own understanding and its horizons of comprehension did or did not really and fully coincide in its actual declaration with what it really meant to teach authoritatively.

All tradition is always a unity of divine and human tradition, a unity which cannot be absolutely thought out to the last detail. Every phase of the development of dogmas and of the history of theology confirms this fact. Every concrete tradition demands, therefore, a criterion for the theological reflection concerning it and appealing to it, a criterion about what in its concrete reality can really be addressed as *traditio divina* and what can only have the value of *traditio humana*. The actual tradition does not of itself clearly bring this distinction with it, especially in cases where one is looking for clarification about a proposition which may possibly be definable as a truth of faith and which until now in tradition has not been explicitly put forward *as* such a truth, and also in other until now debated questions which are to be clarified by the magisterium. On the other hand, this distinction is not given at all in scripture: it is (if we may put it this way) pure *traditio divina*. Scripture can, therefore, function as (at least one) criterion for this division within the rest of tradition (which does not, of course, exclude the possibility that such a process of clarifying distinction may take a long time, since the employment of this criterion does not happen like a physical chain of events or a merely logical operation, but is itself history).

Scripture, like any other human truth, is naturally also characterised by historicity; it uses a whole way of conceiving things which was already present before it arrived on the scene and which need not be simply and under every respect the best way for what is to be expressed in scripture. It sees the truth which it attests from certain aspects and viewpoints which are not the only possible ones. Its statements may in many respects have a historically conditioned format. The scriptures propose a truth which will have a further history, in fact the history of dogmas. There are, of course, other possible or actual writings of the apostolic age apart from scripture. Not every part of the New Testament is older than some other actual or possible non-canonical writings of Christian content, and these writings are not necessarily distinguished with regard to their canonicity or non-canonicity simply through their writers, since even the writers of the New Testament were not always apostles. The scriptures, however, are the pure objectification of the divine, humanly incarnated truth; the knowledge of the divine truth has in them indeed a divine-human origin, but not, as can be the case in 'unpurified' tradition, in the sense that one would have from the very start to exclude certain human elements so as not to miss the truth even in its beginnings. Hence scripture is indeed something which has to be expanded in theology in the spirit and under the direction and guarantee of the Church and her magisterium, though this interpretation is not really a critical procedure applied to scripture but rather to the reader. Even the magisterium which interprets scripture authoritatively with the assistance of the Holy Spirit does not thereby place itself above scripture, but under it; it knows that *scripture*, understood as something effected by the Spirit and read by it with the assistance of the Spirit, tells *it* what is right. Thus scripture remains the *norma non normata* for theology and for the Church.

4. *Biblical theology and dogmatic theology* (and other types of 'systematic'

theology). What we have seen so far will help us to look at the position of biblical theology in relation to dogmatic theology. On the one hand, dogmatic theology (and precisely from the starting-point given here) cannot renounce engaging in biblical theology itself. If dogmatic theology is the systematic, reflex listening to God's revelation in Jesus Christ (and not merely a theology of conclusions *from* the already *presupposed* principles of faith taken as premises, such as medieval theology understood itself in theory and contrary to its actual practice), then it must above all engage in this reflex listening to revelation where it finds the most direct and ultimate source of Christian revelation, viz. in scripture. It naturally always reads scripture under the direction of the magisterium, since it reads it in the Church and hence always already instructed by the Church's actual proclamation of faith, i.e. by the magisterium. To this extent, theology always reads scripture with an already given knowledge which in this form is not to be found simply in scripture, since the theologian must always be already engaged in theology under the inspiration of the Church's actual consciousness of faith and since there has been a real development of dogma.

Nevertheless theology has not simply the imposed task of expounding the actual teaching of faith of the ecclesiastical magisterium, understood as something which can be legitimated by scripture, by subsequently finding the *dicta probantia* for the Church's teaching in the scriptures. Its inter-dogmatic task goes beyond the task thus conceived (although this is often unfortunately far too exclusively its practice), and this in a two-fold respect with regard to scripture. It must not be overlooked from the very start that the actual Church is herself always the Church who reads, proclaims and commands others to read the scriptures. In other words, it is not as if only that belongs to the actual teaching of the Church's magisterium which is taught in the Church in councils, encyclicals, catechisms, etc. Scripture itself is also always actually proclaimed officially in every age. If, therefore, the actual teaching of the Church is assigned to the dogmatic theologian as the direct object of his reflection, scripture too is thereby assigned to him as the direct object of his dogmatic efforts. Hence, scripture is not a *fons remotus*, i.e. merely that source to which the dogmatic theologian eventually retraces the Church's teaching, but the precise object with which he has to occupy himself directly, since he really cannot ultimately distinguish scripture as 'another' object and source from the actual teaching of the Church. Furthermore, the theological occupation with God's revelation as found in the actual proclamation of the Church and the magisterium, and in the Church's consciousness of faith of one's own day, must lead back to scripture even where this proclamation is no longer identical in the present-day Church with the reading of scripture. The full understanding of present-day teaching always demands a renewed return to the source from which, according to its own testimony, this teaching is derived, i.e. a return to the teaching whose exposition and actualisation it itself means to be, in short a return to the scriptures.

Biblical theology, therefore, is an intrinsic element of dogmatic theology itself; it is not merely one element among others in 'historical' theology but an absolutely outstanding and unique element of dogmatic theology. Yet this is not meant to dispute the fact that biblical theology may also quite legitimately and for various reasons establish itself as a proper science in the whole complex of theology. This is, even for practical reasons, perfectly in keeping with its proper status, since in the concrete a dogmatic theologian can only very rarely be as expert an exegete as he would have to be if he wanted to administer biblical theology on his own. Furthermore, the outstanding position proper to biblical theology within dogmatic theology in distinction to its other efforts (patristic theology, medieval-scholastic and modern scholastic theology) is brought out better if biblical theology is not practised only within dogmatic theology. Perhaps, as a result of the reform of ecclesiastical studies, we may some day get a special subject in which biblical theology is carried on, not as a mere continuation of normal exegesis nor as a mere element in dogmatic theology, but as a science on its own which represents the correct mediation between exegesis and dogmatic theology.

9

SCRIPTURE AND TRADITION

THE occasion for this treatment of the question of 'scripture and tradition', is the discussion of it which has already begun at the Second Vatican Council. You will know from your reading of the daily Press that during its first session the Council was presented with a draft dogmatic decree entitled 'The Sources of Divine Revelation'. Although this schema did make certain statements about the relationship between scripture and tradition, this relationship itself did not represent the real and central theme of the draft. The question had not yet really been systematically formulated in the Council debates on this whole schema. Yet it may be supposed that even such individual questions as this were already appearing in the background of the Council Fathers' deliberations, and that perhaps even this very question of the statement in the draft decree about the relationship between scripture and tradition had an influence on the very critical attitude adopted by the Fathers towards this draft. As you know from the daily Press, this critical attitude finally led to a rejection in practice of this draft.

How this question will be treated further later on, what the Council will finally teach on this question, whether the Council will even answer it by an authoritative statement, all these questions we cannot yet answer today. It may quite well be that this question will in the end be left open by the Vatican Council as being still too theologically imprecise.[1] Nevertheless, you will see even from this very brief background history of our common reflections that this subject, on the one hand, is in no sense a particularly central and important theme for the Council as such and that, on the other hand, it nevertheless can demand a certain interest from those who are in any way interested in the themes of the Council. Seen purely from the dogmatic point of view, this question of the relationship between scripture and tradition is undoubtedly a very important and significant

[1] In fact this is what happened. – *Tr.*

subject, since the question about the source of the individual Christian's knowledge, and above all about the Church's own knowledge, about the divine revelation made in Jesus Christ, is undoubtedly one of the basic questions of Christian theology as such.

We do not intend in this lecture to enter directly into the question as posed in the Council but want to attempt, to the extent in which this can be done in such a short time, to introduce you from a Catholic point of view into the actual objective problem at stake here.

First of all, a few – but really only a few – very modest indications about the history of this problem. Most recently there have appeared two important works on the subject by J. R. Geiselmann in Tübingen and by Johannes Beumer in Frankfurt o.M/St Georgen;[2] in these works, the historical materials about this question of the relationship between scripture and tradition are spread out exactly and in great detail, so that I can simply refer you to them and limit myself to a few remarks and indications which are simply meant to serve as an introduction to our real problem itself.

Let us begin with the notion of tradition. Tradition means transmission: something is transmitted by one generation to another. When we speak of tradition today in Catholic theology then, by a curious and not at all self-evident narrowing-down of this notion, it is almost unconsciously taken for granted right from the start that it refers to a teaching-tradition: some teaching is handed on, in certain circumstances authoritatively; a certain magisterium with a definite teaching authority proclaims a particular proposition which is communicated to the generation of the day in such a way that even the next generation is thereby taught authoritatively and thus a dogmatic proposition is handed down from generation to generation. There is, of course, such a notion and it is quite a legitimate one, but we only really come closer to the real mystery of Christian tradition when we begin by widening this notion or, respectively, when we come to its proper root.

After all, what ultimately is Christianity? Undoubtedly, it is God's truth which is proclaimed to us. Yet precisely this revelation of the divine,

---

[2] Cf. J. R. Geiselmann, *Die Heilige Schrift und die Tradition, Quaestiones Disputatae* 18 (Freiburg 1962) (English Translation: *The Meaning of Tradition, Quaestiones Disputatae* 15 [Freiburg & London 1966] – *Tr.*); J. Beumer, 'Die mündliche Überlieferung als Glaubensquelle', *Handbuch der Dogmengeschichte* 1/4 (Freiburg 1962).

saving truth is not a proclamation which occurs primarily in doctrinal propositions or catechetical texts. It is a proclamation in events. What is proclaimed in Christianity is not a general, necessary, abstract truth which could be attained equally well from any point in history because it shines forth in eternal sameness and clarity in the heaven of ideas; no, Christianity is primarily the event in which God in his grace acts on us. It is a free event, an event of his powerful love, an event which cannot be derived from anywhere else but must be experienced in its free historical reality and which therefore has also to begin with a perfectly determined spatio-temporal situation in the history of man. Revelation in the proper, original sense is the revealing *deed* of God in historical concreteness, in historical spatio-temporality; this does not exclude but in fact includes the fact that the Word belongs to the constitutive elements of the act of revelation *itself*. It follows then that, if such a saving event takes place at a perfectly determined point, if the Word becomes flesh precisely of the Virgin Mary, in Jesus of Nazareth, if we are redeemed into the glory of God precisely by the fact that this particular man hung on the cross at a particular point in time and in a particular place, under Pontius Pilate, then this saving event must come towards us from this particular point in time and place if it is to reach us not only in the depths of our grace-filled being beyond all our own historical experience but also in the dimension of our spatio-temporal historical life; it must, as it were, move through this spatio-temporality of the historical existence of humanity and in this way come towards us. Hence, the concept of *paradosis*, of *traditio* or handing-down – from a biblical point of view – has its ultimate and deepest meaning and reality not so much in the handing down and transmission of *propositions* but in that *paradosis*, handing-over or transmission in which the Son of God become man, the divine Logos in the flesh, always hands himself over and delivers himself up to us anew in the celebration of the sacred mysteries, the Lord's Supper of the Church, in the Eucharist, proceeding from the event of the Last Supper (in union with his death). This is the event in which tradition primarily takes place, in which the once-and-for-all salvation-event of the death and resurrection of Christ delivers itself ever anew to men in their humanity while always going on and extending further. In so far as and because such a real tradition of the event of revelation to all times obviously and necessarily includes also the Word as a constitutive element of this saving reality itself, its handing on to man and its reception by man – and this of necessity in view of the nature of the event of revelation and in view of the recipient of revelation – then the fact of God's historical, saving act continuing to hand itself over and delivering itself up to all generations is also necessarily a tradition of the Word. This after all is why the sacraments, through which the saving reality communicates itself to men, are saving signs which take place in the Word, and why words are constitutive elements of these saving signs themselves. Since the saving event, which is the act of God in man, takes place once and for all in history and yet this unique event wants to hand itself over historically to all men, and since such an event in its origin and arrival always necessarily takes place with us in words, *traditio* is also tradition in the usual sense of that word today.

Having seen this, we must now take a further step. The saving event on which our life, death and eternal hope rest is called Jesus Christ, the Son of God, the Word of God who has appeared among us in the flesh, found in all truth as a man like ourselves, who like us was born and died. Since this reality which wants to hand itself on is the reality of the eternal Logos of God himself and hence is the unsurpassable, permanent and no longer replaceable eschatological event of salvation, it is obviously and necessarily the kind of event which does not transmit itself in such a way that it could really annul itself in its true reality in this tradition; this is of course the way other historical events continue to be effective but only by annulling themselves in a sense and being replaced by something new or revolutionary, by something which ushers in a new aeon. It follows from this, however, that Jesus Christ – not only in an abstract sense but in his concrete appearance, his particular concrete time, just as he is – is also the absolute norm for every future tradition since he is the absolute reality. This self-tradition of Jesus Christ in his being, his actions, his death and resurrection, and so in everything – and hence also in his words to humanity – is such a deliverance of himself that it must necessarily attest itself in the Word, in the authoritative word of those whom we call apostles; it follows directly from the fact of Jesus Christ and his concrete appearance which cannot possibly be derived any further, that this deliverance of himself takes place first of all in the spoken word, in the living word in which one person encounters the other, by which a person opens himself, his person, his freedom, his decision, his love towards another human being, and so is available for the other. It naturally follows from this that now, in this completely comprehensive sense, the *traditio Jesu Christi* in his reality, action and word is an oral tradition and that as such it is an absolutely normative and permanently eschatological tradition. This tradition, heard, accepted and believed in his own day (understood in a wide sense, of course), means the community of believers who have directly experienced Jesus Christ at least in their own contemporaries, and who have received this word and testimony of Jesus Christ directly through the living word of the very witnesses who saw and heard him; in short, it signifies the Church. The Church, taken as the apostolic Church of the first generation, of the apostles themselves, is nothing other than the really heard and absorbed *traditio Jesu Christi* to humanity. This Church – and this follows from everything we have said – is obviously the normative norm for all subsequent ages. What was heard, celebrated, received and believed there, is and remains the standard which must be handed on, since it is the eschatological saving event of Jesus Christ himself and since we are speaking here in the true sense of the primitive Church. The Church – we may say quite correctly – in so far as it has Jesus Christ in her midst, i.e. the Church of the apostles, is what is handed on. She is handed on, of course, not only in her teaching but in what the Church is herself, what she believes and celebrates, the Church in her sacraments, in her concrete life, her experience, her Lord's Supper and of course also in the reflex expression of what she has heard and what she lives herself, in the word of the apostles.

We know – quite apart from whether we can prove it more precisely metaphysically from the nature of man – that this apostolic Church, understood as the permanent, insurpassable, normative measure which hands itself on in reality and in word to all future ages, has objectified itself, has settled down, made itself concrete and has expressed itself in what we call Holy Scripture. We have to ask: where does the apostolic Church become tangible for us in its own reality, its own faith, in so far as this tangibility is to be based on human possibilities and means? In reply to this question we may and must say at least once in a positive, if perhaps not yet exclusive sense: she is tangible in the sacred scriptures. There the apostolic Church interprets itself for later ages. There is written what she has said, and what she has believed and lived, in a way which is still tangible and readable for us today.

If what we have just said is fairly correct, then it can also be understood from the outset that this word of sacred scripture is always the word of the living Church which makes things concrete and that it necessarily continues to be supported by the living self-tradition of the Church as it goes forward into its future; in short, that it continues to be borne by the living witness of the tradition of this Church herself. This Church brings the sacred scriptures and offers them as God's scriptures to future generations. The reality of Holy Writ with regard to its inspiration and its scope, its canon (as it is usually called in theological terminology) continues necessarily, and in the very nature of things, to be borne by living tradition, i.e. simply by the living existence of the Church which possesses sacred scripture as its own book and which carries it through the ages, attesting its nature and its scope, all of which in the last resort cannot be known from any other source than precisely this living witness of the Church. If, therefore, we understand tradition in this wide, complete and original sense which we have just tried to indicate, then what follows is really quite clear. On the one hand, holy scripture is itself a result and a mode of the tradition in which the saving event of Jesus Christ is received and handed on in the Church; it is also a mode of tradition and an objectification of tradition, one which always remains attached to the total process of this – if you like – even oral, i.e. living tradition of the Church.

Up to this point, in our opinion, there cannot be any doubt among Catholic Christians and theologians and this in accordance with the teaching of the Church, and we believe that today, even though perhaps with difficulty, agreement can be achieved to this extent even with Protestant Christians. But this does not yet give us a clear picture of the special internal Catholic problem of the relationship between scripture and tradition. There now arises the question: does the oral tradition go beyond scripture merely in so far as it supports the scriptures, or does this so-called oral tradition have material contents over and above its witness to scripture, contents which are in *no* way attested in scripture as such? Unfortunately, I cannot put this somewhat tricky question in much simpler terms. If (in order to clarify the question a little further) we ask the ordinary theology of the last centuries within the Catholic Church, then it undoubtedly looks as if scripture and tradition were two tributaries flowing in a somewhat parallel manner and bringing us materially different contents of the faith, so that one can perhaps, to begin with, find and determine certain truths only in scripture and then other truths – and this is the real crux of the problem – only in oral tradition. The question therefore is whether this concept of the relationship between scripture and tradition is correct. Before we start thinking about this question and try to work out an answer, we must first clarify matters still more precisely in three respects.

First of all, for the individual Christian as such, the Church's living witness of faith, i.e. the witness of the Church's authoritative magisterium, is undoubtedly a doctrinal norm which in his Catholic understanding he cannot replace by scripture. In other words, if we may on this occasion more or less identify the magisterium and oral tradition by a somewhat inexact use of words, then we can and must say that one cannot abolish a *formal* authority of tradition in favour of scripture. This follows quite logically for the Catholic understanding of faith even from the mere fact that scripture itself must be attested by the Church as being her own objectification, the objectification of the apostolic Church, for otherwise there could not be any certainty about its inspiration and canon.

Secondly, it is also self-evident for a Catholic understanding that even starting from scripture as such, there is a true development of the Church's teaching which cannot be merely the development of an ecclesiastical theology but absolutely speaking is also in certain cases the development, unfolding and clarification of the dogmatic teaching of the Church, of the real faith of the Church. The dogmatic teaching of the Church and the direct word of the scriptures are not simply identical for the Catholic understanding of faith, not even when – as we can perfectly well suppose – this whole dogmatic teaching of the Church rests on scripture. In other words, a formal authority of tradition and at least an explicative function of 'tradition' in relation to sacred scripture is self-evident for the Catholic understanding of faith.

Thirdly, in so far as even the attestation of the nature of scripture takes place through tradition, tradition in the Catholic understanding of faith is also, at least in this respect, a constitutive material source and norm for faith. The question about the relationship between scripture and tradition, which has occupied Catholic theology especially during the last twenty years, is a question about whether over and above this formal authority and even constitutive function of tradition, we must accept a further, material insufficiency of scripture with regard to its contents and as compared with tradition, or whether one can deny this without coming into conflict with the Catholic principle of tradition.

If, in view of the question clarified in this way, we look into the history of the Christian self-understanding, we will have to say on the whole that we cannot find any really clear traditional answer to this precise question.

In other words, a clear, fully thought-out, universally accepted answer to this precise question is not to be found in the tradition of Catholic theology but that – in so far as one can find any answer at all to the thus formulated question – different opinions and conceptions have been held right up to the present day. This is due first of all to the fact that this question was simply not posed in the past with the precision we have just tried to give to it. It was asked for instance, in a very general way, whether tradition contains things which are not to be found explicitly in scripture. When this question was then answered by an 'obviously yes', this is really no answer at all – neither in a negative nor in a positive sense – to the question just posed by us. Obviously, in our opinion, every Catholic Christian must say that tradition contains matters which are not immediately tangible in holy scripture, viz. at least the very fact of scripture, its inspiration and its scope itself. Yet an answer formulated in such a general way does not answer precisely the question as to whether there are other such matters over and above those mentioned in this answer. The question, however, is not usually given this precision. In addition, there is a second reason for our not being able to expect a clear, unambiguous, generally accepted answer in the average history of theology to the question we have posed above. A really reflex, historical understanding for what we today call the development of dogma and the history of dogmas did not exist in Catholic theology – again on the whole – before the nineteenth century and indeed, for understandable cultural reasons, could not exist. Now, wherever the question and the knowledge about genuine historical development of the Church's consciousness of faith are not seen clearly and with all the possibilities inherent in such a development, our question also cannot really be answered either in one way or the other. Of course, there have always been theologians – for instance, in the Middle Ages – who say that holy scripture obviously cannot be materially.all-sufficient on its own, for there is this and that matter which is not contained and cannot be found directly in holy scripture. Nevertheless such theologians just did not know as yet what immense possibilities of development can and must be possessed even by a truth such as those found in scripture, if we are to give any even approximately theological explanation of the development and history of Christian dogma and of the Church's consciousness of faith. The theologian who (often even still today) has the impression that tradition must be called upon as a substitute for an apparent insufficiency of holy scripture, had (and has) in most cases also no conception of the number of matters contained in today's consciousness of faith which are also not immediately tangible in the earlier tradition of the Church. In other words, he usually has, in addition, no conception as to the fact that even under the presupposition of a material independence of oral tradition, the problem does not really become any easier, since even today's sharper historical consciousness finds it no easier in practice to retrace to an earlier tradition of the Church contents of today's consciousness of faith which cannot be easily traced back directly to holy scripture. In other words, the appeal to oral tradition for explaining why this or that modern dogmatic proposition can be traced back to the divine revelation of the apostolic age, does not in fact lead more easily to a conclusion than when the other 'party' (if we may put it that way) tries to trace these modern truths of faith back to scripture. These are the reasons, it can be said, why the investigation of tradition does not throw a great deal of light on the answer to our precise question. It will not be possible to speak of a really clear *consensus unanimis* in one direction or the other either in the patristic age or in medieval times right up to the Council of Trent. It will be perfectly possible, however, to say that there was in the old Church and also in the theology of the Middle Ages, e.g. in St Thomas Aquinas, a real living consciousness of faith with regard to the surpassing importance of holy scripture and its basic function for *every* belief of the Church. It will be entirely possible, therefore, to deny that the old tradition before the Council of Trent is a really theologically qualified testimony for the opinion that the so-called oral tradition hands on material contents which belong to the faith of the Church, to the apostolic deposit of faith, and yet are in no way contained in the scriptures. Such a *consensus* with regard to a thus understood significance of oral tradition, in the sense of a particular material source of faith beside scripture – such an unambiguous tradition – does not exist before the Council of Trent. We will then have to say furthermore that the Council of Trent did not give a decision on this precise question even in the polemic contrasting of the Catholic Church with the Protestant principle of *sola-scriptura*. The Council of Trent says nothing more in its binding statements than that scripture and tradition are norms of the Church's faith and that in *this* respect (but not in every respect) they must be accepted and respected *pari reverentia*. *How* scripture and tradition are related to one another, however, and what exact relationship they have with regard to their formal authority – and with regard again to their material limitation relative to the attestation of the nature of scripture itself, on the one hand, and the attestation of the material contents of faith, on the other hand – all these are questions about which the Council of Trent did not say anything and indeed did not wish to say anything and about which it has intentionally, one may rightly say, chosen a foundation which leaves this question open. We will not be able to doubt or dispute the fact that in post-Tridentine theology the main trend of thought has been to maintain, on the basis of an anti-Protestant front, that there is not only the truth of the inspiration and of the canon of scripture but that there are also other truths of faith which are not to be found in scripture, so that for them oral tradition is a materially distinct source of faith. It cannot be said, however, that this question was really posed even after the Council of Trent with the precision which we have just attempted to develop; nor can one say that the theological tradition of the schools and this theological trend are something binding, nor that during this time the question was answered unanimously in favour of a wider idea of the material insufficiency of scripture. Only most recently, in the last ten or twenty years, has this question come up again for debate, especially in a controversy between Joseph Rupert Geiselmann and the Roman theologian Lennerz, and later on in a wider discussion among other theologians; and it has been shown that in this question Catholic theology is not in agreement. I would think, therefore, that it must be expected that, given the present state of the question, the Second Vatican Council will also be unwilling to answer this question.

I would like, however, to try in the last part of our reflections to bring forward certain reasons for our not needing to accept – not even from a Catholic point of view – a constitutive material function of tradition which goes beyond the testimony of the nature of scripture; that we can say conversely, therefore, that it is entirely possible to formulate a Catholic *sola-scriptura* principle with regard to the Church's deposit of faith, *provided* that we understand this in a Catholic sense and therefore understand it to involve also an authoritative attestation and interpretation of holy scripture by the living word of the Church and her magisterium, and an attestation of scripture itself and its authoritative interpretation which cannot be replaced by scripture itself. If these two – not limitations but precisions arising out of the nature of things – are borne in mind then, I think, one can perfectly well speak of a Catholic *sola-scriptura* principle; this is always presupposing, of course – and this must be stated once more – that one does not interpret this principle of the *sola-scriptura* in an unhistorical and petrifying sense as meaning a prohibition of a living development of the faith of the Church. If, however, these three conditions are observed, then it seems to me that there can be a perfectly correct Catholic principle of *sola-scriptura*.

First of all (this is, of course, an extrinsic reason and one which theologically speaking does not carry much weight), we have a duty towards the experience of faith and the theology of our Protestant brethren to take the Protestant principle of *sola-scriptura* as seriously as possible; after all, it is backed up by a genuine religious experience and, in my opinion, even a genuine theological tradition going back into the Catholic past. We must therefore take this principle so seriously that, as long as we are not forced by any real Catholic truths of faith to deny it, we ought to fight to be able to understand and accept it in a Catholic sense. This is not an inner-theological objective reason; yet, in our own Christian situation of today, it is an extremely serious consideration. We have no right and no duty to see separating trenches between us and our Protestant brethren where we are not absolutely forced to see them. In this respect, I would say, the *sola-scriptura* principle with the given precisions (and not really limitations) is not a principle against which we must necessarily protest.

There are, however, also inner-theological objective reasons which argue for a correctly understood adequacy of holy scripture. To begin with – to return to something already touched on in passing above – the theological situation, i.e. the theological possibility for the Catholic theologian to prove that the faith of today's Church is all part of the apostolic deposit of faith, is not made any easier by supposing a material 'plus' in oral tradition over and above scripture. Why? There is certainly the feeling (behind the defence of such a material 'plus' of tradition beyond scripture) among many Catholic theologians even right up to the very present that we could not prove the Catholic, now already defined truths of faith to be contained in the apostolic tradition without this thus understood principle of a 'plus' of tradition. Now, it is quite immaterial as to which truths of faith we might mention here, whether it be the possibility and necessity of infant baptism, or the bodily assumption of the Blessed Virgin into heaven, or the sevenfold number of the sacraments, or the sacramentality of marriage, or certain principles of moral theology, or that in spite of Our Lord's words one may under certain circumstances seriously swear an oath, etc. In all these cases one gets the impression among these theologians that such truths, which cannot be doubted by a Catholic by reason of the magisterium, could not be traced back to the apostolic tradition if one had to trace them back to scripture. This is the really live reason why many Catholic theologians dispute a principle of *sola-scriptura* even when understood in a Catholic sense.

But what is the real position? I think that with regard to the matter just indicated, an overestimation (if one may put it this way) of oral tradition as opposed to scripture does not really help at all. It does indeed go without saying for any Catholic theologian that, if the Church's actual consciousness of faith as it is *today* testifies and firmly holds to a truth *as* really believed with divine faith and as an apostolic tradition and declares it to be such by an infallible pronouncement by a pope or a Council, then in virtue of the indefectibility of the faith of the Church this conviction must be true even when the individual theologian or believer has not yet proved this truth historically and has not yet made it explicit. Yet even in the case of such a *dogmatic* evaluation of the present state of the Church's doctrinal proclamation and hence of oral tradition, the Catholic theologian obviously still retains the right and beyond this the *duty* to show *historically* how the Church's dogma as believed today has come down to us from the apostolic age in a genuine, historical tradition and development. This historical proof of the origin in the apostolic age of a content of the faith of today's Church – a proof which is even obligatory on the Catholic theologian – does not in fact become any easier by trying to trace it from an oral apostolic *traditio* rather than from holy scripture, and this for a quite simple reason. It is quite feasible to say that we have no material theological sources from (let us say) the first three centuries, i.e. sources which while being materially and at the same time theologically binding, go beyond *those* contents which are also attested for us in holy scripture. This means, however, that whenever we now profess something explicitly which we do not find expressed explicitly in scripture, we are also unable to prove this explicit contemporary truth to be something explicit in the rest of the tradition of the first two or three centuries. In other words, we have in any case to fall back on a process of explanation whose exact nature, possibilities, limits and scope I naturally cannot develop more exactly here. The appeal to an oral tradition does not, therefore, ease the work of the Catholic theologian in the face of his historical and historico-theological conscience. This basically means that the driving force of the theory just mentioned does not really exist by any objective right.

Furthermore, if (which we are at the moment again unable to do) we bring the fact of the inspiration of scripture into closer connection with the fact that holy scripture is the normative objectification of the normative faith of the apostolic Church, then it really follows from this that this scripture must also be sufficient – if this is to have any meaning at all – wherever a contrary inadequacy does not follow from the *nature* of things. Put differently and quite simply, this means that if God has in fact really worked the miracle of scriptural inspiration and of a divine scripture, then he cannot – apart from the attestation of this miracle itself – let certain truths of the Church not be attested in scripture, since this scripture was inspired precisely in order to attest the truth of the apostolic Church for later generations. Scripture – to put it in a different way again – cannot indeed really attest itself by itself, but if it is there at all and is meant to be inspired divine scripture, then it must attest every other part of the faith of the Church. Otherwise one cannot really see why there should be this whole miracle of divine inspiration and of divine scripture; one could not understand either why otherwise there would not enter into the one and homogeneous reality of the Church's faith a difference which one does not understand and which is unbearable. After all, the doctrine of a material inadequacy of scripture over and above its attestation of itself would mean that there would be truths in the Church's faith which would be explicitly or implicitly pronounced by the divine word of scripture itself and hence would have quite a different dignity and power to convince than other truths, and besides this there would then be other truths which would indeed appear also with the claim of being divine revelation and yet would not have this origin and dignity of being directly attested in the Word of God itself; this, however, is a conception which one cannot really seriously carry through.

One will no doubt be allowed to say, furthermore, that the teaching concerning a continuing material inadequacy, looked at basically, has far too doctrinaire and positivistic a conception of the content of faith proclaimed by the Church. There are, of course, many truths of faith; obviously one must not glance over the material plurality of these truths of faith in any existential or demythologising sense, as if wanting to remove all this so as to reduce the whole faith to some sort of abstract formality. Of course there are things which God must say positively and whose propositional truth is known to us, since and in so far as they are attested by the Word of God; yet this one whole truth of faith has an internal homogeneous character, an inner unity and inner mutual consistency in the plurality of truths of faith. The faith which we believe and live is not a collection of propositions arbitrarily brought together, a collection which is held together only by an abstract, formal authority of the revealing God; rather, these truths together really form an inner unity, they belong together, each refers to the other, and the faith in any one of them is always merely faith in one aspect of the one truth, and is always possible only in the one totality which is comprehended in its historical development through the ages by the one living consciousness of faith of the individual and of the whole Church. If one really has a living understanding of the unity of the reality of faith and of the object of faith, then it becomes rather absurd to say that this whole faith of the Church is largely attested by scripture (which no one can deny) but that this or that particular proposition is, as it were, so different from the totality attested in scripture that one must absolutely derive it from a completely different source.

No, the one consciousness of faith of the Church, supported by the Spirit of God, embraces the inner unity of the reality of faith and distributes and unfolds this one faith from the one centre. This unfolding is a historical process but it always returns again to its origin, viz. the faith of the apostolic Church which has been deposited in the divinely inspired scriptures. This objectification can come down to us only in the tradition of the Church, in which it hands on its own reality, the body of the Lord, and hence also his truth. This reference back to scripture is possible only in the self-accomplishment of the Church in which this scripture attests itself, but this also means conversely that this self-attestation of scripture in scripture and with scripture has really objectified itself – apart from the process of the self-attestation itself – in scripture itself and that, therefore, it is quite possible in this sense to have a Catholic principle of *sola-scriptura.*

In a word, the unity of the object of faith, the inner interconnection of the many God-revealed truths, makes it at least unlikely and ultimately impracticable from a religious point of view simply to presume two materially different sources of faith, two means of transmitting the faith, one of which is called 'scripture' and the other 'tradition'. In view of their origin, of the divine life delivered in grace to men, of the way in which the word-tradition has been deposited in sacred scripture, of the necessary attestation of scripture through the living Church, these two realities belong much more closely together than the somewhat comfortable and primitive theory of two materially different means of transmitting the faith would admit.

This is the point with which I wish to close. May I say: pray God's Holy Spirit to help the Church, in true self-restraint, to leave this question open in the Second Vatican Council; nothing more is needed. We theologians who desire this will then be quite content. Precisely from our point of view, we simply cannot expect or want to expect that the Church should go beyond this present stage of her consciousness of faith and take sides with us. It will be quite sufficient if the Church says again what she said in the Council of Trent: scripture and tradition are Catholic elements of the one *traditio fidei*. Then we theologians and the future consciousness of faith during the next decades or centuries can think about how the more exact relationship of these two realities is to be determined on the basis of the ultimate understanding of faith. Let us hope this is what will happen.

10

REFLECTIONS ON THE CONTEMPORARY INTELLECTUAL FORMATION OF FUTURE PRIESTS

THERE is no doubt that for us in Central Europe (and in the world as a whole) there exist – or at least should exist – serious and unresolved questions and difficulties regarding the right theological training of future priests in keeping with the intellectual situation. The conciliar schema *'De institutione sacerdotali'* is so brief (about 130 lines altogether) and must therefore remain so much on the level of generalities that one may not indulge in the pleasant deception that the questions referred to here will be solved by it, especially since theological studies as such are merely touched on in thirty-seven lines.

When the present author tries to put forward a few reflections on this subject here, he takes up anew a subject about which he has expressed himself before, but without success, many years ago.[1] His hopes of finding

---

[1] Cf. K. Rahner, 'Der Theologe. Zur Frage der Ausbildung der Theologen heute', *Sendung und Gnade* (Innsbruck ³1961), pp. 334–358 (originally: *Orientierung* XVIII (1954), pp. 149–152, 165–168; also Italian in: *Missione e grazia* (Rome 1964), pp. 505–540; English translation: *Mission and Grace* II (London & New York 1964), pp. 146–181). Cf. also Georg May, 'Die Ausbildung des Weltklerus in Deutschland', *Tüb. Th. Quartalschrift* CXLIV (1964), pp. 170–215; J. Allendorff, 'Zur Wissenschaftlichen und aszetischen Ausbildung unserer Theologiestudenten', *Theologisch-praktische Quartalschrift* CXI (1963), pp. 305–309; F. Klostermann, 'Überlegungen zur Reform der theologischen Studien', *Theologisch-praktische Quartalschrift* CXII (1964), pp. 273–313 (where further bibliography will be found). Cf. also Card. Franz König, 'Theologische Fakultät', *Wort und Wahrheit* XX (1965), pp. 329–341. In the meantime, public and private discussion of the thoughts proposed here has begun. It is not surprising that in these discussions individual thoughts have become separated from the context of these reflections and have come to stand on their own feet. This is true above all of the idea of the 'Basic Course'. I can only draw attention once more to my exposition. It would still be premature at present to enter into the questions and hesitations put forward in letters, orally and also in published form. There remains even apart from this the main danger of the present efforts of reform,

more interest or even agreement this time are therefore more than modest. Furthermore, he is very conscious of treating only a very small part of the whole many-sided matter and that, therefore, even for this reason alone, he may not imagine that he can put forward any concrete plan. He hopes, however, to touch on a central point of the whole problem.

PRESUPPOSITIONS

We will be concerned here about the right foundation of the first theological training of the pastoral priest. In order to grasp this properly, four points above all must be noted to begin with.

The pluralism of sciences in general and of theological sciences as such in particular

Under this title, it is first of all necessary to see and understand soberly a previously quite unknown situation in the history of the human mind; we refer to today's situation in which the individual sciences – including the theological sciences – have found such an extension of their problems, materials and complexity of their methods that the individual man – to put it maliciously – only really knows something about less and less, since he understands more and more about less and less. Today one can at most know something in one discipline or in one small sector of a subject; only in this sense can one be a specialist today who is able to appreciate seriously the questions and answers of a particular discipline and who can take part in its discussions and pass critical judgements. All honour to the teamwork and co-operative effort of many sciences in the practical field! Naturally even a theoretical 'synthesis' will always remain a task of the sciences among each other; in the realm of the natural sciences there may even be synthesising results and successes which suddenly simplify many things again so that they can be mastered by the mind of the individual. All this does not change anything, especially in the realm of the sciences of the spirit, in the basic situation indicated above, particularly since team-

---

viz. that they might not preserve that absolutely necessary patience required for any process of maturing. Post-conciliar work will perhaps leave more room and time for common dialogue and discussion. In the last analysis, however, the present outline can be made clear only through a concrete plan of a 'basic course'. (Note added at the time of the inclusion of the essay in this volume.)

work in these sciences is in the very nature of things confined within very narrow limits. The insights of the sciences of the spirit cannot be communicated by means of material apparatus or definite formulae without one having to know their proof oneself, but must either be found together with their proofs in one and the same mind or be simply non-existent for it. One can, of course, let oneself be instructed in a popularising manner by the specialist, let us say, about nuclear physics or the history of Tibetan medicine . . . but then one can not only not take part in discussions but also cannot permit oneself to make any objective and at the same time personal judgement about these things.

All this may be of little importance in many branches of science since in them one need not have any judgement of one's own. But what about the case where a personal decision in life is unavoidable and yet it becomes less and less possible even for the 'educated' person, who inevitably becomes less and less educated all the time, to have a reflex, scientific basis for this decision? This might be the case, for instance, in politics, economics, and in the profession of a religious creed. The situation we have in mind here applies also in the realm of a 'world-view'. Let us not have any pious illusions: one may have been engaged in theology for forty years and yet be no longer able to take part in the discussions of central questions (as they are treated in contemporary work and with modern methods), questions which from a reflex fundamental-theological point of view are of basic importance. If, for example, I am a dogmatic theologian and am proficient in this field, how can I possibly imagine nowadays that I could scientifically form an independent, competent judgement in accordance with the principles and methods of modern exegesis – a judgement which I have myself critically examined and proved – about the meaning and scope for the 'primacy text' in Mt 16:18? This is perhaps still possible today for an exegete, but it certainly is no longer possible for a dogmatic theologian; even the exegete can do this only after long study which by far exceeds the normal period of training for the average priest today. Yet the question just mentioned is of basic importance within the perspectives of the fundamental theology practised even today. This means, then, that in modern scientific work and its methods, it is no longer possible for the young theological student to construct a fundamental theology for himself for which he could be held responsible before the tribunal of his knowledge of the truth – a fundamental theology which is reflex and gained by a scientific method – if one understands by fundamental theology and its work what one must understand by it in accordance with the evidence of its textbooks.

The young student of theology would have to be a historian of religion, a philosopher of religion, an exegete and many other things, including the unlimited specialisations which each of these disciplines has once more gained for itself. He cannot be or become this. It is of no use to him to present him with the results of these sciences in a basically popularised form (in the way in which one tells a non-physicist about the results of nuclear physics). His situation is after all quite different from that of the 'layman' who lets the specialist tell him something about nuclear physics and accepts it on faith; the young theologian should not accept this basis of his faith provided by fundamental theology 'on faith', relying on the authority of the specialist; rather, he should know and understand it and make it his own as a specialist in his own right. Unlike the natural scientist, he is faced with 'results' which are and remain disputed in these theological sciences and sciences of the spirit, whether we regard Catholic theology on its own or in company with the many theologies and philosophies of today. He is left standing helplessly before its problems without being able to say to himself that he could and may work out a position for himself by independent judgement, a position which he can then also defend responsibly when others do not hold the same position. The usual fundamental theology with its philosophical and historical branches has not indeed been abrogated in itself (as a justified and necessary science and method); it will and must go on. But it has been taken *ad absurdum* if and where it intends to be the scientifically reflex basis of the faith for the young theological student, which is something it had until now always clearly intended to be in the business of theological training. Of course, basically it had to be said even previously that such a scientific foundation of the faith was never intended or able adequately to work up and catch up with the existential, pre-scientific basis of the faith in the presence of the individual's conscience about truth, that the ground of the personal faith of each individual always contained more than what it was possible to objectify in scientific reflection. Nevertheless, what has been until now traditionally called fundamental theology, in the sense of a reflex question about the foundations of the faith, can no longer be achieved by the reflex, systematic provision of reasons for the faith in the time available in practice to any individual. Where it is possible here and there (which we do not mean to deny), it happens because the professor involuntarily changes the until now usual subject matter and method and, perhaps without being fully conscious of it, follows a path about which we can only speak here later on in our discussion.

This is the reason why contemporary textbooks of fundamental theology, although really better in themselves and not worse than previously, make a terrible impression on today's young student of theology. How, for instance, is he to get a scientifically reflex conviction from it about the 'historical Jesus' – the founder of the Church, the person who instituted the Last Supper, the risen Christ and so on – in such a way that he clearly understands this kind of proof on his own and critically without being (since he cannot be) an expert in the Jewish theology of the time of Jesus, a Qumran specialist, a form-historian, a historian of ancient religions and many other things besides? If he honestly becomes at least conversant with the contemporary problems in all these questions, must he not get the impression of always remaining a pitiful amateur, supposing that he is expected to work out for himself the basis of the faith in the usual way of a slow synthesis which should lead bit by bit through the most complicated philosophical and historical researches which he cannot and does not know how to carry out himself? Will he not basically – perhaps quite unconsciously but nevertheless effectively – adopt a Protestant attitude in order to carry on, and will he not also see it implicitly at work in his teacher: instead of looking for a 'rational basis for faith', why not take the 'existential', absolute leap into faith?

It will have to be stated later on why the outlined situation does not affect only fundamental theology but also dogmatic theology (and hence also that exegesis which does not intend to be merely philosophical and historical, and concerned with the history of religion, but means to make a positive and effective contribution to the construction of a basis for the faith, i.e. to be a dogmatically fruitful exegesis leading to the understanding of the Church's contemporary teaching of faith). Presupposing this, however, it must be said that the necessary and unavoidable pluralism of today, and the enormous branching out and deepening of problems in the sciences in general and also in the theological sciences in particular, mean that the theological subjects at their core (fundamental theology, dogmatic theology, and dogmatically interested exegesis) become un-suited to constituting in themselves and directly that theology which is to communicate a first basis for the faith and a first systematic construction of the knowledge of the faith to the young student of theology.

The existential situation of the young theologian

Even a mere thirty years ago, what was the situation when a young man started his theology? Usually (granting exceptions and individual critical cases brought out by the study of theology) the young theologian came to his study of theology with a firm, and on the whole unproblematic, substance of faith. The family and the rest of the surroundings of his life (for the most part a peasant or small artisan milieu), which had on the whole remained homogeneous, had already given a fairly firm foundation to the young personality even before he started his study of theology. The theological science which he then heard and studied was able to cement and deepen but was not really required to build up the personal substance of faith; this was present already and theological reflection did not change it very much; hence, the personal spiritual life also was not very much influenced by the study of theology. The science was too often simply a hurdle of things to be learnt, a hurdle which one had to pass in order to be admitted to Orders; it was a superstructure and not a foundation, a training for one's calling later on and not (or only very remotely) a formation of one's own religious personality which was dealt with rather by the ascetic training of the seminary. In the case of a student with good capabilities, it was therefore also possible to engage in theology with that dialectical unconcern and subtlety which was very often met with in neo-scholasticism: there was no need for science to provide a completely basic mastering of existence with all its distress and in its threatened nature, since this distress and threatened condition were not really felt; thus it was possible to do theology speculatively or historically (according to one's bent and talent) with a touching lightheartedness and in the spirit of a theological *art pour l'art* attitude, such as one can still find frequently among theologians of Latin countries who write long dissertations about whether Mary already knew about the mystery of the Trinity when still in her mother's womb!

Today – again on the average – things have changed. The young theologian (above all the talented one, but not only him) suffers from a real poverty of faith. He has grown up in an absolutely pluralistic milieu. He no longer has convictions of faith accepted as foregone conclusions in such an undisturbed manner as in the past, attitudes which were conditioned rather by tradition and milieu than by the grace of faith. He has a threatened, attacked faith: threatened and attacked on all levels of his existence. This does not stand in contradiction to his interest in the world of the Faith nor to his religious vocation; both of these may be given an impetus precisely by this distress of faith. Yet if one looks at the situation soberly and honestly as it is, then one will have to say that today the young theology student necessarily looks for a fundamental basis and strengthening of his faith; he necessarily and rightly demands from his theology something different than what was demanded by the theologian of earlier generations; he does not look for an intellectual superstructure on top of the already unquestionably possessed faith of his youth and of his Christian surroundings which are firmly based in tradition, but rather for the reflexly responsible substructure of a threatened conviction of faith in the midst of surroundings indifferent to belief or unbelief, for this is the inescapable milieu of his believing existence and of its permanent questioning. He does not normally bring this basis with him from the junior secondary school. The religious instruction in senior secondary schools is accorded too little time, and suffers from the milieu of pupils who frequently just sit through it and are not really interested in religion; attention to it is hampered by the encyclopedic variety of other school subjects. Rectors of seminaries would have a tale to tell about the primitive theological knowledge of young people entering our seminaries today.

Seen from this point of view, the questionableness of the traditional fundamental theology becomes even more acute for the young theologian. That kind of fundamental theology tries to build up a basis of faith by undertaking to work out positively and directly all 'in themselves' pertinent questions of the philosophy of religion and history, questions which in themselves and objectively, purely in the nature of things, have to be answered for a rational justification of the faith. This, however, is impossible for the young theology student of today, at least in the short time available for his studies and in view of the immensely complicated nature and material and methodical difficulty of all the questions to be treated in fundamental theology. Yet he requires such a foundation for his faith with quite a different urgency and necessity than was the case with the young theologian of earlier times for whom all this was a theoretical and not an 'existential' matter, so that it was not at all as important for him to what extent such a merely theoretical science, which removed all 'methodic doubts', 'appealed' to him and agreed with him. The dilemma can no longer be overcome by improving the didactic element in the question of fundamental theology. To repeat, we do not question here or even dispute the fact that there are teachers of this theological science who actually solve this problem and offer their young theologians the answers which they must look for and find in this science today. What we say is that if such a professor is successful in accomplishing this task, then (quite apart from whether he clearly knows it or not) he has turned the traditional fundamental theology into something else, the nature of which we will have to reflect on more particularly later on. What he offers is certainly no longer a fundamental theology in the old sense even though of course many individual themes of the old fundamental theology and this new science – which is still trying to find its proper character – may be the same materially. The old science, however much it remains right and necessary, of its very nature is not in a position to offer by its method and general subject matter the reflex, concrete foundations for the faith of the young theologian which for him are a matter of life and death. To give another example, we need only look at normal day-to-day practice in exegesis and biblical theology as it really is, viz. as an inner moment of an historically orientated fundamental theology: the exegete loses himself in his problems and when it comes to the question of faith, he refers his students to the faith already provided elsewhere or to the magisterium, or (where he does more, i.e. does want to contribute something positive to a fundamental theology) he actually becomes 'apologetical' but with a bad conscience, giving himself and others the impression of 'oversimplifying the problems', of watering down the difficulties and of no longer facing up honestly to the non-Catholic exegesis of today. How, for example, can one communicate to the young theologian the problem of the 'historical Jesus', of his relationship to the 'Church', of his 'eschatologism', in such a way that he gets a 'scientific', independent insight into this and thus gains rational and historical *praeambula fidei*?

The level of intelligence of the theological student

Of course, even today, there is still great talent among theological students entering our seminaries ... yet we could be deceiving ourselves if we were to close our eyes to the fact that their percentage has decreased in comparison with the past. The trend of the highest intelligences does not lead to theology today. We need not be unhappy about this: the suitability for the calling of theologian and future priest – quite differently from that of the nuclear physicist or aeronautical engineer – is more directly co-determined than in other callings by other factors besides intelligence; by such factors as a desire for selfless service, love of men, a well-balanced character, the inner relationship to the world of God, etc. Such a person, even though he may not be a genius, can later on as a priest be important even to the intellectual who is superior to him in intellect, since even for the intellectual the ultimate problems of life neither arise nor are solved simply in the sphere of the reflecting reason. Nevertheless, we must not overlook, simply because it is embarrassing to admit such a thing quite realistically, a fairly substantial lowering of the level of intelligence among the general run of today's theological students. One must also see then, however, that the formative situation of the young theologian has become considerably more difficult than in the past: he is intellectually less talented than before and is faced with a scientific task which has become enormously more difficult than in the past. How then is he going to be able to accomplish this task? He will inevitably get the feeling that too much is demanded of him, and this feeling gives rise to a bad conscience and represents a grave danger to the joy in his calling. There must be a healthy balance between what is demanded and what can be accomplished. If at the same time what has been said above is true, then this healthy balance can no longer exist today unless it is supposed that the previously greater talents were not by any means exhausted by the previously smaller task, a point which obviously was not noticed in the past. As those of us who are familiar with this situation know, it follows that the examination of the theologians (apart from the few doctorate examinations) are made much easier than they should really be in view of the highly scientific nature of the lectures and seminars. Even this consequence shows once more in the concrete that there is a disproportion between the average intellectual level and the science which is offered to the young theologian who is therefore not really able to cope with it taking into account what it is and what he is.

Orientation towards practical pastoral care

In itself, there is of course nothing in the strictest science of theology which could not be made fruitful directly or indirectly for pastoral work in the concrete. This is even true simply because the pastor should be concerned also with those who are highly formed scientifically in any discipline whatsoever. It is, however, clearly presupposed for such an apostolate that the theologian has been able to acquire any of these sciences in such a way that he can dispense them as something belonging to him personally. Form-history, for example, could certainly be useful for exegesis in his preaching, provided he has really been able to gain an inner understanding of it and has acquired the independent capacity of using such understanding. But can he really have this? For a great part of the theology taught and offered to the young theologian, this question may be answered unhesitatingly in the negative.

This is not meant as a plea for a merely practical, 'unscientific' formation of the future priest as a subordinate, routine ecclesiastical functionary. Yet if what we have said is true, then it means that in the contemporary scientific situation and given the personal position of his faith, the young theologian in great part is not offered that scientific knowledge which he will need for his pastoral work later on. This is true even for the simple reason that his later care of souls is essentially conditioned by his own personal capacity to believe, a capacity which, however, does not receive that help from the theological science of today which it requires. I am fully aware of the fact that such statements run the danger of paralysing the young theologian's determination of will and patience to 'get down to' this science and to study industriously, even though he cannot yet estimate fully how he might be able to 'use' and 'apply' later on what he is learning just now. Yet these statements must be made. It is true, and we must find remedies for the fact, that our young theology students are not being sufficiently formed for their future pastoral activity in a manner suited to their own potentialities. Theology is becoming more and more 'scientific'; it develops in accordance with the immanent laws of science 'in itself'; it branches off into ever new subjects and is concerned with many matters which previously were left to practice and experience; it proliferates its subject matter so that it can no longer be taken in by one person on his own; in short, the study of theology at the present moment is structured as if it were intended to train future professors of theology. Nothing is changed in this by the fact that similar problems are appearing also in other faculties and that the tension between the university as a place of research and as the bearer of vocational formation is in itself an important and healthy characteristic of German universities which is copied also by other places of theological formation, sometimes in a praiseworthy manner and sometimes badly, without any proper goal of formation being thereby reached.

THE BASIC THEOLOGICAL DISCIPLINE

What is meant here by this heading has often been attempted under different names without anything ever becoming quite clear as to the proper nature of this discipline. One has demanded a kerygmatic theology for the formation of the future pastor of souls, with the simple theoretical intention of putting this kind of theology side by side with scholastic theology and making it in practice the formative or basic training for the future priest. This theory itself became tied up with too many problematic epistemological theories; it did not seem to do sufficient justice to the strict and sober scientific nature of even a basic training and seemed to contain too many misconceptions about the kerygmatic origin and orientation of every true theology. Consequently, this programme did not appeal very much.

Prescinding from such theories, the demand has often been made for a basic course of theology which would be intended primarily for *all* theologians or just for the future pastors of souls (not including those students destined for academic work later on); such a course would be clearly orientated towards future pastoral care and should be adapted to the intellectual capacities of the students, leaving the introduction proper to real scientific work and research to other and 'higher' courses not meant for all students of theology. Yet even these efforts have always been strangled at birth. The suggested structure cannot be incorporated into the usual framework of lectures as it has always existed in the universities. It was feared that it would mean a debasing of the greater mass of theology students who would appear to be branded by this suggestion as a herd of lesser talents. There was uneasiness also about a possible lowering of the intellectual standard in the formation of theological students. The impression was current that such a basic course could be nothing other than a primitive, watered-down version of the theology offered to and required from theological students till then, all of which of course was not calculated to arouse any great enthusiasm for such an idea. No one wanted a theological 'polytechnic' or 'junior secondary course' of theology in place of an academic formation (and thus one did not recognise either that in fact one had not been achieving anything more than such a theological polythechnic even on the academic level, a fact which becomes particularly obvious at examination time). The fundamental difficulty experienced, even though only vaguely, in connection with such suggestions, consisted in the fact that one could only picture such a basic course as something derived from the procedure, content and method of what had been done before and hence could not help regarding it '*ad usum delphini*'; as simply a different version of what had gone before.

This 'basic course'[2] of theology, however, is recognisable in its essence from the presuppositions we have reflected on above without having to be conceived as a popularised and watered-down version of the traditional fundamental theology (and dogmatic theology), and this in such a way that this course is seen to be an answer to the questions we have posed.

It must be possible to give an introduction into the nature of Christianity and of its truth which is not identical with fundamental theology such as it is in fact understood today (and which is in itself also justified in the nature of things).

This means to say that there is a basis for faith (naturally understood with all those more precise interpretations and reservations which are what is meant in the Catholic understanding of faith by such a rational justification of faith, but which is something we need not enter into here)[3], because even today there is a real exercise of faith and this cannot pass muster before the moral conscience of truth without having been rationally justified. Hence also, such a basis for faith cannot simply be in its origins the subsequent result of a methodically reflex, scientific reflection, even

---

[2] We should be conscious of the danger of misunderstanding this initially indispensable concept. It is not a question of an introduction to some other discipline from which this introduction might borrow its meaning, method and standards (even though in a somewhat simpler, popularising manner). Rather, we are dealing here with an absolutely autonomous discipline, a discipline which is to be justified more exactly in what follows from the point of view of scientific theory; nevertheless, it is a discipline which – without detriment to its scientific character – can serve as a theological 'basic course' for the young theologian, and this out of its own most proper nature and not merely by an introductory adaptation of this science for 'beginners'. This basic discipline, therefore, is *not* a matter of what one has been doing until now under the title of an 'introduction into Catholic theology', of a 'theological introduction' or of a kind of 'theological encyclopedia'. It would be possible, of course, to take this old discipline which is hardly taught any more and transform it (there actually are tendencies in this direction) in such a way and so basically as to give rise to something like the basic discipline envisaged here.

[3] This proviso must not be overlooked. This is not the place to describe the nature and limits of this 'rational basis for faith' more exactly and to defend it against the kind of rationalistic interpretation which, since the nineteenth century, was (and still is) met with only too often in Catholic fundamental theology.

though it always of course contains such reflex moments right from the start, moments which are not far removed from a properly scientific and methodical reflection.

This originally unreflected but 'lived' justification of faith, such as it is to be found today in the average believer within the contemporary intellectual situation on the 'academic' intellectual level, must now be brought out and reflected on in a strictly methodical, scientific manner.

This grounding of the faith on the level of the pre-scientific and also of the scientifically reflex datum is not simply identical with the grounding given by the traditional fundamental theology. It is obvious that many of the themes and proofs of the traditional fundamental theology cannot be found in this new approach even in a pre-scientific, unreflected manner and that nevertheless this grounding of the faith is existentially authentic and sufficient, since otherwise it would be impossible for the exercise of the faith to be existentially authentic and sufficient. This, naturally, is not meant to dispute the fact that many of the contents, themes and methods of this grounding of the faith (on both levels) do coincide materially with the contents, themes and methods of the usual fundamental theology. The basic difference, however, remains: basically the old fundamental theology reflected scientifically on everything which is actually and objectively given as content and reasons in the total statement of the Faith. The new 'fundamental theology', conceived as a 'basic course', reflects scientifically and basically on what – at the same time less and more than the object of the old fundamental theology – must be given in the pre-scientific existential basis for the faith of the educated man of today (if faith is to be 'reasonable'), on what is given (since there is reasonable faith) and what is sufficient (although this grounding-of-the-faith of today does not and cannot contain many of the things which are – and rightly so – the object of the traditional fundamental theology).

This new 'fundamental theology', if properly carried out, can perfectly well fulfil the concept of a strict and objective science. 'Science' is had when a legitimate question is posed and answered with all methodical precision and clear reflection. The question, however, about why (and what) I believe as a man of today and as a Christian, is such a question. Only at a superficial glance do this question and its answer coincide with the whole range of problems dealt with by the traditional fundamental theology; for, as has been said, this question, in view of the fact that my faith is already well-founded, is not intended to furnish an initial basis of faith (not even from a methodic point of view) but rather intends to raise this real and existentially already given basis to the level of 'scientific' reflection. Hence this question means to ask only about what is given here and now (even though frequently only very implicitly) as the basis of faith. It must also, therefore, ask about many things which were not asked in the old fundamental theology or were even directly covered up as questions there (e.g. even the precise question as to why I can rightly believe even before having directly mastered and worked out many of the philosophical and historical problems of the old fundamental theology; the many questions which are imposed on us by today's 'world-view', although they are not made explicit in the traditional fundamental theology). Further reflections are required and useful to explain what is really meant by this 'basic course' envisaged here for today's training in theology, this course which we have provisionally called the 'new fundamental theology' for want of a better term. Naturally, even the reflections which follow cannot here be carried to the point of giving an exact and detailed programme for this 'basic course'. Still, we can advance a little further than we have done so far in the description of what we mean.

The traditional fundamental theology is not very well adapted for an existentially successful grounding of the faith of the kind which has been demanded, and this above all because it develops the proof of the event of revelation proclaimed by the Church in a purely formal manner and without the material contents of what is revealed itself. In other words, normal fundamental theology proves the actual occurrence of revelation and the existence of its magisterial transmission and bearer. What is revealed, however, does not interest it and is left to 'special dogmatics'. This itself could already bring us to ask whether existence and content of revelation are really as indifferently separate as is surely presupposed by this method. Is it not rather the case (at least in the concept of an eschatologically completed revelation, with which we are after all concerned since there was no fundamental theology before this stage of revelation-history) that these two moments mutually condition one another and render one another intelligible? Thus, for example, it can be seen that there really is revelation and that it has real existence only if one looks at what is revealed, viz. the absolute self-communication of God. Quite apart from all this, the man of today (at least at some time in his life) experiences the question about the actual communication of a divine revelation as a real question, not so much from the point of view of its abstract concept (such as: *'locutio Dei attestans'*) but from the point of view of its content; this is the point of view which makes revelation-history problematic for him. Anyone, for instance, to whom the 'idea' of an incarnation of the divine Logos, of a unique historical God-man, appears to be an unrealisable myth, will discover a sufficient number of not at all insignificant reasons within the research into the history of the historical Jesus for disputing that Jesus intended himself to be understood as such a metaphysical Son of God. In short, 'fundamental theology' is an inner moment of dogmatic theology itself, since the latter must prove the internal credibility of the content of revelation just as much as fundamental theology must prove the credibility of the event of revelation in its abstract concept, and since both these tasks are for the man of today mutually demanded by and inextricably interrelated in the reflex proof of his faith. This does not mean that there cannot and must not be a special dogmatic theology in which this aspect of fundamental theology recedes into the background and appears only on the fringe, a dogmatic theology whose proper task consists in a more precise rational examination of the statement of faith and of the way in which it can be traced back to the 'sources of revelation'. It does mean, however, that the 'basic course' we are looking for – since it is the scientific reflection on modern man's basis for the faith as it is lived existentially today – must reflect on the proof of the content of the faith; this proof is in no sense exhausted by simple reference to the statement that the historical revelation has taken place and that this or that is contained in it. All this shows, however, that this 'basic course' of a new fundamental theology is also in strict unity a basic course on the fundamental statements of faith themselves. It is also one, therefore, with a basic course of dogmatic theology, in which the full norm of the structure of absolute revelation and the ultimate themes of its expression mutually mirror and illuminate one another and render one another credible. It must again be emphasised, however, that the exact proof of the possibility of such a course cannot be given here. This would mean carrying out this basic course itself . . . which cannot reasonably be expected here.

We would like at this point to return to a reflection which was briefly indicated above so as not to obscure the structure of the proof that a new 'fundamental theology' is necessary. The possibility of a 'new fundamental theology' is based on the fact that the extent of the contemporary, existentially and unreflectedly exercised reasons for faith does not coincide with the range of reasoning which is systematised in the usual fundamental theology; instead there is an 'overlap' on both sides: much of what is of decisive significance for the exercise of the faith today does not become explicit in today's fundamental theology; many things are very central in it (and this quite rightly since they are worthy of questioning) and yet are not in question for an existential grounding of faith or at least are things merely peripheral to it, since they cannot really be worked out in a properly exercised, reflected existential grounding of the Faith (corresponding to the amount of time available, talent, etc.), given the pluralistic complexity of the theological sciences; in any case, they need not be worked out in the 'new fundamental theology' since they do not belong to the essential points of any prereflexive existential basis of the Faith. There is this diastase. Even previously, every *'analysis fidei'* had already been aware of this question at least on the fringe of its reflections, when it asked why even *'rudes'* can believe in a rationally justified manner, even though they understand little or nothing of the usual fundamental theology. Given the modern 'progress' of the theological sciences, one has simply to admit quite soberly that the individual is becoming more and more of a *'rudis'* in the face of these sciences taken in their totality and complexity; the more he studies, the more he comes to see how he can really understand little or nothing of many of the problems of this fundamental theology in his own tiny mind which cannot be switched off or replaced, and when the time and energy available are so limited. In many particular cases he will say: I believe this simply because it too belongs to the content of my Christian and ecclesiastical faith, although 'in itself' it is also an object of fundamental theology (and hence can be 'known'). This can be the case even in very important matters.

But, you may ask, what remains of the reasons for his faith in such a situation? For the man of today, there is a certain canon of reasons for the possibility and duty of his faith. To reflect on these, and only on these, and this in their unity, coherence and possibility of achievement, is the task of the 'new fundamental theology'. This reflection does not need to be conceived in a modernistic sense as a reflection on a merely 'irrational' need for faith, but it is certainly a reflection on an original ground of faith. Part of this reflection almost from the outset is also reflection on the fact that man can and indeed always must legitimately achieve his existence believingly in an existential decision before he has adequately worked out and become conscious by reflection of the reasons for his decision. These reasons include a transcendental anthropology regarding the dependence of man on history and the possibility of salvation history. These reasons will certainly contain also certain historical elements, given a Christianity which is really met by God in the history of salvation. If, however, there is faith today and, included in it, a rational basis, then the immediate historical reason of faith in its existential exercise certainly cannot in individual cases lie directly and indisputably in those proofs with which the historical theology of the life of Jesus, of his self-knowledge, etc., is concerned. The experience of the spirit concerning the concrete reality of the Church and within the concrete reality of the Church is also a historical experience which can be reflected on and which, while it does not play any part in the old fundamental theology (despite Dechamps and Vatican I), is part of the central subject matter of the 'new fundamental theology'. This does not deny the fact but rather includes it (although as background and not as the direct ground of faith in every particular situation and for every particular believer) that this historical experience refers back to its historical origin and renders it credible.

Since it reflects on the really existentially exercised and possible grounds of faith today, such a 'new fundamental theology' ought to be to a great extent 'transcendental', i.e. it ought to reflect on the conditions within the believing subject which make it possible to realise the contents of faith. Modern dogmatic theology frequently retreats too quickly into a dogmatic positivism: this or that proposition is simply revealed and hence it is guaranteed by the authority of God revealing. This then is often taken to mean the same as stating that it is to be found in Denzinger. Often dogmatic theology does not pay sufficient attention to the fact that there is already theology within the sources of revelation, i.e. in the Old and New Testaments. It can be asked (and today it must be asked) whence and how the bearers of revelation (the prophets and scriptural writers) know what they say; it can and must be asked how and why what they say can often be quite simply traced back to a few quite simple basic assertions, while the multiplicity of dogmatic propositions appears as the theological development (even though guaranteed by revelation) and as the articulated interpretation of these basic assertions. If this were asked and one therefore 'reduced' the multiplicity of dogmatic propositions (without impoverishing their content) to a few basic mysteries of revelation, then one could get a much clearer view of the correspondence in these basic mysteries between the formal being of revelation as such and its Christian 'content'. A 'transcendental' proof makes it possible for the 'new fundamental theology', however, to pass over many (even though not all) of the historical proofs with which the usual fundamental theology had to concern itself; furthermore, it would make it possible to develop the central themes of dogmatic theology in one go and thus reflect the total grounds on which a contemporary conviction of faith actually rests.

THE BASIC THEOLOGICAL DISCIPLINE IN THE FRAMEWORK OF THE WHOLE OF THEOLOGY

The position of philosophy

Whenever one thinks seriously about the theological formation of the future pastor of souls, the function and position of philosophy appears as a difficult problem. According to the official instructions of the Church on Catholic theological training, the course of theology proper is supposed to be preceded by a course of pure philosophy. One can agree with this when and where there is time for at least a two or three year course of philosophy. Such a course, however, presents its own problems in view of the difficulty of presenting a philosophy which is really up to date, with all the difficulties involved in this, to students who for the most part do not have any philosophical bent. Things become even more problematic if, as is the case in Germany, one simply presents the theologians with a kind of introduction to philosophy lasting only one or two terms with an hour or so a week, a preparation which at the most can only very vaguely claim to be philosophy. The whole study then either degenerates to a merely formal exercise in a few concepts originally of a philosophical kind which will be needed later on in theology, something quite unattractive and without any hope of kindling any philosophical Eros, or one gives a genuine course of philosophy which most of the students are incapable of following.

In this situation, it would seem, to begin with, to be much better to do philosophy within the initial fundamental-dogmatic course; this is basically what was done in the Middle Ages. Philosophy is then studied within the reality towards which the student of theology has an authentic personal relationship; more and more basic philosophy can be demanded of him in this basic course than has been the case in our normal practice until now; no philosopher can seriously maintain that one cannot genuinely philosophise in this way (for otherwise a St Augustine or a Pascal would be without any philosophical significance); 'pure' philosophy can then still be taught – and indeed more profitably – in the later years of the course. Through the basic course one could then philosophise first of all in the area in which the real existence of the young theology student is grounded. Does a Christian have to be ashamed, or even merely regard it as unphilosophical or hold it as something not sufficiently 'without presuppositions', if philosophy is for him to begin with the exact, methodically precise reflection on his real and full exercise of human existence, so as – later – to release the 'pure' philosophy from this starting-point out of the whole of Christian existence into its authentic freedom as the presupposition presupposed by theology itself? A philosophy for theologians, which would be taught after this basic theological course of 'fundamental-theological dogmatics' (as we may also call it), would at any rate arouse more interest and would have a greater chance of success than the rather impoverished philosophical introduction which most frequently is given today at the beginning of our theological studies. It would then also be easier to recognise who among our theological students is suited for such a 'pure' philosophy, and the real professors of genuine philosophy would find more joy in such students than is normally the case in the early terms.

'Old' and 'New' fundamental theology

It should be stressed once more that a partial material identity between the traditional fundamental theology and special dogmatic theology, on the one hand, and the here outlined basic course of 'fundamental dogmatic theology', on the other hand, is not only not denied but appears as a quite self-evident fact. This basic course, however, has a really proper 'formal object' and within this a principle of choice and structure by which it is clearly distinguished from the other disciplines referred to. It is the scientifically exact and methodical reflection on the reasons existentially effective today for faith in the real event of Christian revelation and its central contents; this reflection makes the basis a datum by looking simultaneously with it at the reality grounded by it and by thinking about the possibility of its existential realisation.

'Mystery of Christ'

We read in No. 12 of the Conciliar schema of Vatican II, *'De institutione sacerdotali': Studia vero ecclesiastica inchoentur generali introductione in mysterium Christi, quod totam generis humani historiam afficit, in Ecclesiam iugiter influit et in ministerio sacerdotali imprimis operatur.*[4] The author does not wish to maintain that this simple but profound statement simply and directly expresses what he has tried to indicate here as the basic and naturally also central discipline of theological instruction. Yet it will no doubt be possible to say that if this *generalis introductio in mysterium Christi*, understood as the beginning and basis of the whole of theology on which, as the text immediately continues, the other disciplines are to be centred, is not to be merely pious talk which simply fishes a few bits and pieces out of the material of the traditional theological disciplines and then at best presents them simply in the manner and with the method of these known disciplines (the well-known danger of the usual 'introductions') – and if this *introductio generalis* is understood on its own (as it must be) after the original manner of scientific theory and not merely in a pedagogico-didactic way – then nothing else will remain but to understand the *introductio generalis* demanded here in the sense in which we have understood the basic theological science we are looking for: as the basic and central discipline of theological formation. If attention is paid in this basic course to the fact that it is a question of the possibility of the existential exercise of faith today and therefore concerns precisely those who can attest this faith in the name of the Church, then the *mysterium Christi* is seen automatically as the mystery operative in the priestly ministry, without this aspect simply degenerating into a small, individual dogmatic or edifying point which would really have little to do with an *introductio generalis* to the whole of theology. The transcendental reflection on the conditions of the possibility of faith – which must always also reflect on the ultimate reason for this faith, viz. God's self-communication in grace understood as a permanent existential dimension – shows immediately and in an original manner that the *mysterium Christi* suffuses and finalises the whole history of mankind, so that this supernatural

---

[4] 'Ecclesiastical studies should begin with a general introductory course into the mystery of Christ, a mystery which affects the whole history of the human race, influences the Church continuously and above all becomes effective in the priestly ministry.' Although this text is not yet final, the definitive text will no doubt express materially the same thing. (This it in fact does. – *Tr.*)

transcendentality appears ever more clearly in history until it finds its highest and unsurpassable manifestation in Christ.

Unity of formation

Every formation, if it is to have that unity which alone can be formative necessarily and in a genuine sense, must have a central discipline towards which the multiplicity of subjects is orientated as to their preparation, articulation and sequence. This is true above all of theology, the highest science of the spirit. It has often and rightly been said today that the study of scripture is the 'soul of theology'. Yet in the concrete and quite unavoidable practice of the contemporary introductory science and exegesis, it will be quite impossible to say in any practical sense that exegesis can be the central discipline of theology. Exegesis carries on its business today, even on the Catholic side, in such a way that the kerygma of today's Church and the teaching of the magisterium are in practice no longer anything more than merely a *norma negativa*; until the results of exegesis have been translated directly into the kerygma of today and into the personal substance of faith, it requires such a great deal of 'translation' work in view of the distance between scripture and the spiritual situation of the man of today, that this work cannot in practice be done to any sufficient extent by exegesis itself. In those cases in which exegesis and biblical theology do such work of 'translation' in a most praiseworthy and successful manner today, this work (even though it may still be called exegesis) is bound up and shot through with so many philosophico-theological reflections that it is no longer distinguishable in principle from the kind of work dogmatic theology ought to be doing today. This, however, shows clearly that 'pure' (i.e. principally historically and philologically orientated) exegesis is indeed a very important and indispensable discipline in theology, but that it cannot be the central discipline in which the decisive act of theology is achieved, viz. that listening with all one's spiritual powers to the revelation of God, in such a way that this revelation will make a direct impact on the conscience of faith of the man of today.

There is no basic reason in principle, however, why dogmatic theology as such should be denied the dignity of such a central discipline within the sphere of the theological sciences. It may, therefore, quite rightly claim this dignity. Nevertheless, it can be said, on the one hand, that it is so much divided up in its present-day business (and not without reason) into historical inquiries (i.e. exegesis, history of dogma and of the magisterium) that it finds it very difficult to achieve a synthesis which brings revelation to be heard directly and enables it to be accomplished. On the other hand, the envisaged basic discipline of a 'fundamental-theological dogmatics' intends to be truly dogmatic theology; it tends to be this in a way which will bring the unified whole of the message of faith in its basic structure and credibility to the level of scientific reflection, so that one need have no qualms about granting it the dignity of the desired and necessary central discipline. If a genuine '*introductio generalis*' is given only when one starts to grasp the whole out of its radical unity, then this '*introductio generalis in mysterium Christi*' is also at the same time and necessarily the central discipline of theology, and the individual tracts of special dogmatic theology can then be regarded as its branches (at a second remove). Other theological disciplines have from the very start no claim to be considered as the central and unifying discipline. Granted that there has to be such a central discipline in theology which synthesises everything else, and this in the very nature of things and for didactic and pedagogical reasons, then it would seem that we have such a discipline in this basic course of fundamental dogmatic theology. This – without ceasing to be theology and science by being the systematic reflection of this kerygma – would then also border most immediately on the one salvation-kerygma of the Church.

Further practical considerations

We will now try to round off our considerations. The fundamental-theological dogmatic basic discipline envisaged in its scientifico-theoretical and theological form would be intended as the basic course for all theologians. This would presumably make it superfluous to pose the question as to whether one would have to institute two parallel courses (one 'academic' and one 'seminaristic') in the central subjects according to the difference in levels of intelligence and in view of differences in the eventual work to be done once the theologians have finished their studies. The basic course we have in mind obviously must and can correspond didactically to the average level of intelligence of the students, so that its *niveau* will have a certain variation in scope. It can, however, be given as the same for all: being a basic course, it addresses itself to listeners who are all beginners, its theme is directly and in practice of the highest importance and urgency for all, and it leads at the same time into questions which are so profound and have to be explained in such a scientific-ally exact manner that even the more talented students will not find it monotonous. Given the obscurity still remaining with regard to such a new basic discipline even after these explanations, it is of course rather difficult to say what length such a course would have to be in order to achieve what it has in mind. It can be supposed, however, that three to four semesters of four hours per week would be sufficient and necessary, plus seminars arising out of this subject.

Given real co-operation, a common understanding of the nature of this new basic discipline and an objectively common basic conception (especi-ally regarding the general philosophical aspects and contents of this discipline), there should be no basic difficulty about several professors dividing the lectures between them. If it were possible (which it is not within the present context) to give a more exact outline of the content and the course of this basic discipline, then it would presumably become even clearer that it is objectively and technically possible for several lecturers to divide the work between them without any damage being done to the unity of this discipline. In more modest circumstances, of course, even one professor alone must be in a position to present this discipline.

Basic discipline and other subjects

Naturally, even in this conception, other 'subjects' besides this basic discipline would have to be studied from the very beginning, and these would step into the foreground 'optically' and in terms of time. We cannot treat here of the problem (which is not merely a didactic but also very basically a scientifico-theoretical one) as to what should be the exact objective division of theological subjects and how time and labour should be divided among lectures, seminars and private study. At any rate, the cancer-like growth by which ever more new subjects arise within the framework of theological studies and fight over the time available for lectures, is a great evil which can be overcome only by really keeping in mind the inner unity and structure of the one theology. Still, given that there are these subjects in sensible division and order according to rank and weightiness, they should be grouped meaningfully around the basic discipline. Introductory sciences to the Old and New Testament, exegesis and biblical theology, should accompany the course of the basic discipline from the very beginning. In order that not too many different subjects have to be taught in the first terms, the bible-sciences should be given plenty of room during these terms. It would be conceivable that during the first four semesters there would also be a course in Church history, taken as the other part of historical theology. After completion of the basic course, and in a kind of second phase of studies, the emphasis would shift to special dogmatic theology (together with the history of dogmas) and moral theology. A third phase of studies would be given over to practical theology (canon law, liturgy, pastoral theology, ecclesiastical sociology, etc.) and to 'pure' philosophy in which, if properly carried out, certain essential aspects of the basic course would automatically be repeated but on a deeper level. We have already touched on the question as to how individual themes of the traditional fundamental theology would be treated in so far as they are outside the subject of the basic course. It should be remembered in this connection that many of these themes can perfectly well be incorporated into special dogmatic theology as long as it can be presupposed that this dogmatic theology offers a sufficient ecclesiology.

As far as existing university regulations and distribution of professorial chairs is concerned, the suggested structure of theological studies need not encounter any insurmountable obstacles. The incumbent of a chair of fundamental theology, without in the least coming into conflict with his teaching commission, could understand and teach his fundamental theology in the sense of this 'new fundamental theology'. We would like to repeat an old wish in this connection: that the theological colleges of the religious orders, which are much freer in law and in organisation than the State or episcopal institutions and hence have the duty and right to be more elastic and open to new experiments than the latter, ought to have the courage to look for new ways of theological formation and not merely to copy often rather pitifully – the theological faculties of the universities. Perhaps they could try out in practice whether the idea proposed here has anything to recommend it.

Theology and the spiritual life

The basic course, with all its soberness and scientific strictness necessarily proper to it, might nevertheless be suited for building a bridge between the science of theology and the spiritual life of the young theology students. The gap between these two sectors of their life is for the most part extremely wide, indeed far too wide. Such an *introductio generalis in mysterium Christi* could make it clear to the young theology students that it should also help them to reflect on the significance of his spiritual life, so as to foster it, and to remember that this science is acquired personally only if it is supported by a religious exercise of what is reflected on in it. If this basic course is really taught the way it should be, then it should not be necessary, as has been considered in various quarters, to have a longer ascetical preparation before starting theology, a sort of 'novitiate' for the theology students going on for the secular priesthood, intended to make them more suited to reap the benefits of theology and to overcome the danger of the disintegrating process of mere problematising in theology. If something like a 'novitiate' is held to be important, it could perhaps come in rather later (in the actual seminary, in prolonged retreats, etc.), once the theology students have reached a certain theological maturity. A real contact between the 'fundamental theologian' and the 'spiritual director' could be very useful for both of them.

Lay theologians

One could now go on to consider whether such a basic discipline as we have tried to outline would not be suited also to act as the basic course of the 'lay students' who are studying at the university in preparation for becoming secondary school teachers later on and who, besides their particular secular subjects, are also taking theology in their course so as to be able later on to teach religion in the schools. It will be impossible to deny that their training for teaching religion in secondary schools is often quite pitiful. In most cases they are of course quite unable, in view of their other studies, to give as much time to the study of theology as a normal theology student who is going on for the priesthood, and yet they will later on be able to teach in a way not permitted to every curate. It would, therefore, be of advantage both for them and for their future pupils if their training could at least show a certain compactness and emphasis on the most decisive questions. It would seem, therefore, that the basic discipline outlined here could be of the greatest benefit to such lay theologians.

No matter how one may judge the value of the reflections expressed here, one thing at least should be recognised: the question of improvements in the study of theology is not merely a pedagogical, didactic and organisational one. It must not be presumed that we already know quite evidently and clearly what 'subjects' make up theology and that it is merely a question of a somewhat greater co-ordination and balancing out of these subjects among themselves. Before any such practical considerations, there is a scientific theoretical question which itself is again merely the formal aspect of the question as to what is the real meaning of theology and what it must be all about. As long as one is busy merely organising, no satisfactory answer will be found to the question about the right structure of theology.

PART THREE

Theological Anthropology

II

THE SECRET OF LIFE

I T is really perfectly obvious that in a general discussion about the nature of life, the theologian too should make his contribution. In his realm, too, the word 'life' is a key concept which he cannot do without and towards which his most immediate sources, namely the writings of the Old and New Testaments, draw his attention most forcibly over and over again.

I

Before we turn to the actual theological concept of life, we will attempt to make a few remarks on the question of the possibility of theology taking up a position towards the biological concept of life. Almost everyone in Catholic scholastic philosophy is a supporter of vitalism, i.e. the doctrine which teaches that life is based on a substantial form or entelechy (or whatever else one might call this principle) which is irreducible to the physico-chemical and its inner possibilities. Naturally, one emphasises in this connection also the substantial unity of this principle with matter, its correlative ontological principle. Scholastics have therefore welcomed the revival of this so-called vitalism in biology, as for instance in Driesch, and have appropriated its arguments. In this way one also feels in agreement with a basic conception which endows biology with the dignity of a basic science and thus does not in practice think of biology as merely an extension of biochemistry and hence of 'inorganic' chemistry and physics. Also, it must not be overlooked that this neo-scholastic zeal to defend a certain form of hylemorphic vitalism had a certain element of theological pathos. Below the surface there was no doubt the impression that in vitalism one possessed certain outer defences for the bastion from which one defends the dignity of man against materialism. But, prescinding from the question about the possible meanings and reasons vitalism in all its different forms might have objectively and on its own basis of natural philosophy, it will have to be said that the question of vitalism is in no way directly relevant to a Christian world-view and theology and that Christian dogmatics can therefore remain neutral on this matter. If we prescind for the moment from man as such, the Old Testament makes rather a radical connection between biological life and the 'earth', regarding the former as a product of the latter, even though only under the creative 'breath' of God which, however, must not be confused with a new created substantial principle. Today's basic Christian conception of the world, of its history and its relationship to God, thinks of God in the realm of nature as the creative, dynamic ground of a development which (at least if one is thinking of man) does indeed recognise factors of essential self-transcendence into something radically new under the creative dynamism of God; it does not, however, understand God as the categorial cause which intervenes at certain points in the time and space of natural history without any created causality being operative at all, and which *in this way* makes natural history progress by something which is in no way any longer also the result of the world-causality itself. The fact that man cannot be reduced to anything merely material and biological is safeguarded, without injury to his real connection with the total biological evolution, by man's knowledge 'from within' about his absolute transcendentality, his spirituality and freedom, even before he has understood anything about the mere biosphere and its relation to the inorganic world. The self-transcendence of the inorganic into life (always supported by the creative but transcendent, uncategorised dynamism of the absolute being of God) may be seen and acknowledged. Whether it implies a hylemorphism in the classical sense or whether it can at this point of transition be interpreted in another quite different sense, is a further question that is very difficult to answer. The vitalism of neoscholasticism itself has left so many open questions with regard to its more exact interpretation, the nature of what it calls the 'entelechy', its precise relation to matter and its individual origin, that even for this reason alone it cannot have any dogmatic and apologetic significance for theology and Christian anthropology. This does not yet represent any judgement about its truth content. It merely tells us that vitalism is not a theological question as long as it refers merely to the biological sphere as such. The above-mentioned 'outer defences' may in themselves represent an absolutely correct position, but they are unnecessary precisely *as* the 'outposts' of Christian anthropology against materialism.

In these few words everything that theology as *such* has to say on the subject treated so far at this congress seems to us to have been said. Hence, the theologian may now turn his attention immediately to the question dealing with the notion of life recognised by theology as applicable within its own field.

II

This theological notion of life is, of course, connected with the ordinary experience of life. It could not possibly be otherwise, since it is quite impossible to have absolutely different and completely new basic concepts in theology if theology is to be in any way capable of making itself understood by man in his existence which is always in the world. This ordinary experience of life, however, is that of the living man as such himself. The Old Testament in particular is indeed aware that animals too are living (it hardly reflects in this connection on plants); often it even regards human-animal life with an almost terrifying naivity from the same point of view, both with regard to the earth which supports this life and also with regard to the sovereignly vivifying or destructive God ... but when it comes to the question as to what scripture thinks about ordinary 'life', then it casts its regard on man and on him alone.

The most exciting thing about this notion of life from a theological point of view is that it has its own history within the history of revelation. This history starts off from the concrete experience of human life and death and in the end arrives at that 'life' which we still confess today at the end of the Credo as 'eternal life' and which, therefore, has become one of the most decisive key-concepts of the Christian revelation and faith. This does not mean that the original concept of life has at some time been 'transferred' and 'metaphorically' applied to a completely different situation, so that the new reality is simply somewhat similar to and comparable with the original meaning of life. No, what is referred to even in the last stage of this conceptual history is the originally signified thing itself, the genuinely experienced life. Yet precisely in this conceptual history, which constitutes the progressive self-unfolding of the original thing itself, the depth and radical nature of the original experience become ever clearer: the life lived by man in his unity and as a whole is the becoming, the preparatory stage of eternal life, if it is understood not merely as one but as a whole in its complete perfection of being. It can easily be seen that it is not a question here, biblically speaking and in a Christian sense, of the history of a pictorial metaphor or analogy but of the historical unfolding of the always one and same reality. The 'eternal life' we profess is also the 'resurrection of the body', i.e. the perfection of life, which was the starting-point of the history of this concept. The beatific, perfect community-with-God of personal human existence which we profess in hope, is also the perfection of the life which we experience bodily here below and which we must slowly pass through and experience in all its human breadth and depth. This does not mean, of course, that 'life' is the only possible key-concept for the perfection of man and hence for an anthropology. Starting from this concept, the personal, free, responsible and dialogic aspects of this life remain some-what unexpressed. Hence this concept must always be seen in unity with other central concepts which call upon the whole of the self-understanding of man in accordance with revelation, such as the 'kingdom of God', 'community', 'knowledge face to face', 'love which remains for ever'. Yet it is nevertheless characteristic of the scope of the concept of life that the concept 'ruach', pneuma, spirit, which appears above all in the New Testament as the divine good of salvation, is ordained from the very outset to the concept of life and thus is associated with the history of the latter. 'Ruach' is the divine life-giving force and thus becomes slowly and more profoundly understood as God's power and the content of eternal life, as the holy pneuma of God himself which in this way powerfully fills man with grace right up to the transfiguration of the body (1 Co 15:45; Jn 6:63; 1 P 3:18) as πνεῦμα τῆς ζωῆς (Rm 8:2).

This concept of life starting from man and his experience – and under-standing what the scriptures say[1] about the *unity* of the one man which does not permit of any dualistic separation into two independent sub-stances – certainly envisages also the concrete earthly side of (human) life: the man who yearns for 'length of days' (Ps 21:5; 91:16; 119:17, 37, etc.; 143:11), for 'good days' (Ps 34:13), associated with peace, joy, happiness, fruitfulness of the land, health, and abundance of children.

[1] Cf. for the Old Testament texts: H. Fries, *Handbuch theologischer Grundbegriffe* II (Munich 1962), pp. 25–27.

Already however this earthly life, accepted and defended in unashamed affirmation of life, has an inner theological depth in scripture; it comes from God who is absolutely alive (Ps 18:47), it is awakened by him who is the 'fountain of life' (Ps 36:10) by his *'ruach'* (cf. Ps 104:30; Is 42:5), so that this life is always experienced as dependent on God, and as transient in spite of all the inner vitality and autonomous power of man. Seen in this light, it becomes understandable that the bodily life of man is experienced from the start as incorporated into the personal, dialogic history of salvation and damnation which takes place between God and man. Even the earthly life is not seen as a neutral, profane matter but as the appearance of the salvation of Yahweh and of man's peace with God in obedience to his commandments (Dt 4:1, 40; 5:30; 6:18; 8:1; 11:8 *sq.*; 30:15–20; 32:46 *sq.*; Ps 37:9, etc.). It is indeed true that in many places in the Old Testament death is accepted unproblematically and in silent, unquestioning obedience, presupposing merely that one may be permitted to die 'in old age and when tired of life', contemplating the gift of posterity, and not having to experience the end of this life before one's time and violently. If one wants to do justice to the *whole* expression of the Old Testament and the New Testament, it must be said nevertheless (if we may formulate it in this way) that man cannot ultimately see death except as something that should not be, as something that does not belong to God's original idea of man and which therefore can originate only in the guilty separation of man from the God of life at the beginning of his history. Thus it happens that life and death take on a radically theological meaning, that death becomes the appearance and the judgement of sin, and that the history of salvation and damnation becomes clarified as the battle between life and death. It must always be remembered in this connection that man is such a unified being for scripture as a whole that scripture cannot limit the absolute claim to life, which constitutes the depth of his existence, to man's 'soul', as if the history of his life and death were merely the history of the relationship of an 'immortal' soul to God. There is always reference to the one, whole man who fulfils his ultimate living nature in corporeality. Hence the motto for the *victory* of the one life which he experiences bodily but also simultaneously as the personal history with the living God, is not the immortality of the soul but the resurrection of the body where, however, for this very reason the 'body' does not refer merely to the biological dimension of man but to the whole man in his mortal nature and the radical desire for life awakened in him by the *pneuma* of God; in this resurrection, it is just as much a question of the 'soul' having to be saved out of the destroying separation-from-God of the 'underworld' (*scheol*) as it is of his corporeality being given back to him. This view of the eschatological saving good of life in the resurrection of the body is therefore a view of the total finality of the one, whole man who perfects himself in free dialogue with God; it is a view which comes through ever more clearly in the history of revelation (having started in the Isaiah-apocalypse [Is 25:8; 26:19 *sqq.*], it asserts itself in Dn 12:2; 2 M 7:9 *sqq.*; 12:43 *sqq.*; 14:46). It is perfectly true, however, that this view accompanied reflection on the fact that this bodily eschatological life must be accomplished by passing through the radical transformation of death, thus does not represent a return to an earthly bodily existence and hence can no longer be 'imagined' (1 Co 15). Wherever the history of the theological concept of human life in its wholeness has reached its climax, this life disappears, transforming itself radically and thus withdrawing into the unspeakable mystery of God. Yet the whole man hides himself into this mystery, 'body' and 'soul'. Precisely in this way man, as it were, returns to his initial experience of 'life'. The last is still the first. He has no longer any right not to take anything about himself seriously; he may not, for example, regard his *human* 'biosphere' as something merely provisional which he must simply leave behind or could possibly reject when the perfect state dawns. The final 'transformation' of history is the salvation of everything, even of matter, even of the bodily life, but it is of course a salvation into the mystery of God.

On the one hand, man knows about God only by experiencing how God acts in him and thus knows of 'God in himself' because God in Himself gives Himself in self-communication by grace. On the other hand, man's experience of himself in the history of salvation offers him 'life' as the beginning *and* end of his self-experience, as the key-word (darkly and in metaphors, of course) for the whole of his own existence. This being so, it is understandable that he is right in saying of God: He is *the* living being. He is 'living', not merely because he is 'the fountain of life' for us, as we read in Ps 36:10, and because all living creatures owe their existence to the '*ruach*' of God (Ps 104:30; Is 42:5): this must always be seen, even at this stage, to mean that it is not a question here of a mere retracing of our life to its ultimate cause but is also a question of the statement that our life remains continuously subject to the sovereign providence of God, of Him who is, who takes and who gives life (Rm

4:17; 1 Tm 6:13; Jn 5:21; 6:57; Lk 12:20; 2 Co 1:9; Jm 4:14 *sq.*)[2] He is also not merely the Living Being in contrast to 'dead' idols, i.e. God who works of himself and is experienced as working in distinction from the idols which man creates for himself and in which he wants to experience himself as a 'creative ideologist'. God is living in himself, he is life. He is this, first of all, because the radical affirmation of life, such as man experiences it ever more clearly both as an individual (in the experience of the spirit) and collectively in the history of salvation and revelation, implies a basic indestructibility and absoluteness which, absolutely and quite apart from the dialectic counterpoint with death, can belong only to the eternal God who therefore is alone the absolutely Living One. He is ξῶν (Rm 9:26; Mt 16:16; 26:63; Ac 14:5); he has life in himself as its source (Jn 5:26), lives eternally (Rv 4:9 *sq.*; 10:6; 15:7), he alone has ἀθανασία of himself (1 Tm 6:16); life itself is so much the property of God as such that God is introduced on oath by his highest property, viz. life (Nb 14:28; Dt 32:40; Rm 14:11) and that even man swears by this highest possible good, viz. by God's life (Jg 8:19; Rt 3:13; 1 S 19:6; Jr 5:2); He *has* life originally and before his creation of the world and salvation (in him, the divine Logos, 'was' the life, says St John in his prologue 1:4) and hence he can give it to us by the fact that this Logos comes into the world and into the death-destined '*sarx*' of our existence and thus this divine life itself appears to us as the 'light' (Jn 1:5), truth (Jn 1:14) and 'love' which he is himself (1 Jn 3:1; 4:7–21 *sq.*; 2 Co 13:11). This inner aliveness of God unfolds itself for us in ἀλήθεια and ἀγάπη, and these two sides of this life to which no further, equally original sides can be added on the basis of the New Testament, refer back to the mystery of the Trinity of the one God in which the Father (itself a concept in the meaning-range of life) who is life (Jn 5:26), generates a Son as Logos (Jn 1:1) to whom the Father communicates life (Jn 5:26), and from whom proceeds a Holy Spirit (1 Co 2:10 *sq.*) who knows the depths of God and who is the Spirit of Love (cf. Jn 6:63: πνεῦμα καὶ ζωή as the one good of salvation in the words of Jesus to the believer).

Seen in this light, the *Christological* side of the New Testament concept of life also becomes intelligible. In Jesus Christ, God with his whole *self*-communication becomes historically tangible for us and is rendered

[2] Cf. for the New Testament texts: *TWNT* II (Stuttgart 1935) (English Translation: *Theological Dictionary of the New Testament* II [Michigan 1964] – *Tr.*)

present in his irreversible victory. If, however, God is life itself *in se* and *quoad nos*, the 'life has appeared' in Christ (1 Jn 1:2); he is the Logos of life (1 Jn 1:1), the life-giving *pneuma* (1 Co 15:45), the ἀρχηγὸς τῆς ζωῆς (Ac 3:15).[3] When, therefore – in one of his emphatic, high-priestly I-am-expressions which are the parallels to the 'I-am(there)-who I-am (there)' of God (Ex 3:14 *sqq.*) – the Johannine Jesus wants to say who he is in himself and for us (both of which coincide), he can say simply: 'I am the Life', 'I am the resurrection and the life' (Jn 11:25; 14:6), just as his absolute 'I am He' (Jn 8:24, 28, 58; Mk 6:50; 13:6; Lk 21:8) can be clarified by 'Truth', 'Way', 'Bread of Life', 'Light of the World'.[4] Thus 'Life' in St John can really be seen as the comprehensive salvation-concept[5], containing everything brought by the Saviour of the world; thus St John speaks thirty-six times of life, of 'eternal life', and emphasises that this 'life' is granted even now to those who believe and love (Jn 3:36; 5:24; 6:53 *sq.*; 1 Jn 3:15; 5:13; Ep 2:5), even though it is still hidden with Christ in God (Col 3:3). This Christ is not merely life for us; he has himself participated in our history which goes through death into life, so that the statement regarding the resurrected Christ: 'he lives', is the very centre of the Christian proclamation (Mk 16:11; Lk 24:5; Ac 1:3. Rm 6:10; 14:9; 2 Co 13:4).

III

Let us look back once more and in the process translate what we have said into a language which is perhaps more directly the language of today and which draws our contemporary understanding of the world even more clearly into the understanding of what has been said. The contemporary world-picture is characterised by a pre-decision for unity and development; it sees matter, life and spirit as held together in one single history of evolution. Such a concept is not necessarily false as long as it remains discreet and realistic and does not play down essential differences within this unity. Actually, the idea of evolution does not exclude but includes an

---

[3] *TWNT* II, 866

[4] Cf. on this *TWNT* II, 866, 871; *LTK* VI, 855/856.

[5] Cf. especially F. Mussner, *Ζ Ω Η. Die Anschauung vom 'Leben' im 4. Evangelium unter Berücksichtigung der Johannes-Briefe* (Munich 1952). Further bibliography above all in *LTK* VI, 856. Cf. also H. Schlier, *Besinnung auf das Neue Testament* (Freiburg 1964), pp. 260 *sqq.*, 278, etc.

essential self-transcendence[6] continually going on within it, since otherwise nothing would ever really become new. This self-transcendence has been conserved in some sense even within dialectical materialism under the idea of the 'qualitative leap'. The Christian philosopher and the Christian theologian will always conceive this self-transcendence, by which a being surpasses and 'elevates' itself into something essentially higher, as happening under the dynamism of the divine being and under the continuous divine creative power. Under this presupposition, however, evolution and essential self-transcendence (seen as the manner of the former) is an absolutely possible way of conceiving matter, life and spirit as one connected reality and history and even to regard the divine self-communication to the rational creature by the grace of God's *pneuma* as the highest, freely given unsurpassable step and phase of this one evolution. In such a pre-decided world-picture, *that* concept will be most easily suitable for understanding the content of the one evolving history which (a) expresses the reality in which it is given to us most immediately within this whole unity, and which (b) always makes what precedes and what follows this reality still comprehensible by means of this one history. Such a reality is 'life', as we experience it in our own human life. Starting from this life, which is most close to us, is the most likely way of rendering matter and sub-human life intelligible, and this concept is also, as shown by the Bible, the creed and dogmatic theology, suited for expressing the ultimate good of salvation, the perfection of man in God himself. It now becomes clear also that the concept of life actually enables us to have a continuous even though, of course, also gradual and analogous understanding of this one history of created reality.

We should look at life as a form first of all from the point of view of an inner unity and in a heterogeneous (i.e. physico-chemical and spatiotemporal) manifoldness which is not simply co-ordinated but hierarchically subordinated. Add to this the fact that this form has an 'interiority' which governs and preserves, as from a central point, the self-construction, self-preservation and relation to the environment, which at the same time separates and opens itself for the rest of the surroundings in a final and

---

[6] On this concept, cf. more closely and in detail the next chapter in this volume which tries to provide a speculative basis for these theses expressed here. Cf. also P. Overhage-K. Rahner, *Das Problem der Hominisation* (Freiburg ^{2}1963) (English translation of part of this work: K. Rahner, *Hominisation: The Evolutionary Origin of Man as a Theological Problem*, Quaestiones Disputatae [Freiburg & London 1965] – *Tr.*)

spontaneous relationship, and which conserves itself, incorporates, causes itself to appear in the whole and in all the parts, has the source and end of self-movement within itself and has a living-space and inner time-form all its own. Looking at life in this way, we will get a description of (to begin with, biological) life (without going into the distinction between animals and plants) which can be used as a model for understanding both higher and lower reality: i.e. the one whole being and history of experienced reality.

To begin with then, we can understand inorganic matter as the first elementary step, as a collection of instruments, as a kind of vocabulary of biological life, as a boundary condition and value, and at the same time as a 'deposit' for life. 'Dead' matter is then the asymptotic zero-condition of life in which the interiority and openness-to-the-other of life approaches equally to the lower boundary-value; the individual material thing is *apparently* quite open to the totality of material reality, since it is a pure function of the whole and is completely tied up in the causal chains external to it. Yet precisely in this way it has no true openness for the whole or reality; it exists merely as a moment of this reality itself since it has not (yet) that interiority and that concentration in itself (at least as 'form') *vis-à-vis* the whole (at least of an environment) which characterises the living; it is lost in the other and hence in this absolute self-alienation it is also incapable of experiencing the other *as* such; it is not truly 'open' since it is not interior to itself. It has already, nevertheless, at least the passive possibility for such an interiority and openness, a possibility which grows in the same measure as it can be built up into heterogeneous systems which, if the 'miracle' of self-transcendence towards self-posses-sion and self-assertion should happen to them, signify precisely the interiorised form of the organic. Put in a different way, one could say and in this hit on the interconnection and distinction of the inorganic and the living in one blow: when the heterogeneous material system, built with a view to a unified, prescribed effort (at least of self-preservation) appropriates its orientation as such to itself, i.e. interiorises itself, then we have something living.

Starting from the concept of life, it is quite possible to understand the spirit and person as the radicalisation and self-surpassing of life. The environment becomes simply the world, interiority becomes existence as a subject, assimilation of the environment by assimilation of nourishment becomes appropriation of culture and the machine, all through harmonisation of the environment beyond the properly biological sphere; interiority of consciousness becomes self-consciousness; finite openness to the environment becomes infinite transcendence towards being as such. It must be remembered in all this that we know of no personal subjectivity in our experience which is not in itself biologically alive and which does not presuppose itself as its own condition; it must be remembered that the fact of having to allow itself to be encountered which belongs to the 'other' of the world, which is essential for commencing finite subjectivity, is precisely the nature of the biological, of the sensibility of the spirit *per definitionem*. It must be noted that this is not contradicted by the Christian doctrine of the angels, since even they can be perfectly well conceived as mundane and cosmic beings, so that materiality and biosphere are merely different words for the sphere of the necessarily receptive spirituality and for inter-subjectivity.

Seen in this light, the unity of nature of the finite, even though also transcendentally and infinitely open spirit and of matter is once more confirmed. Biological life and spiritual life have something in common in that they both constitute the unity of the one human life which is biological and sensible *so as to* be capable of being spiritual; even if the biological existed for itself alone, it would therefore remain valid that the openness towards the 'other' grows in the same measure as, and not in inverse proportion to the degree of self-possession and self-direction arising out of an inner unity. Where the openness of such life becomes unbounded and there thus appears the inner unity in the form of self-disposition, proper subjectivity and freedom, there is the real life of the spiritual person. Even this is always still 'life' in the genuine 'biological' sense, a life which man has not simply 'in addition' side by side with his life as a spiritual person but rather as the inner, necessary moment of the life of the spiritual person itself. Hence his spiritual life in his transcendence towards meaning in general, towards the world as such and its secret ground (God), is still always supported by corporeality, by *environment*, by spatio-temporal encounter, by sense experience, by witness, bodily intercommunication, and sociability. In short, it is true that the spirituality of man is and remains life in the very hard and sober everyday sense, and conversely, that his life is always and everywhere opened towards the breadth of the spirit. In him it is impossible to live the biological life itself without the personal life, nature without culture, and natural history without the history of the spirit. Since, however, this inner unity of life is given in the form of *bios* and of spirit in that biological life constructs itself in a directly recognisable way into an ever greater and more complex interiority and into an ever wider environment (and both at once), it can be said without hesitation – presupposing any *essential* self-transcendence to take place under the divine dynamism – that life, transcending itself, unfolds itself in the history of nature into spiritual life itself.

According to Christian teaching, this one life finds its highest summit in the self-communication of God. God is not only the ground and innermost dynamism of this one history of nature and the spirit. He is also its goal, not merely as the asymptotic final point towards which this whole movement is orientated but also in the sense that he gives himself in his most personal, absolute reality and infinite fullness of life, to the life of man as its innermost power (called grace) and as its innermost goal which communicates itself in its own proper reality. This is a sovereignly free, unowed self-communication but is as such the final fulfilment of life, because that towards which life is opened now becomes also its innermost ground and most interior possession, since the world of life becomes the life of life itself: *vita aeterna*. Even here, this life of man does not leave behind or reject the corporeality of the one being of man as if it were something non-essential. Whether one's biological side can still be called 'biological' when man is perfected in God is ultimately an indifferent question. The whole man (and hence also his spirit) will be changed. The whole man (and hence also his corporeality) will be saved. That we cannot imagine the preserved salvation of the bodily man is not surprising: the whole glorified man is withdrawn from us in the absolute mystery of God.

The self-communication of God, however, together with the divine Trinity given with it and with the historical appearance of this self-communication in Jesus Christ, constitute the whole of what Christianity professes and hopes for, and towards which the Christian lives. Because and in so far as the possession of this divine self-communication can be understood as the highest, most absolute stage of life, Christianity can be understood quite correctly as the teaching about life as such, as the profession of God, the Living and of eternal life. For this reason, we always conclude the Credo with the words: *et vitam aeternam. Amen.*

12

THE UNITY OF SPIRIT AND MATTER IN THE CHRISTIAN UNDERSTANDING OF FAITH

THE subject of the following reflections is: the unity of spirit and matter in the Christian understanding of faith. We say 'in the Christian understanding of faith' so as to emphasise from the very start that this is neither a controversial theological subject disputed among the Christian denominations, nor a properly philosophical investigation and far less still a political controversy. This is true even though it will be shown that it is necessary to think also along theological lines and to employ philosophical concepts if one wants to make it clear what one really believes and what not. Of course, the posing of the question is co-determined by the fact that there is today a world-wide materialism which disputes the foundation of the Christian faith. Christianity must think its positions through anew in the face of such an opponent, an opponent who must not be underrated in so far as the precision of his philosophical argumentation is concerned, an opponent who at least apparently can call up even in us Christians of today an experience of the absence of God, of the necessity and at the same time rational transparency of the evolution of the material world even when taken as the basis of consciousness and of human society. In the face of such an opponent, Christianity has no reason and no right to act as if every question raised by today's materialism has already been completely worked out and answered simply because there has always been materialism. The present reflections are intended to be a very modest contribution to this debate. As has been said, they are based on the conviction that we Christians have an absolute duty and right to face up to certain basic attitudes of the man of today, and quite simply to assimilate them, and that, as long as we do this properly, we become better Christians with a more Christian faith. The ultimate reason for this is that the basic structure of the contemporary understanding of the world is not at all as unchristian as its overhasty and illogical interpretation of itself in materialism, but that in the ultimate analysis it has grown out of Christian roots. It is, of course, quite unavoidable in such an attempt that certain things which are said will appear to the decided Christian as a false or dangerous or superfluous concession to the opponent, and that to such a Christian the simple, solid and bitter contradiction of materialism appears as the only proper attitude that has any hope of success. Such a person should reflect as to whether, even in the judgement of those who believe in God's providence in the history of mankind and in the light of the Logos who enlightens all men, such a world-wide materialistic outlook so widespread in the West as well as in the East can contain only error and guilt. Christianity and its theology must certainly be on their guard against making lazy compromises with false philosophical systems and with the spirit of the age in which also the powers of evil and sinful darkness are always at work. A real theology must not, nevertheless, refuse to learn anew and must not think that it itself in its existing form does not bring with it clouded and one-sided elements, elements which originated in the unchristian spirit of earlier centuries and which have not become Christian simply because we have become accustomed to them and so do not clearly experience their contradiction to basic Christian positions. This short contribution cannot, of course, enter directly into the further question of God's existence and its philosophical knowability. It is simply intended to give an outline, in the first part, of the immediate data of the Christian proclamation which presents us with a unity of spirit and matter. In the second part, then, we will try to communicate a few theological reflections which, arising out of the immediate data of faith, pointed out in the first part, attempt to clarify the meaning and scope of this unity of spirit and matter.

I

The Christian faith recognises a unity of spirit and matter by their very origin, in their history and in their final end.

1. The Christian faith recognises a unity of spirit and matter on the basis of their origin in so far as it professes that this origin is one and the same for both, viz. the infinite, absolute and one reality of Him whom we call God. In making this assertion, we must first of all be quite clear

in our minds that when we speak about God, we do not mean something which is already known to us before our experience of the material world and of the spirit; God is not a reality which is already open to us in its existence and nature even independently of the spirit and of matter as if, *because* we already know God, we would also say of him (almost as an afterthought) that he has also created the material world and that reality which we call spirit: it being quite indifferent, to begin with, how we determine its relationship to what we call the material world and it being also indifferent as to what exactly we mean when we speak of matter and the material world. We mean by God rather that absolute mystery which, whether we want to or not, we always associate at least implicitly in our spiritual encounter of the world with the presupposition and ground of objects and subjects. In the assertion of the Christian faith expressed above, God therefore stands as the ground and all-embracing, pre-given unity of the experience of the spirit and the material world in their unity. It is therefore precisely asserted in this proposition that we do not merely postulate God as the creative cause of two completely separate realities but that, because we have already discovered an original reference of both realities to each other as something given in our experience, we call him one and the same cause of matter and spirit. Without such an ultimate affinity of spirit and matter in the unity of a real and meaningful, even though analogous concept of being, and without the experience of the unity of spirit and matter in the very act of human knowledge, man could not come to recognise that these seemingly so opposed and disparate realities have their one origin and source in the one God and that both are upheld by the permanent actual power of that infinite and necessary being whom we call God. As the history of philosophy and of the attack on the Christian dogma of creation shows, this affirmation about God, the Creator of matter and spirit, is not absolutely self-evident, no matter how originally it is not only a dogma of faith but also a basic proposition of human existence as such. Again and again, matter has been experienced as something dark, anti-divine, obscure or chaotic; again and again, it has been seen as something which stands in contradiction and bitter combat against the spirit understood as the true image and representative of God in the world, a combat which constitutes the history of nature and of the world. Again and again, Christianity has protested against these conceptions as incorrect and hasty interpretations of human experience and, even though not everything in this falsely interpreted human experience was wrong, has condemned them as error and heresy. Matter itself, together with everything meant and implied by it, has its origin in the same ultimate ground from which arises the created spirit. Matter itself, even in its finiteness, temporality and spatio-temporal differentiation and in its history and its distinction (even though not contradiction to) the spirit arises out of God's creative act itself. This act reaches directly to matter itself so that it is equally directly present to God and is not really a kind of more distant, secondary product of an evolution in which merely the becoming of the spirit itself is thought to have been inaugurated by God. Matter is good; it expresses its origin in its own way and, if the gnostic error is to be rejected that there is a tragic inner contradiction within God himself, it cannot therefore ultimately be the opponent to the spirit. If it is frequently added to this statement of faith about God, the Creator of spirit and matter, that God the Creator of 'heaven and earth' is himself spirit, then this statement, which of course bears a correct sense, must be understood carefully. God, in the Christian metaphysical understanding, is not a part of this world but rather is its all-embracing ground directly bearing all its differentiated realities; He is not simply the unity of all realities brought about by the parts of the world, but the previous ground of the possibility of this unity, the ground which therefore also exists before this duality of subjectivity and objectivity which we call spirit and matter. God's 'spirituality' is therefore from the very start of a qualitatively different kind from that to be found within the world; the latter is what is different from matter, that which presupposes but does not create materiality, whereas the former is the ground of spirit and matter in the world, the ground which has an equally immediate relationship to both. This ground is called 'spirit' only because the 'spirituality' experienced by us rightly appears as the higher reality within the world. This intramundane spirituality already includes the transcendental and conscious relation to that ultimate ground which bears all being in its own and which we call God. The 'spirit' therefore (by this intentional infinity) does not positively include in its nature the negativity of the simply, absolutely and in every respect, finite and hence can be more readily used to characterise God than the materiality of the individual, and in every respect finite, thing. To what extent, apart from this, materiality – even as such – can also be used for an analogous understanding of God, even though naturally not in exactly the same way as the spirituality of the transcendental subject, can only be ultimately explained more exactly once we have clarified the precise relationship of created, worldly spirituality to matter. If this were to or does result in the conclusion that created spirituality is quite unthinkable without reference to materiality as a condition of its possibility – even though this relationship must be conceived differently for different kinds of spirituality – then it would or will become very clear that (and why) the characterisation of God as a spirit is to be understood only very analogously and can really only be made by always taking one's starting-point for knowledge of God as a spirit simultaneously *per viam negationis et eminentiae* also from matter. This is, however, something we cannot yet speak about. At any rate, the Christian dogma of the creation of 'good' matter and of spirit and the rejection of any kind of dualism and gnosticism which see matter as something a-divine or anti-divine and anti-spiritual, means also the affirmation of an innermost and ultimate unity and relationship of spirit and matter. As to how more precisely this relationship and unity between spirit and matter are to be conceived, the Christian dogma of creation – purely in itself – does not say very much but the subject does nevertheless represent a decisive challenge to thought about how, even in their history and their goal, these realities belong together.

2. Spirit and matter have a unity in their history. Regarding this fact, it is not possible here to give more than a few hints. These indications, however, show that the basic Christian conception of the non-divine reality rejects any ultimate, radical dualism of spirit and matter. Indeed, if one wanted to conceive the material world in its physical and biological sphere as a kind of neutral stage on which is enacted the history of spiritual persons, of their culture, salvation and damnation and the process of their eternal perfectioning, one cannot even do justice to the Christian understanding of faith; the conception referred to here means that this 'stage' itself would remain untouched by these spiritual events or that the history of nature itself would be merely accidentally and in addition, as it were, the scene of such a history of the spirit. Such a conception, obviously, will always try to break through again on account of the pluralism of human experience. Naturally, it will always seem to man time and time again as if the process of nature is uninterested in man and his history and as if man is a stranger within a natural history, a stranger who plays a very brief role in this history in order to retreat as quickly as possible out of this world into the realm of the pure spirit, of the beyond and of God, while the history of nature, untouched by all

this, continues its iron march. Of course, the basic Christian assessment regarding the unity of the history of matter and spirit has not yet been thought through in all its aspects, either with regard to the inclusion of the history of nature in that of the spirit or conversely with regard to the cosmic conditioning and significance of the history of the spirit for the history of nature. The fact that a lot remains still to be done in this respect is not really surprising: man's reflection cannot really run ahead of actual history in its real concreteness.

Nevertheless, the ultimate basic assessment of a true unity of spirit and matter in their history is given quite clearly as a fact of experience. We do not intend, to begin with, to develop it speculatively with a view to presuppositions and consequences which are not, or at least are not yet clearly present, in the explicit consciousness of faith of Christianity; we simply mean to point out here a few indications for this unity of history of spirit and matter which are inevitably tangible in Christian dogma.

In so far as this is possible even within the establishment of these explicit statements of faith, we must first of all remove a difficulty, a difficulty which repeatedly tries to force its way through against a clear and consequential conception of this unity. The Christian faith speaks of the existence of angels; these are characterised in a platonic formula as 'pure spirits'. From both these facts there then arises the impression in the average, ordinary understanding of faith (which must not be simply identified with the dogma) that there is a created kingdom of finite spirits which carries on its own history quite independently from the material world and its history; and that this shows that spirit and matter are only very partially connected with one another even within the realm of created reality. On this basis, it is then almost inevitable, psychologically speaking, that one ends up with the conception of the world as the merely accidental and ultimately superfluous scene of an itself again also matter-less history. It is here unfortunately impossible to say anything sufficiently adequate either about the dogma or the theology of the angels. It is even more impossible here to attempt to show that the dogma of the angels has nothing to do with the almost fairy-tale, mythological and – for contemporary man – unimaginable conception of the angels current among ordinary people. Here it can merely be a question of showing briefly, first of all, that the Christian doctrine of angels contains quite sufficient elements which permit and indeed urge the inclusion of the angels and their history in the history of the cosmos. Theologically speaking, it is an absolutely controverted and open question as to whether or not the creation of the world coincided in time with the creation of the angels. If one justifiably allows the creation of the spiritual world of the angels to coincide with that of the material cosmos (of course, always in the sense in which the positing of the temporal world by a non-temporal cause can be conceived to take place at a 'point in time'), then the space of time of spiritual and material history is the same at least from this point of view. Furthermore, the theological data (into which we need not enter here in detail) show that the history even of the angels and the history of the world are at least interlaced in many respects. The common goal of both is the eternal kingdom of ·God; the granting of grace to men as citizens of the material world and to the angels is the same; in the Christian teaching the angels, whether they are to be thought of as good or bad, certainly exercise functions in this world; in particular, since they reach down to or into the material world, these functions must ultimately be based in the nature of the angels; the angels can be understood quite correctly, even according to scripture, as cosmic (even though personal) powers of the order of nature and of its history; Christian theology has always seen the object of the personal decision of personal spiritual powers, called angels, to lie in Christ and in his salvific function for the history of mankind and hence of the material world. If one looks at these data, it will be quite legitimate to be of the opinion that, first of all, the doctrine of the angels understood as 'pure spirits', no matter how materially correct, unjustifiably lends too much support to a platonic and non-Christian removal of the created spirit from this world. Furthermore, it will have to be said that the angels, in spite of their differences from man, can be conceived in such a way that, in their own way and of their own most proper and original nature, they are powers of the one and hence also material world to whose material nature they are genuinely and essentially related. It may rightly be said, at any rate, that the Christian teaching about the angels does not basically bar the way to a decided and consequential conception of the unity of spirit and matter in their common history. Since ultimately we really know very little that is certain about the angels and demons, we have the perfect right after what has been said to look at the unity of spirit and matter as we experience it directly in the history of man and also as interpreted in a way compatible with revelation, and to look at this unity as paradigmatic in principle for the unity of spirit and matter in the created sphere as such.

Seen in this way, a basic unity of the history of spirit and matter is no problem for Christian theology. Man in the Old Testament writings is very undualistically and unplatonically a unity in his being and history, and the world is seen from the very beginning as an environment intended for man. Man comes quite unashamedly from the earth and is therefore seen even in scripture, without detriment to the fact that he is also known to be the spiritual, responsible partner of God, called directly by God, as (to express it in a more modern idiom) the product of the material cosmos, without scripture thereby allowing this one man in the para-doxical duality of his origin to break up into two quite independent realities called spirit and matter. Consequently, for the Old Testament writings in particular, the whole man is made to suffer by death; the earthly spatio-temporal life is the life of the personal spirit for whom no other life, either before or after this life of material spatio-temporality, is available for the shaping of his freely achieved finality; and the fulfilment, to which man looks hopefully, is not a liberation of the spirit into an existence removed from matter but is the 'resurrection of the flesh', i.e. a fulfilment of human existence in which, even though in an unimaginable manner, the one whole man composed of spirit and matter reaches his perfection. Consequently, the whole turning away from God at the beginning of the history of mankind took place within the material of the world and the autonomous mastery over intramundane goods, and not in a corruption of an a-cosmic relationship of man to God. Consequently, the Christian commandments are never concerned with a merely interior ethics of intentions but contain concrete material demands which always are also aimed at the mastering of tasks of the one, bodily and hence also socially-bound man. Accordingly, what we call Christian redemption is achieved in the acceptance and patient bearing of what is also a biological happening in death. Accordingly, the climax of salvation history is not the detachment from the world of man as a spirit in order to come to God, but the descending and irreversible entrance of God into the world, the coming of the divine Logos in the flesh, the taking on of the material so that it itself becomes a permanent reality of God in which God in his Logos expresses himself to us for ever. Accordingly, the salvation history of the individual, however much it means a unique personal decision in every case, always rests in the Christian sense on the will of God for a united humanity, for the covenant, for the social communication and tangibility of salvation both in the spatio-temporal history of the Church and in tangible sacraments and social institutions. Always and everywhere, man is regarded by Christianity, precisely in the history of his relationship to God, as a bodily, material and social being who can always only have this relationship to God in this the material constitution of his existence. By the very fact that he is always the theo-logical and theo-nomous being only by being the cosmic being, it is already implied that his history – understood as the history of a direct relationship to God, the origin of all reality, and as the history of a material being, i.e of a being which cannot be thought of other than as a factor in the cosmos (even though it signifies a personality and hence the unique totality of this world itself in each individual) – is always also the history of the material world itself and vice versa. The unity of spirit and matter – since each in their own way have a history – is itself a historical reality; it develops, it reaches its decisive stage in man and achieves itself in the fulfilment of man. Spirit and matter have a unity in their history which grows and furthermore (as will have to be explained more in detail in a moment) both historical processes reach their completion in one point.

3. In consequence of what we have seen, the Christian message also knows of a unity of matter and spirit in its achievement and goal. To begin with, the Christian faith knows nothing about the fact that what we call matter and experience as such belongs to a merely provisional period of the history of the created spirit and freedom, a period which must in the end be definitely surpassed. Matter for the Christian mind is not a watchword for a limited period but a factor in perfection itself. In the main, it is perhaps a merely platonic and not very Christian prejudice that finds it easier in the case of the limited created spirit than in that of matter to conceive of a state of perfection in which history in its spatio-temporal extension into finality is left behind. This perfection for the world as a whole is also not the final point which can be planned and achieved from the side of the world itself, a final point which would be a factor in history itself; rather it is the stopping of this history, foreseen in faith and hope, by God's deed itself by whose power the world surpasses itself and thus enters into its goal. Yet precisely this means that this fulfilment cannot be concretely imagined either for the material world or for the spirit but must for this very reason be simply thought of as the fulfilment of that world which we experience concretely, the world in its unity constituted of matter and spirit in one united – which does not

mean 'uniform' – history. Hence Christian eschatology does not know merely, or even first and foremost, the atomised salvation of each individual for himself in the beatitude of his own soul, but rather the kingdom of God, the eternal covenant, the triumphing Church, the new heaven and the new earth. No matter how many figurative elements all these expressions may contain, however much all these propositions of faith must be understood in their merely analogous meaning, they always contain the basic conviction that the material world in its history and the history of the personal spirit in man find their goal in one and the same point and that, because they are borne along by this dynamism to the one goal, they constitute a genuine unity with one another.

II

The facts which we have so far simply collected together from the theology of the faith must now be thought through in the second part of our reflections so as to reach a conclusive and basic understanding of the unity of spirit and matter. Of course, such a philosophising systematisation of these data of faith and the dogma itself are not one and the same thing. The systematisation works necessarily with extrapolations and various auxiliary suppositions which, not even for the believer, are covered by the dogmatic teaching. It is sufficient for such a systematisation if, after having been judiciously unified, it does not come into contradiction with itself or with the actual doctrine of faith.

   1. Regarding the difference of spirit and matter. Up till now we have spoken a great deal about the unity of spirit and matter. In all we have said, unity has never meant uniformity, but has simply envisaged the fact that in the realm of the one and yet pluralistic reality of the world, in so far as it is distinct from God its absolutely one ground, what we call spirit and what we call matter are at least in the actual order of reality irreversibly related to one another and that together, in spite of their differences, they constitute the one reality of the world, and that they do not exist merely one beside the other as if enclosed merely by an empty space. Before we try to consider this unity of spirit and matter more systematically and in detail, we must first of all refer explicitly to the difference of spirit and matter. The Church's magisterium emphasises in the general doctrine of creation, in the doctrine of man in general and in view of the question of hominisation, that spirit and matter are not

the same, that the spirit is not simply the secondary product of matter as such, something which can be derived from it; it emphasises that man, because he is a spirit, takes up a metaphysically irreducible position in the cosmos and that therefore his origin in his spirituality cannot be simply out of matter as such, but that as a spiritual person, i.e. in view of his 'soul', he is directly referred to God as to his source. The Church's magisterium does not really define the concepts of spirit and matter employed in such statements, but rather presupposes them as known. Even this fact gives rise to tasks of a basic kind for a systematic reflection on the difference and unity of spirit and matter. If these statements are to be understood properly, it will be necessary to know what spirit and matter really signify. Only then can one understand the statement that spirit and matter are not the same; only then can one understand the statement correctly, i.e. without falling into an absolute dualism which would no longer be capable of understanding spirit and matter as a unity in origin, history and goal. Even though it requires a further interpreting reflex articulation, what is meant by spirit is an *a priori* datum of human knowledge; it is only from this *a priori* datum that we can determine metaphysically what is really meant by 'material' and 'matter'. It would be an unmetaphysical and, in the bad sense, materialistic prejudice to think that man is occupied first of all with matter, that he knows exactly what it is and must then subsequently, laboriously and most problematically discover 'spirit', and hence that he can never quite know whether what is meant by this cannot be reduced ultimately again to matter, with which he deals primarily and with full questionless knowledge. In reality, the primary thing with which man deals is himself understood as the one who deals with something other than himself, viz. the world, both in knowledge and in action; in other words, man in a unity and distinction from the knowing subject and encountering object, where the unity, distinction and inexchangeability of these elements are equally original. When a materialist says that there is only matter, he has merely to be asked what exactly he understands by this matter which he maintains is the only reality, in order to recognise that within a materialistic system, in which that which originally and alone gives being and norm lies outside the unity of subject and object, the first and last statement of such a system has no definable meaning at all. Truly scientific expressions are always limited to stating merely functional connections between different factors: if there is A, then B takes place. If everything is matter, then it becomes scientifically inexpressible and indeterminable what this 'everything' is, i.e. what matter is. By definition there cannot be anything by which this 'everything' in its intended sense could be determined as a function of something else. The attempts to define matter as everything could only end up in declaring the pure formalism of the network of functional declarations as the 'essence' of this 'everything', which would be a most idealistic interpretation of the nature of matter. It would at least throw up the question as to whether this nature is simply the *a priori* structure of the knowledge of the knowing subject and thus has nothing whatsoever to do with 'reality in itself'. Or, the nature of this matter might be said to consist in the purely empirical data of experience as such, data which are said to be ordered by these mathematicised functional relationships without being completely reducible to them. This, however, would be even less of a statement about *the* matter, since these purely *a posteriori* and empirical data are precisely as such different from one another, *as* such do not represent anything 'unified', and hence of themselves do not permit any statement about matter *itself*, much less permit the thesis that there can only be exactly the same matter as what we have experienced until now. The proposition, therefore, that everything is matter has no positive meaning in the mouth of a purely scientific materialist, since within his system and with his method, it is basically impossible for him to say what he understands by matter. Hence, if the statement that there is only matter is to have any meaning at all, it could only refer to the pure postulate and heuristic principle that an absolute and completely irreducible plurality of absolutely and, in every respect, disparate realities which cannot be reduced to any common denominator but which at the same time are said to be objects of the one possible knowledge of one and the same man, is from the very outset a logically and objectively impossible conception and metaphysical non-sense. This principle is perfectly correct. If, however, it is formulated in the way just indicated, then 'matter' is objectively identical with the concept of 'being'. It would be possible in itself to adopt such an identification without thereby asserting anything absolutely false, since this principle states nothing further than that there is only being, and that at least a few statements can be validly made in common and for every being about absolutely everything that can be thought. One could even try positively to recommend this initial terminological definition by pointing out that even for a Christian philosophy, in distinction to platonic and idealistic philosophy, what can be expressed by sense experience, and in this sense the material, is what man encounters first in his knowledge, that which he rightly regards, therefore, as the starting-point of his knowledge and as the model of the possible objects of his knowledge. It would nevertheless have to be said against this recommendation that it must first of all confine itself clearly to the postulating and heuristic principle, and that there remains perfectly reconcilable with this principle the possibility of differences within this one 'matter' by which the individual realities within the one 'matter' are differentiated from each other in such a way that they cannot really be reduced to each other; this, of course, still leaves open the question as to whether the unity of these irreducible, essentially distinct realities is a unity in principle or in fact, however this is to be conceived, a merely logical unity. Secondly, one would have to oppose to this recommendation of the principle in question the fact that what is really given first of all in human experience is not the material in and for itself but the unity of relation of one questing subject, within a boundless horizon of questioning, with a self-manifesting, sensible, *a posteriori* object which is contained within the transcendental horizon but is not deducible from it. This original reality of experience, therefore, is the unity itself. It does indeed already betray and affirm the inner reference, relationship and unity with the subject and object in spite of and indeed within their very difference, and hence gives us also the right to bring the subject and the object under one common concept and word. This original reality in its unity does not, however, permit us – after the manner of a pan-psychism or of a dialectical materialism or of a consequential psychophysical parallelism – to postulate such a unity of relation of a subject-object kind for everything itself individual which is met within this unity, since this would obviously initiate a meaningless regress to infinity or would cancel out again the difference of subject and object to be found in this unity. From the point of view of the first assessment, especially in view of the historically loaded nature of words like 'matter', etc., it is not advisable to subsume the subjectivity which is met with in this unity under the word 'matter', since the equally originally discovered difference in this unity between the subject in its unbounded transcendence and the merely encountered object would at least be obscured. The refusal to use this terminology is, therefore, not a pre-decision in favour of a platonic conception of the spirit as something simply opposed to matter or something completely alien to it. It is also far from being a prejudgement about whether in the 'world', i.e. within the space of possible experiential individual objects, there can be objects which can be absolutely and in every respect exempt from all the 'material' laws which we discover in our empirically experienced reality of a material kind, or whether this is unthinkable. Even if we postulate a consequential and necessary correlation between spirit and matter within the space of the world, this does not yet make us materialists in the sense of an interpretation rejected by Christianity. We have already said that God, the cause of every reality divided into the distinction of subject and object, i.e. of spirit and matter, transcends this intramundane distinction of spirit and matter. We have also pointed out already that the Christian doctrine of the angels does not permit us to conclude necessarily that there are created spiritual realities which have absolutely nothing to do with matter. The exact nature of matter, therefore, is not at all as immediately evident as it might seem at first sight. The spirit, however, is already posited with the question about it and is already experienced in its nature; its meaning can be deduced from the question itself by a transcendental deduction. What matter is in general and on the whole, is not a question for natural science as such but a question of ontology on the basis of an existential metaphysics; such an ontology can answer this question because it already knows what spirit is and thus on the basis of this metaphysical experience of the spirit can state what the material as such is, viz. that which is closed in its individuality to the experience of the transcendence of being as such. On this basis also, it must then be made clear that 'spirit' cannot basically be deduced from any combination of the material, however it might be conceived, i.e. from something cut off from itself and its reference to being as a whole, and that therefore there exists an essential difference in this sense between spirit and matter.

2. The unity of spirit and matter. We have seen that it follows from the origin of human knowledge that spirit is a proper, original reality which cannot be derived from anything else and can be understood and approached only in its own proper experience, and from which alone it can be said what matter in itself really is. We have also seen that for an existential ontology and metaphysical anthropology it is consequently quite clear from the very start that the very question about a possible deduction of the spirit from matter has no meaning, since one would be trying to deduce what is logically and ontologically prior from what is posterior in both these senses and would be of the opinion that what is

anterior for the temporal series must by this very fact also be the onto-logical ground of what is later and sparser in the spatio-temporal order. All this, however, does not yet exhaust the question about the relation-ship of spirit and matter. This relationship must be determined not only negatively but also positively. Now, when treating of the question of the essential distinction between spirit and matter, we have already hinted that such a distinction cannot be conceived nor may even be merely legitimately conceived theologically as simply an absolute metaphysical separation of the two realities. If spirit and matter are said to be found in mutual correlation in one and the same original experience, then they cannot be absolutely separate from one another. This is so not only because they can be apprehended only by being brought together under definite formal principles by this one apprehension, but also because apprehension – properly understood – is not merely the ideal cognisance taken by a knower of an object which stands over against this process of appre-hension in a completely external and unconcerned manner; it rather pre-supposes the real communication between reality and the capacity to apprehend for the possibility of apprehension or is in actual fact, at least in the original form of apprehension, i.e. of knowledge not mediated by any other, such a communication and such a real process of events: the object communicates itself in a real, ontological process and builds itself really and ontologically into knowledge. If this is to be possible, however, then there must be an inner relationship between the knower and the known, even when the known is something 'material'. This reflection is also in no way weakened by saying that something material is not grasped by the spirit but primarily by man's sense perception. If sense perception is to be recognised as a material and yet conscious reality, then this already admits in principle what is at stake here. Moreover, sense perception is to be understood merely as the condition for the possibility of spiritual knowledge which the latter creates for itself by distinguishing it from itself, and thus asserts once more the 'relationship' between spirit and matter. The classical theological and philosophical tradition of Christianity has in fact always recognised this relationship and mutual correlation of spirit and matter and has always (often under heavy struggles of thought) repeated it again and again. In the Christian con-ception, matter is retraced in its whole nature and being to the creative act of God who is called Spirit. The emphasising of the creation of matter also implies of course that the reality of matter does not simply, as in a pantheistic view, flow from the being of God (which, however, is equally denied of the created spirit) and cannot be simply interpreted as an expression or as a part of the reality of God. Nevertheless, the origin and what develops out of it, even taken as something created, cannot be simply and completely separate and dissimilar. This is all the less so since this materiality is created by God from the very start for the sake of and in view of the spirit and thus, even from the point of view of finality, matter cannot rest incommensurable beside the spirit. Christian philosophy and theology rightly dispute that God 'could' create a material world on its own, since this would be quite meaningless. They must then, however, recognise the really 'meaningless' as the ontologically impossible, since the distinction between a physical and a merely moral impossibility is a stupid anthropomorphism when applied to God. Thus matter and the material are thinkable for a Christian theistic philosophy and theology only as a factor connected with and directed towards the (finite) spirit. Hence it will not be permissible to say that Christians are merely interested in bringing out the difference between spirit and matter and that they have overlooked the inner ontological essential relationship and the relation of mutual conditioning. What we call material has always been seen, at least in thomistic philosophy, as a limited and in a sense 'frozen' spirit, as limited being whose being as such, i.e. prescinding from the real negativity and limitation of this being (commonly called *materia prima*, which of itself does not signify any positive reality), is exactly the same being which outside such a limitation means being-conscious-of-itself, knowledge, freedom and transcendence towards God. This limitation in material being, of course, its not-becoming-conscious-of-itself in transcendence towards absolute being, is of a metaphysical kind that is constitutive of the essence. In other words, it must not be imagined that this inner, real negativity belonging to the nature of a particular material being considered merely as such can be overcome by this being of its own power and that it could thus change itself into spirit by a merely intramundane process of becoming. Since this inner negativity, in so far as this being is merely material, is the activity of the transcendent causality of God and thus belongs to its nature, all its activity is always and from the very start and necessarily imprisoned by this limitation that is imposed by God as the basis of its nature. Its action moves, therefore, on the ground of this negativity, a negativity which consequently can never be overcome effectively by this being itself. There is therefore no independent leap from the material into the 'noosphere' by any means belonging to its essential constitution or by any power inherent in the essence of the material being. This unlimiting of the limited (called matter), however, does happen in the spirit, and this above all where the spirit itself enters so closely into materiality that it differentiates it from itself *and* keeps it as a factor of its own becoming as a spirit, of its becoming-conscious-of-itself, viz. in man. What is thus lifted out of its negativity in and by the spirit is precisely the spiritual reality and positivity of the material, and not just anything ultimately which would be known in its objectivity as alien to the spiritual; on the contrary, it is a moment of the spirit and of its fullness of being itself. Only in this way is it possible even in a Christian philosophy to explain the Christian dogma which tells us that the spiritual soul (precisely as spiritual) is the form of the body; for thomistic philosophy this ultimately means that every reality in man, including even every positive material reality, is the reality and expression of his spirit. Thus the bodily nature of man is necessarily a factor in man's spiritual becoming; it is not something alien to the spirit, but a limited moment in the achievement of the spirit itself. This is valid then even of the rest of the material world, particularly since this must be conceived from the start as the environment and as the broadened corporeality of the spirit. Ontologically it is quite indifferent in this whether these realities – in this purely external-temporal aspect – present themselves as existing simultaneously or as following one another in time. This is true especially since it has not yet by any means been established that God could also have created the material world without the inner necessity of simultaneity and unity with those spiritual beings whom we call 'angels'; with regard to the angels, we have already said that it is an absolutely open question whether they too are not of their very nature necessarily related to matter, without their having to be bodily beings on this account in the same way as human beings. It has also been said in the first part of these reflections that the spirit (at least in its finite form) can never be conceived in the Christian sense in such a way that it must move away from anything material in order to become perfected, or that its perfection actually grows in proportion to its distance from matter (which is the eternal temptation of a false platonic interpretation of Christianity); the spirit must only be conceived in the sense that the finite spirit searches for and finds itself through the fulfilment of the material itself. Today, from a Christian interpretation of the present experience of man, we can say perfectly well that this perfect achievement of the spirit takes place in a turning towards the material world, and this not only in a theoretical sense but also by an active transformation of this world, in which man is no longer merely an object but also becomes an active subject in the real history of nature. All this holds water only if – from the point of view of the essence of both – spirit and matter do not simply exist side by side as alien to one another. If, however, matter is interpreted as frozen spirit, i.e. interpreted spiritually, then this also necessarily implies a highly 'material' explanation of the finite spirit. This becomes clearest if we think once more about the incarnation of the divine Logos. A Christian theology and philosophy which does not wish to subject this basic truth of Christianity to the suspicion of mythology, must ask itself today why precisely the Logos who is infinite becomes material when he steps out of himself into the sphere of the finite and when he wishes to make his own being appear in this sphere and its history, and why, even in the consummation of this his finite appearance, he does not strip off this materiality but retains it eternally. A more precise philosophical reflection on this basic dogma cannot stop at the statement that the Logos has 'assumed' this or that finite reality and presuppose in this that the peculiarity of what is thus 'assumed' is already something firmly established in itself and requires no further explanation, something which ontologically precedes the 'assumption' (which in a purely external, temporal sense is of course quite correct). We must remember rather the Augustinian recognition that the creation of what is thus 'assumed' is only a movement in the 'coming-to-appear' of the Logos in his own being, a moment in his self-expression projected into the dimension of the finite. This means, however, that the matter which is 'assumed' and which remains valid even in the appearance of the Logos as such, must be regarded (if and by the fact that the Logos even as such brings himself to appear and shows himself in the otherness of the extra-divine and finite) as the appearance of the Logos, i.e. of the spirit, and as an essential moment in what becomes. Matter is, therefore, the openness and the bringing-itself-to-appear of the personal spirit in the finite world and hence is from its very origin related to the spirit, is a moment in the spirit, and indeed a moment of the eternal Logos as he freely but in fact exists, and this for all eternity. This is not meant in any way to turn matter idealistically into spirit, for by the same statements the spirit is equally originally 'materialised'. It comes to be seen, rather, that spirit and matter cannot, like any two objects of our individual experience, be thought of as existing side by side in alien disparateness from one another. Objects of our experience are dull facts existing side by side in all their difference. Spirit and matter, even though distinct from one another, must rather be thought of – as in the first original experience – as factors of created reality indissolubly referred to one another. Thus the Christian can only really be a materialist and a spiritualist at the same time if these two words are meant to indicate that spirit and matter are not ultimately words referring to particular regions of the total reality, regions which lie side by side, but refer to factors which wherever encountered, though essentially different, are everywhere correlative constitutive moments of the one reality.

3. Regarding the unity of the history of the spirit and of matter: the two realities we are looking at in their mutual relationship and unity are not static realities but created being in becoming. They have a history and develop. The concept of historicity is a most profoundly Christian concept. That the world has a history in a unique, irreversible and orientated flow is already, at least with a view to the history of mankind, a fundamental assertion in the Old Testament. Furthermore, Christianity knows a divine providence, a community of all men in origin, determination and goal, a fullness of time, a history of God's revelation, the God-man seen as the centre and climax of history, it has hope seen as one of the basic conditions of Christian man, it has the eternal kingdom of God in which, at the end of history, God is all in all; to this extent, history, historicity, time, development (in the widest sense of the word) – even for the New Testament and Christianity as such – belong also to the basic categories of existential understanding. The explicit recognition that nature itself also knows development and hence, in its own way, history, may not yet be clearly tangible in the Old and New Testaments, especially since the work of the six days at the beginning of scripture belongs rather to the means of representation than to the content itself of what is stated. Since, however, scripture and the Christian understanding of faith recognise at the very least that the world was created for the historical existence of man, that it is changed by the activity of man himself and that it enters into the completion of the history of mankind by participating in it, the developmental character of even the extra-human world and nature has at least an inner relationship with the basic convictions and categories of Christianity and, as soon as the natural experience of man has recognised the

becoming and development in nature as the environment of man, it can easily be assimilated into a Christian world-view. In accordance with the essential difference between spirit and matter, the developmental character also is naturally different in each case, but this need not be discussed more closely here. In accordance with the mutual reference, relationship and unity of spirit and matter in the one world of creatures, the becoming and development of spirit and matter are also intertwined with and conditioned by one another.

Up to this point, there is no special problem with regard to the developmental nature of spirit and matter in general. The real problem, as it occupies the minds of men today, becomes visible only once we reflect on the fact that the spirit, in the sense of proper self-consciousness and freedom, only appears or at least seems to appear at a very much later point in time in the world of our experience than the material world and the sequence of its development. One could indeed, from a Christian point of view, point to the angels as both personal beings and cosmic potencies and thus raise the question whether there has ever really been, even in a merely temporal sense, a spiritless and merely material world or whether the Christian doctrine of the angels does not imply the spiritual orientation of the whole history of nature. Still, we are going to prescind from this question here, even though – in view of the supra-individual structure of the biosphere inexplicable by purely physico-chemical elementary data – one can perhaps raise the question as to whether such an entelechial formation of nature and its history is an hypothesis which lies absolutely beyond natural human experience. We limit ourselves, therefore, to taking as the starting-point of these reflections the affirmation that the human spirit came into being only at a very late point in time and presumably also at a very limited point in space within the history of nature. Thus there arises the question whether the history of nature and the history of the spirit do not merely form a unity if and in so far as both are already presupposed as given but also form *one history*, i.e. in a sense still to be determined more exactly, the spirit itself may be regarded as the result of the history of nature when it has arrived at a certain point of its history, or whether this is quite irreconcilable with a Christian understanding of the distinction between spirit and matter and of the creative relationship of God to man being in an absolutely special sense. This is the question with which we must now deal. In answering it, in the framework of a modest lecture like the present, we must of course take certain things as already proved and accepted, matters which in a different context would themselves have to form the object of philosophical and theological reflection. One of these propositions which must be presupposed here is obviously and above all the assertion that all reality experienced by us is grounded in its existence and nature, in its becoming, activity and self-achievement, in an absolute being which we call God and which is the original creative and always active ground which posits everything in its own being and activity. Another of these presuppositions (which we have earlier on tried to clarify at least briefly) is also that concerning the essential difference between spirit and matter.

It seems that, with this assertion of the essential difference between spirit and matter, the newly posed question is already answered in the negative. It is also conceded that the average theological interpretation of the dogmatic statement that God is the direct creator of man's spirit understood as the constitutive element essentially different from the material, also already signifies a negative answer to the newly posed question. Since, on the one hand, the spirit cannot be simply regarded as the immanent product of material development and evolution, it originates from a new creative initiative of God; this is an absolutely indisputable fact for a theist with regard to the world as a whole and hence does not present any special difficulties even as a new and absolutely original initiative.

Yet, for a Christian, the question now posed need not be decided in the negative as quickly as it appears to have been from what we have just said. First of all, it is not at all as straightforward even for the Christian understanding of the relationship between God and the world as already built up by Thomas Aquinas in his teaching that God as creator of the material world is the transcendental ground of everything but not the categorial and spatio-temporally localisable cause for a determined individual thing and indeed is seen to be working rather through 'secondary causes' in this respect. There are difficulties even for this Christian understanding if the coming into existence of the individual spiritual souls at particular points in space and time were in no way the result of the world and of its natural development due to secondary causes and if, as it were, God's creative activity could be grasped '*in vacuo*' and in a 'worldless' sense, so that God's causality would be an activity in the world *beside* other activity of creatures, instead of it being the ground of all the activity of all creatures. Furthermore, the negative answer to this new question corresponds little with the non-dualistic basic outlook of the Old Testament in which the one man is a being of the earth and the result of the creative act of God, without scripture – in order to make this comprehensible – dividing man into a being originating directly from the earth and a soul coming directly from God alone. Furthermore, this division of man into a part which is the product of the evolution of the world and into another which must be kept away from such evolutionary thought, looks too much like a compromise to the feeling of the modern natural scientist, a compromise which seems rather to belong to the bad variety of compromise rather than to the good. Finally, such a negative answer which divides man into two parts only related rather too extrinsically to one another, and an answer which does far too little justice to the real essential unity of the constitutive elements of man, makes it difficult to understand what after all is today an observed fact in paleontology, viz. that man has a long preparatory history which, in ever higher steps of living forms endowed with psychic life, at least leads very closely to him.

In order to make any progress in this question and to reach a positive answer under quite determined presuppositions and with conceptual precision, it will to begin with be necessary to clarify here somewhat abruptly the notion of active self-transcendence.

(a) There is becoming, and this becoming is ultimately not just the merely spatially, temporally and quantitatively transformed combination of basic elements which remain statically the same, but is the becoming of something really new which has an intramundane origin and yet is not simply the same as that from which it originates. Becoming is, therefore, always and of its very nature a self-transcendence of the cause, effected by the lower itself; it is an active surpassing of self. It is unfortunately impossible here to bring out clearly the transcendental source of a genuinely metaphysical concept of cause and becoming; this source lies in the movement of the spirit itself experiencing itself as the most radical case of the surpassing-of-self in its transcendence to being as such.

(b) Thus, real becoming is not just duplication but a surpassing of self in which what becomes really becomes more than it was and yet this 'more' is not simply something added to it from outside (which would cancel out the notion of genuine intramundane becoming). If this is so, and if such becoming in which more comes into being is to have a reason for this 'more', then this effectively becoming self-surpassing can only take place by the fact that the absolute being is the cause and basic reason for this self-movement of what becomes, in such a way that, on the one hand, this self-movement has this basic reason within itself as an inner moment of the movement and thus there is true self-transcendence and not merely a passive 'being-surpassed': yet, on the other hand, it is not for this reason the becoming of the absolute being since this, even as an inner moment of the self-movement of the self-transcending development, exists at the same time feely and untouched above what becomes, moving it without moving itself. It follows precisely from this, however, that movement does not cease to be self-movement when it becomes self-transcendence but that precisely in this case it attains its proper nature. Since every finite causality works in virtue of the absolute being within the finite and this always and essentially, so that the finite being has its own being and activity precisely through the existence of the absolute being within it, we can and must grant causality to the finite being; even causality for what is more than itself and towards which it surpasses itself. Within these metaphysical presuppositions, and given certain precisions, it can be said without qualms that a finite being can bring about more than it is. A denial of such possibilities can only basically make sense as an attempt to emphasise and clarify that such an active self-surpassing by something finite in its active development cannot take place except by the power of the absolute being seen as the absolute act which without thereby becoming a constitutive element of the finite being itself, is interior to the finite being in its becoming and activity.

(c) Thus the nature of each particular being with whose transcendence we are concerned is not the boundary of what can happen in this self-transcendence, but it is an indication that (i) something becomes and must become out of a limited potency, something which is not always realised already, i.e. an indication of something still having to become and that (ii) without prejudice to the real self-transcendence of the point of departure of the movement, i.e. the nature of the being moving itself, always remains also the limiting law of what can directly come out of it. The point of departure, even though it is surpassed, can very well be an indication of the goal towards which the transition is orientated and an indication of how far it can go directly. Presupposing this, however, the ontologically valid concept of becoming understood as really active self-transcendence also implies the basic possibility of going beyond oneself by surpassing one's *nature*. This can be said already because for a thomistic metaphysics different essences, in spite of their essential difference, are to be conceived as different grades of the limitation of being and not as absolutely disparate magnitudes. A lower being in its positivity is not, therefore, a disparate opposite of a higher being but merely a relatively narrower limitation of being by this lower being in relation to a higher one. Hence, when it surpasses itself in the process of its becoming, in the sense of a self-transcendence beyond its own being, then this does not mean the positing of an absolutely separate and essentially alien existent in the sense of a simple *generatio aequivoca*. Rather, it is immediately clear from this thomistic starting-point that the new existent can and must preserve within itself, as its own proper characteristics, all the positive realities of the nature of the old existent from which it originates. All this does not exclude but, on the contrary, includes the fact – even in such an essential self-transcendence – that the point of departure of this kind of self-transcendence, i.e. the proper nature of what becomes by thus surpassing itself, is the *a priori* limiting law for what can come to be here and now. Becoming, therefore, understood as an essential self-transcendence in virtue of the absolute interior but supra-essential being, does not exclude but rather includes the question about the precise sequence of the stages of this becoming which is unlimited in the forward direction. What and how things in such an evolutionary series can come in direct sequence one after the other, can only be determined in an *a posteriori* manner and is in the nature of things a difficult question. Precisely in the case of an essential self-transcendence, the notion of surpassing oneself always means a partial non-continuity which cannot and may not be avoided if we are not to deny basically genuine and qualitatively new becoming of being. On the other hand, the limit of what can become, which is given together with the finite nature of what becomes by transcending itself, demands that the non-continuity is not conceived in too wide a sense; indeed, it signifies the heuristic postulate requiring us to keep the 'leaps' as small as possible and the transcendence as fluid as possible, without of course intending thereby to give an 'explanation' of the higher development in which the essentially new would be explained away. Hence, if such an essential self-transcendence cannot be directly observed, it will never no doubt be completely possible to pass beyond a duality in one's methodic position: one will without qualms take into consideration all such 'leaps' and such self-transcendence to a new metaphysical being and hence will not at all demand an absolute continuity (which would be a metaphysical nonsense), while one will still continue to go on looking for new inter-mediate steps which will create more fluid transitions.

Given the ontological and Christian legitimacy of a self-transcendence, even one which goes beyond nature, and granted that the description of spirit and matter presented so far is held to be correct in its basic outlines, then it can also be said without hesitation that a development of the material in the direction of the spirit and the self-transcendence of the material into the spirit is, both philosophically and in the Christian sense, a legitimate conception. We have seen that becoming is really self-transcendence, and this in certain cases even towards a new nature even though this happens, of course, by the power of the dynamism of the absolute being, all of which, however, in its turn does not deny the fact that this is a question of a genuine, active *self*-transcendence. We have seen furthermore, that matter and spirit are not simply disparate things but that matter is, as it were, 'frozen' spirit whose only meaning is to render real spirit possible. Finally, we have seen that the spirituality of the creature always remains spirituality in materiality right up to its absolute perfection. Given all this, a development of matter in the direction of the spirit is not an impossible notion, presupposing merely that the notion of develop-ment is understood in the sense of that essential self-transcendence under the dynamism of the absolute being which we have briefly tried to outline. If, under the movement by the absolute being, there is any becoming at all in the material world by which the material surpasses itself, then – since this absolute being is spirit, self-possession and freedom – this self-surpassing can take place only in the direction of the spirit. The history of nature and the history of the spirit can be seen as *one* history without having thereby to deny the essential gradation of the world and of its development, and without having to embed the development of nature and the free personal history in dire opposition to one another. The highest grade of all productive becoming is the human spirit and matter tends towards it as towards its final principle of nature and form, for man is the goal of all generative becoming. This statement is already found in St Thomas Aquinas (*ScG* III, 22). Matter and spirit have a unity in their starting-point, in their history and in their goal. Both of them remain eternally valid before God and form for ever, now and in the state of perfection, the mutually correlative, non-separable constitutive elements of the one created reality.

13

THEOLOGY OF FREEDOM

WE have been asked to say something here about the theology of freedom. The lack of space available will not permit us to make a survey of the dogmatic and theological history of the doctrine of freedom. For the same reason it will also be impossible to collect together more precisely the theological statements about the nature of freedom as found in the theological sources of the scriptures, tradition and the Church's magisterium. Both of these things are impossible here. We must therefore be satisfied with giving a synthesis of what arises objectively from revelation about the nature of freedom.[1]

Even though man exercises them unsystematically in every one of his acts, he becomes only slowly aware of the systematic and objective nature even of his essential characteristics in the course of his individual and collective history. Hence, the history of salvation and revelation (including the history of Christian theology) is also a history of man's systematic reflection on himself as a free being. Thus it is not as if man always already knows adequately and systematically what human freedom is and uses this concept, always already given, in the expression of revelation and theology without changing and deepening it. The average scholastic theology may often give the impression that this is what man does but in reality it is not true. Obviously we cannot here give even a

---

[1] For a more detailed exposition of what can often be merely indicated here, it may be permitted to refer to the following essays of the author in previous volumes of 'Theological Investigations': 'Freedom in the Church', II, pp. 89–107; 'The Dignity and Freedom of Man', II, pp. 235–263; 'The Theology of Power', IV, pp. 391–409; 'The "Commandment" of Love in relation to the other Commandments', V, pp. 439–459; also (certain thoughts have been taken over from this too) to J. B. Metz, 'Freiheit – theologisch', *Handbuch theologischer Grundbegriffe*, ed. by H. Fries (Munich 1962), I, pp. 403–414; 'Freiheit als philosophisch-theologisches Grenzproblem', *Gott in Welt* I (in honour of K. Rahner) (Freiburg 1964), pp. 287–314.

brief account of the history of the Graeco-Western notion of freedom, but it is worth mentioning that even the real freedom of choice as such – i.e. the freedom which consists not only in the fact that man cannot be forced from without but also in that a free decision about himself is demanded from him which, therefore, is rather a demand and a task than freedom – can alone already be seen quite clearly in Christianity. Only in Christianity is each person completely unique and of eternal value – in God's personal love for man – and hence a personality which must be accomplished through the highest personal responsibility and hence in freedom.

The history of revelation has entered into its final, unsurpassable eschatological phase in Jesus Christ. The intramundane finality of this phase is not merely the actual way things are (because God does not want to reveal anything new any more) but is already given with the newer being of this phase itself, since – basically – it can only be surpassed by the direct vision of God. Given all this then, this characteristic of the history of revelation in Christ must also be applicable to the self-consciousness of man as a being of freedom: freedom as it is continually, creatively granted to man by God is not one of the 'objects', with regard to which a neutral freedom of choice is activated among other things, but the one who in this absolute act of freedom first appears to man and in whom alone the nature of freedom itself attains its full essential achievement.

I. FREEDOM IN THE THEOLOGICAL SENSE IS FREEDOM RECEIVED FROM AND DIRECTED TOWARDS GOD

It would be a complete misconception of the nature of freedom to try to understand it as the mere capacity of choice between objects given *a posteriori*, among which, besides many others, there is also God; so that God would only play a special role in the choice made by this freedom of choice from among these many objects on account of his own objective characteristics but not on account of the nature of freedom itself. Freedom only exists – as was seen explicitly already by St Thomas – because there is spirit understood as transcendence. There is unlimited transcendence towards being as such and hence indifference with regard to any particular, finite object within the horizon of this absolute transcendence only in so far as this transcendence in every individual act concerned with a finite object is directed towards the original unity of being as such. Moreover, this indifference exists only in so far as this act of transcendence (considered as the ground of every category of behaviour towards a finite subject and also towards the infinite represented in finite concepts) is supported by a conditional opening and extending of the horizon of this transcendence starting from itself, and of its goal, which we call God.

Freedom, therefore, has a theological character not only when and where God is represented explicitly and side by side with other objects in the objectivity of categories, but always and everywhere by the nature of freedom itself, since God is present unthematically in every act of freedom as its supporting ground and ultimate orientation. When St Thomas says that God is recognised unthematically but really in every object, then this applies equally to freedom: in every act of freedom God is unthematically but really willed and, conversely, one experiences in this way alone what is really meant by God, viz. the cognoscitively and appetitively incomprehensible orientation of the one original transcendence of man unfolding itself in knowledge and love.

The orientation of transcendence cannot be mastered but consists in the infinite, silent mastery over us in that moment and indeed always when, by making a judgement on it, we begin to master something by making it subject to the laws of our *a priori* reason. It is not given merely as the *goal* of transcendence itself (which means that, since this goal is not experienced in itself but is only known unobjectively in the experience of subjective transcendence, every thesis of ontologism is already avoided from this point of view alone) – and its presence, furthermore, is the presence of such a transcendence that it is always given only as the condition of the possibility of a knowledge in categories and not by itself alone. One can never go directly towards it. One can never reach out to it directly. It gives itself only in so far as it directs us silently to something else, to something finite as the object of direct vision.

It is decisive for the Christian understanding of freedom, however, that this freedom is not only made possible by God and is not only related to him as the supporting horizon of the freedom of choice in categories, but that it is freedom *vis-à-vis* God himself. This is the frightening mystery of freedom in its Christian understanding. Where God is understood in categories as merely one reality among others, as one of the many objects of freedom of choice - understood as a neutral capacity which is arbitrarily occupied with this and that -- the statement that freedom of choice is choice even with regard to God would present no particular difficulty.

That freedom, however, is freedom *vis-à-vis* its all-supporting ground itself, that in other words it can culpably deny the very condition of its own possibility in an act which necessarily reaffirms this condition, is the extreme statement about the nature of created freedom which in its radicality leaves the usual neutrality of categories far behind. It is decisive for the Christian doctrine of freedom that this freedom implies the possibility of a 'yes' or 'no' towards its own horizon and indeed it is only really constituted by this. This is true not merely and not even primarily when God is given and represented systematically in concepts and categories but also when he is given unsystematically but originally in our transcendental experience as the condition and moment of every activity directed towards the contemporary world in which we live. It is true in this sense that we meet God everywhere in a most radical way as the most basic question of our freedom, in all things of the world and (in the words of scripture) above all in our neighbour. Why then, more precisely, is the transcendental horizon of freedom not merely the condition of its possibility but also its proper 'object'? Why do we not act in freedom not merely towards ourselves, our surroundings and the people around us either in conformity to reality or in a destructive way within that infinitely wide horizon of transcendence from which we freely confront ourselves and the world in which we live, and why is this horizon itself also the 'object' of this freedom in our yes or no to it in itself? This horizon is once more *per definitionem* the condition of the possibility of saying no to it. This means that in such a 'no' it is unavoidably negated as the condition of the possibility of freedom and is also at the same time negated as an unthematic 'object' or even (in explicit or practical 'atheism') as a conceptually mediated object. Thus, in the act of the negating freedom there is present a real, absolute contradiction in the fact that God is affirmed and denied at the same time; in it this ultimate monstrosity is both withdrawn from itself and, by the fact that it is necessarily made objective and mediated in the finite material of our life in its temporal extension, made relative by being introduced into temporality. The real possibility, however, of such an absolute contradiction in freedom cannot be denied, though it is indeed disputed and doubted. This happens in ordinary everyday theology whenever it is said that the only thinkable mode of freedom is that the infinite God in his objectivity can only evaluate a little 'bending' of finite reality, the offence against a concrete and merely finite natural structure, for what it is, viz. something finite; he therefore cannot evaluate it by an absolute prohibition and an infinite sanction and cannot characterise it as something directed against his own will as such. The 'will', against which such a sin really offends (such a theology would say), is after all the finite reality really willed by God, and to suppose an offence against God's will over and above this is to falsely turn God's will into a particular category of reality alongside the finite thing which is willed. Yet there is the possibility of a free 'no' towards God. Otherwise freedom would basically have no real orientation to the subject (of which we will have still to speak explicitly), i.e. the fact that freedom is concerned with the subject itself and not just with this or that thing. Let us grant that the act of freedom is really concerned with the subject itself, since this subject is transcendence. Let us grant furthermore that the individual intramundane beings encountered by us within the horizon of transcendence are not events within a space which remains untouched by what is in that space, but are the historical concreteness of the encounter and projection of this source and goal that support our transcendence. In this light freedom towards the encountered individual beings is always also a freedom towards the horizon, the ground and abyss, which allows them to present themselves to us and lets them become the inner moment of our receiving freedom. In so far as and because the horizon cannot be indifferent to the subject understood as a *knowing* subject but is systematically or unsystematically that with which this knowing transcendence is concerned, particularly if this '*ad quem*' is not its explicit object, to that same extent and for the same reason *freedom* – even though it is always exercised on the concrete individual things of experience and through this becomes what it is – is primarily and unavoidably concerned with God himself. Freedom in its origin is freedom of saying yes or no to God and by this fact is freedom of the subject towards itself. Freedom is either indifferent to this or that, the infinite repetition of the same or of the contrary (which is merely a different kind of the same), a freedom of eternal recurrence, or the same 'wandering Jew', or it is necessarily the freedom of the subject towards itself in its finality and thus is freedom towards God, however unconscious this ground and most proper and original 'object' of freedom may be in the individual act of freedom.

We must add a second reflection to this, a reflection which alone brings to light the ultimate theological reason for freedom as freedom towards God, but one which can only be briefly indicated here. The supernatural and historical concreteness of our transcendence is never given as something merely natural but is always embraced and taken up by a supernatural dynamism of our spiritual being which tends towards the absolute nearness of God. In other words, God in the concrete is not present merely as the horizon of our transcendence, one which always withdraws itself and refuses to give itself; rather, understood as this horizon, he offers himself to be directly possessed in what we call divinising grace. Given all this, the freedom in transcendence and in the yes and no towards the ground of this transcendence is given a directness towards God by which it becomes most radically capable of saying yes and no to God as such. This happens in a way which would, of course, in no way be already given by the abstract formal concept of transcendence directed towards God as the merely distant and repelling horizon of our exercise of existence and it is such that it cannot be derived from this concept alone.

II. FREEDOM AS TOTAL AND FINALISING SELF-MASTERY OF THE SUBJECT

Freedom, as we have said, cannot be viewed in a Christian sense as an in-itself neutral capacity to do this or that in an arbitrary order and in a temporal series which would be broken off from outside even though, from the point of view of freedom, it could go on *ad infinitum*; freedom is rather the capacity to make oneself once and for all, the capacity which of its nature is directed towards the freely willed finality of the subject as such. This is obviously what is meant by the Christian statement about man and his salvation and damnation when he, the free person, must answer for himself and the totality of his life before the judgement seat of God, and when the eternally valid sentence about his salvation or damnation in accordance with his works is passed by a judge who does not regard merely the appearance of his life, the 'face', but the freely governed core of the person, the 'heart'. It is true that man's formal freedom of choice and decision is more presupposed in scripture than used as an actual theme. It is true also that the explicit theme in scripture, especially in the New Testament, is for the most part the paradox that man's freedom, while remaining responsible and without being destroyed, is enslaved by the slavery of the demonic powers of sin and death and to some extent even of the law, and must first of all be liberated to make way for an inner inclination towards the law (we will discuss this later). Yet it cannot be doubted that for scripture both the sinful and the justified man are responsible for the actions of their life and to this extent are also free and that freedom, therefore, is a permanent constitutive of man's nature. The proper nature of freedom, however, appears precisely in so far as freedom is the basis of absolute salvation and damnation in Christian revelation, and this finally and before God. For a merely profane every-day experience, freedom of choice may appear merely as the characteristic of the individual act of man, which can be attributed to him in so far as it is actively posited by him, without this positing being already causally predetermined and in this sense forced by some inner condition of man or some external situation. Such a concept of freedom of choice atomises freedom in its exercise and thus distributes it exclusively to the individual acts of man, acts which are only held together by a neutral, substantial identity of the subject and of the capacities positing them all, as well as by life's external space of time. Freedom in this sense is merely freedom of acts, imputability of the individual act to a person who remains neutral in himself and hence (as long as the external conditions are given for this) can always determine himself anew. Once we see in a Christian sense, however, that by his freedom man can determine and dispose himself as a whole and finally, the idea of responsible freedom is changed and deepened immensely. This means that man does not merely perform actions which, though they must be qualified morally, also always pass away again (and which after that are imputed to him merely juridically or morally); man by his free decision really *is* so good or evil in the very ground of his being itself that his final salvation or damnation are really already given in this, even though perhaps in a still hidden manner. Freedom is first of all 'freedom of being'. It is not merely the quality of an act and capacity exercised at some time, but a transcendental mark of human existence itself. If man is to be really and finally able to be master over himself, if this 'eternity' is to be the act of his freedom itself, if this act is to be really able to make man good or bad in the very ground of his being, and if this goodness or badness is not to be merely an external, accidental event happening to man (so that this act would merely, contrary to its goodness, draw something which remains good into damnation), then freedom must first of all be thought of as freedom of being. This means that man is that being who is concerned in his very being about this being itself; he is always a being who already has a relationship towards himself, a subjectivity and never simply a nature; already a person . . . never just 'something there' but always already 'for himself', 'existing'. Nothing happens to this being which does not affect its relationship to itself in some way, or if it does, it becomes subjectively and salvifically significant only in so far as it is freely 'understood' and subjectively taken over by the free subject as such in a quite definite way; its 'ego' cannot possibly be passed over, it simply cannot be turned into an object and can never be replaced or explained by something else, not even by its own reflex representation of itself; it is genuinely original, never based on something else and hence cannot be derived from or proved by anything else. Its relationship to its divine origin must never be interpreted according to the notion of causal and formal relationships of dependence as operative in the categories of the realm of our experience in which the source keeps and binds and does not set free, and in which therefore independence and dependence grow in inverse and equal proportion. Man, by his freedom of being, is always the incomparable being who cannot be adequately classified into any system and cannot be adequately subsumed under any one concept. He is in an original sense the untouchable, but therefore also the lonely and insecure, a burden to himself, who cannot by any means 'absolve' himself from this once-and-for-all lonely self-being and who can never 'unload' himself on others. Hence, freedom is originally also not primarily concerned with this or that which one can do or not do; freedom is not originally the capacity of choosing any object whatsoever or the ability of adopting an individual attitude towards this or that; it is rather the freedom of self-understanding, the possibility of saying yes or no to oneself, the possibility of deciding for or against oneself, which corresponds to the knowing self-possession, the understanding subject-nature of man. Freedom never happens as a merely objective exercise, as a mere choice 'between' individual objects, but is the *self*-exercise of the man who chooses objectively; only within this freedom in which man is capable of achieving himself is man also free with regard to the material of his self-achievement. He can do or omit this or that in view of his own self-realisation that is inescapably imposed on him. This self-realisation is a task he cannot avoid and, in spite of all the differences within the concrete material of his self-achievement, it is always either a self-realisation in the direction of God or a radical self-refusal towards God.

It must of course be realised that this basic nature of freedom is achieved over a whole period of time and that the total project of human existence, one's own total self-understanding or *'option fondamentale'*, frequently remains empty and objectively unfulfilled. It must be borne in mind that not every individual act of freedom has the same actual depth and radical nature of self-disposal and that, although each individual act of freedom wants to venture total and final self-disposal, all such acts always enter into the totality of the one, total act of freedom of the one, whole temporally finite life, precisely because each one of these acts is exercised within, and receives its weight and proportion from, the horizon of the whole of human existence. Correspondingly, the biblical and Augustine concept of the heart, the concept of subjectivity in Kierkegaard, the notion of *'action'* in Blondel, etc., shows understanding for the fact that there is such a basic act of freedom which embraces and shapes the whole of human existence. This act is indeed realised and can be exercised only by means of those individual acts of man which can be localised in space and time and which can be objectified with regard to their motives. Yet this basic act cannot be simply identified by an objective reflection with such an individual act; it does not represent either the merely moral sum-total of these individual acts nor can it be simply identified with the moral quality of the last of the free individual acts exercised (before death). The concrete freedom of man by which he decides about himself as a whole by effecting his own finality before God, is the unity in difference of the formal *'option fondamentale'* and the free individual acts of man no longer attainable by reflection, a unity which is the concrete being of the subject of freedom having-achieved-itself. In all this, to emphasise this once more and explicitly, freedom – precisely speaking – is not the possibility of always being able to do something else, the possibility of infinite revision, but the capacity to do something uniquely final, something which is finally valid precisely because it is done in freedom. Freedom is the capacity for the eternal. Natural processes can always be revised again and directed along a different path and are therefore for this very reason indifferent. The result of freedom is the true necessity which remains.

III. FREEDOM REGARDED AS A DIALOGIC CAPACITY OF LOVE

This self-perfecting of freedom into the eternal 'moment' is, as we have said, its self-realisation before God. Freely posited salvation or damnation, consisting in the gaining or loss of God, must not be understood as a merely external reaction of a judging or rewarding God but is itself already performed in this freedom. Freedom, if it is to be able to effect salvation or damnation and hence the determination of the whole man, of itself brings into play the whole man with his mutually interactive relations to his origin and future. Freedom is always self-realisation of the objectively choosing man seen in view of his total realisation before God. In this way, considered as the capacity of the 'heart', it is the capacity of love. This answer is not so self-evident if we ask: what is the basic act of man into which quite absolutely he can synthesise his whole nature and life, the act which can embrace everything and incorporate everything within itself, everything which goes under the name of man and the life of man, happiness and despair, everyday life and starlight hours, sin and redemption, past and present. Yet this is really the case: the love of God, and this love alone, is capable of embracing everything. It alone places man completely before the one without whom man would be merely consciousness of radical emptiness and nothingness; it alone is able to unite all man's many-sided and mutually contradictory capabilities because they are all orientated towards that God whose unity and infinity can create the unity in man which, without destroying it, unites the diversity of the finite. Love alone allows man to forget himself (what a hell it would be if we were not able to do this in the end); it alone can still redeem even the darkest hours of the past since it alone finds the courage to believe in the mercy of the holy God. Love alone reserves nothing to itself and therefore can also decide about the future (which man, in the anxiety about his finiteness which must be used sparingly, is otherwise tempted to save up). Because it loves the one who has never regretted the venture of such a world of guilt, malediction, death and fruitlessness, love can also love this earth together with God. Love of God is the only total integration of human existence, and we have only grasped it in its dignity and all-embracing greatness if we have understood it to be this and once we suspect that it must be the content of the moment of eternity in time and hence the content of the eternity with God himself which is born out of it.

This love is not a determined, assignable performance which one could define exactly, but rather that which every man becomes in the irreplaceable characteristic of his always unique realisation of nature, something which is known only once it is accomplished. This is not to say that there is in no sense a universal concept of love, as seen in the statement that man is obliged to love God and to say that the whole divine law consists in this. Man is, in spite of all this, obliged to love God with his *whole* heart . . . and this one heart which man must stake, the innermost centre of his person, is something unique. What it bears within itself in its uniqueness, what is staked and given away in this love is known only once it has been done, at the stage when man has really caught up with himself and thus knows what is in him and *who* he is in the concrete. In this love, therefore, man enters into the adventure of his own reality, an adventure which to begin with is veiled from him. He cannot survey and evaluate from the very start what is really demanded of him. *He* is demanded, he himself is ventured, he in the concreteness of his heart and his life which, only when accomplished, reveals what this heart is that had to venture and squander itself in this life. In the case of all other efforts, we may know what is really demanded of us. It is possible to gauge, compare, ask oneself whether the stakes and the gain are worth it. One could justify such a demanded effort by something else, by a result which shows it to make sense, but in the case of love this is impossible. Love itself is what justifies love, but this only in any real sense when with the whole heart and with all one's might it has been carried to the very end.

The Christian ethos does not basically consist in the respecting of objective norms imposed by God on reality. All structures of things are *lower* than man. He can alter them, bend them as far as possible; he is their master and not their servant. The only ultimate structure of the person which manages to express it completely is the basic capacity of love, and this is without measure. Thus man too is boundless. Every sin is at root merely the refusal to entrust himself to this boundlessness; it is a lesser love which, because it refuses to become the greater, is no longer love at all. Of course, so as to know what this means, man requires objectifications which he encounters in the multiplicity of commandments. This is true but everything which thus appears in this multiplicity of commandments is the objectification or partial accomplishment or preliminary beginning of a love which itself has no norm by which it could be measured. One can speak of the 'commandment' of love as long as one does not forget that this 'law' does not command man to do *something* but imposes a person as a task on himself, that person who can love only by accepting that love belonging to God in which God does not give something but himself.

God, however, in spite of – no, because of – his absoluteness is no impersonal 'It', no asymptotic stationary take-off point of the transcendence and love of the spiritual person but the 'living God' in whose regard every action of man is essentially a response to his call. This ultimately is the basis of the historicity of the person. The historicity of man can only be taken perfectly seriously once man knows himself to be exposed in something *essentially* (and not merely *de facto* and *per accidens*) indisposable; in other words, when he understands himself as someone existing within the sovereign freedom of God against which there is no appeal. This essential reference of human self-understanding to .God's freedom and the thereby given 'essential history together with God' is ultimately nothing else but the anthropological expression of the fact that everything created remains always actually dependent on God. This is so since it means man remains dependent on God in that self-understanding which characterises his human *existence*, i.e. that he can never build God into this self-understanding as a disposable element. The experience and affirmation of inexhaustibility, of the mystery of God and of his freedom belong to the human self-affirmation as a creature. Man, therefore, accepts that dependence of a creature proper to him by the fact that he does not simply interpret himself in his self-understanding as something which is definitively available of itself (*after the manner of* 'pure nature', for instance) but rather patiently awaits a *historical* interpretation by God.

In this historical interpretation there becomes concrete what has been said above about the interpretation of the transcendental and categorial exercise of freedom. Human freedom, even in the case when it prepares to be directly and explicitly freedom *vis-à-vis* God, is always freedom with regard to some category of object and *vis-à-vis* some intramundane Thou, since even *such* an act of an explicit yes or no towards God cannot conduct itself directly in relation to the God of original, transcendental experience but only to the God of explicit, conceptual reflection, to God in the concept and not directly and alone to the God of transcendental presence.

God's Word, if it is to take place in intramundane tangibility, can only be spoken by man as a finite word. It is equally true '*in converso*', 'in the opposite direction', that the relationship to God in its directness is necessarily mediated by intramundane communication. The *transcendental* opening out requires a *categorial* object, a support as it were, so as not to lose itself in empty nothingness; it requires an intramundane Thou. The original relationship to God is ... love of neighbour. If man becomes himself only by the exercise of love towards God and must achieve this self-mastery by a categorial action, then it holds good – and holds good perfectly in the order of grace – that the act of love of neighbour is the only categorial and original act in which man attains the whole of the concretely given reality and finds the transcendental and supernatural, directly experienced experience of God.

The historicity of dialogic freedom, however, becomes even clearer in this relationship with one's fellow men, by the fact that it is not merely concerned with the sovereign God but also with the uncontrollable decisions relating to one's surroundings, and by the fact that it is determined by them and must in the concrete decide itself in determined situations.

Freedom, then, is not merely the capacity of knowing principles but is also the call to obey 'imperatives', to make decisions, decisions which cannot be derived from universal norms and eternal laws (although they may not contradict them) and yet do not leave man free to choose in any way he likes but rather make a total demand on man . . . out of the situation of his 'hour', of his call.

It is impossible here to develop a logic of the concrete understanding of what should be done at each moment, an ethics which does not simply stop at the rejection of situation ethics but reaches towards a genuine individual ethics. It must suffice simply to mention it . . . and to point out that only such an understanding can preserve the mystery of freedom.

IV. THE MYSTERY OF FREEDOM

Freedom is a mystery first of all because it comes only from God and is directed only towards God, who is essentially the incomprehensible mystery which as such is precisely the source and goal of freedom as such. The ground of freedom is the abyss of the mystery, which can never be conceived as that original datum of our transcendental experience in knowledge and freedom which in its self-evident and permanent incomprehensibility is the reason for the possibility of understanding every individual reality as such which it meets within this horizon.

We must abstain here from going on from this starting-point to pose the empistemological question about the real knowableness of freedom. Freedom is not a datum of any empirical psychology. Such a psychology can merely determine functional interconnections of individual facts within the horizon of experience as a whole, whereas freedom previously

to such an experience of objects is always already grasped as the form of
transcendental experience as such by the fact that the subject knows itself
to be incapable of being turned into an object and thus knows itself to be
free.

This radical mysteriousness of the freedom of the subject continues also
into the free act of the subject as such. The individual act of freedom
participates in the mystery of its origin and goal and in so far as it can
never be absolutely objectified in its freedom and hence also never in its
ethical quality. This characteristic does indeed already arise directly out
of the strictly subjective nature of freedom, but is also emphasised
explicitly and objectively in the statements of revelation. These statements
contain an ultimate non-objectifiability of freedom and of the free,
concrete decision. The total decision by which man decides definitively
about the whole of his reality, i.e. posits this totality itself in its freely
determined finality (and an individual act can be called really and completely free only in so far as this happens), is a total decision that according
to revelation belongs to the judgement of God alone. Man does indeed
come ever closer to his finality in freedom and as a *conscious* subject, but
he cannot once more objectify this result of his freedom for himself, i.e.
judge himself and even less others in their total quality before God. The
Catholic doctrine of faith declares that man cannot, while still a pilgrim
on earth, have an absolutely certain judgement about his state of justification or eternal salvation. Even the *Protestant* doctrine of justification is
not ultimately at variance on this point (in spite of all controversies)
since, even for the Lutheran doctrine of justification, absolute fiducial
faith always remains subject to temptation. This means also, therefore,
that man cannot adequately reflect objectively and with absolute certainty
on his free decisions. It means that freedom is really subjectivity and that
subjectivity is in itself and in its self-presence a more original reality than
individually existing objects which can be clearly determined by a
previously conceived co-ordinate system of universal ideas. *In* the deed
of his freedom itself man knows who he is and wants to be in freedom
but precisely this knowledge is strictly identical with himself and hence he
cannot separate this knowledge from himself as something objective and
manipulable and so once more say clearly to himself what he declares
himself to be in his freedom towards God. This declaration which he is
himself disappears for him, as it were, into the *mysterium* of God. An
absolutely certain, propositionally objectified declaration about a man's

exercise of freedom in a determined act located in space and time is basically impossible for this man with regard to himself and even more so for others. This does not indeed mean that freedom and responsibility are in no way realities to be found within the space of human experience and reflection and in the realm of inter-subjectivity. Freedom, even as the concrete total self-determination of the free subject about itself in the direction of finality, always takes place by means of a pre-given particular category of material; subjectivity and the person always fulfil themselves in the natural. This shows the created nature of human freedom. It is equally clear that man, without injury to the impossibility of an *adequate* self-reflection, is always also the reflecting, the self-objectifying being who places himself under the norms of universal validity. It is a Catholic and also, in view of the material ethics of the Bible, a completely biblical doctrine that it is not merely possible to develop *formal* principles of the subjective exercise of freedom of the subject with regard to its correctness or wrongness but also absolutely material norms of an objective and universally valid kind with regard to the right or wrong exercise of this subjective freedom within the categories of the nature of man and of his world. It then becomes self-evident that man is empowered as well as obliged to make a certain reflex and objectified self-judgement about his moral condition, i.e. to make a judgement with regard to the presence, rightness or wrongness of his exercise of freedom in a particular material act. This understanding of oneself which one can pronounce to oneself and examine critically, and in view of which one can attain a certain valid result, is qualified precisely by the characteristics of the pilgrim existence of man in this life, in which freedom is still at work and hence every trial is itself once more an act of freedom which cannot be adequately examined by reflection. It is a real knowledge which gives *that* kind of 'certitude' which can be given within the space of the historical and of freedom: as a demand to place freedom itself under obligatory moral norms. One has the right and duty to include this knowledge about oneself and ultimately also that about others in the calculations of one's life and of one's active decisions and actions, since otherwise one cannot exist and since absolute abstention from such judgements would not avoid the risk of such judgements but would itself be once more a free decision full of risk. Yet this judging, deciding, risking, objectifying knowledge about freedom does not understand itself as something final, absolutely certain and beyond appeal. In this objectifying knowledge, and in his reflex self-understanding which is once more an act of unreflected freedom, man accepts himself and, precisely as the one who understands himself in this way or that, he makes himself answerable to the mysterious judgement of God that takes place in a hidden way in the unreflected act of his freedom. Freedom is mystery.

V. CREATED FREEDOM IN AN UNAVOIDABLE SITUATION OF GUILT

The freedom of man is indeed free self-realisation into finality. Yet in spite of its peculiarly creative character, it is a *created* freedom. This can be seen from two facts. In its transcendental nature this freedom experiences itself first of all as borne and empowered by its absolute horizon, an absolute horizon which it does not form but by which it is formed. The transcendentality of the spirit must not be conceived as residing either in the knowledge or in the freedom of love as if the spirit projects and determines its orientation or 'goal' by itself. Its 'goal' itself, in the peculiar manner of something withdrawn, opens itself of itself to the knowing and willing spirit (without – as has already been said – this implying that open realisation maintained by ontologism); the goal is experienced within the realisation of spiritual existence itself as the real moving force; the active self-projection of the spirit towards its goal and its future is experienced as taken up by the goal which opens itself of itself and over which the spirit has no control since he does not grasp it fully but is rather constituted by it as something lying beyond it. The characteristic of the transcendentality of freedom, understood as freedom borne and empowered by its goal, right away indicates the created nature of this freedom of which freedom is directly conscious in its exercise. In so far as this empowering of freedom, towards the absoluteness of being, is experienced as the empowering by grace to the absolute *nearness* to this goal – in its direct self-communication (called divine grace) – the character of created freedom comes through more strongly and clearly through the empowering self-opening of this goal (even though this experience can be made clearly objective only through its interpretation in the supernatural revelation of the Word and by faith).

The experience of the created nature of freedom is shown secondly by the fact that this freedom, understood as a self-disposing by the subject towards finality, is necessarily mediated by an environment and intersubjectivity which of themselves are *a posteriori*, uncontrollable and ultimately unplanned. Man always exercises his original freedom towards himself by merely accepting and passing through the history pre-given and imposed on him. Freedom is the free answer of yes or no to necessity and once more experiences in this its created nature.

According to Christian teaching which is contained above all in the implications of the doctrine of original sin and concupiscence, the fact that created freedom is conditioned by situations and that it only becomes conscious of itself by going out into the world is characterised by the fact that this situation is always and unavoidably co-determined by guilt. The doctrine of sin at the very source of the common history of the world and of humanity and the doctrine of concupiscence signify that there is never a situation and material for man's freedom (if this situation and material are regarded adequately and without any arbitrary abstractions) which is not right away, even before each person's own positive or negative moral decision, co-determined by the guilt in the history of mankind, and that it will never be possible – right to the end of history – to eliminate completely this mortgage of guilt that is objectified in the situation of freedom.

In so far as freedom must always objectify itself in an alien material in order to find itself, it becomes alienated from itself. As has already been shown, it can never look at itself so clearly in what it has done for its own self-realisation in the material of the situation as to be able to recognise in this exactly and with absolute certitude what it is in itself, viz. the yes or no to itself and to God. This can be seen to be true even by the mere fact that there is no objectification of which one could say with absolute certitude that it could only have arisen in its concreteness out of freedom and not by natural necessity. Being created and mediated freedom, this freedom necessarily becomes in an ultimate sense ambiguous in its objectification; it therefore becomes a mystery to itself and as such it must surrender itself to God. This characteristic of ambiguity in the objectifications of freedom is heightened by the circumstance that the material imposed on freedom and entering into its exercise is always already co-determined and formed by guilt from the very beginning of the history of the spirit. The freedom of the individual, of course, can still understand this material co-determined by the guilt of others (which does not remain external to the free act) either in the sense of ratifying the guilty determination of this material as the embodiment of its own 'no' to God, and thus make it the objective manifestation of its own guilt, or by suffering and overcoming it as a participation in the Cross of Christ with its 'yes' to God. Yet precisely this ambiguity of the imposed situation and its material for freedom makes the original free act once more something which cannot be absolutely understood, a mystery for freedom which cannot be solved; it veils within the unsearchable judgement of God the meaning and quality of the individual life as well as of the history of humanity as a whole.

VI. FREEDOM AS LIBERATED FREEDOM

In so far as freedom is always and in every act freedom directed towards the mystery of God himself (that mystery by which it is supported and empowered), the act of freedom is always essentially the act of man's self-surrender to the uncontrollable providence of God and in this sense it is always essentially a trusting venture. How God transmits himself to this freedom which if it does not want to refuse itself to him must entrust itself absolutely to him in its venture into the unpredictable, it can appear only slowly in the history of the self-experience of this freedom. This whole matter becomes even more acute on account of what we have called the guilt-situation of freedom. Even though according to Catholic teaching human freedom was not destroyed by original sin, yet it was profoundly 'wounded' by it; hence, even though God's promise does not need to create it completely anew, it certainly does require his loving assistance. The injured freedom must (freely) *accept* this help and yet is not capable of this acceptance by its own power. Even for this it must be liberated by the 'prevenient grace' of the unsearchable decision of God who when he 'wants to show mercy does so, and when he wants to harden someone's heart does so' (Rm 9:18) but of whom we are bound to believe at the same time that 'he wants everyone to be saved' (1 Tm 2:4).

God has manifested this final, irrevocable decision to liberate freedom in his Son. Hence the history of the experience of freedom with God is – by his will, against which there is no appeal – salvation- and revelation-history; it is the experience achieved in Jesus Christ that God has given himself to the freedom of man as the absolute nearness and as the ground of the free acceptance of this nearness in what we call divinising grace. God has surrendered himself in his innermost divinity to the freedom which surrenders itself into the unforeseeable ways of God; God is not merely the distant horizon towards which man projects his free self-understanding as to something always distant but He has become in absolute immediacy the space and 'object' of this exercise of freedom. This exercise of freedom made possible and elevated in Christ is that liberated freedom which St Paul proclaims as the 'freedom of the children of God', the real Christian freedom. The love of the Father which has been revealed in the Son (Jn 8:36) become flesh, the aletheia, makes us free (Jn 8:32), because where His *pneuma* is, there is freedom (2 Co 3:17). This freedom is a freedom from sin (Rm 6:18–23; Jn 8:31–36), from the law (Rm 7:3 *sq.*; 8:2; Ga 2:4; 4:21–31; 5:1, 13) and from death (Rm 6:21 *sq.*; 8:21): from sin, in so far as sin is in a thousand different ways the free achievement of self-assertion in oneself and in the world without openness towards the love of God; from the law, in so far as the law, although it is the holy will of God, becomes the thorn of his own self-assertion against God or before God for the man without grace (whether this man be wounded or self-gloriously fulfilled in his work); from death, in so far as death is merely the phenomenality of guilt. Man makes this freedom which is and is given by Christ his own by the fact that, obedient to the call of this freedom (Ga 5:13), man subjects himself by faith (and its tangible sign which is baptism) to that happening which breaks open the prison of the world: the incarnation, death and resurrection of the Son.

It has also been revealed in this experience of freedom that man's no to God, as far as the whole history of human freedom is concerned, was permitted by God in His yes to His own self-communication to created freedom and that it remains embraced by this yes of God which remains victorious in the history of salvation as a whole. The freedom of man is liberated into immediacy to God's own freedom of being. It receives the power for its highest possible act, one which is rooted in its formal being but is not demanded by it. The freedom towards God and originating from God as the source and future of freedom, and the freedom that is seen as the dialogic capacity of love, is achieved in the highest imaginable form of these aspects: as the freedom which is taken up by God's self-communication in personal love and which accepts God himself, so that the horizon and object of this love liberated for itself are identical.

14

GUILT – RESPONSIBILITY – PUNISHMENT WITHIN THE VIEW OF CATHOLIC THEOLOGY

I

THE subject of this chain-lecture is 'Guilt – responsibility – punishment'. No one, however, will take umbrage at the theologian if he changes the sequence of these three themes and speaks about responsibility – guilt – punishment, for he unlike the jurist does not look at these themes from the point of view of the penal significance of his knowledge and judgements but from the point of view of the original nature of things. It is obvious, after all, that there can only be guilt in the theological sense where there is freedom and responsibility, no matter how obscure to begin with the notions of freedom and responsibility and hence also of guilt may be. Under these presuppositions, we would like first of all to make a few preliminary remarks on the method to be adopted in the theological treatment of this subject. The Catholic theologian will certainly include responsibility – guilt – punishment within the sphere of his questions and declarations even in the sense in which they enter into the realm of the life of the ordinary citizen, that of jurisprudence, that of ordinary inter-human relationships and that of the humanistic appreciation of man and his deeds. The Catholic theologian is of the opinion that the divine revelation which he tries to follow in his thought in no way merely makes statements about a realm of objects which lie absolutely beyond human experience but that it throws light and passes judgement on the concrete world in which man lives his concrete existence. Hence, Catholic theology – basing itself on divine revelation – also claims the right, for instance, to make statements about historical events; it also claims this right with regard to those ultimate essential structures of man which would belong to his competence even if there were no divine revelation and no vocation of man to a direct, 'supernatural' partnership by grace of the individual and God: essential structures from which we derive the so-called natural law which is the unchangeable moral norm for man. From this it is self-evident for Catholic theology that, out of its most proper source of knowledge and with its specific methods of knowledge, it also makes statements about responsibility, guilt and punishment even in the sense in which these notions are understood in the realm of ordinary life, and that it does not simply connect contents with these concepts which from the very start have nothing to do with the ordinary understanding of these particular concepts. Thus it is also understandable that even in every theological statement there is and must be presupposed a pre-theological, profane understanding of these provisional concepts. If we did not know at all by pre-theological knowledge what is meant by freedom, responsibility, guilt and punishment, it would also be completely impossible to have any theological understanding of these concepts. It is not a simple matter of revelation and its theological reflection simply constituting anew the ultimate, basic conceptual elements even of the language of revelation and of theology; rather, the language of revelation always picks up concepts already known in the ordinary sphere even though these concepts can also then be given a more profound, changed or new meaning by the fact that they are put in a new context. From what has been said it follows that, on the one hand, we must here presuppose a pre-theological understanding of the concepts to be dealt with and that, on the other hand, we must show what new and deeper content these concepts attain within the theology and its decisive statements and, finally, how from this starting-point theology clarifies and judges the profane use of these concepts by affirming them positively and also putting them critically into question. This closed circle of a pre-theological and general human understanding of these concepts, of a metamorphosis of these concepts by their being drawn into a theological context, and of a critical theological clarification of their profane use, must (as far as is possible here) determine all our reflections.

II

We start with a theological reflection on the concept of responsibility. Responsibility, in the sense intended here and in the only sense in which it can be the basis for the theological concept of guilt and punishment, presupposes freedom as the characteristic of acting being in general and as the property of that particular way of acting for which the acting being is supposed to be responsible. Whether a different concept of responsibility is possible in the nature of things or not – such as, for instance, in the administration of justice or under the presupposition of a psychological or theological determinism – need not concern us here. For Catholic theology, at any rate, responsibility and freedom are mutually clarifying concepts (at least terminologically), both of which appeal in the same way to the experience of the human subject in its actions. Hence, if we wish to know what is meant by responsibility in the theological sense, we must always, without having to try anxiously to keep the concept of freedom and responsibility strictly apart, look at the same time at the phenomenon of the experience of freedom and its theological interpretation.

From our introductory remarks it already appears that Catholic theology presupposes quite freely that we always already know what freedom and responsibility are even before theology starts to undertake the task of describing this pre-theological general human and profane knowledge about freedom and responsibility and to investigate the history of man's self interpretation in the history of the more precise understanding of these concepts. The understanding of these concepts in the history of man's self-interpretation has no doubt a long and variable history to which also belongs precisely the history of revelation and of Christian theology. Christian theology nevertheless presupposes a permanent nature in man which is preserved throughout the whole history of mankind even though it only becomes gradually conscious of itself in that history. It therefore presupposes also a permanent common knowledge about responsibility, even though this too has its own history. Otherwise, all men could not really be the subject and object of the one divine salvation on the part of one and the same God in Jesus Christ within one unified history of salvation. For this theological reason and not merely for lack of time it will perhaps be permissible here simply to presuppose this pre-theological knowledge about freedom and responsibility. In this connection it should merely be noted (without going into this more deeply here) that it is quite possible to presuppose in a Catholic theology that an authentic, even though provisional experience of freedom and responsibility which has not yet quite caught up with its true nature, is quite conceivable and something which really occurs; this is an experience in which the reference of freedom and responsibility to God and his law – however much it must be implied – need not yet be the subject of explicit reflection; it is therefore perfectly possible in certain circumstances to have an atheistic ethics of freedom and moral responsibility and that this can, precisely in a Christian understanding, be the source of a genuine and original understanding of what is really meant by God and the divine law.

Thus we simply presuppose this pre-theological, ordinary human understanding of freedom and responsibility, and ask ourselves what new and deeper interpretation these concepts undergo when they are brought into a theological context. We will first of all try to determine very simply the theological locus of the interpretation of these concepts and will then ask ourselves what results from this for the deepened understanding of these concepts. As far as the theological locus – understood as the origin and horizon of the understanding of these concepts and of the reality meant by them – is concerned, we may perhaps put it quite simply as follows: man disposes over the totality of his being and existence before God and this either towards Him or away from Him. Man does this in such a way that his temporal decisions determine the eternal finality of his existence either in absolute salvation or damnation: on account of his freedom, man is responsible for his eternal salvation or damnation. The meaning of this simple statement must now be unfolded so as to show what it involves for the nature of freedom and responsibility. Yet let it be stated in advance on this subject (since we will have to pass this over later on) that the experience of freedom and responsibility illuminated by revelation experiences and knows this freedom precisely as a gift of God's grace both in its basic condition and in its proper exercise. From the outset, therefore, it understands freedom as an autonomous self-possession of man before or even against God, but not in the sense that God's grace and mastery and the responsible exercise of freedom are realities encroaching on each other – in the sense, for instance, of a Pelagian synergism – as if they were realities of which the one could assert itself or grow only at the expense of the other. The divine freedom and mastery are experienced from the outset as the reason for the possibility of the creature's responsibility and freedom, so that both grow in equal and not in inverse proportion. Having stated this in advance, it must now be said what is meant more exactly by freedom considered as the whole subject's capacity and necessity of being responsible itself with regard to final salvation and damnation before God. This is obviously what is meant by the Christian statement about man and his salvation and damnation if he must, and must be able as a free person, to answer for himself and the whole of his life before the divine judgement seat and if the eternally valid sentence concerning his final salvation or damnation is passed according to his works, on the part of a judge who does not regard the mere appearance of life, the 'face', but the freely disposable core of the person, the 'heart'. It is true that man's formal freedom of choice and decision is more presupposed than treated of as a proper subject in scripture. It is true also that the explicit subject of scripture, and especially of the New Testament, is to a great extent the paradox that man's freedom, while remaining responsible and without being destroyed, nevertheless falls under the slavery of the diabolical powers of sin and death and to some extent even of the law, and that freedom must first of all be freed by God's grace for its real task of loving God in an inner inclination towards the law. Yet, although all this is true, it cannot be doubted that for scripture, the sinful and the justified man are both responsible for their life's action before God and hence are also free . . . at least to the extent that the freedom of choice is a permanent constitutive element of human nature. Its true nature, however, is made to appear for the first time precisely in so far as in the view of Christian revelation this freedom of choice is the basis for salvation or damnation, and this finally and before God. For to a merely profane experience this freedom of choice may appear merely as the characteristic of the individual human act which is imputable to man only to the extent in which it is actively posited by man himself, without this being causally determined beforehand and in this sense forced by an inner condition of man or by an external situation preceding the active decision. Such a notion of freedom of choice distributes freedom in its exercise exclusively and in an atomising fashion over the individual acts of man which can thus be held together only by a neutral, substantial sameness of the subject positing them all and by life's external space of time. Freedom in this experience is, therefore, only the freedom of acts, the imputability of the individual act to a person who in principle remains neutral and hence can always determine himself anew (as long as the external conditions for this are still present). Yet, seen from a Christian point of view, the idea of responsible freedom changes greatly and becomes immensely deeper when it is seen that man can determine and decide about himself as a whole by his freedom, and this with finality, and that he therefore posits acts which must not merely be qualified morally and then pass away again (being imputed to him thereafter only juridically or morally), but that he really and truly *is* so good or evil in the ground of his reality itself that in this way his final salvation or damnation is already given (even though perhaps in a still hidden manner). Freedom is then seen to be first and foremost freedom of being. It is not merely an act which is sometimes posited in its exercise, but a transcendental characteristic of the being of man itself. If man is really to be able to decide finally about himself, if therefore eternity is to be the act of his freedom itself, if this act is not to be able to draw something which remains good, contrary to its goodness, into a ruin which simply contradicts this permanently good reality, if therefore freedom is to be able to make man really good or evil in the very depth of his being, and if this being good or evil is not merely to be an external accidental condition of man . . . then freedom must first of all appear as freedom of being.[1] This means that man is that being who is concerned in the depths of his being about this being itself, the being which always has a relationship to itself, which is a subject and never merely a nature, which is always already a person, never simply there but always already personally existent. In this being nothing happens to him which does not touch his relationship to himself. His 'I' can never be jumped over, it can never be turned into a mere object, can never be replaced or explained by something else, not even by its own reflex representation of itself. It is authentically original, not based in its turn on something else, and hence also cannot be derived from something else or be justified in view of something else. Man, by his freedom of being, is always the incomparable who cannot be pigeon-holed in any system or completely subsumed under any idea. He is in an original sense the untouchable, and also the lonely and exposed individual, someone who is his own burden and who cannot 'absolve' himself by any device from this unique, lonely self-being. Freedom also, therefore, is not originally and primarily concerned merely with this or that which it can do or not do. Freedom of choice is not primarily the ability to choose any object whatsoever or to choose any particular attitude towards this or that; it is

---

[1] The author gratefully uses here and in what follows the exposition of his good friend J. B. Metz, as found in: H. Fries, *Handbuch theologischer Grundbegriffe* I (Munich 1962), pp. 403–414 (article entitled 'Freiheit, theologisch'). Cf. now also 'Theology of Freedom' in this volume, pp. 178 *sqq.*

the freedom of self-understanding, the possibility of saying yes or no to oneself, the possibility of deciding for or against oneself which is parallel to the knowing self-consciousness and the knowing subjectivity of man. Freedom never occurs merely as an objective exercise, as a choice 'between' individual objects, but as the self-achievement of the objectively choosing human being, and only *within* this freedom in which man is master over himself is he then 'free' also with regard to the material of his own self-realisation that is inescapably imposed on him. This self-realisation is an unavoidable task and, in spite of all the differences in the concrete material of this self-achievement, it is always a self-realisation towards God or a radical self-refusal with regard to God. The salvation or damnation that consists in the gain or loss of God posited in freedom (we will have to return to this more at length later on) must not be understood as a merely external reaction of a condemning or rewarding God but is itself seen to be already achieved in this freedom. Freedom is therefore capacity for wholeness; if it is itself to be able to effect salvation or damnation, i.e. the determination of the whole man, then it must of itself bring into play the whole man in his origin and future and this within the interplay of his relationships to himself, the world and God. Freedom is always the self-fulfilment of the objectively choosing man in view of a total achievement, a total disposal of his existence before God. It must certainly be remembered for this that in many cases each envisaged total project of existence, one's own total self-understanding, the *'option fondamentale'*, remains empty and objectively unfulfilled. It must be remembered that not every individual act of freedom has the same actual depth and radical nature of self-disposition. It must be realised that, although every individual act of freedom intends to venture a total and final disposal of oneself, each of them always surrenders itself into the whole of the one and complete act of freedom of the one human, temporally finite life precisely because each of them is accomplished within the horizon of the whole of existence and receives its weight and proportion from this. Accordingly, the notion of the heart as conceived within the biblical and Augustinian mould, the notion of subjectivity in Kierkegaard, the notion of *'action'* in Blondel, etc., all show understanding of the fact that there is such a basic act of freedom which embraces and moulds the whole of existence. This act does indeed realise itself and can only be achieved by means of the individual human acts which can be placed in space and time and can be objectified with regard to their motives, yet it cannot be simply identified by objective reflection with such an individual act, nor does it represent the merely moral sum total of these individual acts, nor finally can it be simply identified with the moral quality of the last of these posited free individual acts. The concrete freedom of man in which he decides about himself as a whole before God by the realisation of his own finality before God is the unity in difference – which can no longer be reflected upon – of the *'option fondamentale'* and the individual free acts of man, a unity which is the concrete being of the free subject which has fulfilled itself.

The subject of freedom is responsible because in freedom the subject as such, really itself and not just something belonging to it, is responsible to itself. It cannot exculpate itself by throwing the blame on something other than itself and God could be defined precisely as the one who can give freedom in this sense without thereby being the limitation of this freedom, as is the case with anything falling into the category of cause.

There is a still further peculiarity of this responsible freedom in the theological sense to be brought out. It does indeed already arise directly out of the strict subjectivity of freedom, but it is also explicitly and objectively emphasised in the statements of revelation; we refer here to the impossibility of any ultimate objectification of freedom and of the concrete free decision. The total decision in which man finally disposes of the whole of his reality, i.e. posits this totality itself in its freely determined finality, is according to revelation subject to the sole judgement of God. Man does indeed mature in freedom, i.e. he brings his finality to maturity as a conscious subject, but he cannot once more objectify *this* result of freedom to himself, i.e. judge himself or others in their total quality before God. In so far as the Catholic dogma of faith declares that man in the state of pilgrimage is denied any absolutely certain judgement about his state of justification or his eternal salvation – and in so far as the Protestant teaching on justification also ultimately and on this point does not contradict this (in spite of all the controversies) since even for the Lutheran teaching on justification fiducial faith always remains subject to temptations – it is also stated by this that man cannot objectively and adequately reflect on his free decisions with absolute certitude. He knows in the act of his freedom who he is and wants to be in freedom but precisely this knowledge is about him himself and hence he cannot detach this knowledge from himself as something objectifiable and manipulable and thus once more tell himself clearly what he declares himself to be in his freedom before God. This declaration which he is himself disappears, as it were, into the *mysterium* of God.

It must now be remembered, however, that for a Christian understanding this freedom is precisely the proper nature of freedom in general even where it is not seen in this systematic theological form; for there really is no peculiarly civil-profane freedom and, side by side with it, theological freedom before God but the latter signifies the true nature of the former. If this is correct, however, then it follows absolutely necessarily that a completely certain statement about the realisation of a man's freedom in a determined, spatio-temporal act is basically impossible. This does not indeed mean that freedom and responsibility are in no way matters which are found within the space of human experience and reflection and in the field of human inter-subjectivity. After all, we have already indicated that the concrete total self-disposal of the free subject over himself always takes place in a pre-given, particular category of material and that subjectivity is achieved in the realm of nature. It is equally clear that man, without prejudice to the impossibility of an adequate self-reflection, is always also the reflecting, self-objectifying being who puts himself under universally valid norms. It is a Catholic doctrine and, in view of the material ethics of the Bible, also a completely biblical doctrine that it is not merely possible to develop formal principles of the subjective exercise of freedom but also material, objective and universally valid norms for the right or wrong exercise of this subjective freedom in the categorised material of the nature of man and of his world. From this standpoint it is then, however, obvious that man not only has the power but also the duty to make a certain reflex and objective judgement about his own moral state, i.e. with regard to the fact and rightness or wrongness of his exercise of freedom, in a particular material act. This self-knowledge which one can communicate to oneself, and which one can examine critically and with regard to which one can come to a certain final conclusion, characterises precisely the property of the pilgrim existence of man in this life in which freedom is always still at work, and hence every examination is itself once more an act of freedom which has not been and cannot be adequately examined consciously. It is a real knowledge, it gives certitude, and one has the right and duty to take account of this self-knowledge, and ultimately also of the knowledge about others, in the calculations of one's life and of one's active decisions

and actions, since otherwise one cannot exist at all and the complete
abstention from such judgements does not even avoid the risk of judging
but would itself be once more a free, risky decision; yet, this judging,
deciding, risking knowledge is not to be taken as final, absolutely
certain and beyond appeal. In it man accepts himself in his own self-
understanding and hands himself over – precisely as the one who understands himself in this or that way – to the mysterious judgement of
God.

In this way, man's judgement about the existence and the quality of a
free decision in his own case or that of others is, even in ordinary social
life, accorded its full character by theology and thus not merely on account
of a sceptical or careful psychology. Scripture and tradition presuppose
that there is the possibility and necessity of such judgements. Man, if he
wishes to live and act in a Christian manner, may not simply take refuge
in that scepticism that is so easily aroused today psychologically which
maintains that basically one knows nothing about the freedom and
responsibility of a particular person in his particular actions. Otherwise,
for example, the Church could only lay down general principles about
good and evil in her internal ecclesiastical discipline but could not, for
instance, put an ecclesiastical ban on the individual action of a particular
person or give the individual person material and yet binding precepts
for his conduct in the concrete. Yet, on the other hand, man must know
in accordance with the same attitude of the Church that these judgements,
which he cannot avoid and which have absolutely practical consequences
for him, are provisional judgements subject to the final pronouncement
by God, that they are risky judgements for the very person who passes
them, so that the correct and false judgements of man, the exercise of and
abstention from a judgement must once more be submitted to God's
pronouncement of judgement. In view of their results one may apply the
name of moral certitude, in contrast to metaphysical certitude or some
other label, to these reflected and critical judgements. The fact remains
that man is basically obliged to reach a reflex and knowing decision
with regard to the existence and quality of his exercise of freedom and
that nevertheless this decision itself, and not a sceptical abstention,
is the expression of one's self-commitment to knowing freedom in
God.

Before we apply what has been said about freedom and responsibility
to the concept of guilt, we must finally make a further, additional remark

about the theological concept of freedom and responsibility. Even, and perhaps especially, the theological concept of freedom and responsibility is subject to an inner variability and gradation in freedom and responsibility. It is not only everyday life, psychology and jurisprudence that know about the different degrees of responsibility and freedom. Theology too knows it, and knows it from her own point of view. This is not self-evident. Such a conception finds its place quite easily, of course, in a purely formal psychological notion of freedom of choice: the sovereignty of the subject in his free decision about opening itself actively towards the motives trying to move him is determined by causes pre-existing the free decision. The number of thus offered possibilities for freedom is always finite, can be very limited and thus can so hem in freedom materially without destroying it formally that it becomes almost or even absolutely nil, since in a concrete case there may no longer be a plurality of motives among which one could choose. The problem of degrees of freedom and responsibility becomes much more difficult from the theological point of view. Freedom in the theological sense has, after all, shown itself precisely in its initial step as that surrender of the subject to itself by which it can decide about itself as a whole definitively for or against God. Given such an initial step, the notion of freedom seems really to be *in indivisibili*, and it seems to be impossible to have a 'more-or-less' with regard to freedom, since the subject either decides or does not decide about itself as a whole definitively and hence the concept of the totality and radicality of the subject's being affected by his free decision does belong to the nature of freedom. In fact, it will have to be said also in view of this basic theological starting-point (which remains completely unsystematic in Catholic moral theology) that the decision of freedom which takes place in the *whole* of a life, does not actually admit of degrees, that in it the subject has decided completely about himself and that the possibility of freedom which was imposed on the individual subject is really completely converted into this definitive decision. This does not imply (so as to meet at once a likely dogmatic objection against this thesis) that the manner and degree of perfection of each individual must be the same and equally great if these perfections are compared among themselves. Every man, if the thesis referred to is correct, does indeed use up and exhaust all the possibilities granted to his freedom. Since, however, the freedom of the creature is always the freedom of a subject predetermined in itself in its peculiar nature in view of these predetermined, finite and different realities for different individuals, such a formal equality in the totality and radicality of every fulfilment of life does not signify equality of the result of the finality of the exercise of freedom since after all the predetermined, finite and differentiated material enters as a constitutive element into the finality of this result. Hence it will not be permissible to dispute this thesis of the formal equality of the intensity of everyone's total, free fulfilment of existence from the basic theological starting-point of freedom, especially since otherwise it would be impossible to make it comprehensible how by this freedom in time the *whole* man could be brought *definitively* to salvation or damnation if as a result of such a free decision there still remained open and unused possibilities in both directions. Theology does not prevent itself nevertheless by what has been said from gaining the insight into a gradation of freedom and responsibility as we know them from life, psychology and jurisprudence. Indeed, as has been said, it demands such a gradation by its own principles. First of all, there is no need to dispute, on account of the basic theological principle, the fact that the objective material offered to freedom by the inner dispositions of man and the external situation in which the personal decision of freedom, understood as self-mastery over oneself, realises and must realise itself, can be finite, variable and greater or less. This can, however, go so far that, for example, the material offered for a concrete free choice embraces only objects which are completely evil and forbidden according to the standards of objective morality. In such a case, we could at times no longer talk about freedom of choice and imputability according to the *a posteriori* criteria of everyday life and of psychology, although it could always still remain open whether there could not be a decision for or against God even with reference to such material. Furthermore, it must be noted that the characteristic of the total decision about the *whole* of life cannot be simply ascribed wholly and without reservation to the individual act within this life, in so far as this act can and must be regarded as merely a part of the whole life and it is ultimately impossible for the subject to make an adequate judgement about its relationship to the one totality of the decision about life. Since, for theological reasons, an adequate and definitive self-estimate remains denied to the subject, it is impossible to unconditionally attribute the radicality and totality belonging to freedom in principle to the individual act taken as a merely partial quantitative factor of the whole of life, and this impossibility is not necessarily merely an external gnoseological moment but is an inner moment of this act itself. It may be merely a partial moment of the whole, total decision about life in the form of a preparation for it or as a merely particular manifestation of the total decision which has already taken place in the depth of the free subject. In contrast to the usual conception in Protestant theology, Catholic theology emphasises that even where freedom is really given in a formal sense, the difference in the radicality and totality of free acts can be not merely gradual but so essential that two acts no longer coincide univocally with regard to their freedom, responsibility and disposal over the subject, but can merely be placed under one common *analogous* concept of a free act. Catholic theology is aware of the difference between mortal and venial sin. In the former, when it is really subjectively present, there is a real decision of the subject about his salvation before God, and to this extent it realises the proper theological nature of freedom (even though such an act has its finality only in the totality of the decision about life and from the '*option fonda-mentale*'). In the latter, i.e. in venial sin, there is still indeed freedom in the formal sense of an active choice between two possibilities but this in such a way that a real self-disposal of the subject with regard to its goal and hence the totality of its existence does not take place. We cannot enter here into the theological reasons for this difference and into its ontological presuppositions in the nature of the spiritual-corporeal man. We simply wished to point out this distinction so that it will become clear that theology is also conscious of the essential gradation of freedom and responsibility for *inner* theological reasons.

III

What has been said about freedom and responsibility must now be applied to the concept of guilt.

Before doing this, however, it must at least be noted briefly that precisely for theological reasons and not merely for reasons taken from a metaphysics of freedom, the objectively and subjectively morally right action of freedom and the objectively and subjectively wrong and reprehensible free decision may not be regarded merely as two equal, co-existent species of realisation of simply one and the same nature of free action. The bad act of freedom does not merely fail to attain the object properly associated with it, viz. the good, what is proper to nature and what is willed by the absolute will of God; it also fails to attain the most proper and innermost nature of freedom itself, since the morally evil realisation of freedom is also indeed a free but evil, unsuccessful realisation of freedom itself because God has not created freedom as the possibility of the creative positing by a subject of what is good and evil but as the possibility of creatively positing what is good; hence freedom fails also to attain itself, which indeed it 'can' do, when it is bad freedom. In addition there is the fact that in every space in which God has already freely decided on the victory of love and salvation, then – previous to any created freedom but without cancelling it out – the bad decision of freedom and human evil, in spite of and indeed within its simultaneously heightened radicality and dangerousness, is subject to a peculiar powerlessness which makes it once more impossible to regard the evil decision as an equal realisation of freedom and responsibility on the same plane as the free decision for good.

With this reservation it must be said, however, that guilt regarded theologically is primarily and in its most proper essential ground the total and definitive decision of man against God, the self-understanding of the subject in the 'no' against his supporting ground and this *vis-à-vis* the horizon within which it is accomplished inescapably in 'yes' or 'no'; guilt in this sense is theological and metaphysical suicide but one which does not thereby allow the subject to escape from itself into nothingness. The Christian teaching about guilt considered as sin contains the possibility, which always existentially threatens man's existence, of such a radical self-denial in self-closure before God. That this is at all possible brings us to that *mysterium iniquitatis* which man can indeed experience in the depth of his conscience but from which he always runs away again by all the means of self-deception, displacement, excuses and by utilising the in themselves legitimate means of psychology wherever he does not allow himself to face up to this most impossible possibility of his existence by the testimony of revelation. Of course, this capacity, this possibility of denying sin and guilt understood in this way, has its reason once more in the fact that man simply cannot always and everywhere bring the totality of his existence under the control of freedom in the concrete partial exercise of his spatially and temporally extended existence and that he is thus capable of real sin before God in the full sense. Since he cannot in principle attain an adequate objectifying judgement about his own decision of freedom – since he cannot really judge himself – he also does not even have the last word about his own guilt, and precisely this constitution gives him — from a theological point of view — the last, never surpassable possibility of doubting or denying the realisation of something like guilt in man. In addition, there is the fact that, in the sphere of the eschatologically victorious grace of God in Christ, guilt can only in truth be experienced as an already disarmed guilt even though it must be left an open question as to whether the freedom of the individual does not intend to remain in that empty helplessness of guilt which attaches to it since the time of Christ and which constitutes both its ultimate disorder and its ultimate horror. There can be and there is in fact guilt in the just mentioned theological sense according to the testimony of revelation in history even though we should be permitted to hope that such guilt will be eventually overcome in all men.

This theological nature of sin is realised — *if* it is realised at all — in those shapes and forms which we usually qualify as guilt even in the ordinary everyday sense. This brings us to the question about the more exact relationship between guilt in the theological sense and guilt in an ordinary sense. First of all, it must be repeated once more that in spite of its all-embracing character and in spite of the impossibility of localising it at any particular point of existence in space and time, the absolute definitive 'no' of the whole of existence towards God takes place for reflex consciousness in perfectly determined, concrete acts of life. Sin takes place in sins. Sin does not take place in a merely transcendental interiority of a noumenal subject but in the works of the flesh which are obvious and tangible: in fornication, indecency, debauchery, idolatry, sorcery, feuds, wrangling, jealousy, bad temper, quarrels, disagreements, factions, envy, drunkenness, orgies (Ga 5:19–21): in actions which, as St Paul says, exclude from the inheritance of the basileia. All this is, at least to begin with, quite understandable: man as spirit is not an abstract subject but an embodied, historical spirit who achieves his transcendence precisely by means of the material of the world, of its bodily corporeality and history, and this in such a way that, as is shown by the Christian doctrine of the eternal value of the 'flesh', this material is not merely (as, for instance, in Hofmannsthal's '*Jedermann*') the always external opportunity for proving a formally good will, but itself enters as an intrinsic constitutive factor into the permanent validity of this free act of the subject. If, however, the relationship between guilt in the theological and in the ordinary sense is to be defined exactly, it must not be overlooked that it is not given to man to pass any ultimate judgement about guilt before God in the form of a reflected objective statement either in his own case or in that of others. Hence it is impossible, even from the objective material, the spatio-temporal tangibility and the objective quality of human action, to get any clear idea for such a definitive judgement about such a really existing guilt before God. This means that in principle an action may be objectively bad and yet may not be a realisation of guilt in the theological sense, and that someone may realise his 'no' against God in a form which from the point of view of an objective impersonal ethics gives rather the impression of being the fulfilment of a divine commandment. We cannot avoid this basic and ultimate ambiguity of all concrete actions of a man with regard to the question of the presence or absence of guilt by taking refuge in the classic distinction between intention and external acts (achievement). This distinction certainly exists, as is shown even by ordinary everyday experience in which a good intention is often carried out by objectively wrong means or, vice versa, a bad intention unintentionally achieves something objectively good. The intention, however, in so far as it is said to be identical with the real total being of man before God and hence, when bad, is supposed to signify real guilt, cannot be adequately objectified by objective reflection, and all in it that is really applicable for an objectifying judgement is precisely the 'external' action; this presupposes, of course, that one understands by 'external' (as one must, metaphysically speaking) everything and anything basically accessible to an objectively working reflection or science, so that even the 'inner' but conscious motivation, etc., also belongs to this external action, since even all these elements still lie within that indissoluble unity of the subject and its decision which cannot be adequately reflected on. To this extent is it possible to speak in an ordinary, expressible and demonstrable sense of guilt but only in that provisional open sense in which man can and should have a reflex objective knowledge of his free decisions and active responsibility. This knowledge about guilt and responsibility in the ordinary sense cannot, on the one hand, bypass an ultimate relation to guilt in the theological sense as something completely irrelevant for its own understanding, since even freedom and responsibility in an ordinary (and in any designable genuine sense) is impossible without some reference to transcendence, real subjectivity and hence reference to God (no matter what one may call this transcendence and its final point of reference). On the other hand, however, this ordinary knowledge about guilt is naturally dependent on criteria which are not of a directly theological kind and it is interested in factors of this freedom, responsibility and guilt which are of an intra-mundane character; in the case of judging the free action of someone else, this ordinary knowledge about guilt is even more difficult and problematical with regard to the certitude and clarity of such a judgement than where a subject reflects on his own freedom, responsibility and guilt, and hence one requires also much stricter standards than for judgements about oneself if one is to draw any practical conclusions for such a judgement about others.

It cannot be the task of a theologian here to develop the principles according to which practical life, e.g. juridical practice, judges the question of imputability or non-imputability. It can and must be said, however, from a properly theological standpoint, that even for theological reasons (since man could not otherwise be a subject who decides about his salvation at all) the existence of a formal freedom must basically be pre-sumed until the contrary is proved, even though such a presumption must be employed most carefully as soon as it is a question of seeing this basically existing freedom of being of a subject realised in a particular individual act and thus of also recognising guilt in an individual act, even if this is only in the merely provisional sense and does not anticipate God's judgement which alone makes such a judgement even possible. Even for psychological, 'internal' reasons, the concrete act may be in no sense or only in an essentially diminished sense a realisation of basic freedom and it may be that the imposed choice of material possibilities for freedom was already so limited that the act which must be qualified as objectively bad is no free act at all in an ordinary sense because this objectivity which alone is of ordinary interest and which in the particular case was an offence against the intramundane and civil order was in the concrete the only possibility of acting open to the subject. On the other hand, theology will always have to remind the person, who necessarily and rightly judges in the ordinary sense, that it is true even in the secular sphere that no matter how conscientiously a sentence may be passed, it will necessarily bear that ultimate uncertainty which necessarily attaches, and this for theo-logical reasons, to the theological sentence of guilt imposed on man, since ultimately the material presupposition for guilt is the same in both sentences; after all, proper freedom even in the secular sphere is freedom precisely by reason of the transcendence by which man disposes over himself as a whole before God for salvation or damnation. No matter how much ordinary life must judge, the words of the Sermon on the Mount are paradoxically addressed to it also: 'Judge not, that you may not be judged.'

For lack of time, we simply refer the reader back to the more general descriptions of freedom and responsibility for what should be said further about guilt from a theological point of view.

IV

We now come to the notion of punishment. This notion is, of course, very important even in theology, a theology which cannot give up the idea of God as the founder and guardian of the moral order, the sanction of the moral order, forgiveness, damnation, etc., and hence also the concept of punishment for the freely culpable offence against the divine law. Yet it must also be admitted that the concept of punishment in theology has still to be thought through very much more exactly. For when it comes to the theological concept, the model of punishment in its secular and juridical uses always pushes itself too quickly and automatically into the foreground; God's punishment is understood too hastily and univocally in the sense of the punishment imposed on offenders against the civil order by civil, secular society. Once this happens, ironically, the content and validity of the secular concept of punishment is – quite unintentionally – given inversely that sovereignty and religious absoluteness which basically pertain only to punishment in the theological sense. To see what is really meant by this methodological difficulty, we need only reflect on a factor which necessarily belongs to punishment in the civil and secular sense, and to ask ourselves whether this factor also pertains to punishment in the properly theological sense, to the divine punitive sanction for the definitive 'no' of man against God. It is characteristic of punishment in the secular sphere that it does not result directly from the nature of human guilt itself but is imposed from without on the lawbreaker by a new and proper act and decision of the other, i.e. the civil society of the State, and that therefore guilt and punishment are not merely formally but also materially and really distinct from each other. Yet it can now at least be asked seriously on the theological plane whether what is meant theologically by divine punishment, damnation, etc., must really necessarily be conceived of as an external, *additional* punishment or whether this can be doubted without injury to the Christian dogma. We think that the latter is quite possible.

Three points must be remembered in this connection. Firstly, personal freedom of its own nature means to be and under certain presuppositions also is a definitive decision of an irrevocable kind – that, in other words, the obduracy of the sinner must be conceived, with Thomas Aquinas, as an inner moment of the reprobate's own free decision and not properly speaking as the moment of his punishment as such. Secondly, a man's free decision takes effect, and must take effect, in dimensions and strata which, on the one hand, really belong to man and yet, on the other hand, are not simply identical with the subject of freedom in its subjective origin and thus can still assert themselves as consequences of true guilt in the whole man even when the free decision as such has been revised. Thirdly, on account of the continuing mundaneness and corporeality of man, the subjective decision which enters into the whole reality of man always and necessarily encounters the obstacle of the objective structure of these media of personal decision and hence necessarily creates suffering for itself. If we keep these three points in mind, then there will no longer theologically speaking be any insurmountable obstacles to the thesis maintaining that all divine punishment is a connatural consequence of guilt flowing from the proper nature of guilt and need not be specially added by God: and that therefore God is the punisher of sin by having created the objective structures of man and of the world. It is impossible for us here either to describe this thesis more in detail or to defend each part of it or to prove its reconcilability with certain particular propositions of the traditional and binding Christian dogmatics. The thesis itself, however, had to be stated here because, if it is correct, it will be seen that the characteristic of human punishment in the civil field precisely must not and cannot appeal to the parallel of divine punishment but that its justification – which ought to be absolutely indisputable – must be made theologically credible from some other source. One cannot, to put it in ordinary words, tacitly or explicitly think that prisons and death sentences must be justified simply because a hell or other divine judgements exist. The characteristic of human punishments consists precisely in the fact that the evil, which punishment is and must be if it is to be true punishment at all, does not flow connaturally and simply of itself from the evil of guilt but that the person who punishes adds the evil of punishment to the evil of guilt and that one can therefore ask how one can over-come one evil by creating another. It will be seen, therefore, that the moral justification and the moral boundaries of civil punishment must be derived from elsewhere. This means also that from a Christian and theological point of view one must take care not to ascribe a properly retributive character to human punishment simply because this is certainly one of the characteristics of divine punishment. The vindictive character of divine punishment is simply objectified and given in the indestructibility of the concrete nature of man and of the world, in their absolute validity (at least in the spiritual subject), so that what we intend here is already given when we say that the dignity and sovereignty of the moral law in itself and as such already demands punishment for the one who dares to offend against this law. Human punishment, however, precisely has not got this vindictive character arising out of the nature of the clash between reality and guilt. If it is to be attributed to it, nevertheless, then this would at least have to be proved on its own and based on objectively different reasons. In the concrete, the Christian will therefore also be quite justified in saying that the meaning, purpose and limits of punish-ment in civil society are derived from the right and duty of civil society to maintain the objective order of society: in other words, that the moral fault of a man is to be punished only when and in the measure that it is a question of the defence of the common good. At least in practice, punish-ment in the civil order must be regarded — even from the viewpoint of these theological reflections — as a self-defence of society against the encroachments of the individual and thus can and ought to confine itself to this self-defence even though such self-defence against someone in whose case subjective guilt can be presupposed with sufficient moral certitude takes other forms and has wider limits than merely that of self-defence against someone who without subjective guilt offends against the objective goods of society. This also makes it comprehensible why we cannot demand too absolute a certitude in the case of civil punishment with regard to the presence of guilt. For if an, as it were, collective scrupulosity were to bring it about that the safeguarding purpose of punishment which is always and even of its very nature prophylactic were no longer attained, then this would destroy the very meaning and purpose of punishment in the civil order. A certain sober calculation of the risk involved with regard to the 'justice' of the punishment is perfectly permissible since without it the secular purpose of punishment cannot be attained at all and since an absolute certitude about the subjective guilt in the proper, which means also theological, sense is unattainable for man. The time available is too short to treat of the question as to what conclusions might be drawn from these general reflections regarding the problem of the death penalty.

15

JUSTIFIED AND SINNER AT THE SAME TIME

IN the Church, and indeed in Christianity, everyone must learn from everyone else; everyone testifies to the gift of grace which has been granted to him, to the Christian experience which he has, so that the spirit and heart of others may be enlarged in order to experience the riches of grace more deeply and fully. There is, therefore, not merely an ecumenical dialogue in the field of dogmatic theology, of the constitutional life and practical activity, but also in the field of the spiritual life. Indeed, it should be there above all. In this field, in the original Christian experience, there seems to be – beyond all merely external critical positions which have given and still give occasion for division – the vital point for the separation and also the possibility of an encounter which would prepare for the unification of Christendom. Only if we understand one another in the direct exercise of Christian *existence itself* is there any hope that the reflex expressions of this exercise, i.e. the dogmatic theologies, may be brought to coincide in unity.

One of the basic religious experiences is undoubtedly the experience that we are sinners but that we may also at the same time console ourselves about being justified before God in Christ. Whether we Catholic and Protestant Christians understand one another on this point is a question on which depends the richness of the Christian experience of grace in our mutual communication and learning as well as the possibility of our ecumenical dialogue. It must indeed be admitted and this has been expressed in sober honesty most recently, especially on the Protestant side, that man today is no longer terribly bothered about the question as to how from being a sinner – which he does not think he is in the first place – he becomes someone justified before God and finds a merciful God. Yet if the man of today suffers rather from the agony of existence, its darkness and worthlessness than from guilt, and if he tends to ask how

God justifies this situation in the face of agonised man rather than to ask how he can go on existing before God, this sums up precisely what is a common concern of all Christian denominations: for *all* Christians have to confess that man is a sinner and is justified by God's grace alone. *All* Christians have therefore the task of asking themselves *how* they can fulfil this fundamental task *vis-à-vis* the spirit of this age. The old inter-Christian controversy about the nature of justification and of the state of being justified before God is indeed given a new angle through this, viz. the angle of the search for the right way of proclaiming this in the present age (which is no longer that of the Reformation and Counter-Reformation); yet it is not thereby outdated or without importance. Also there are still sufficient Catholic and Protestant Christians for whom the question about the nature of justification is absolutely central, even prescinding from how the answer to this question can be proclaimed in a way which will do justice to the present age. There seems to be a mutual dependence between both these points of view from which this question can be looked at, so that one must perhaps say: only if the separated Christians can make the 'pagans' of today understand that the problem is not how God can exist before man but how man can exist before God and through God alone, will Christians then also understand each other in this question of justification. *And*, vice versa: only if Christians agree on this question, will they also find the right way to give a convincing witness of their experience of justification in the face of the spirit of their age.

What the Reformation formula about the experience of justification can tell us Catholic Christians is a genuine question for our spiritual life and not only for our theology.

I. THE REFORMATION FORMULA

Reformed Christianity was, in the deepest and most radical sense, a Christianity of the frightened conscience of the sinner before God. It believed – quite rightly – that one can become and be a Christian only if one capitulates radically before God. When man begins to realise the infinite sanctity and justice of God, then he becomes most profoundly the frightened sinner. He cannot be saved of himself and by his own power. Grace, justification and salvation arise from God's mercy alone. Man is always and everywhere dependent on this justifying mercy of God. This is the correct starting-point for the Protestant formula: '*simul justus et peccator*'. This man of the Reformation always stands and continues to stand as a sinner *vis-à-vis* God. If he looks at himself, his dispositions and works, then always he can only tremble before the infinite judging holiness of God, since he falls infinitely short of God's total demand and always experiences himself again as a sinner. He does indeed hear of God's grace in the message of the gospel: in the doctrine of baptism and justification by faith. He has been justified by God in spite of his sinful condition, he has been saved by Christ's redemption and has been made a sanctified and well beloved child of God. Yet when man looks at himself again, he recognises himself always and permanently as a sinner. When he hears the absolving word of God and believes in it, when he accepts justification by grace, he knows himself to be justified, although not by his own deed but by the unfathomable and unmeritable grace of God. Thus he reaches the conviction that the ultimate and most basic Christian experience consists precisely in this fact that he is at the same time a sinner and justified before God. He does not baulk at this paradox. He thinks that only this twofold statement about man can really express the true Christian understanding of man. The sinner who remains a sinner before God down to the last fibre of his conscience, stands startled before God because he does not consider himself to be of any worth at all, does not place any trust in himself and finds nothing good in himself which he could maintain before God and by which he could protect himself before God. Yet, in an immense venture of faith and hope, and in an unlimited trust in the message of God, he knows that he is justified.

Reformation Christianity says that treason is committed against the real Christian understanding of man whenever any attempt is made to soften this paradox. Man always comes from himself as a sinner to God. If he looks at what he is of himself, then he will see himself as a sinner completely at the mercy of God's judgement. Of himself he cannot bring any claim before God on the basis of which he could be saved by God. Out of this abyss of an almost hellish despair and in pure faith in the grace of God, trusting in nothing else, man knows that he has been saved.

In the course of the history of Reformed Christianity, the elemental power of this experience was able to weaken. The radical consciousness of being a sinner over and over again fell into the danger of disappearing. Man in his humanistic mollification felt himself to be a being who takes it for granted that he lives under the sky of a loving Father. Again and again, however, Reformed Christianity awakened to the consciousness that the essence of Christianity and of Christian existence consists in the paradox of this formula: 'Justified and sinner at the same time'. Only where the radical experience of permanent sinfulness is combined with the consciousness given by faith of being nevertheless someone justified by the saving deed of God, is one a Christian, in the faith in this alone, i.e. in an ever new leap away from oneself, in an ever new capitulating admission of being a sinner.

It should be noted that we have intentionally taken some trouble to understand the Reformation formula and have tried to avoid simply registering a formal logical and very easy Catholic protest against this formula. We have intentionally avoided characterising justification by God as something merely extrinsic, 'forensic', as a pure 'as if'. This we have done because all these subsequent theological interpretations, both on the Catholic and on the Protestant side, can only obscure the original starting-point of this formula.

II. THE CATHOLIC REJECTION OF THE REFORMATION FORMULA
'Simul justus et peccator'

In what then does the Catholic 'no' to this formula consist?

(a) Justification as an event of salvation-history creates something new which cannot exist 'simultaneously' with the old state. Salvation-history is a really genuine history, not only as total history in the order of objective salvation but also as the individual history of salvation. This means: something happens and takes place here which is now but was not before. Since this history is an action of God on man, it knows real caesuras, revolutions, genuine new creations. It *becomes* something by the power of God which once did not exist in this man. '*See, I make all things new*'; '*See, a new creation*'; '*The old is past, the new has come to pass*'; '*You were dead and are now created anew in Jesus Christ.*' Even in the history of the individual it is therefore a question of genuine saving events and not only of an ever growing consciousness of something always remaining the same and always true, even though it remains true that this becoming conscious, made possible and supported by God's grace, is a moment in this history and not just a moment of coming to know which remains external to it. Hence Catholic theology must emphasise that everything does not always exist in its fullness at the same time but rather that something new enters in which may not be placed under a permanent 'at the same time'; a simultaneity in which a permanent dialectical relationship between equally necessary existentials of human existence would be revealed.

(b) Since justification is decisively God's deed, the reality of justification and the experience of justification do not necessarily coincide. According to Catholic teaching, God's deed is the decisive factor in justification and not the deed, the experience or the faith of man. The question, therefore, about the sense in which man is justified before God, cannot be judged solely from the point of view as to how and to what extent the divine deed is experienced by man. Experience of faith in the everyday sense of the word 'experience' (if we prescind, therefore, from an 'experience' – which may exist – in which man experiences precisely his inclusion in the unreflectable depths of the mystery of God) and reality of faith do not coincide and this precisely because God's own power alone is the really effective and decisive factor in the justification of man. For Catholic theology and the Church's magisterium, therefore, the declaration as to what actually happens in justification cannot be made simply from the *experience* of justification alone. The experience of justification and of faith, in so far as it is given in *propositions* for the experienced man himself and for others, can never catch up with the whole depth and radicality of the divine saving deed exercised in man, once we presuppose that God's deed effects the reality of justification. So as to give God's grace and power the glory, the Catholic doctrine of justification will always emphasise that we become and are God's children through God's grace, that in justification the Holy Spirit is given to us, that we *are* the temple of God, sons, anointed and beloved of God through God's grace. This reality is not merely an ideological fiction, not merely an 'as if', but the true reality of man himself. Justification, understood as God's deed, transforms man down to the deepest roots of his being; it transfigures and divinises him. For this very reason the justified man is not 'at the same time justified and a sinner'. He is not simply, in a merely paradoxical and dialectical suspense, sinner and justified at the same time. By justification, *from being* the sinner he was, he becomes in truth a justified man which he was not before. He ceases in a true sense to be a sinner. The Catholic doctrine of justification believes that only in this way does it do justice to the real historicity of the event of salvation, to the real primacy of God's deed in man, to the difference between the experience of salvation and the reality of salvation, and to the intrinsic veracity and validity of God's action on and assurance to man which grasps man interiorly and changes him. On this basis, the Catholic and anti-reformation attitude and teaching at the Council of Trent rejected the formula *'simul justus et peccator'* because this formula with its simultaneity of justification and sinfulness fails to understand the real nature of Christian justification. At the very least, the real becoming, the becoming new, the inner justification by God's act on man does not become sufficiently clear in this formula. This is *one* aspect of the Catholic position with regard to this formula.

Catholic theology, therefore, rejects the formula 'just and sinner at the same time' because it does not render the state of man in an objectively correct and adequate manner. The ultimate, basic formula of human existence is not a suspended dialectic between sinfulness and holiness. Man has really crossed the boundary of death. In the ultimate view, in view of God's action which has become effective in him, man is no longer sinful and justified at the same time, but justified and nothing else.

III. THE PROPERLY UNDERSTOOD CATHOLIC 'YES' TO THE FORMULA *'Simul justus et peccator'*

The rejection of the Reformation formula is a basic one in so far as it has to describe that 'in itself' and that 'objectivity' which is effected by God himself and on which we must and may rely more than on our own 'subjectivity'. Even our true 'subjectivity', when it achieves its ultimate being, is the letting-oneself-go towards a reality which we can no longer survey or administer and which we do not appropriate to ourselves but to which we become appropriated as to the mystery of God himself. *If* justification has really taken place, then this man is no longer a sinner but the justified and sanctified man.

(a) *Uncertainty of salvation*

Can the individual, however, maintain with absolute certainty about himself that *he* is really someone justified and that, precisely because he is this, he is no longer a sinner? According to the teaching of the Council of Trent there is no absolute individual certitude about salvation. Let us not misunderstand this teaching of the Council of Trent. It does not say that man must live in a trembling, cowardly fear about his salvation, a fear which mistrusts God himself. Rather it means that man must look away from himself towards God's unspeakable grace. He should *trust* that, in the midst of the experience of his inner weakness and poverty, he always is nevertheless in all truth the much loved child of God borne by the grace and mercy of God. He must possess the joy, the confidence and the all-conquering hope of the saved. It is a great sacred duty to leap over his own continuously experienced wretchedness by the virtue which we call Christian hope and to trust in God's unfathomable mercy. Man cannot indeed qualify, in any objectified way such as is possible for dogmatic faith, the reality expressed in the statement: I am clearly and certainly justified. He must not take up the attitude of someone who takes possession of himself absolutely, who examines himself through and through, who draws up the complete account of his own existence and is perfectly sure of himself. He must not have this attitude, but this does not mean that he should and indeed may be cowardly, restless, fearful and distrustful towards *God*. On the contrary, he must really deliver himself up to God with a firm hope, and this by passing over everything he experiences about himself and of himself, precisely because, in spite of the experience of his own uncertainty about salvation, he must trust in God with complete generosity and as a foregone conclusion. This courageous and unconditional hope imposed on him demands precisely that he must not twist the attitude of complete confidence in God's grace into a theoretically reflected certitude of salvation. This precisely would make him again independent of God, and, on account of the certitude of its expression, would dispense him again from this complete confidence in God. Since, however, man cannot attain absolute certitude about his own salvation of a believable, theoretical and objective kind in the act of hope, it follows that even for this reason he always knows himself to be a sinner. It follows from the impossibility of an absolute, radical self-assurance that he always experiences himself again as a sinner, as someone threatened and unsure, and that he may not push this experience to one side as something of no account and theologically irrelevant, but merely in the hope in which he takes the leap away from himself towards God must he overcome it and by this very fact always accept it again. Even though Catholic theology cannot accept the abstract ontological and objective formula of '*simul justus et peccator*', this formula is nevertheless justifiable if it is understood as the expression of the experience of the individual person. Even though he must and may hope with all firmness that he is personally justified before God, he must at the same time fear, in spite of, and within this hope, that he is a sinner.

(b) *The sinfulness of man through 'venial' sins.*

Since the time and in the words of St Augustine, the Church emphasises 'not merely humbly', 'but in all truth', that man is and remains a sinner. This teaching also has not been cancelled out by the Council of Trent's declaration that in a certain sense the formula *'simul justus et peccator'* is not right. Yet how can the justified be and remain a sinner if he remains at the same time in the state and attitude of the justified? Every Catholic will answer this by saying that, even while remaining someone justified, he keeps on committing 'venial sins' and hence must always fly again as a sinner to the forgiving grace of God.

The Catechism and theology state that the justified who commits sins remains in the state of sanctifying grace as long as he does not sin mortally in an objective and subjective sense. Although this statement is perfectly correct, it must be understood very discreetly. It is in fact much less simple than would appear to the average Catholic consciousness. Certainly, many think, one is always still a sinner to some extent. One commits one's daily faults, omissions, the small offences against God's law and will. For this reason one must acknowledge oneself to be a poor sinner. Yet such an understanding of the doctrine of the distinction between mortal and venial sin and the reconcilability of the state of grace with venial sins and venially sinful attitudes surely essentially underestimates the real depth, threatened condition and darkness of Christian existence.

According to Catholic teaching, there is really a both objectively and subjectively radical difference between mortal and venial sin. In biblical terms, there are sins in the existence of the justified, the beloved child of God, which do not destroy this child relationship; there are also, however, sins which – if they are really committed with the necessary clear knowledge, consent and responsibility – exclude from the kingdom of God, as St Paul says, and from the inheritance of heaven and make man a child of the wrath of God, as long as he obstinately remains in this state of sin. Yet, however justified this doctrine of the objective distinction between mortal and venial is, we must not abuse it to turn Christian existence into something completely harmless. We say far too easily that venial sin does not destroy grace, that it does not annul justification and does not condemn and damn man. After all, these are only moral weaknesses, little shadows over our relationship to God, small imperfections which do not change the real basic attitude of man to God. In so far as it is really only a question of venial sins, it is possible to say this, even though only with very serious reservations. But do we know exactly that our supposedly merely venial sins are really just venial sins? Naturally one can say that certain happenings in our life, regarded simply in themselves and measured by objective norms, are really only venial sins, as for instance some unfriendliness towards our neighbour, a lack of devotion in our prayers, a little impatience; these are undoubtedly things which can indeed weigh upon Christian existence but which on the other hand may not and cannot rob us of the joy of being redeemed, of the grace of being safe in God and of our sanctification by the Holy Spirit. Lapses of everyday life are certainly in this sense objectively venial sins.

It cannot be denied, however, that it is a onesidedness in Catholic moral theology and confessional practice to regard each of the individual events of our moral activity on their own, almost in an atomised fashion. We often overlook in this way the total structure of our moral position, our ultimate attitude towards God, and our basic religious condition. Man does not posit individual acts on the basis of the substantiality of a soul of a purely objective kind, individual acts which he strings up on the thread of external time, but rather the one whole man lives out of a basic outlook which is either directed towards God or is turned away from Him. This ultimate, decisive and all-informing basic outlook is, nevertheless, not at all so easily open to man's reflection. Indeed, it simply cannot be *adequately* reflected on, since otherwise it would be possible to have that reflected theoretical certitude of salvation which according to the Council of Trent is denied to the Christian. We can look at the individual acts of our life but we cannot throw a glance directly on the ultimate source of these acts in our heart. Seen in this light, the question about venial sins takes on quite a different seriousness than we are perhaps inclined to think. Could not this or that apparently harmless unkindness towards our neighbour, when regarded in itself, be deep down merely the distant echo and summer lightning of an ultimate and basic egoism which in the end is really mortal? Could not such an attitude of egoism which perhaps does not express itself at all in any externally very ugly deeds which would be very objectionable even according to a civil moral code, be exactly

what we call a mortal sin? Could it not be that the coolness of our
religious life, this easy and apparently harmless indifference towards God,
although it does not really manifest itself in clear acts and activities,
arises nevertheless from an ultimate, free, terrible, mortal indifference and
coldness towards God? And this is after all quite different from a venial
sin. It certainly does not mean an individual action associated with a
determined point in the time and space of our life. May it not, however,
signify an ultimate lost condition, an ultimate and basic 'no' to God?
And this would be precisely what we in fact call a state of mortal sin. In
this way we could point out still other things which in appearance are
merely so-called venial sins but which in reality are the concealed and
dissimulated signs of the ultimate, mortal turning away of man from God
which man does not admit to himself and which he has exercised as it were
anonymously and with the left hand and yet has done in the depth of his
freedom. Since, however, we always go on commiting venial sins, must
we not then be frightened and ask whether we are not sinners in a far
deeper and more radical sense, i.e. men who in the depth of their heart do
not want to have anything to do with God, even though externally and in
a thin bourgeois sense they still want to be pious and decent people who
'keep their plate clean'? This would put quite a different face on the
doctrine that every man is a sinner at least in so far as he commits venial
sins. On the other hand, this does not mean that we must think of ourselves as lost, as excluded from the kindgom of God and deserted by the
Spirit of consolation, even though we trust in God's grace with an honest
heart and always turn again to God. The conception that we are sinners
takes on a new appearance only in the sense that we must ask ourselves
fearfully whether we who hope to be God's beloved children must not
always also fear again that we may be something quite different, as long as
the basic roots of our heart continue to bring forth fruit which is not
really the fruit of the Spirit.

Thus the teaching of the permanent sinfulness of man by venial sins
represents a continuous question for us as to what we really are deep down.
We must always answer this question in a positive sense, placing our
hope in the grace of God but we can never do this proudly and self-
assuredly with a theoretical certitude of salvation.

Hence we must somehow pass beyond the distinction between mortal
and venial sin, however much it is materially and objectively correct,
since it cannot be carried through completely in concrete reflection on

our own existence. On the one hand, we are in fact sinners who hope always to be allowed to escape again out of their sinfulness into the mercy of God. On the other hand, there is justice, and if it is really in us through God's grace, it is always also threatened and tempted and hidden from us.

The doctrine of permanent, habitual justice through infused sanctifying grace must not be understood as if this justice were a purely static possession or static quality in man. Rather, this justice is always tempted and threatened by the flesh, the world and the devil. It is always dependent again on the free decision of man. In spite of its character of a state it is suspended, as it were, on the point of the free grace of God and on the point of man's freedom. The grace of justification must always be accepted and exercised anew again, since basically it is always given anew again by God. This permanent condition of grace is always exposed to the freedom of man. The freedom of man in its turn can accept and preserve God's grace only in and through the free grace of God which God has granted and must grant to us ultimately without any merit whatsoever on our part. Since our justice is always under attack, it must always be given to us anew by God's favour and grace. It is therefore also the ultimately indisposable justice. Certainly we believe in God's salvific will . . . but this salvific will, when referred to and having become effective in each of us, is the immense and incomprehensible miracle of God's absolute favour. Man's free 'yes' to God's liberating grace is itself once more a gift of God's grace. Thus we must declare our own freedom to be once more a grace of God, a freedom which is not only a capacity for acting in a salvific way but also an act which really opens itself towards God. Of ourselves *alone* we cannot do anything at all which could make God direct his grace towards us, for our prayer for grace is based on unasked for grace which must give us both the power to pray and the act of praying itself. God must always anticipate us with his grace. Even when we think we are doing, and actually do, the most personal and original things, we experience precisely in this the earlier and more powerful deed of God in us. Of ourselves we are always sinners. Of ourselves we would always turn away from God if God's grace did not anticipate us. In view of the completely uncontrollable grace of God, of tempted justice, uncontrollable justice, we are always sinners. In this sense, it is possible to find an always true and decisively important Catholic sense in the formula 'Just and sinner at the same time'.

(c) *Man the pilgrim is just and sinner at the same time*

Even when justified, man remains a pilgrim. As such he has not only an external space of time to live through, but he is 'on the road'. In his personal history of salvation he is in search of something permanent, indestructible and final. We are on pilgrimage in the faith. We possess God only on the ground of hope. We reach out in hope for what is to come, that which is not yet given to us. Thus possession is given by hope, and by this same hope possession is also withdrawn from the free direct grasp of man. By our free personal history we must first catch up with what by God's deed which justifies us we already are. We are pilgrims in faith and hope, in ever new temptations and trials, by always accepting God's grace anew in freedom. We come from Adam and the land of darkness and look for the eternal light and bright perfection. Since the one great movement of our existence out of our lost condition towards God always still carries within itself the source from which this movement originates, we are 'just and sinners at the same time' by being sinners in the state of becoming who are still in search of perfection. This does not mean, as has already been said, that these two things, remaining always the same, confront one another in a simple static dialectic. Yet the concrete salvific activity of man is always simultaneously characterised by the starting-point from which we came, by our own lost condition which we have left behind, and also by the goal which we already possess in hope but towards which we also still reach. Here is realised the being-by-becoming of the creature. One can only recognise created man in his historical being-by-becoming, in his tension between beginning and end, by pointing to the beginning and the end. Every moment of this becoming is characterised by both, since this movement has an *a quo* and an *ad quem*. Seen as a future citizen of eternal glory, man always moves between the beginning and the end. This 'at the same time' is not a simultaneity of beginning and end, but an 'at the same time' in the tension between both.

Thus the Reformation formula of the *simul justus et peccator* – if only the factors of a Catholic 'no' to this formula remain clear – has a perfectly positive meaning for Christian existence. The Catholic Christian especially should not interpret himself as the 'good man' who basically and really, unless he steals silver spoons or poisons his neighbour, lives from the very start as a good man in grace, so that, as modern sentiment often maintains, it is really God who must justify himself before man and explain why there is so much suffering, darkness and confusion in the history of the world. The Christian must have understood that of himself he is nothing but nothingness and that left to himself he is nothing but sin. Wherever he discovers something good in himself, he must acknowledge it as a causeless free grace of God. Hence even the Catholic Christian should not spread out his justice before God. He should rather from day to day accept his justice, which in fact divinises him, as an unmerited gift of God's incalculable favour. If he wants to express this by saying that he is always and of himself a poor sinner and always someone justified by God's grace as long as he does not close himself to this grace of God by disbelief and lack of love, then he is quite at liberty to do so.

Even Catholics like St Theresa of the Child Jesus have done this. When they dared to stand before the countenance of God, they came of and for themselves with empty hands and confessed themselves like St Augustine to be sinners. In this consciousness of their own sinfulness they discovered in themselves that miracle which means that God fills our hands with his glory and makes our heart overflow with love and faith. Anyone who confesses that of himself he is a sinner, experiences precisely in this that grace of God which really and truly makes him a saint and a just man. Then God absolves him from all sin so that he is really and in truth, to the last root of his being, a holy, just and blessed child of God.

16

REFLECTIONS ON THE UNITY OF THE LOVE OF NEIGHBOUR AND THE LOVE OF GOD[1]

YOUR Association has given itself a strangely adventurous and at the same time sacred task: it has the audacity to try to organise what cannot really be organised, to try to give to what is always new a permanent presence and to try to keep in the public eye what is hidden, what God alone sees and estimates. After all, it has only one real object – to love our neighbour in deed and in truth. You want to love by giving real help, but a help which is not merely an organised effort and effect of socio-political organisation but which in truth remains love. Such love, however, where it truly exists and remains and *thus* really supports the social efforts between men – even though these efforts can also exist, be demanded and organised without real love – is not the function of secular society but itself constitutes a completely new society of men even where it has no name; it allows the eternal kingdom of God to begin in secret and is the miracle of the birth of eternity. Yet for this very reason this venture is strangely adventurous and daring. According to the Apostle, it is completely possible to give all one's goods to the poor and yet lack charity. This means surely that no matter how important and wonderful, and how 'useful' socio-political action may be, it alone does not yet represent what is precisely the decisive factor of this undertaking; by this kind of action alone – without this mysterious love – your 'Association' would sink to the level of a function of secular society and would become *that* which belongs to the age of a world which passes

---

[1] In this essay, the author takes up in greater detail and more exactly reflections which he has used for the question of the veneration of the Saints (cf. *GuL* XXXVII [1964], pp. 325–340, on the question of possibility). Cf. also: K. Rahner, 'The "Commandment" of Love in relation to the other Commandments', *Theological Investigations* V (London & Baltimore 1966), pp. 439–459.

away. Hence, however much such love as is meant to govern here must think about how it can avoid the danger of becoming an empty feeling and nothing but talk and become a tangible helping action, we must also inquire here about what love is in itself. Even though we know basically what love is only by the fact that it takes place and thereby forgets to ask about itself, there is nevertheless – according to scripture – the Word, which commands it to act in God's name; hence there is also the responsible right to reflect about love itself, even though such reflection – unlike the commanding and promising word of love which goes out from the altar of the highest event of love, the cross – cannot bring with it the power of grace for that which is ultimately itself.

We intend to inquire into charity here by reflecting on its unity with the love of God. Precisely what is not meant, however, is that charity loses itself in the depth of the love of God by dissolving itself or by becoming unimportant as such, or that two ways of fulfilling human existence, although each could be understood and carried out on its own, become subsequently associated. In the case of this unity the important thing is to understand rather that the one does not exist and cannot be understood or exercised without the other, and that two names have really to be given to the same reality if we are to summon up its one mystery, which cannot be abrogated.

Active love as the illuminating situation of modern man's existence

The question about the essential unity of love of God and neighbour which alone brings it about that the two 'commandments' are equal (Mt 22:39) and the realisation that on both together hang the Law and the Prophets (Mt 22:40), is more urgent today than ever before both for the living action and the theoretical reflection which is carried by that action and at the same time necessarily illumines it. To get some idea of this urgency, we need only take a look at the situation of contemporary philosophy. There is talk of the end of metaphysics; it seems that, in some mysterious and profound sense, we are also already questioning again the transcendental philosophy of the pure subject, with its openness to the Absolute (in the form of the epoch-making conversion of the Greek cosmocentricity into a Christian, modern anthropocentricity), whose meaning and also permanent significance is only being slowly assimilated by Christian philosophy and so will also no doubt be preserved by this in its permanent meaning. Sociology is making an attempt to replace metaphysics or to convert philosophy into an ontology of intercommunication. The orientation of the philosophy of cognoscitive transcendence towards a beyond which is always valid seems to want to turn in the direction of hoped-for future events; action is not now experienced as the derived consequence of knowledge but rather knowledge is seen as the event of self-consciousness which dwells only in action itself. The God of the beyond of the world is suspected to be a non-verifiable ghost which must be laid, since he does not exist there where we experience, achieve and suffer ourselves and where we suffer *ourselves* in solitude as the only real bottomless abyss. One tries by thought and action to demythologise everything and to destroy taboos in everything until the only thing left is what seems to survive all this: the incomprehensible something which is experienced as the absurd something which one would like to honour by shocked silence, or as the honest and bitter minimum of everyday duty in the service of others, if one is still inclined to act on and talk about an 'ideal' at all.

Be that as it may, it must be placed over against the words of the gospel and the liberating grace of the living God or over against a sector which retains the courage not to despair and to withstand the impatient disappointment regarding every naturally always finite formula of human existence. Yet if Christianity is not to be merely 'objectively' right but is also to say something right by its judgements to the man of *tomorrow* who must understand himself *where* and *in the manner* in which – after all – he exists, then it must obviously be made comprehensible to him that the *whole* truth of the gospel is still hidden and in germ in what he finds most easily as a deed and then as truth, viz. in the love of one's neighbour. If Christianity is faith, hope and charity, and if these three are not realities added to each other externally, each with a different origin and a different nature, but if love is rather the one word for the perfection of the one reality which we signify by these three names, then love could be the valid topical word for today which calls the whole of Christianity in the man of tomorrow into the concreteness of life and out of that depth into which God (and not ourselves) has immersed it by his offer of grace, the grace which He is Himself. This presupposes, however, that it can really be said seriously that the love of God and the love of neighbour are one and the same thing, and that, in this way and in this way alone, we understand what God and his Christ are, and that we accomplish what is the love of God in Christ when we allow the love of our neighbour to attain its own nature and perfection.

Love of neighbour understood as love of God: The declarations of scripture

The realisation we are groping to reach, if we examine it honestly and soberly, is not as directly and clearly attested in scripture and tradition as one might think. They speak after all of *two* commandments (Mt 22:39; Mk 12:31), of the second of which it is said merely that it 'resembles' the first. Nevertheless, the two together are valued in the Synoptic tradition as the life-giving (Lk 10:28) epitome of the Old Testament revelation in the scriptures and the prophets (Mt 22:40), greater than which there is nothing (Mk 12:31). Furthermore, in this Synoptic theology of love, it certainly must not be overlooked that in the eschatological discourses about the Judgement, love of neighbour is given in St Matthew as the only explicit standard by which man will be judged (Mt 25:34–46), and that the cooling down of *this* love is represented as the content of 'lawlessness' among the afflictions of the last days (Mt 24:12). In addition, there is that puzzling saying in the Synoptic tradition that what is done to the least of his brethren is done to Jesus, a saying which cannot be explained by an arbitrarily altruistic identification which according to many commentators Jesus himself undertakes as it were merely morally and juridically in a mere 'as if'. The understanding of this text must certainly first of all proceed from the absolutely unique position Jesus attributes to himself as the Son as such, as the presence of God and of his *basileia* among us, and must in general try to bring out clearly the unity of *this* Son with man. If we do this, we will no doubt be led back again to the doctrine of the mysterious unity of the love of God and of neighbour and to its Christological basis and radicalisation. This doctrine becomes most radical (though without any explicit reflection on this fact) in St Paul: love of neighbour (understood as the sovereign commandment: Jn 2:8) is declared to be *the* fulfilment of *the* law (Rm 13:8, 10; Ga 5:14), and hence as the 'bond' of perfection (Col 3:14) and as the better 'way', i.e. as the Christian form of existence simply and finally (1 Co 12:31–13:13). In St John, we find then a first reflection on the justification of this radical elevation of the love of neighbour to being the totality of Christian existence, a radical elevation which otherwise might appear to be a pious exaggeration, as it is in fact watered down in the reflective processes of the Christian exhortation to virtue to the point that love of neighbour is a single part of the Christian demand without which, in spite of its difficulty, salvation is lost. According to St John, we are loved by God (Jn 15:12) and by Christ *so that* we may love one another (Jn 13:34), a love which is the *new* commandment of Christ (Jn 13:34) which is his specifically (Jn 15:12) and which is the command imposed on us (Jn 15:17). Thus for St John the consequence of this is that God who *is* Love (1 Jn 4:16) has loved us, not so that we might love him in return but so that we might love *one another* (1 Jn 4:7, 11). For we do not see God – he cannot be truly reached in gnostic-mystic interiority alone, in such a way that he would *thus* be really attainable by love (1 Jn 4:12) – and hence the 'God in us' by mutual love is the God whom alone we can love (1 Jn 4:12), to such an extent that it is really true and that, although it is usually not at all clear to us, it is a radically convincing argument for St John that 'a man who does not love the brother whom he can see, cannot love God whom he has never seen' (1 Jn 4:20).

Many things remain undefined and unclear in the explicit wording of this attempt to make the concentration of the whole Christian relationship to God in the love of our neighbour comprehensible. Is perhaps even here the love of neighbour still merely the 'proof' of our love of God simply because God, who is to be loved, has given us precisely this commandment to love our neighbour; and is, therefore, its fulfilment merely the best touchstone for us as to whether we are serious about the love of God, the whole matter resting ultimately nevertheless in two different partial fulfilments of Christian human existence and in two commandments? Is the word about the brother whom we see and about God whom we cannot see, merely – after all – a simple *argumentum ad hominem*, an inference from the easier (which has not been achieved) to the more difficult (which will then certainly and *a fortiori* not be fulfilled)? Or may we take the words of St John absolutely seriously, so that the 'God in us' is really the one who alone can be loved and who is reached precisely in the love of our brother and in no other way, and that the love of neighbour encounters the love of God in *such* a way that it moves itself, and us with it, closer to the brother near by and attains both itself and the peak of perfection in the love of this brother, i.e. specifically as love of neighbour, and brings us to God and his love by the love of our neighbour?

Even though we cannot give a sure answer in the purely exegetical sense to this question of biblical theology, theological reflection in tradition gives us a little more courage to answer it in favour of the second part of the above alternative, i.e. in the direction of a radical identity of the two loves. It must be noted in this connection that while, on the one hand, even this theological tradition with its theologumena does not give us any absolutely convincing solution to this problem yet, on the other hand, it does bring data of biblical theology[2] into play for our question which are not given their full effect in *these* texts or scripture itself which touch precisely on our question.

The teaching of theology

The tradition of the schools in Catholic theology has already held fast for a long time and this unanimously to the fact that the specific Christian love of neighbour is both in potency and in act a moment of the infused supernatural theological virtue of *caritas* by which we love God in his Spirit for his own sake and in direct community with him. This means, therefore, that the love of neighbour is not merely the preparation, effect, fruit and touchstone of the love of God but is itself an act of this love of God itself; in other words, it is at least an act within that total believing and hoping surrender of man to God which we call love and which alone justifies man, i.e. hands him over to God, because, being supported by the loving self-communication of God in the uncreated grace of the Holy Spirit, it really unites man with God, not as He is recognised by us but as He is in Himself in His absolute divinity. Three things must not be overlooked in connection with this thesis of scholastic theology which identifies the love of God and neighbour at least in their supernatural potency of the one infused supernatural theological virtue of *caritas*. (1) Scholastic theology does *not* overlook (in principle quite correctly) the fact that such a *caritas* can be also a mere impulse for certain modes of relationship to others by personal love which are not themselves formally acts of charity but merely its *actus imperati* restricting themselves more to a merely human dimension. (2) Scholastic theology, when giving a more precise interpretation of its radical thesis, will presumably often fall short of it, especially when it tries to give reasons for it; it will realise this thesis and will give reasons for it in such a way that it really remains a thesis in words only, and it will not really catch up with the existential, onto-logical presuppositions of this thesis. (3) If scholastic theology were

---

[2] For example, when scripture declares that the love of neighbour is supported by the same *pneuma* (Ga 5:22).

asked explicitly whether this identity is absolutely valid, it would no doubt answer that every act of charity towards our neighbour is indeed formally, even though perhaps only implicitly, love of God since the act is done after all by definition 'for the sake of God loved with a supernatural love'; but scholastic theology would probably deny that conversely every act of the love of God is formally also a love of neighbour (even though it naturally includes also the *readiness* for this). Above all, most theologians today would still shrink from the proposition which gives our fundamental thesis its ultimate meaning, its real clarity and inescapable character, viz. that wherever a genuine love of man attains its proper nature and its moral absoluteness and depth, it is in addition always so underpinned and heightened by God's saving grace that it is also love of God, whether it be explicitly considered to be such a love by the subject or not.

Yet this is the direction in which the understanding of the thesis of identity as it is meant here leads us, since we hold it to be objectively correct and of basic significance for the Christian self-understanding of the future. What is meant by this requires a more detailed even though unavoidably still very summary explanation.

Love as a reflected and explicit mode of action and as an unconceptualised transcendental horizon of action

If we are to keep our ideas clear and avoid the most gross misunderstandings of the envisaged thesis from the very start, it is first of all necessary to distinguish in a human spiritual act between its explicit object represented in a determined concept and category, which is envisaged in a systematic way both by the intellect and will, on the one hand, and the *a priori* formal object, the transcendental horizon or 'space' within which a determined individual object is encountered, on the other hand. The transcendental horizon is, on the one hand, the subjective possibility for the individual object to show itself at all; it is, as it were, the system of co-ordinates within which the classified object is given its place and which makes it comprehensible. On the other hand, the transcendental horizon is that which is itself given only in the encounter with the object of a concretely historical experience (it itself in transcendental experience), which of course does not mean that this experienced transcendental horizon of the categorised individual experience must be for this reason already systematically, explicitly and objectively represented and named.

The latter is, of course, not usually the case. Indeed, even where this transcendental horizon of objective knowledge is reflected on and where it is therefore systematised, conceptually represented and named, and hence is itself made the explicit object of knowledge, this happens once more in virtue of this same horizon which as such must once more be given in an unconscious manner. The representation of its concept cannot dispense with this horizon itself in its unconscious exercise.

This distinction being presupposed, it must be said, of course, that not every act of the love of God is also a formal act of love of neighbour, if and in so far as the love of neighbour means an act in which our neighbour is envisaged and loved as the conscious object in its categorised and conceptual representation. If one relates oneself explicitly by prayer, trust and love to God, then this is in *this* sense an act of love of God and not an act of love of neighbour. Moreover, measured by the object, such an act of love of God has, of course, a higher dignity than an act of reflected love of neighbour. Yet where the whole 'transcendental' depth of interhuman love is realised and represented (which, as has been said, *can* at least be *caritas*, as is quite certain from tradition), there such a love is also necessarily a conscious love of God and has God as its reflex motive (even though this is of course true once more in very different degrees of clarity). In this case our neighbour, and he himself, must then also be really loved and must be the formal object and motive of this love, no matter how one may explain the unity of the two then given motives. (The neighbour, through God's love for him, is 'one' with God, etc.) Yet this still leaves open the other question which also occupies us here, viz. whether all interhuman love, provided only that it has its own moral radicality, is also *caritas* (i.e. love also of God), since it is orientated towards God, not indeed by an explicitly categorised motive but (and this is the question) by its inescapably given transcendental horizon, which is given gratuitously by God's always prevenient saving grace.

The anonymous 'Christianity' of every positively moral activity
A second preliminary remark must therefore be made: we presuppose here in what follows a theological opinion[3] which is not indeed commonly

[3] Cf. on this, e.g., K. Riesenhuber, 'Der anonyme Christ nach K. Rahner', *ZKT* LXXXVI (1964), pp. 286–303; A. Röper, *Die anonymen Christen* (Mainz 1963); K. Rahner, *Zur Theologie des Todes*[4] (Freiburg 1963), pp. 79–86 (English translation: *On the Theology of Death*, Quaestiones Disputatae 2 [Freiburg & Edinburgh-London 1961] – *Tr.*).

held in Catholic theology but which has a sufficiently serious basis to allow it to be presupposed here, even though it is impossible here to develop this basis. This opinion states that wherever man posits a positively moral act in the full exercise of his free self-disposal, this act is a positive supernatural salvific act in the actual economy of salvation even when its *a posteriori* object and the explicitly given *a posteriori* motive do not spring tangibly from the positive revelation of God's Word but are in this sense 'natural'. This is so because God in virtue of his universal salvific will offers everyone his supernaturally divinising grace and thus elevates the positively moral act of man. Furthermore, the thereby already given, supernaturally transcendental even though unconscious horizon of the spirit (its *a priori* orientation towards the triune God of eternal life) includes an element of (transcendental) revelation and possibility of faith which also gives such an act that sufficient character of 'faith' necessary for a moral act being a salvific act. This opinion states, therefore, that wherever there is an absolutely moral commitment of a positive kind in the world and within the present economy of salvation, there takes place also a saving event, faith, hope and charity, an act of divinising grace, and thus *caritas* is exercised in this, a fact which still remained an open question above. There is a possible logical but not a real distinction between a moral act and a salvific act. Yet all this does not mean that we have proved our proper basic thesis about the strict mutual identity of the love of God and the love of neighbour. It still remains questionable whether such love of neighbour is just *any* one of the moral acts among many others of equal rank which we must interpret as saving acts, or whether this love has a special, all-embracing position within the whole of morality, in such a way that it must be taken as the basis and sum total of the moral as such and hence – when divinised by grace – can be regarded as *the* saving act of explicit love of God in the sense that even conversely every act of explicit love of God is truly and form-ally (though in a sense still to be determined more exactly) love of *neighbour*.

Love of neighbour as the basic moral activity of man

It is the second part of this alternative which must be affirmed. Love of neighbour, even and especially if we regard it to begin with as a *moral* phenomenon and do not yet ask about the theological virtue of charity at all, is not to begin with just any of the many co-existing morally right reactions of man towards his own reality and that of his surroundings, but is the basis and sum total of the moral as such. Why and in what sense is this so? In the external multiplicity of his surroundings man encounters at a first glance a colourful, apparently arbitrary, juxtaposed variety of objects towards which his moral activity too can be referred in each case and which – as is shown, for instance, by the systematisations of special ethics – are then subsequently and somewhat arbitrarily collected together and ordered in groups. Yet still, the world encountered by man (we prescind from God at this point) is in many respects more originally *one* world of man. This is already seen to be true by the fact that the true and proper surrounding of man is his personal environment. This environment of persons is the world through which man finds and fulfils himself. (by knowledge and will) and . . . gets away from himself. From a personal and moral point of view, the world of things is of significance only as a factor for man and for his neighbour. This follows first of all from the *a priori* structure of the one whole man (in knowledge and will), a structure which imposes a unified law of its possible knowledge on the external variety of possible objects and which thus systematises this variety as it is known and willed. Knowledge is, however, of its nature a 'being-within-oneself', or rather a return to one*self*, and freedom is not simply the capacity to do this or that but (formally) a *self*-disposing into finality; the subject (from a formal point of view) is always concerned with itself. Hence it must necessarily be the secret *a priori* law imposed on the multiplicity of the possible objects for man that they can be concerned with and be ordered for man's knowledge and freedom, precisely in so far as they can serve this 'being-within-*oneself*' and this self-disposal. It follows from this, however, that the world of things can be a possible object for man's concern only as a moment of the world of persons. In the traditional teaching this is seen also in the axiom: being and the good are identical; the objective *moral* good is given in a *personal* being; thus a good which is not the person or something referred to the person as such cannot be regarded as an objective value of moral action. Nevertheless it must be added immediately that this formal nature of knowledge and freedom, understood as self-possession and self-deed, refers to the *formal* nature from a certain point of view and must not be misunderstood in an egocentric sense. Materially – even merely on account of the mundaneness and *a posteriori* historicity of man – the *a posteriori* object is the necessary mediation of the knowing subject to itself and so, presupposing what has just been said, the known personal Thou is the mediation, the 'being-within-oneself' of the subject. This condition is even clearer and more radical in the case of freedom: the free self-disposal, when morally right and perfect, is precisely the loving communication with the human *Thou* as such (not as mere negation of nor as something different from the 'ego' which wants merely to find *itself*, even though in the other). Yet since knowledge (being itself already an act) attains its proper and full nature only in the act of freedom and therefore must lose and yet keep itself in freedom in order to be completely itself, it has a fully human significance only once it is integrated into freedom, i.e. into the loving communication with the Thou. The act of personal love for another human being is therefore the all-embracing basic act of man which gives meaning, direction and measure to everything else. If this is correct, then the essential *a priori* openness to the other human being which must be undertaken freely belongs as such to the *a priori* and most basic constitution of man and is an essential inner moment of his (knowing and willing) transcendentality. *This a priori* basic constitution (which must be accepted in freedom, but to which man can also close himself) is experienced in the concrete encounter with man in the concrete. The one moral (or immoral) basic act in which man comes to himself and decides basically about himself is also the (loving or hating) communication with the concrete Thou in which man experiences, accepts or denies his basic *a priori* reference to the Thou as such. Everything else is a factor in this or a consequence of it or an impulse towards it, but in the present order of salvation, i.e. one having a supernatural goal, *this basic* act is, according to what has been said, elevated supernaturally by a self-communication of God in uncreated grace and in the resulting basic triune faculty of the theological virtues of faith, hope and charity, whereby theological love necessarily and of its very nature integrates and saves faith and hope into itself. Hence the one basic human act, where it takes place positively, is the love of neighbour understood as *caritas*, i.e. as a love of neighbour whose movement is directed towards the God of eternal life.

Love of neighbour as man's manifestation of his wholeness and essence
The reduction of the spiritual knowing and willing reality of man to that love of his neighbour which is *caritas*, when seen as man's basic act, does not of course limit this act to the obviously and transparently ordinary

everyday events but, even if we prescind to begin with from its theological aspect, gives this act a quality of mystery. When we say that a self-under-standing of man – understood as the assembling of his knowledge and as the free self-determination of man with a view to finality – takes place in the act of loving communication with the Thou (in this and in nothing else) so that everything else is a moment, presupposition, initial stage or result of *this*, then we also say of course *eo ipso* and conversely that the whole incalculable mystery of man is contained and exercised in this act of love of neighbour; it means that *all* anthropological statements must also be read as statements about that love which is not merely a 'regional' happening in the life of man but is the whole of himself in which alone he possesses himself completely, meets himself completely and falls into the ultimate abyss of his nature.

His corporeality, his temporality and historicity, his final incapacity to catch up with himself by reflection, the unfathomable and adventurous character of his existence, the anticipation of his future in hope or despair, the bitter impossibility of his perfecting and fulfilling himself and the disillusion proper to him, his continual confrontation with the nameless, silent, absolute mystery which embraces his existence, his readiness for death which after all can also be seen – in a very peculiar way – as the basic act of existence . . . all these together are necessarily also the essential traits of *love* for another person. The love of neighbour is not something which everyone always already knows reflexly in the depth of his being; rather, it is that which is sent to man only through the experienced and suffered wholeness of life and still remains even then, indeed especially then, a nameless mystery. It would be necessary to show by an empirical and descriptive phenomenology of love, responsibility, loyalty, venture, and of the unfinished and eternal quality inherent in love, what breadths and depths are implied by love of the Thou, how man really experiences in it who he is, how the 'no' to it imprisons the *whole* man within the deadly lonely damnation of self-created absurdity, how the totality of reality, which freely gives itself and is accepted and understood as the blessed incomprehensibility – which is the only self-evident thing – opens itself only if man opens himself radically in the act of love and entrusts himself to this totality. It would be necessary to show more empirically than is possible here what is the mutual relation of dependence between the transcendental openness and readiness for unlimited communication with the Thou, on the one hand, and the concrete encounter with the concrete Thou, on the other hand. This would make it more comprehensible that in the act of love for another, and in it alone and primarily, the original unity of what is human and what is the totality of man's experience is collected together and achieved, and that the love for the other concrete Thou is not just something which also exists in man among many other things but is man himself in his total achievement.

If it would thus become clearer by the description of love of the other Thou that this love is really the fulfilment of the total and hence also spiritually transcendental nature of man, then it would also become easier to grasp that it occurs in the present economy of salvation only in the form of *caritas* for *caritas* means nothing else than the absolute radicality of this love in so far as it is open to the immediacy of the God who communicates himself under the form of grace.

Normally speaking, we merely say quite abstractly in our teaching on grace that the absolute, infinite transcendentality of the spirit is the '*potentia oboedientialis*' for grace and that it is liberated by grace – in its infinity which of itself belongs to this transcendentality – from being the *mere* condition of the possibility of grasping a certain categorised object to being the possibility of immediate presence to God as he is in himself. This declaration, however, would have to be made concrete in the knowledge that from a more concrete point of view this *potentia oboedientialis* is precisely the transcendentality towards the other who is to be loved and who first of all is one's fellow man. Even by theological reflection we must arrive at the point where we can say: if in the present economy of salvation and on account of the universal salvific will of God *every* radically free moral act becomes a saving act through grace and is thus orientated towards the immediate presence to God (as has already been said), then this must be true *a fortiori* of the basic moral act which integrates everything, viz. the love of our neighbour. Even though this the supernatural nature of a saving act cannot be grasped reflexly by an arbitrary introspection alone[4] (but this is to be ascribed to that systematisation into themes which takes place precisely in man's history of salvation and revelation), it would nevertheless be possible to show, by

---

[4] The supernatural character of the saving act is also not simply what is beyond consciousness, as is held by a nominalistic tendency in theology even to our own day (outside the thomistic school). Cf. on this: K. Rahner, 'Gnadenerfahrung', *LTK*[3] IV, pp. 1001 *sq.*; K. Rahner, *Theological Investigations* III (London & Baltimore 1967), pp. 86–90; J. Alfaro, *LTK*[3] IV, pp. 207 *sq.*

such a phenomenological description of the empirical, authentic love of neighbour, the elements in it which are elevated and liberated by grace to their absolute perfection and which are then also experienced as such unsystematically. Furthermore, it is not the place here to describe the different concrete forms of love of neighbour. Suffice it to say explicitly here that, even when we are talking about *caritas*, it must always be a question of real love and that it is therefore not just a matter of fulfilling a commandment which guards and defends the other against our brutal egoism; 'love for God's sake' – to be precise – does not mean love of God alone in the 'material' of our neighbour merely seen as an opportunity for pure love of God, but really means the love of our neighbour himself, a love empowered by God to attain its ultimate radicality and a love which really terminates and rests in our neighbour.

The encounter of the world and of man as the medium of the original, unobjectified experience of God

We must now finally give thought to an objection against any thesis which understands the love of neighbour as the one all-embracing basic act of human existence, viz. that the *religious* act directed towards God is the basic act of human existence or at least stands equally entitled and equally original, indeed with higher rank, beside the act of loving communication with another person. This objection is, however, a misunderstanding. It must be noted first of all that, at least for the original experience of God, God is not one 'object' besides others either objectively speaking or in the subjective intentionality of man (in knowledge and free action and their unity). God is not an object towards which the intentionality of man can be directed in the same fragmentary and particular way as it is towards the multiplicity of objects and persons encountered within the categories of intramundane experience. God is not originally given in the way in which – as if by chance, externally and without it having to be thus by the nature of human intentionality – a flower or Australia are 'given'. We must not consider man as unconcerned about God until he systematically conceives the notion of God as one reality 'besides' others and this in the merely dividing distinction from these other realities. In the original act which precedes all reflex systematisations, God is always given as the subjectively and objectively all-bearing *ground* of experience, a ground which is beyond this world; he is therefore given indirectly in a kind of boundary experience as the origin and destination of an act which is objectively directed towards the world and which, therefore, as will have to be said more in detail below, is a loving communication with (or 'no' to) the Thou in the world. God is primarily and originally given in (or as) the transcendental, unclassified horizon of the knowing and acting intentionality of man and not as an 'object' represented by an idea within this horizon. Moreover, even where God is made the subject of religious and Christian reflection – hence, where and in so far as (over and above such a philosophico-religious reflection) He is given (transcendentally) in the 'horizon' of the spirit opened up or maintained in its absolute manner by divinising grace (as the goal of this transcendentality which transmits itself supernaturally) and where he speaks himself (in categories) through the revelation of the Word in salvation history, and where in both these ways he becomes a 'partner' in a personal and direct relationship between himself and man – this revelation of grace and the Word and the real self-communication by grace always happens *vis-à-vis* and through man who is already 'in the world', i.e. who is given to himself in freedom by entering in love into the world around him, and by personal encounter and communication with the Thou of intramundane experience.

The (naturally and supernaturally) transcendental experience of God which is also the necessary presupposition of the historical revelation of the Word and both is and remains its supporting ground, is possible only in and through man who has *already* (in logical priority) experienced the human Thou by his intramundane transcendental experience (of his *a priori* reference to the Thou) and by his categorised experience (of his concrete encounter with the concrete Thou) and who only *in this way* can exercise the (at least) transcendental experience of his reference to the absolute mystery (i.e. God). The classical thesis of scholastic theology (against ontologism and the innate idea of God) which maintains that God can be known only *a posteriori* from the created world, does not ultimately mean to imply (if it is properly understood) that man merely comes upon God like any object given to him purely accidentally (e.g. this flower or Australia) with which he might just as well not be concerned (from the point of view of the *a priori* structure of his knowledge) but it does mean that the transcendentally original *a priori* experience of his original reference to God and thus of God himself (an experience which must in some measure also be objectified in categories) can be made only in an always already achieved going-out into the world which, understood as the world of man, is primarily the people *with whom* he lives. Precisely because the original reference towards God is of a transcendental kind and hence does not fall into any category but is given in the infinite reference of the spirit of man beyond every mere object of his personal and material surroundings, the *original* experience of God (as distinct from his separating representation in an individual concept) is always given in a 'worldly' experience. This, however, is only present originally and totally in the communication with a 'Thou'.

Since every conceptual reflection on the transcendental conditions of the possibility of knowledge and freedom is itself based once more on these same conditions, then even the *explicit* religious act in which God becomes the reflex theme of knowledge and love is once more under-pinned and taken up by that act which offers a transcendental, inclusive experience of God (of a natural-supernatural kind) and this *by the fact* that this act – in our turning towards the people we live with, and therefore in our explicit communication with them – lets us also experience un-reflectedly the transcendental conditions of this act (i.e. the transcendental reference to God and the transcendental openness to the human Thou).

The act of love of neighbour is, therefore, the only categorised and original act in which man attains the whole of reality given to us in categories, with regard to which he fulfils himself perfectly correctly and *in which* he always already makes the transcendental and direct experience of God by grace. The reflected religious act *as such* is and remains secon-dary in comparison with this. It has indeed, as has already been said, a higher dignity than the reflected act of love of neighbour, if and in so far as the latter is measured by the particular explicit, conceptually represented object of the act in question. Measured by its 'horizon' or its transcendental possibility, it has the same dignity, the same 'draught' and the same radicality as the act of explicit love of neighbour, since both acts are necessarily supported by the (experienced but unreflected) reference both to God and to the intramundane Thou and this by grace (of the infused *caritas*), i.e. by that on which the explicit acts both of our relationship to God and of our love of neighbour 'for God's sake' reflect. Yet this does not alter the fact that the primary basic act of man who is always already 'in the world' is always an act of the love of his neighbour and *in this* the original love of God is realised in so far as in this basic act are also accepted the conditions of its possibility, one of which is the reference of man to God when supernaturally elevated by grace.

Love of neighbour as the primary act of love of God

We are now in a position to give a direct answer to the basic question of our whole reflections. This was the question about the identity of the love of God and the love of neighbour. More exactly, it was the question about whether the love of neighbour understood as *caritas* is ultimately only a secondary moral act (one among many) which more or less proceeds objectively from the love of God as an *'actus imperatus'*. In other words, does the love of neighbour have God for its 'motive' (just as in the explicit love of God) in such a way that this love of neighbour really 'loves' God alone and hence, in accordance with the will of God who is really loved, is well disposed towards its neighbour and does good to him? *Or* is there a more radical unity between the love of God and of neighbour (taken as *caritas*) in such a way that the love of God itself is always also already love of neighbour in which our neighbour is really loved himself? We can now answer: the categorised explicit love of neighbour is the primary act of the love of God. The love of God unreflectedly but really and always intends God in supernatural transcendentality in the love of neighbour as such, and even the explicit love of God is still borne by that opening in trusting love to the whole of reality which takes place in the love of neighbour. It is radically true, i.e. by an ontological and not merely 'moral' or psychological necessity, that whoever does not love the brother whom he 'sees', also cannot love God whom he does not see, and that one can love God whom one does not see only *by* loving one's visible brother lovingly.

Finally, we would simply draw the reader's attention to the fact that we should really go on to reflect now explicitly on the 'Christological' and 'eschatological' aspects of this situation. If in 'recent times' (and only then) one has learnt to see and love the Father whom one does not see in the man Jesus whom one does see, then the unity of the love of God and of neighbour on which we have been reflecting becomes even more radical from a Christological and eschatological point of view and thus reaches its climax; thus the man Jesus takes on and continues to have an eternal significance for our relationship to God right into the 'direct' vision of God.

The relationship to God through man is thus not merely a 'mediation' in time but also in eternity, and therefore the same is present 'subjectively' as is present 'objectively' through the never reversed acceptance of humanity by the Logos. Unfortunately we cannot enter further into this here, otherwise it could also be shown how a love of neighbour which has reached an absolute (supernatural) perfection of being also includes Christology.

The topical significance of the love of neighbour for modern man's knowledge of God

This whole laborious reflection may appear as if it only considers some-thing which, if true, is valid *always* and everywhere (at least in the Christian order of salvation). This is quite correct yet our reflections have particular significance for the historical 'moment' in which we live *today*. A natural-supernatural knowledge and love of God of an existen-tially authentic kind, in which the reality of God is truly experienced, is in the very nature of things an act which can only be posited by man as *a whole*. Everything he is and with which he is concerned must be included in this, otherwise the absolute ground of reality, the ground of the know-ing and acting spirit, would not be encountered in it and God would not appear in it as God, as a Person, as Freedom and as absolute mystery. This reality, however, which achieves itself as a whole towards God, has nevertheless different aspects in different periods for the man who fulfils himself historically, privileged aspects under which it presents itself and transmits itself to man. Each epoch has different 'catchwords', 'primitive words', under which the one totality of the experience of God is summoned up and comes towards us anew out of the totality of our experience of reality and of ourselves.

Already in scripture, and then also in the course of the history of faith and salvation, there shows itself a variety of such catchwords which always mean and imply the whole and yet appear at the same time as many *different* gateways which form *the* particular approach to this whole according to the spirit of each particular age or as particular characteristics of the Christian religious experience of particular men. For St Paul, for instance, the 'catchword' is 'faith', but this is not the same for everyone or every age, even though no one can come to God without faith. It could be asked whether the trilogy of the three divine virtues does not *also* already indicate a sphere of such a change of 'root terms' for a religious experience in a particular period, just as the key-word for everything in St John is not faith but love, while the Synoptics replace even this by 'conversion' (*metanoia*). Today, at any rate, when by reason of its enormous numbers, its concrete unity and in its necessarily new social forms, mankind must learn to love completely anew or go under; when God opens out anew as the silent incomprehensibility so much so that man is tempted to honour him now simply by silence and nothing else and when all atheism, which today really exists for the first time, is simply the mistaken adolescent form of this opportunity and the temptation given to us as regards God's incomprehensibility; when an extremely worldly world is coming into being, a world which man creates for himself and which ought not indeed be sacralised but which must be experienced and acted in the depth *sanctified* by God, i.e. opened towards him . . . at the dawn of such a new epoch, 'love of neighbour' might easily be the root-word which really moves people and the key-word for today. Nevertheless, if we want to say today that anyone who loves his neighbour has fulfilled *the* law as such – namely that if we love one another, then God's final salvation is within us (as one might translate 1 Jn 4:12) – then we must understand absolutely fundamentally why the love of neighbour, provided it is genuine and accepts its own proper incomprehensible being to the very limit, already contains the whole of Christian salvation and of Christianity. This must indeed still be unfolded in that complete fullness and breadth which we know and preserve, but whenever someone loves someone else truly and 'to the end', it is already grasped in its original root.

PART FOUR

Contributions to a Theology of the Church

A. THE PILGRIM CHURCH

17

THE CHURCH OF SINNERS

THE topic of the 'Church of Sinners' usually receives a very cursory treatment in Catholic dogmatics. In truth, there are more important and more glorious things to say about the Church. Perhaps the reason why the Church as a Church of sinners does not appear very much in the forefront of theological interest lies in the fact that it is only too clearly a matter of everyday experience. Nevertheless this topic is materially of the greatest importance in our doctrine about the Church, not only because we are here concerned with one of the most agonising questions of ecclesiology which persistently recurs throughout the history of dogma, but also because it is a question of such consequence for the individual's life of faith. Ultimately, however, the question acquires importance because it is not intended as a question of everyday, superficial experience, but as a dogmatic one, that is to say as a question which has to be answered in the light, not of human experience, conceited, questionable, and distorted by sin, but of God's revelation.

We said it was here a matter of an agonising question which persistently pervades the whole history of dogma. Christianity has always declared, 'I believe in the holy Church.' Again and again in the course of history the question has arisen where this Church is to be found which so confidently declares itself to be a holy Church, therefore the Church illuminated by the light of God's own holiness. Again and again, on the basis of this article of the Creed, the concrete Church has been rejected as sinful; again and again some new Church has been founded as the true and holy one, and declared to be the true Church of God and of his Christ. Already Tertullian maintained that the universal Church of his time was not the true Church of the Spirit and of spiritual men but a house of whores, because she did not cast adulterers out of her communion once and for all. Somewhat similar was the thought and teaching of Montanism and Novatianism in the third century, of Donatism in the time of Augustine, of Messalianism and other heretical movements within monasticism, movements like that of the Cathari, of the Spiritualism of Joachim of Fiore, of the Spirituals among the Franciscans, of the Hussites in the Middle Ages. All of them wanted a 'holy' Church instead of the unholy Church of their time. And even the Reformers of the sixteenth century, who were so insistent in teaching the sinfulness and corruption of all men, made a large part of their attack on the Catholic Church consist of diatribes against the corruption of the papacy and the unholiness of the Church in general.

In the life of the individual, too, the experience of the unholy Church nearly always plays a significant role in his inner struggle to come to terms with his faith. Whenever complaints are heard against the clergy, what else is usually the matter of reproach, but that their lives contradict what they preach? Is anything repeated more frequently than that church-people are no better than others, that the Church too has failed? And these reproaches and the troubled temptations against faith that arise from them have, from the purely human point of view, a certain amount of right on their side. There stands the Church, and she declares herself necessary for salvation, she comes to us in the name of a holy God, she declares herself to be in possession of all truth and grace, she claims to be the one ark of salvation among the flood of sin and corruption, she believes herself commissioned to convert and save all men. And this very Church which comes to us with such claims, why, look at her! – so they will say – look how she seems to use two different yardsticks: she proclaims to poor, troubled humanity the Sermon on the Mount with its 'impossible' demands, but her official representatives seem to let these demands rest very lightly on their own personal shoulders. Don't they all seem to live pretty comfortable lives? Aren't they often avaricious or arrogant or overbearing? Isn't there a continuous succession of scandals, even in the ranks of her religious orders, who after all are supposed to be striving for holiness and perfection? Are the bad popes a mere catch-phrase or aren't they a historical fact? And haven't even her holiest things been continually misused in all sorts of ways for sinful purposes: the confessional and the sacraments in general, the papacy used for transparently political purposes, and so on? That we are all human –

so this plaint or complaint continues – that is not to be wondered at; and that the men of the Church also, even her official representatives, are human and sinful, that too is in itself nothing to cause surprise. If this were all, then it would admittedly be quite unjust to comb through the corners of Church history in order to lay bare the sins of the Church. But – the Church puts herself forward as being something essentially greater than a merely human organisation in which it is unavoidable that things often happen in a human and too human way. She claims to hold the place of the all-holy God in the world, to be the holy Church; she goes so far as to assert that her 'extraordinary holiness and inexhaustible fruitfulness in all that is good' is in itself a powerful and permanent motive of credibility and an irrefutable testimony to her divine mission.[1] It is precisely here that the contradiction is to be found: if the Church were more modest – so goes the eternal objection of unbelief – then one could be mild in one's judgement of her and forgive her everything that one forgives in oneself. But because she declares herself to be holy, she must also permit her life and her history to be measured by standards that are higher than the merely human. And what then? Is not then the claim to holiness which she puts forward a singular presumption which proves precisely the opposite of her inordinate claim?

We said our topic is of importance from quite another point of view as well. For us the question is not at all one of how we as Christians who believe in the holiness of the Church manage to deal with our *purely human* experience of the unholiness of the Church. Rather, the question asked is a dogmatic one: namely, what does Revelation itself have to say about the unholiness of the Church? In other words, we are not concerned with listening to the voice of outraged humanity, (perhaps we know better now than did earlier times that this kind of 'public opinion' even when fairly unanimous is a highly doubtful matter, and that usually each one finds in his experience whatever corresponds to his expectations); we are concerned with examining the self-witness of the Church regarding her own unholiness. For the fact that she is a Church of sinners is itself a piece of the Church's consciousness of her faith. Because if someone with an all too superficial optimism were to hold the Church to be completely 'holy', the Church would not say, 'Thank God! here at last is someone who holds me in just esteem!' No, she would on the contrary have to say to him, 'You are a heretic, and the truth about me

[1] First Vatican Council, Sess. III, cap. 3, cf. *DS* 3013.

is not to be found in you; your mildness is of the Evil One, and you have not grasped what the Spirit of God thinks either about the holiness which he has really bestowed upon me, the holy one, or about the holiness which I, the unholy Church of sinners, do not possess; you do not have in you that holiness which you should have, otherwise you could not think that you had found it in me, any more than someone has it who disappointedly arraigns me for not in fact possessing it.'

Accordingly there are two things in question: the Church of sinners, and sinful man before the holy Church of sinners.

I

The Church of God and of his Christ is a Church of sinners. What is meant by this will be explained in two groups of ideas: sinners in the Church, and the sinful Church.

1. Sinners in the Church

It is an article of faith that sinners are members of the Church. Even sinners who are destined to be lost can truly and really belong to the Church. This is a truth of our faith which the Church has constantly taught, in patristic times against Montanism, Novatianism and Donatism, in the Middle Ages against the Albigenses, against the Fraticelli, against Wyclif and Hus, and in modern times against the Reformers, against Jansenism and the Synod of Pistoia. The proposition that sinners, those deprived of grace or those foreknown by God as destined to be lost, are not members of the Church is a formal heresy which has been definitively condemned by the Church.

And let us not be over-hasty in asserting this to be a self-evident truth which could only be doubted by an idealistic visionary. It is not at all a self-evident truth. All that is self-evident is this: there exists a socially recognised 'religious association' called the Catholic Church, to which belong according to the register papers not only those who can be said to be in a very civic and superficial sense 'respectable people', people who have 'no previous convictions', people who can be set up as examples of virtue, people who can even (if one wants to use such a high-sounding title) be described as 'saints'. This is certainly very much self-evident; but it in no way penetrates to the real meaning of the word 'Church' in this Catholic dogma, nor to what meaning is here attached to the word 'sinner'.

For the word 'Church' signifies in this connection the visible presence of God and his grace in this world in sacramental signs, it means the historical embodiment of Christ in the here and now of the world until he comes again to 'appear' in the glory of his Godhead; 'Church' signifies here what is human, which while it is really distinct from what is divine is yet inseparably united with it. And 'a sinner in the Church' does not here signify a person who has been in conflict with the police (this can happen occasionally even to the dearest friend of God), but 'sinner' in this article of the faith signifies a person who is in reality devoid of God's grace, a person who is wandering far from God, a person whose destiny is perhaps moving with fearful consistency towards an ultimate eternal damnation. And *this* sinner belongs to *this* Church: he is not merely entered in her official register but is her member, a part of the visible presence of God's grace in the world, a member of the Body of Christ! Is this perhaps something self-evident? Is this something which is already unmistakably and without difficulty a matter of our experience? Or is this not rather a truth which in sheer incomprehensibility far outstrips anything which unbelievers can bring forward in their accusations against the Church and their protests at her unholiness?

Yet it is this revealed truth which is clearly taught in scripture and tradition. The kingdom of Heaven is like a net which hauls out of the sea of the world good fish and bad. Only on the shore of eternity at the end of time will the angels of judgement separate the evil from among the good and cast them into the furnace (Mt 13:47–50). At the wedding banquet of the kingdom of Heaven there will also be found seated among the guests those who have on no wedding garment and who will at the end be bound hand and foot and cast out (Mt 25:1–13). There are 'brothers' who by their disobedience to the Church ultimately become as the heathen and public sinners (Mt 18:17). Even the servant who has been set over the household of his lord can be condemned (Mt 24:45–51).

The apostles, too, bear witness to the doctrine contained in these images used by our Lord: there are sinners in the Church, people to whom the Spirit says, 'I know your works; you have the name of being alive and yet are dead' (Rv 3:1 *sq.*). This is the terrifying part of it: one really has the name of being alive and yet is dead.

The Church of the first centuries found it difficult enough to grasp this truth of faith without trembling, and even as late as St Augustine, who by his struggle against Donatism has become for the history of dogma of the greatest importance in this question, it is not always altogether clear whether in his theory of the wheat and the chaff and of the intermingling cities of Jerusalem and Babylon he unequivocally and definitely regards the dead members as true members of the mystical Body of Christ, or whether he merely means that while the borderline between the two cities is always undoubtedly there, it will be revealed only at the end of time. As regards this matter the Church's consciousness of her belief has subsequently been clarified in the course of time towards the full truth of faith that there are sinners, and that they belong to the Church. There is within the Church sin and failure. And those who sin and fail form a part of the embodiment and manifestation of that divine salvation and that divine grace which we call 'Church'.

It is true that this 'belonging of the sinner to the Church' must be viewed from another side as well, that is, it must be negatively delimited, for the sinner does not belong to the Church in the same full sense as the justified person.

To begin with, it is surely self-evident that one can and must speak of a membership of the Church in all the directions and dimensions into which the Church herself extends, and that consequently whoever does not belong to the Church in *one* of these dimensions cannot be regarded as her member in the *full* sense. Now both Leo XIII in his encyclical *Satis Cognitum* (1896) and Pius XII in the encyclical *Mystici Corporis Christi* (to indicate only the more recent expressions of the Church's magisterium) emphasised that it would be an ecclesiological Nestorianism and a rationalistic Naturalism if one were to see in the Church nothing more than an external, juridical organisation, merely a visible society, a 'confession' in the civico-social sense of the word. She is much rather the living Body of Christ, animated by the Holy Spirit of God, to whose reality belong divine life, grace, and the power of the future aeon. But since the sinner does not possess this Holy Spirit, it is self-evident that he does not simply belong to the Church in the full sense of the word 'Church' which we have indicated. This proposition in no way contradicts the propositions we set out above from the doctrine of the Church which simply declared the sinner to be a member of the Church. In those propositions the word 'Church' is in fact taken in the sense of the external society; for only on this supposition can the absence of an inner state of grace in the sinner be without effect on his membership of the Church.

That this concept of the Church does not contradict the teaching of

Leo XIII and Pius XII referred to above is certain from the following considerations.

The Church has, to a certain extent, a sacramental structure. But in a sacrament we must distinguish between the sacramental sign as such (and the conditions for its 'validity') on the one hand, and the sacramental sign in so far as it is really the cause of sacramental grace and filled with it, on the other. The two concepts must be kept carefully distinct; for it is possible to have in certain circumstances a 'valid sacrament' which in point of fact does not cause any grace in the recipient of the sacrament. Now in a certain sense the Church is the basic sacrament (*Ursakrament*); hence in her case we must make a distinction between her visible appearance as a body in so far as this is a sign of grace, and this visible appearance in so far as it is a reality filled with grace, and accordingly also between a (merely) 'valid' and a 'fruitful' membership of the Church. The sinner has the first kind of membership of the Church, but not the second. But by making this distinction the continuing membership of the sinner in the Church is not being reduced to a harmless formality of an external, juridical kind. It is true that the sinner still belongs to the visible appearance of the Church, but his visible membership of the Church has ceased to be the efficacious sign of his invisible membership of the Church as a living, holy community. In a certain sense the sinner has turned this sign into a lie (rather like someone who receives a sacrament validly but unworthily); for he has robbed his continuing membership in the Church of all the meaning and effect to which it is by its entire nature ordered: the inner, living union of men with God and with each other in the Holy Spirit.

2. With this we come to establishing the express point which this doctrine primarily enunciates in all its clearness: *the Church is sinful*. After what we have just said it is already impossible to maintain any longer as consistent with the faith that there are admittedly sinners 'in' the Church as an external confessional organisation but that this fact tells us nothing about the Church herself. For we have already seen that these sinners, according to the teaching of the Church, are real members, parts, and therefore integral pieces of the visible character of the Church herself. We must now elucidate this a little further.

In order to see our way more clearly, we must keep in mind two things. If we were merely to say, 'Certainly there are sinners in the Church, but this fact has nothing to do with the real Church', we would be assuming an idealistic concept of the Church which from a theological point of view is very questionable. 'Church' is then an idea, an ideal, an ought-to-be, something to which appeal can be made from the concrete reality, something which is meant to be reached only asymptotically, as it were, by slow approximation. That is something which we can of course always love, to which we can fearlessly commit ourselves; it is something untouchable, beyond the reach of the wretchedness of daily life. But this is not really the meaning of the theological concept of 'Church'. In this latter concept the Church is something real: it is the one and only Church which exists and in which we believe, in all cases always including the visible and juridically organised assembly of the baptised, united together in the external confession of their faith and in their obedience to the Roman pope. And it is precisely of this Church that it is impossible to say that she has nothing to do with the sins of her members. Obviously she does not approve of sin; obviously there will always be within her ranks men (and perhaps many men) whom we must call, in some real sense of the word which we need not discuss further here, holy men. But if she is something real, and if her members are sinners and as sinners remain members, then she herself is sinful. Then the sins of her children are a blot and a blemish on the holy mystical Body of Christ itself. The Church is a sinful Church: this is a truth of faith, not an elementary fact of experience. And it is a shattering truth.

Furthermore, we must consider a second fact. If what we said is true, then it is also self-evident that the official representatives of the Church, those men whom a superficial theological consciousness especially among the Catholic laity likes to regard exclusively as 'the' Church (as though the laity, too, were not the 'Church', as though they represented merely the object of the Church's ministration, an error emphatically opposed in Pius XII's encyclical on the Church), that those men too can be sinners, and in fact have been and are in a very noticeable way. But then it is again even clearer that the concrete Church is sinful (and once again, only in the concrete is she the 'Church'). For it is surely beyond dispute that the sins in question do not occur merely in a realm of the 'private life' of these ecclesiastics, but may also influence very substantially their concrete mode of action as official representatives of the Church. When the Church acts, gives a lead, makes decisions (or fails to make decisions when they ought to be made), when she proclaims her message, and when she is obliged to proclaim it in accordance with the times and historical situations, then this activity of the Church is not carried out by some abstract principle and not by the Holy Spirit alone, but rather this whole activity of the Church is at the same time the activity of concrete men. And since they can in fact commit sin, since they can be culpably narrow, culpably egoistic, self-satisfied, obstinate, sensual or indolent, this sinful attitude of theirs will naturally affect also those actions which they initiate precisely *as* ecclesiastics and in the name of the Church as acts of the concrete Church. There exists no dogma according to which the assistance of the Holy Spirit which always remains with the Church would limit the effect of the sinfulness of the men who administer the Church to their purely private lives and not permit it to have any influence on those events which must be characterised as unmistakably acts of the Church, if the concept of the Church is not to evaporate into the abstract ideal of an invisible Church. It is true that the Christian's conscience can, if he thinks himself capable of attempting it, discover such motivations; he can also, indeed he *must*, refuse obedience in a case where he is commanded what is sinful, but he cannot withdraw himself from obedience to the Church as long as he himself is not commanded to do anything sinful (even though he may think that the command springs at least partially from sinful narrowness, obstinacy and love of power), and above all – and this is here the only point – he cannot dispute the fact that such actions of ecclesiastics are actions of the Church. This means it must be conceded that the Church can be sinful in her actions. It goes without saying that this happens in opposition to the impulse of the Spirit and the norms and laws always proclaimed by the Church. But this is surely what is so great about this *faith* in the sinful Church, that she can really do all these things and yet (unlike all human organisations falling away from their original ideals) remain the bride of Christ and the vessel of the Holy Spirit, the only means of grace, from which no one can separate himself by appealing to her own ideal, accusing her of no longer being what she 'once' was (she never was it), or what she ought and claims to be.

Of course we hasten to add that it is not as though the Church were the pure paradox of a union of visible sin and invisible grace. She is holy because she is constantly in a vital contact with Christ the source of all holiness; she is holy, because her whole history with all its ups and downs is constantly pressing forward in the power of her living source, the Holy Spirit, towards that ultimate day to which all her truth, her law and her sacraments are ordered, towards that day when God himself will appear unveiled in his world. She is and remains infallible whenever she makes a solemn dogmatic decision under precise conditions which we need not here further determine. Her sacraments are independent of the worthiness of their ministers, they have an objective validity and efficacy, they are holy and make holy. She never falls victim to the temptation of accommo-dating to the weakness and mediocrity of men the truth and the norms which her very human preachers proclaim. (How far from self-evident is this miracle of the power and the grace of her holy Spirit; yet it is ever renewed through the centuries!) At all times in a sinful world she has championed the holiness of God and of his Christ, and if we had really grasped how easily man tends to regulate his principles according to his deeds, we would recognise in the eternal 'contradiction' between the holy preaching and the all-too-human life of the preacher of the Church's gospel not so much a stumbling-block as a demonstration of the effective-ness of God's Spirit in a holy Church. The Church is also really so holy in so many of her members, and this holiness can be ascertained even empirically, that for the man of good will, enlightened by the grace of faith, even her outward appearance bears all the marks of a constant motive for faith and an irrefutable witness to her divine commission. In a way which is not at all self-evident but extraordinary, she has really been in all ages the eternally fruitful mother of saints, the holy Church, the bride of Christ, whose appearance even now holds out for the man of faith the promise that she will one day be the bride able to enter without spot or wrinkle the wedding feast of the lamb – on that day when the light of eternal life will reveal what in reality she *is* even now under the appearance of the woman of sin.

But all this does not give the Church or us her children the right to put a gulf of arrogance and superiority between her and the sin which is not only in the world but also in the Church and through which she herself is really sinful, and this in a way in which she alone can be sinful (even where she is much better than those who are outside); for she alone can distort by her sin the eternal visible presence of Christ in the world which she is and so wrap a shroud about him – and do this in the face of men who must seek him as a matter of life and death!

If then holiness *and* sin co-exist in the 'image' presented by the Church (and the Church is essentially 'image', a sign making historically accessible the grace of God in the world), this is of course not to say that sin and holiness in the Church have the same relationship to the hidden essential purpose of the Church and therefore belong to her in the same way. The holiness made tangible in her history is an expression of what she is and will remain infallibly and indestructibly until the end of time: the presence in the world of God and of his grace. The Church is always something more than an association, more than a 'juridical Church' and confessional organisation, because the Holy Spirit has indissolubly united himself to her. And this Holy Spirit of God, in himself hidden, recreates over and over again in the palpable holiness of the Church a visible manifestation of his continuing presence capable of convincing the world. In this holiness – not in sin – are we given 'phenotypically' the inner glory which constitutes the permanent heritage out of which her whole character is fashioned. By contrast with all other historical structures, including the 'Church' of the Old Testament, this bodily manifestation of the Church cannot be so distorted by sin that the life-giving Spirit would abandon her or be unable any longer to be historically manifested in her. For the power of death will not overcome her (cf. Mt 16:18). On the other hand, the sin in the appearance of the Church is indeed really in the Church herself in so far as she is essentially 'body' and a historical structure and in so far as in *this* dimension there can be sin. For the existential source of sin, in which it fundamentally subsists, the 'heart', does lie deeper and further than the level of the historical and the social into which it must of course always necessarily erupt when accomplished and where it becomes the sin of the Church. But this sin in the Church is not a revelation of what the Church is in her own, proper, living roots, but on the contrary a contradiction veiling it from view; it is in a way an exogenetic illness in the bodily nature of the Church, not an endogenetic hereditary flaw in the Church herself (even though sin always betrays 'what is in man'). For sin strictly as such is always a contradicting of God and his Christ, who being himself without sin has expiated sin and overcome it, a contradicting of the Spirit of God through whom he has sanctified his bride in the word of life by the baptism of water. Sin is therefore also a contradiction of what the Church is. No one can sin in order to allow God's grace to appear more abundantly and more clearly (cf. Rm 3:5; 6:1), a truth which threatens to be obscured by a dialectical and gnostic kind of mysticism of sin which has been surreptitiously disseminating itself today even among Catholics. And therefore the Church is not sinful in order that God's grace might be revealed more abundantly; sin remains in her a reality which contradicts her nature; but her holiness is the manifestation of her essential being.

It is true that we must make two qualifications in this proposition in order to avoid the appearance of allowing the logical distinction of concepts (which is also an expression of the real situation) to break up the sombre and salutary combination of reality.

First, in the concrete order of salvation whose first and last focal point is the cross of Christ, even the suffering consequent on a sin once it has been committed, the utter absence of remedy from a human point of view, the inconsolable fear which it produces, the earthly darkness which often allows the sin and the suffering consequent upon it to intermingle indistinguishably, can become the manifestation of the cross of Christ in the world and a sharing of its burden: the manifest consequence of sin can in Christ become the conquest of sin. When the Church suffers under sin, she undergoes redemption from her fault, for she suffers her fault in Christ the crucified, particularly since sin, in so far as it exists not in the hidden 'heart' but in the world and so in the Church, while it is sin (because the 'heart' must realise its own action always in the world if it is to exist) is equally already the consequence of sin (because the embodiment of the real and hidden evil in the heart) and since it is carried out as such in the Church gives the Church the possibility of expiating and conquering it. Hence if we encounter sin in the Church we should not forget this. We do not usually take scandal at *sin* in the Church but at the *consequences* of such sin. We are offended, for example, by the 'hard-hearted clergy' not usually because they are empty of love before God, but because they give nothing to *us* or because their 'failure' humiliates *our* pride in the holy Church, as whose members we appear before the heathen, and brings *us* into disrepute in the eyes of those who are without. Why do we not love the Church in such a way as to suffer humbly and silently the ignominy of her sin? This would make her holy much more effectively than our protests against the scandals in the Church, no matter how much they may often be called for and however praiseworthy they may be, and no matter how little the protester should be reproved by anyone who has not previously gone into himself upon the protest, confessed his sin and striven to better himself.

Secondly, if sin in the Church is 'merely' a contradiction of her Spirit, a distortion and illness in her image, this does not make of sin something harmless. For the Church is meant to be the manifestation of God's grace and holiness in the world; she is meant to be the temple of the Holy Spirit. But sinners in the Church make of this figure an expression of the evil of their heart, they make of it a 'den of thieves'. This frightful truth remains, however much it must also be said that sin and holiness in the image of the Church do not have the same relationship to her inner 'truth'.

II

We come now to our second question: *sinful man before the holy Church of sinners*. We are not asking, 'why and in what sense is this Church of sinners at the same time the holy Church?' For this question was dealt with at least by way of general indications in what we have just said. The other question seems to us to be more important at this point, namely the question how we ourselves, the children and members of this Church, come to terms with the fact of her sinfulness. More precisely, what must be our own attitude in order that this eternal scandal of the Church does not become a scandal for us but rather an edification of our own Christian life and so contribute for our part also to the building up of the Church?

Once more, this Church as she is in the concrete is *the* Church, the only Church, the Church of God and of his Christ, the home of our souls, the place where alone we find the living God of grace and of eternal salvation. For this Church is one with Christ and the Spirit of God – not confused with them but inseparable from them. From this Church there is no escape which could lead to salvation. One can flee into a sect or something similar. There one may be less burdened and molested by sin, by narrowness, by scandal. One can then have a magnificent alibi to show that one has nothing to do with 'this' Church; perhaps one is nearer to one's ideals, but not nearer to God. Nor can one appeal against the concrete Church to another ideal; for there is only that ideal which has been eternally identified with this Church and eternally lives in her, and from which one falls away oneself if one separates oneself from the unity of this Church, from her love, her faith and her obedience, in favour of a self-made ideal. It is not possible, so to speak, to want to found the Church anew by a kind of *generatio aequivoca*; for she has been founded once and for all by the one Lord. From her one can flee to her by complaining, weeping, beseeching in anger, accusing in zeal, but one can never be right in fleeing away from her; one can never abandon her without losing to the same degree that which one professes to want to save.

Every spirituality, no matter how deep, which can no longer bear both the figures of the Church as virgin and as woman of sin – in humility and love, with the forbearance and the patience of God – reveals itself after a short period as fanaticism, as the spectre of a spirituality where man in the end remains caught up in himself. One must also give up the illusive desire of continually distinguishing 'accurately' between the 'divine' and the 'human and all-too-human' in the Church. To the extent that the Church herself does this (and she is here in reality broadminded and honest enough, if only we listen attentively to her), we too have the perfect right to lay claim to the freedom of the children of God in theology, in Church art, in practical life, in our method of prayer and our way to God, and no one, as Pius XI said with reference to theological opinions, ought to demand more of us than the Church, the mother of all, really (and not just presumably) demands of all. The more closely we get to know this Church, her life and her teaching, and the more open and unprejudiced is our attention to her directives, the more we will also note how wide this Church is and how much she frees us from ourselves to lead us into the breadth of God, even where she appears to impose limits and speak hard words. But if we begin to distinguish beyond the distinction of divine and human which she herself makes, where can we find an authentic criterion for our distinction? What guarantee is there, that we are not falling victim to our own narrow taste, that we are not rejecting the Holy Spirit (even if only in a particular sphere) when we attempt to trim and to purify the human element in the Church, or when we believe that we must discover and remove abuses and false developments?

Nevertheless, even assuming this primary and fundamental attitude, the honest Christian will see sins and shortcomings, scandals and failures in his Mother. And if he is really a Christian and if his eye and heart have been schooled in the inexorable demands of the gospel, for him perhaps more than for others does the question arise, can he deny the existence of the sins, should he cover them up or minimise them? No. He will of course as a mature person not be one of those who triumphantly try to demonstrate their objectivity and freedom of spirit by sweeping together from every corner of past and present history the scandals of the Church and spreading them out to view at every opportunity before all and sundry, whether they want to know them or not. He will also of course understand that the seamier side of a great history (and the history of the Church is that even from a purely human point of view) does not necessarily have to form the main content of a first elementary text-book for beginners. He will not say that it is a falsification or glossing over of history, if the history of the Church is not turned into a *chronique scandaleuse*; for, even leaving aside all other considerations, the history of the Spirit of God in the Church is still more important and more interesting than the history of human meanness. But even for him there will remain a very noticeable dark patch in the history of the Church; and we will meet this dark patch not only in studying the history of the Church, but we will also come across it in our own lives, especially if we live with the Church and the more we do so. What effect this dark patch has on the individual naturally depends to a large extent on his spiritual temperament. But perhaps it is not even good that we should come to terms with it too easily.

But what is to be our attitude if we clearly catch sight of sin in the face of our holy Mother the Church, if in the sacred precincts of the House of God we encounter failure, corruption, the feathering of nests, the lust for power, gossiping, under-the-counter dealing or narrow-mindedness? We should see these things as men fully conscious from our own experience of being ourselves sinners. When we see the sins of others it is so easy for us to forget that we are all-too-prone to pray, 'Lord, I thank you that I am not as one of these sinners here, like these self-righteous Pharisees in the Lord's House', in other words, that even in the pose of the humble Publican we can be ... Pharisees. If sin in the Church serves first of all to call to mind our own sinfulness, if it shocks us into remembering that *our* sins are the sins of the *Church* – whether we are priests or laymen, powerful or lowly people in the kingdom of God – that we all contribute our share to the Church's penury and want, and that this is the case even though our sins may not figure in any chronicle of the Church's scandals, then we have taken up the proper, that is the Christian, position to see the sins of the Church in their true light. Perhaps we will even then remonstrate, complain, struggle and attempt to better things, in so far as it lies within our power or falls to our duty; but first we will weep over our own sins by means of which we ourselves are crucifying the Son of God in his Church and obscuring the light of the gospel for the world. And we will bear the ignominy of the Church as our own and suffer it, for it is in truth our own, because – whether we want to or not – we belong to her and have sinned in her. So we will comfort ourselves with that divine consolation so incomprehensible to the children of the world, the consoling fact that he has given us – each of us – a Mother whose sin is surrounded by God's mercy, a Mother upon whom, in spite of her daily sins, God bestows holiness and grace, who can never place her confidence in her own power and strength but only in God's mercy, which is grace and not merit.

If we look at the sin of the Church in this light, our eyes will also be ever more ready to observe the hidden and the manifold glory and holiness of this our mother the Church. If we usually see little of this, then the reason is not that we are observing the world and the Church exactly, critically and realistically, but that our eye is that of a still self-centred sinner, that our eye is weak and blinkered. But once we have honestly wept over the sins of the Church and our own sins, if in this confession of our fault it has dawned on us that all true holiness is a miracle of God and a grace and not something to be presumptuously taken for granted, then after being washed clean in the tears of repentance our eye may be capable of seeing clearly the sacred miracle which God daily renews in his Church: that in spite of everything her hands are today as yesterday overflowing with grace, that the entreaty of the Spirit and his inexpressible groaning still ascend from her heart, that the angels of God still carry the prayers of the just in this Church like incense before the throne of the eternal God, that her voice still proclaims the Lord's Word faithfully and unflinchingly with the clear firmness and single-mindedness of love, that she conceives life for her children ever anew in her maternal womb, that the Spirit of God continually wakens men to holiness within her – children and aged, prophets and hidden worshippers, heroes and crusaders – that in her the Lord's act of redemption continually takes place to the end of time. And always we will be able to repeat again, even with tears – whether they be tears of repentance or of joy – the prayer, 'I believe in the Holy Church'.

The Scribes and the Pharisees – they exist not only in the Church but everywhere and in every guise – will always haul 'the woman' before the Lord once more, and secretly delighted that 'the woman' is after all not (thank God!) any better than they are themselves, accuse her: 'Lord, this woman has been discovered in the very act of adultery. What do you say?' And this woman will not be able to deny it. No, it is a scandal. And there are no extenuating circumstances. She thinks of her sins, because she has really committed them, and in doing so she forgets (how could a modest maid do other?) the hidden and the manifest glory of her sanctity. And so she has no intention of denying them. She is the poor Church of sinners. Her humility, without which she would not be holy, knows only of her guilt. And she stands before him whose bride she is, before him who has loved her and sacrificed himself for her in order to make her holy, before him who knows her sins better than any of her accusers. But he remains silent. He writes her sin in the sands of the world's history, which will soon be wiped out and her sin with it. He remains silent for a short while which to us seems to be thousands of years. And he passes judgement on this woman only through the silence of his love which pardons and absolves. Throughout the centuries new accusers stand beside 'this woman', and they always slip away again one by one, beginning with the eldest; for never has anyone been found who was himself without sin. And at the end the Lord will be alone with the woman. And then he will stand erect and look upon this prostitute, his bride, and ask her, 'Woman, where are your accusers? Has no one condemned you?' And she will answer with inexpressible repentance and humility, 'No one, Lord.' And she will be astonished and almost dismayed that no one has done so. But the Lord will come close to her and say, 'Then neither shall I condemn you.' He will kiss her forehead and murmur, 'My bride, holy Church.'

18

THE SINFUL CHURCH IN THE DECREES OF VATICAN II

I F we are to propose for our consideration a theology of the Church which is universal, exhaustive and fully developed in all directions, then there is one theme which can certainly not be omitted from it: the Church of sinners or, as we can also put it right away in order to bring out clearly the whole import and difficulty of the question, the sinful Church.

I

This topic must form part of any ecclesiology which considers its object in a thorough-going and balanced fashion, for that there are members of the Church who are sinners in the sense of living in a state of grave sin, that all the members of the Church,[1] if we exclude Mary, must truthfully

---

[1] That sinners are still members of the Church in a real sense has been substantially defined by the Council of Constance (cf. the errors of Hus and Wyclif, e.g. *DS* 1201, 1203, 1205, 1296, etc.). The history of this dogma is well-known. Movements have constantly reappeared which were in the last analysis 'enthusiastic', like Montanism, Donatism, the various heretical wandering preachers and sectaries of the twelfth century, the Cathari, Wyclif and Hus, which harboured the dream of an utterly pure Church from which are excluded all those who have lost baptismal grace. Cf. R. A. Knox, *Enthusiasm* (Oxford 1950); H. Grundmann, *Ketzergeschichte des Mittelalters* (Göttingen 1963). It was to such doctrines that the Council of Constance finally put an end. Since Constance, however, its doctrine has been handed on in the customary teaching on membership of the Church without any further refinement (in part even in the theology of the Reformers): the sinner in a state of grave sin is quite simply a member of the Church, provided that he has not lost the faith. In this way of viewing things the Church is seen exclusively under the aspect of her visible and social nature and of the historical form in which she appears and from this is determined what constitutes (full) membership in her; it is stated that the sinfulness (even public) of a member does not touch the constitutive marks of the Church in the dimension under consideration and therefore does not alter the structure of membership in her

and humbly[2] confess, 'Forgive us our trespasses',[3] is simply an explicit dogma of the Church.

But then the question arises, how this fact is to be related to another fact which is equally a dogma: the Church is the holy Church. How are these two facts reconcilable, without reducing the holiness of the Church which is professed in the Creed to the invulnerable holiness of her objective institutions, her teaching and her sacraments?

In fact this question was a very live issue in the ancient Church and in medieval theology and it had there a very troubled history. It is a long way from St Paul's declaration that the Church is made holy 'without spot or wrinkle' (Ep 5:27) to the more sober realisation of St Augustine in his fight against the moral pride of Pelagius and Pelagianism, who held the sinlessness of the normal Christian to be a possibility, that St Paul's phrase is applicable in the strict sense only to the heavenly Church in the final consummation.[4] Accordingly, in patristic times and in the Middle Ages one spoke without hesitation of the sinful Church, of the Church

---

and that membership itself. It is noteworthy that the new decree (no. 14, in emphasising the '*Spiritum Christi habentes*') penetrates more deeply and sees more clearly without denying or obscuring what the Council of Constance has defined: the fully adequate nature of the Church includes also her holy Spirit, interior grace, and therefore this must also be called the grace of the individual within her if *full* membership is to be adequately described; consequently the sinner is not simply in the same sense and to the same full extent a member of the Church as the justified person. Between the two modes of membership there exists the same relationship as between a '*merely* valid' and a 'valid *and* fruitful' sacrament. Even the merely valid sacrament is a true sacrament (otherwise it could never 'revive' in certain circumstances); but it is not what it should be and desires to be, namely the appearance of grace actually conferred. So the sinner's membership in the Church (as basic sacrament) is indeed valid, but it does not in fact confer what it signifies, the inner grace of the Church. Yet it remains true that the sinner is in a real sense a member of the Church.

[2] Cf. *DS* 1537.

[3] *ibid.*, Mt 6:12; cf. also *DS* 229.

[4] For the explanation of the text from Ephesians (5:27) given by the Latin Fathers (eschatological explanation), tradition, and modern Protestant and Catholic exegesis cf. especially H. Schlier, *Der Brief an die Epheser* (Düsseldorf 1957), p. 256 *sq.*, particularly p. 258, note 4. For the exposition of the text in patristic tradition cf. E. von Dobschütz, *Das Decretum Gelasianum in kritischem Text herausgegeben und untersucht*, Texte und Untersuchungen 38, 4 (Leipzig/Berlin 1912), p. 236 *sq.* To complete this cf. Hugo Rahner, *Symbole der Kirche: die Ekklesiologie der Väter* (Salzburg 1964), p. 394 *sq.* For the exposition of the text in the early Middle Ages cf. A. M. Landgraf, *Dogmengeschichte der Frühscholastik* IV, 2 (Regensburg 1956), pp. 48–99.

as the woman of sin, and this *not only* in the sense that the mercy of God has turned sinful humanity into the holy Church, that is of the sinful Church in so far as she is regarded in her origins, but also of the Church in so far as she *is* sinful *now*, of her sinfulness as a moral *condition*.

The Revelation of the New Testament at any rate knows that the reliability of a firm faith does not mean a false security. There is no fixation in grace. Even Peter denies the Lord. 'It would be incomprehensible, if such words and events were to have reference only to the acts by which the Church was founded and to have no further significance for her continuance once this had been secured. The New Testament never speaks of the assurances which have been granted to the Church of Christ without placing immediately next to them the threat of misuse, the possibility of defection. Nowhere is the spotlessness of the bride an already achieved fact which the bride only has to accept without troubling herself any further about it.'[5] The Pastoral Epistles already give evidence of defection and backsliding. No sacrament, no mission of the Spirit and no discernment of spirits is a final assurance of salvation, which comes from faith (cf. Heb 6:4 *sq.*).

The problem of the sinful Church is not, it is true, treated *expressis verbis* in the New Testament. There are sinful members of the Church (whether all are in this condition is not stated); it may remain questionable[6] whether the failure of a community can be regarded as the sin of the universal Church. The emphasis is placed – particularly in St Paul and St John – rather on the holiness and ideal figure of the Church. Historically it may be noticed that while we can recognise in the epistles of the New Testament a certain perplexity over the sinfulness which remains in spite of life in Christ, the whole force of the question of the 'sinful Church' as a whole in fact enters upon the scene (even conceptually) only later when in the third century the problem can no longer be by-passed owing to the beginning of an established Church. Yet the frequent parenesis reveals

---

[5] Hans Urs von Balthasar, 'Casta Meretrix' in *Sponsa Verbi: Skizzen zur Theologie* II (Einsiedeln 1961), pp. 203–305, here p. 218. For the Old Testament cf. p. 208 *sqq.*, for the New Testament p. 215 *sqq.*

[6] It remains questionable because we must here prescind from the teaching of St Paul according to which the 'local Church' is not a mere administrative district of the Church, but – and this even with a certain priority – the concrete appearance of the Church as such, so that for St Paul the question can scarcely even be asked whether predicates which are accepted without reservation as applicable to the local Church can be denied of the Church *simply as such*.

how much sinfulness there still was in the universal Church; certainly it is nowhere stated that the Church as such is not affected by it.

Neither are the statements in the New Testament about the holiness and perfection of the Church such as to exclude sinfulness altogether. All the statements about holiness have a strongly eschatological character: the texts about the 'holy People of God' (Ac 15:14; 18:10; Rm 9:25; 2 Co 6:16; Tt 2:14; Heb 4:9; 8:10; 10:30; 13:12; 1 P 2:9 *sq.*), about the 'holy remnant', the 'new Jerusalem', the 'Bride of the Lamb', the 'Temple of God', the 'royal priesthood' (Rm 9:6; Heb 8:8; Ga 4:26; 2 Jn 1:13; Rv 12:1 *sqq.*), and so on, describe the Church to a certain extent from the point of view of her final end and her consummation, from 'above', without thereby wanting to make any statement about the presence or absence of sin in the Church as it actually exists: this would rather be the task of a description from 'below'. This principle of interpretation is applicable at least in part to St Matthew. The Church is continually threatened from within (Mt 24:10 *sqq.*), by false teachers and pseudo-prophets, by the temptation to misuse her mission, something which Jesus was not spared when he was tempted (Mt 4:1 *sqq.*); God grants a place in his Church even to the wicked, the weeds can grow until the time of the harvest, in the fishing-net there are both good and bad fish (Mt 13:24; 13:36; 13:47), all of which is certainly intended to describe not only the relationship of the Church to the 'world' but also an empirical situation of the Church in herself, particularly since Matthew 16 and 18 refers to a penal process against sinful members of the community in which the 'binding' and 'loosing' presuppose a permanent relationship of the community to its sinful members, a relationship which does not exist in the same way towards those who are without (cf. 2 Co 2:5–11; 1 Co 5:1–13). Here as in St Matthew, the effect of Satan's working in the community is being described, as well as the fact that in the Church sin and holiness are interwoven in one texture and will be separated out only at the Judgement whereas now they are inseparable.

In St John and St Paul it is the ideal characteristics in the Church which are clearly brought to the fore. For the sinfulness of the Church perhaps the following can be cited. In general, the present is still the time of weakness, imperfection and temptation (1 Co 4:11 *sqq.* 13:9 *sqq.*; 2 Co 4:7 *sqq.*). In 1 Co 5:1–13, the community as a whole has failed in its duty in the case of the man guilty of incest, as St Paul expressly notes, because it has not cut itself off from the sinner. Quarrels and divisions are other faults which St Paul knows in the communities (1 Co 1:10 *sqq.*). At first sight it might be objected that the situation of 1 Co 5:1–13 cannot be pressed into use as supplying a biblical support for the question of the sinful Church, because the corrective for the community's sin is again an 'ecclesiastical court of appeal', namely the Apostle, who decides upon the definitive giving over of the sinner to Satan (1 Co 5:4 *sq.*; cf. 1 Tm 1:20), and in this way the purity of the community of salvation is restored. Yet precisely this act of the Apostle presupposes that the community as such must have known itself to be involved in the incest of the individual member, for St Paul knows that a judgement of separation such as he has made is quite unnecessary with regard to a heathen and that Christians can have uninhibited dealing with such a one because his behaviour does not affect the community as such (1 Co 5:9–13). In the case of the man guilty of incest the evil member is really in a religious and not merely sociological sense *in* the midst of the community and must therefore be 'got rid of'. His sin affects the community as such. On the other hand, the image of the Body, which is brought out here as in Ephesians, Colossians, Romans, Galatians, cannot be brought forward, as it often is, for the holiness of the Church; it signifies primarily the unity and harmony of the Church. Ephesians 4:15 *sqq.* speaks of a growth to the *pleroma* of Christ, therefore here the perfection of the Church is clearly being understood as an eschatological condition. In Hebrews our question is not immediately answered: while it is true that the people of God is a wandering people on the way and in a state of incompleteness in spite of its firm grip on the ὑπόστασις, the characteristic failing being ἀποστῆναι (Heb 3:12), yet at the same time the people, consisting of 'μέτοχοι χριστοῦ' (Heb 3:14), is no longer as a whole subject to rejection (Heb 10:24 *sq.*). But certainly individuals can lose their membership of God's people through 'sin' and thereby fall back into the state of Israel, the rebel people of God, the state of disobedience. Sin therefore here signifies exclusion from the community of salvation. How far this sin which arises within the ambit of the wandering people of God at the same time affects that people, is a question which is not expressly reflected upon any further.

In the seven letters to the Churches (Rv 2–3) the addressee is always the community as such, together with its bishop (2:7; 2:11, 17, 29; 3:6, 13, 22). Therefore here there is no difficulty in seeing the community itself as sinful, as needing conversion and as threatened by judgement.

The various scenes in the gospel involving sinful women have had from the beginning a great deal of significance for the Fathers of the Church in their view of the concrete, living form of the Church. The whore in Luke 7, the Samaritan woman of doubtful morals with her five or six husbands (Jn 4:17 sq.), Mary Magdalene[7] and in general the dealings of Jesus with publicans and sinners (cf. Mk 2:15–16; Mt 9:11; Mt 11:19 and parallel), the adulteress in John 8 and other words of Jesus (Mt 21:31 sq.) and parables (cf. Lk 15:11 sq.) remain for the Fathers signs of a serious insight into sin and calamity within the Church.

Harking back to the zeal of the Old Testament prophets for the purity of Israel as the people of God, there was an increase in accusation and consciousness of sin but also in astonishment at the wonder of forgiveness and of grace in the face of the faithlessness of the elect people of God in the New Testament. The threats uttered by the prophets against fallen Jerusalem, Sodom and Gomorrah, Tyre and Sidon, Nineveh, the laments and many other fragments from Isaiah, Jeremiah, Ezekiel, Hosea and also from the Song of Songs become symbols of the power and the misery of sin in the Church. Rahab and her house,[8] the marriage of Hosea with the prostitute as a symbolical representation of the people's breach of faith with their Lord,[9] the first act of infidelity by Eve[10] and especially the Jerusalem texts (Ezk 16; 23; Jr 4:29 sqq.) which sound particularly severe,[11] the fate of Thamar and other themes[12] become for the Fathers and for medieval theology warnings for the Church, warnings which are always called out with bitter insistence at times when the passionate zeal of spiritually aroused prophets and of resolute Church reformers protesting against the overwhelming abuses and wrongs of the Church issues a call to repentance.[13] It is true that often there is mention of the sinful provenance of the Church, of the men of the Church (and

---

[7] For a full exposition see U. Holzmeister, 'Die Magdalenenfrage in der kirchlichen Überlieferung' ZKT XLVI (1922), p. 402 sqq., 556 sqq. Cf. also von Balthasar, loc. cit., p. 235 sqq.

[8] Cf. the many texts in H. U. von Balthasar, loc. cit., pp. 222–239; Jean Daniélou, Sacramentum Futuri (Paris 1950), pp. 217–232.

[9] H. U. von Balthasar, loc. cit., pp. 239–251.

[10] loc. cit., pp. 251–257.

[11] loc. cit., pp. 257–280.

[12] loc. cit., pp. 280–289; for the Babylon theme p. 289 sqq.; for the Shulammite p. 297 sqq.

[13] Cf. Yves M.-J. Congar, Vraie et fausse réforme dans l'église, Unam Sanctam 20 (Paris 1950), p. 155 sqq., 170 sqq., 200 sqq., 217 sqq., 220, and especially the third part, p. 356 sq., 539 sqq.

therefore not so often immediately of the Church as such), for in spite of the most vigorous denunciation the spotlessness of the Church[14] is never in any doubt; yet the reference is precisely to such men as constitute the Church and officially represent her, and who are therefore closely bound up with her very essence.

We do not here intend to give an account of the investigations which have been made into this ecclesiology of the Fathers, so that it will be sufficient to refer to the works cited.[15] But even these few indications surely suffice to show that the vital interest in this theological theme grew noticeably less in late scholastic and post-Tridentine theology, although of course it was never denied that the Church must reckon sinful members as still part of her body.[16] In practice the Church was experienced as the established Church of a homogeneous Christian society. It was known and it was stated that many members of the Church were sinners and yet were still her members. But this fact which was admitted almost as a matter of course was not felt to be a vital problem of the Church herself. She herself was seen and praised as holy. If the question was asked why she is holy in spite of her sinful members (and will not just become holy at the end of time, as St Augustine and the majority of the Latin Fathers comforted themselves by saying), then on the one hand the 'objective' holiness of her institutions, her sacraments and her teaching were pointed out, and on the other – particularly in apologetics – it was emphasised with Vatican I[17] that the Church, as is evidenced by the number of her saints and martyrs and her beneficial influence on all spheres of society and culture, has always manifested and still manifests an inexhaustible and incomparable fruitfulness in all that is good; moreover, the Church through admonition, reproof, and all her means of grace works for the conversion of her sinful members.

Fundamentally even the encyclical of Pius XII '*Mystici Corporis*'

[14] Cf. H. Riedlinger, *Die Makellosigkeit der Kirche in den lateinischen Hohelied-Kommentaren des Mittelalters* (Münster 1958).

[15] Cf. also G. Teichtweier, *Die Sündenlehre des Origenes,* Studien zur Geschichte der kath. Moraltheologie VII (Regensburg 1958), pp. 58–67, p. 250 *sqq.*, p. 253 *sqq.*, p. 294 *sqq.*, p. 336 *sqq.*; for St Augustine cf. F. Hofmann, *Der Kirchenbegriff des hl. Augustinus in seinen Grundlagen und in seiner Entwicklung* (Munich 1933), pp. 233–257; M. Seybold, *Sozialtheologische Aspekte der Sünde bei Augustinus,* Studien zur Geschichte der katholischen Moraltheologie XI (Regensburg 1964).

[16] Cf. Pius XII, *Mystici Corporis, AAS* XXXV (1943), p. 238, 202. Cf. *DS* 1201, 1203, 1205 *sq.*, 1221, 2408, 2463, 2472–2478; also 1544, 1578, 1963 *sq.*

[17] Cf. *DS* 3013, 3014.

contents itself with this answer now become traditional. The Church – against the tendency to be found in St Augustine – is somehow, without its being noticed, 'hypostasised', she becomes almost like an independently existent 'entity', which stands as teacher and guide *over against* the people of God; she does not appear to *be* this people of God itself (even though structured hierarchically) in its actual state of pilgrimage. For this reason it is easy to conceive her and understand her as 'holy' without the question arising whether or not (and how far) the sins and failings of her members fall on herself and, if so, how this can be reconciled with her true holiness which is part of the substance of her creed. Much less is it asked in a really radical and explicit way whether and to what extent even her 'objective', 'institutional' holiness in teaching, sacrament and law suffers a kind of reaction from the sinfulness of her members, if these objective realities are viewed not merely in abstraction but in their historical reality and in their actual realisation by human beings in the Church. But traditional theology by applying the distinction between objective and subjective holiness[18] already places these questions in parentheses or else dismisses them as of no consequence because of its apologetic interest inclining to the '*notae ecclesiae*'[19] as the properties which make the Church *definitely* and *clearly* 'recognisable'. The immediate life of the Church has indeed preserved among believers, however nebulously, the consciousness of the constant need of cleansing and penitence in the Church. Evidence for this is given even today, for example, by the collects of the First Sunday in Lent and the Fifteenth Sunday after Pentecost.[20]

[18] Cf. e.g. J. Salaverri, 'De Ecclesia Christi' in *Sacrae Theologiae Summa* (Madrid 1962[5]), no. 1182–1192, 1204–1208, 1228–1263; 'Heiligkeit der Kirche', *LTK* V[2], 128–129 (F. Hofmann). For some further indications cf. K. Rahner, 'The Church of the Saints', *Theological Investigations* III (London & Baltimore 1967), pp. 91–104.

[19] For the concept of '*notae ecclesiae*' and its history, cf. the corresponding article by A. Kolping in *LTK* VII[2], 1044–1048, and especially the indications of J. Ratzinger in *LTK* VI[2], 181; for the history cf. G. Thils, *Les notes de l'église dans l'apologétique cath. depuis la Réforme* (Gembloux 1937), p. 287 *sqq.*; B. Duda, *Joannis Stoiković de Ragusio O.P. (†1443) doctrina de cognoscibilitate ecclesiae* (Rome 1958); A. Lang, *Der Auftrag der Kirche*, Fundamentaltheologie Bd 2 (Munich 1954), p. 154 *sqq.* It would be the task of a further investigation to decide whether the Constitution on the Church also gives in this matter at least implicitly some indications for new perspectives on the '*notae*' or '*conditiones ecclesiae*'.

[20] Cf. *Missale Romanum*, or. dom. XV post Pent.: '*Ecclesiam tuam, Domine, miseratio continuata mundet et muniat; et quia sine te non potest salva consistere, tuo semper munere gubernetur . . .*'

In short, having examined the facts of the case and the history of the Church's dogmas we find the question of the Church of sinners to be a real one, one which has not been fully worked out or even today found its proper place sufficiently clearly in normal ecclesiology. And yet this question would seem to have an existential-religious importance for the life of the individual and of the Church as such. That the guilt of the individual (whether in the ranks of the shepherds or of the flock) has an importance for the *Church* and affects her being, is scarcely a topic which appears in the average teaching about sin in theology and in preaching, and yet it is not merely a theme of the *oldest* tradition beginning with scripture: without this doctrine of the sin and the guilt of the individual in its significance for the Church the whole history of penance with its many ramifications from its roots in the Old Testament and the New Testament right into the late Middle Ages becomes quite incomprehensible.

This theme can and must become of really wide-ranging importance in the religious life of the individual and in the 'awakening of the Church in souls'. And how should the consciousness of the Church as *'ecclesia semper reformanda'*[21] be really alive in all its sharpness and depth (where it is a question of a permanent *metanoia* of the Church and not merely of an adaptation 'to the circumstances of the age' of the liturgy, law and pastoral practice), if one instinctively lives only in the consciousness that the individual persons in the Church could be at times imperfect and even sinful but in the case of the Church everything is always all right, because she is without any doubt 'holy' and no shadow of the shortcomings of her members can ever fall upon her?

This subject has also a great ecumenical importance. Protestant theology repeatedly complains that Catholic ecclesiology proceeds too much 'from above', that it sees the Church merely as an objective institution, an 'institute of salvation', and then glorifies this Church in a Luciferian *theologia gloriae*, instead of placing her, as the community of sinners which constantly flees anew from her ever renewed sin to the pure grace of God constantly re-actuated and which is only thus and in so far as she does this truly the Church, in a *theologia crucis* under the cross so that there she may not boast of her glory but acknowledge her sin and thereby

---

[21] Cf. Y. M.-J. Congar, O.P., *Sainte Église*, Unam Sanctam 41 (Paris 1963): 'Comment l'église sainte doit se renouveler sans cesse?', pp. 131–154 (with many references to the witness of the Fathers and tradition).

alone be 'holy'. Of course a Catholic answer to this 'protest' against a true or a supposed Catholic doctrine of the holiness of the Church, in order to be an adequate answer, has involved the whole Catholic doctrine of the relationship of nature and grace, of the meaning of grace, of the nature of justification, of the truth and falsity of the Lutheran principle '*simul justus et peccator*',[22] of the relationship in Christian existence and in the Church between what is already present and the eschatological reality of the future. But the question how far in our doctrine we really take account of the pilgrim state of the sinful *ecclesia crucis* while acknowledging the holy *ecclesia gloriae*[23] and how far we treat it seriously in our Church life is a weighty question directed to us by Protestant theology. It is for this reason that our topic is also of eminent ecumenical importance.

II

Now the Constitution on the Church of the Second Vatican Council is not, and does not attempt to be, an absolutely complete ecclesiology. But neither is it on the other hand a Conciliar document which in order to repel a new heresy singles out one point or another to clarify and defend it. It discusses the Church in general and attempts to give a reasonably balanced and in some way adequate treatment of the nature of the Church. This is immediately evident from the whole structure of the decree and its sequence of chapters, and may also be deduced from the pastoral aim which the decree sets itself, which can only be achieved by a certain completeness in its treatment of the topic. For this reason it is not an unfair question, or one making from the outset too great a demand on the document, if we attempt to ascertain what it has to say on the 'Church of sinners'.

In the first place, we must note quite simply, merely pointing out a fact and not making a complaint, that the Constitution on the Church does not treat this question with the explicit clarity, intensity and detail which one could perhaps have expected. This topic did not give rise to a single

---

[22] Cf. R. Hermann, *Luthers These 'Gerecht und Sünder zugleich'* (Darmstadt 1960²); W. Joest, *Gesetz und Freiheit* (Göttingen 1961³); R. Kösters, 'Luthers These "Gerecht und Sünder zugleich"', *Catholica* XVIII (1964), pp. 48–77; 193–217: (a review and critique of R. Hermann with many bibliographical references).

[23] A notable attempt at a composite view of glory and cross in the image of the Church is to be found in Hugo Rahner, *Die Kirche, Gottes Kraft in menschlicher Schwäche* (Freiburg 1957).

paragraph, or even to any series of weighty principles. We will attempt to show in what follows, however, that the document does not remain completely silent on this topic, that it does in fact offer some very note-worthy points of departure for a theology of sin in the Church as such. But it can certainly not be said that this question is treated systematically, that it emerges clearly as a 'concern' of the authors of the decree or of the Council, or that the ecumenical importance of the question is made evident in what is said. (It might even be said that the parenetic impulse of the texts, if one may coin this phrase, is in *almost* every case a move-ment from what is good to what is better in virtue, not from sin and its recognition to an ever renewed reaching out towards pardoning grace, which would be possible even on the supposition of an interior justifica-tion, since the justified man always remains a sinner having need of an always new forgiveness by God.) It is in order for us to make this observation if only because in the Council a few Fathers in fact wished for more on this topic, although their suggestion did not make sufficient headway.[24] This fact is perhaps sufficient to show that our observation is not made merely on the basis of an entirely subjective point of view.

On the other hand the fact of a certain deficiency is also understandable; the Constitution was never conceived *from the outset* as the balanced and systematically complete summary of a whole ecclesiology. It grew slowly in an almost accidental way by filling out and adding to the pre-Conciliar schema, which at the beginning after all only set out to treat certain particular topics which were held to be of contemporary interest by that Roman theology which was primarily responsible for it. Furthermore, a

---

[24] These voices did not only make themselves heard among the Fathers in the general emphasis on avoidance by the Church of every form of 'triumphalism'. Council Fathers like Bishop Stefan László (Eisenstadt, Austria) and others expressly demanded that this theme should be dealt with and put forward draft texts. Cf. László's speech, 'Sin in the Holy Church of God' in Y. Congar, etc. (Eds), *Council Speeches of Vatican II* (London & New York 1964), pp. 29–31. It is partly H. Küng's influence which can be recognised here, who already during the time of preparation for the Council drew attention to this subject; cf. e.g. his *Justification: the Doctrine of Karl Barth and a Catholic Reflection* (London 1965), [the German original of which was published in 1957]; *The Council and Reunion* (London 1962), pp. 34–52. Cf. also for this question, besides Congar's work already cited (note 21), Ch. Journet, *L'Église du Verbe incarné*, 2 vols (Bruges 1941, 1951), vol. I, XIII *sq.*; vol. II, 395 *sq.*, particularly 893–894; H. de Lubac, *Katholizismus als Gemeinschaft* (Einsiedeln/Köln 1943), p. 61 *sqq.* The author may perhaps be permitted to draw attention to one or two modest attempts of his own, cf. especially 'The Church of Sinners', reprinted above in this volume.

more penetrating treatment of this topic would not easily have been able to avoid the question whether and in what sense one could speak not only of a Church of sinners, that is of a Church in which there are those guilty of grave sin and in which all others too are in a certain sense sinners because of 'venial sins' (for example, according to the mind of St Augustine), but whether in fact one could also speak, indeed must speak, of a *sinful Church*, that is to say whether one could and must say this *explicitly*. Considering how matters stand or stood in contemporary theology and especially in the Theological Commission where the decree was elaborated, it would have been too much to hope for that a sufficiently large -majority could have been reached in this question without great difficulty. The awareness of many of the Fathers of the immediate theological and mediate ecumenical and pastoral significance of the problem was simply insufficiently developed for this. And in the traditional ecclesiology of the past century this topic was also not far enough evolved (beyond the doctrine that sinners are members of the Church) as to make it appear to a majority of the Theological Commission or of the Council Fathers self-evidently a topic to be treated expressly. This suffices to explain the fact of the Constitution's reserve regarding this question.

Nevertheless, the decree does not avoid the question completely, even though it does not present it all together in one place as a unified continuous statement. It does after all say so much that it offers to future theology plenty of incentive for development. The following considerations are intended to bring out into the open these possibilities contained in the decree itself.

III

To begin with, let us point out the framework which is in fact given in the Constitution for the doctrine of the Church of sinners: the doctrine of the pilgrim Church. The theme of the Church on the march, still making her pilgrimage through the history of the world and not having here any lasting abode, and so while in this state still bearing the 'form of the world' (no. 48), runs through the whole decree. It is indeed true that the decree in bringing out this aspect of the Church is thinking of her historical character and above all of the fact that she is and must be the Church of poverty, humility, temptation, suffering and persecution, following in this way her crucified Lord. None the less she is clearly seen as *ecclesia peregrinans, ecclesia viatorum*, in contrast to the Church of the eternal consummation. And this already implies that the Church is not simply a heavenly entity passing through history as a stranger and untouched by it, not sharing in its life and its sorrow. If in the decree the concept of the people of God with whom God has made a covenant rightly stands in the foreground, almost being preferred to the concept of the 'mystical Body of Christ', and so becomes something of a guide-line for the whole of Conciliar ecclesiology, then with this representation of the Church as the community called together by God room is made or can be made from the beginning for the idea of the Church of sinners much more clearly than if the Church had been seen from the beginning *only* as an 'institute of salvation', which will certainly look after men for their healing, but which is not herself identified with her community (whereas for every individual she is *as* this hierarchically ordered People of God, which is the *fruit* of salvation, also the *means* of salvation).

Within this framework it is in the first place clearly stated that sinners still belong to the Church. The question whether an apostate from the faith still belongs to the Church in the same sense as the believing sinner is passed over. As already stated, in no. 14 the grace of justification is seen also in its significance for incorporation into the Church.[25] In any case, no. 14 declares clearly that there are men who are incorporated into the

[25] Provided (a) that the '*Spiritum Christi habentes*' is understood of the grace of justification; and (b) the '*Ecclesiae societati*' is taken not reduplicatively but specificatively, or that these two possibilities remain in the balance. If the Church is intended *precisely as* the visible society, then of course there can be no question of the grace of justification being a constitutive element of incorporation into this society as such, and the '*Spiritum Christi habentes*' is only specificative: not the reduplicative qualification of the subject of the whole sentence ('*Illi . . .*'). But if '*Ecclesiae societati*' means simply the Church, which is a society (specificative), then the '*Spiritum Christi habentes*' can and must be taken as one of the constitutive elements of 'full' incorporation ('*plene incorporantur*'). The ambiguity of the sentence cannot be avoided by an appeal to the '*plene*', for we can conceive of both a 'full' incorporation into the Church as society and a 'full' incorporation into the Church as a society filled with the *Spirit*, the two of which are not simply identical. If *every* sin did not involve a certain rejection of the Church by the sinner it could not be said that through the Sacrament of Penance a '*reconciliari cum Ecclesia*' (no. 11) is brought about. Cf. in connection with these thoughts K. Rahner, 'Forgotten Truths concerning the Sacrament of Penance' in *Theological Investigations* II (London & Baltimore 1963), pp. 135–174 (with further bibliographical references).

Church but are not justified (*in caritate non perseverans*). It is then explained, making use of an 'Augustinian' expression, that they belong '*corpore*' but not '*corde*'[26] to the Church. It is therefore not overlooked that an incorporation which is absolute and in every respect *full* does imply the grace of the Church. And so at any rate it is stated that there are sinners in the Church, in 'her bosom' (*in Ecclesiae sinu*). By the fact therefore that a man is an enemy of God, devoid of grace, given up to the slavery of sin and to the power of the Devil,[27] he does not cease to be 'incorporated' in the society of the Church (*Societas Ecclesiae*).

It is of course true that of itself the above-mentioned '"*corpore*" *quidem, sed non "corde*" (*in ecclesiae sinu*) *remanere*' permits of many further interpretations.[28] But if one takes into account all aspects of the whole decree and the theological tradition immediately underlying it, one must objectively say that it is a question here of a genuine incorporation which has a positive value for salvation.[29] One might also say that it has the same kind of positive significance for salvation as belongs to a sacrament which has been validly but unfruitfully received (especially baptism), which ought not to have been received in this way, but which can 'revive' and in fact brings with it an obligation and inner dynamism to being revived. This is already involved in the statement that even in the case of the sinner (who is also included in the intention of the whole principle) there is given the *vinculum sacramentorum* (cf. no. 14).[30] But

---

[26] St Augustine, *Bapt. c. Donat.* V, 28, 39 (*PL* XLIII, 197): '*Certe manifestum est id quod dicitur, in Ecclesia intus et foris, in corde, non in corpore cogitandum.*' Cp. also the parallel texts from St Augustine cited in note 12 of the second chapter of the Constitution with the formulation used in the text itself.

[27] Cf. *DS* 1668.

[28] In St Augustine it often has almost the meaning of mere appearance, of something fictitious: chaff on the threshing-floor of the Church. Cf. for this the above-named study by F. Hofmann, *Der Kirchenbegriff des hl. Augustinus* (Munich 1933); J. Ratzinger, *Volk und Haus Gottes in Augustins Lehre von der Kirche* (Munich 1954); H. U. von Balthasar, *Augustinus: Das Antlitz der Kirche* (Einsiedeln 1955²). For the continuing existence of similar formulas among the early Scholastics, cf. A. M. Landgraf (see note 4 above), pp. 60–63, 72, 84, 88, 99.

[29] This can be said because this 'incorporation' still signifies a connection with Christ, at least through the *compago visibilis*, through the *vincula professionis fidei, sacramentorum et ecclesiastici regiminis ac communionis* (no. 14).

[30] This statement can of course raise the question whether the baptised person who has become an unbeliever does not also still possess *this* '*vinculum sacramentorum*' and at least in the case of merely 'internal' disbelief, that is disbelief which does not become socially obvious, still have the *vinculum professionis fidei* (which is something

all this implies conversely that these sinners co-determine the 'quality' (if we may use this word) of the Church herself. They still belong after all – and from the point of view of social life even '*plene*' – to the corpus of the Church (*incorporantur*) and are members of the people of God marshalled in the Catholic Church. The Church does not only stand over against them like an institute of salvation which, while remaining itself quite untouched, regrets that its care did not have more success, but must regard these sinners as a part of herself, as her members.[31] Actually, then, the decree recognises the *fact* that the Church is a sinful Church and not merely that in her (the holy institute of salvation) there are sinners (as object of her ministrations). It is true that the Constitution avoids the expression 'sinful Church'. But it brings out the fact behind the expression, namely that the Church is herself affected by the sins of her members. How exactly this effect upon the Church is to be theologically conceived is a matter about which the decree has nothing to say, so that we must return to this question towards the end of the present article. But that according to the Constitution the Church is affected in this way there can be no doubt. In the first place, it is expressly stated that the sins of Christians 'wound' the Church ('*peccando vulnerare*'). Of course of itself this could be interpreted as meaning that the wounding of the Church consists formally in the (social, public, etc.) *consequences* of sin which are to be found in the Church, not that the Church herself in a *certain* sense is the subject of these sins on the part of her members; in other words that she is only damaged by sin but does not thereby herself become sinful. But it is expressly stated that the *Church* is '*semper purificanda*' (no. 8), that she '*poenitentiam et renovationem semper prosequitur*' (no. 8), that she '*seipsam renovare non desinat*' (no. 9), which must surely at least

---

else than faith itself) and so is still incorporated into the Church just as much as a mere sinner. It seems that with the majority of theologians we can answer this question without any difficulty in the affirmative, without deviating from the decisions reached in no. 14, because this passage does not concern itself with that question. Cf. K. Rahner, 'Membership of the Church according to the Teaching of Pius XII's Encyclical "Mystici Corporis Christi"' in *Theological Investigations* II (London & Baltimore 1963), pp. 1–88, esp. p. 13 *sq.*, and p. 8, note 8.

[31] How far the Constitution on the Church gives us here as in other connections a deeper insight into the significance for salvation of the Church in general, and how far this picture of the Church differs from patristic and medieval ecclesiology and from that which dominated the nineteenth century, would have to be the subject of a special investigation.

include a *moral* renewal,[32] since the whole context makes it clear that the Church by this means is and remains the faithful bride worthy of the Lord. But the Church cannot be the *subject* of her *own* renewal and purification if she was or is not also in the first place and in a certain sense[33] the subject of sin and guilt. It would be a most arbitrary form of hermeneutics to maintain that 'Church' here signifies all of a sudden merely the average mass of individual believers. 'Church' means here what it means everywhere else: simply the Church. She is '*in proprio sinu peccatores complectens*' (no. 8) and therefore has not only external but also internal '*afflictiones et difficultates*' (no. 8), even in the same way ('*pariter*'). It would be quite arbitrary to want to exclude precisely moral afflictions and difficulties.[34]

Quite in accordance with this it is said in no. 65 that the *Church* only in Mary '*ad perfectionem iam*[35] *pertingit, quae est sine macula et ruga*'. So the Augustinian interpretation of Ephesians 5:25–27 is in a certain way taken up and completed here: the *Church* herself as being in a pilgrim state has (apart from Mary) still the '*macula et ruga*'; believers (*Christifideles*)[36] must still '*peccatum devincere*' (no. 65); '*incessanter renovemur*' (no. 7, cf. Ep 4:23). On this basis one can without hesitation understand

---

[32] It is significant that the charisms also serve the '*renovatio ecclesiae*', as is made clear in no. 12. The permanent necessity for the charisms is thus implicitly presupposed.

[33] This sense must be harmonised with the fact that (a) only physical substances which are free subjects can be the subjects of faults and moral renewal in the strictest sense, and (b) the Church is '*indefectibiliter sancta*' (cf. no. 36). It is always to be kept in mind that if, because of (a), one refuses to admit this wider but true and religiously important sense of 'subject of sin and conversion', it will also be impossible to conceive of the Church as the subject of (subjective) holiness, which is something that must be maintained by reason of the whole theology of the New Testament, the Creed and the rest of tradition.

[34] The '*proprio*' in the passage just quoted from no. 8, '*in proprio sinu peccatores complectens*', is emphasised because it is stated by contrast with Christ who – himself without sin – came to blot out the sins of the people. Cf. also no. 42, where it is stated of *holy* people that they are to be found '*in sinu*' of the Church, which clearly presupposes that their holiness is of some significance for the holiness of the Church.

[35] With this '*iam*' the reference must be to the privilege of Mary's complete sinlessness while she was on earth (*DS* 1516, 1573, 2800 *sqq.*), because in heaven the Church is '*sine macula et ruga*' also in the other saints.

[36] The transition in this sentence (cf. no. 65) from '*Ecclesia*' (first clause) to '*Christifideles*' (second clause) is noteworthy. Clearly the redactors of the text here shrank from saying openly that the *Church* still has to conquer the sin within her and so grow to holiness.

the following of the Church *herself,* where it is said, '*Cum vero in multis offendimus omnes* (cf. Jn 3:2), *misericordiae Dei jugiter egemus atque orare quotidie debemus: "Et dimitte nobis debita nostra"* (Mt 6:12)' (no. 40). It is in a way regrettable that the footnotes in the text[37] do not refer to the Council of Carthage of 418[38] and to the Council of Trent.[39] For these texts would really be '*loci classici*' compared to those in fact referred to. Nevertheless, the notes on this do draw attention to St Augustine (besides Pius XII); it was this anti-Pelagian conviction 'we are *all* sinners' of St Augustine and of the Council of Carthage (looking back to St Paul in Rm 3:23; 5:18, etc.) which was the reason for St Augustine's declaring the Church herself to be sinful and promising her the perfection 'without spot or wrinkle' only in eternity. But if the Church herself can be seen as being in a certain sense the subject of the guilt of her members, then it also becomes intelligible how she can be understood as the subject of '*tentationes*' (no. 9: '*per tentationes vero . . . procedens ecclesia*'), where the '*tentationes*' must be understood as temptations to sin and not as mere 'difficulties' and 'trials', as they would otherwise be indistinguishable from the '*tribulationes*' named in the same sentence. This being so, it has an ecclesiological significance and is a statement not merely referring to the individual or perhaps even understood individualistically, when it is said of the lay-people in the Church that they have the duty '*regnum peccati in se devincere*' (no. 36), and when the bishops themselves too are regarded as still having the duty '*mores ad bonum commutare*' (no. 26). Precisely in connection with this service towards the erring and ignorant brother is adduced the fact that the Shepherd, who has himself been taken from among men is clothed with weakness (cf Heb 5:1 *sq.*).

Admittedly the question is not further discussed how the leaders in the Church not only can themselves be sinners but in fact are all such in the Augustinian sense,[40] and above all how this sinfulness inevitably, even though not necessarily in the same degree, has its effect upon the whole exercise of their office and how in this way the Church almost necessarily even in her official sphere is 'sinful' in a quite specific sense: the decree does not go any further into these questions or develop them.

---

[37] Cf. note 3 of Chapter V (no. 40): references to St Augustine and to '*Mystici Corporis*'.

[38] Cf. *DS* 229–230 (can. 7 and 8).

[39] Cf. *DS* 1537 (Decree on Justification, chapter 11).

[40] Cf. *DS* 229–230, 1573.

Since it goes beyond the subject matter of this essay, we only briefly point out the fact that the decree again and again brings into prominence the power of the Church constantly to overcome the sin existing within her, a power given her by God in his Spirit through Christ. Her members can and must fight against the Prince of this World (no. 48), they must transform the world which after all also exists in the Church (cf. no. 31; 35), they must conquer sin in themselves (no. 65). In the Church there exists moreover the *ministerium reconciliationis* (cf. no. 28) and the permanent making present and applying of the one, expiatory sacrifice of the cross of Christ (cf. no. 3; 28).

In much the same way the doctrine of the Church of sinners is found explicitly or implicitly in other documents of the Second Vatican Council. In the Decree on Ecumenism (no. 4)[41] it is admitted that for the separated brethren and for the world the face of the Church is 'less' resplendent because of the lack of Christian zeal and so the growth of God's kingdom is retarded. The Church must every day be 'purified and renewed' until she can present herself to Christ at the end 'glorious and without spot or wrinkle'.[42] Therefore there is no hesitation in addressing the Church herself as the subject of purification and renewal, even if that *from which* she must be purified is indicated in somewhat too careful and mild a way (as a want of that *'fervor'* which gives rise to the duty of striving after *'perfectio christiana'*). But in so far as Ephesians 5:27 is interpreted in the Augustinian way, an indication is also given that the want of 'zeal' and the necessity to strive after 'perfection' have as their reason the sin within the Church. In no. 6 there is talk of the *'renovatio Ecclesiae'*,[43] of a *'perennis reformatio'*[44] of which the Church *qua humanum terrenumque institutum* has constant need, in which is expressly included a reformation *'in moribus'*. But this necessarily involves as the *terminus a quo* a state of sin from which the *Church* must be 'purified' in a permanent 'reformation'. This becomes all the clearer when it is emphasised in this decree that this reformation must begin with the *'interior conversio'*[45] to a *'novitas mentis'* (no. 7).[46]

It is true that a certain timidity becomes evident when the decree explicitly speaks of the sins against unity and of the prayer for forgiveness,

[41] *AAS* LVII (1965), p. 95.
[42] *loc. cit.*   [43] *loc. cit.* p. 96.   [44] *loc. cit.* p. 97.
[45] In no. 8 (*loc. cit.*, p. 98) the expression *'cordis conversio'* is used.
[46] *loc. cit.*, p. 97.

where the subject of the sin and of the prayer for forgiveness is 'we' (no longer the Church!) (*ibid.*). Similarly in no. 3[47] the decree only speaks of the fact that the separations from the Catholic Church took place '*non sine hominum utriusque partis culpa*'. Hence there is fault also on the Catholic side, but it is expressly laid at the door only of her 'men', which does not of course exclude a fault on the part of the Church herself, particularly since the persons immediately concerned in *this* fault are the officials of the Church who act juridically in the name of the Church, so that their fault affects the Church as such in a very palpable way.

IV

On the other hand, according to the Constitution on the Church, the Church is '*indefectibiliter sancta*' (no. 39) and therefore is repeatedly called with the Creed simply '*Ecclesia sancta*' (no. 5:8; 26:32 etc.),[48] '*sponsa immaculata*' (no. 6), '*gens sancta*' (no. 9), '*digna sponsa*' (no. 9), '*sacerdotium sanctum*' (no. 10), '*populus Dei sanctus*' (no. 12). How the Church can be *at the same time* the sinful Church of sinners *and* the holy Church is a matter which the Constitution does not really consider explicitly. Certainly the Augustinian solution alone does not suffice, according to which it is the Church in eternity which will be holy 'without spot or wrinkle' and this is applied by way of anticipation to the Church without qualification. It does not suffice, because in this document it is to the earthly Church that the quality of holiness is ascribed.[49] Clearly the meaning of the Constitution is not satisfied by the 'objective' sanctity of her institutions and doctrines either. For reference is repeatedly made to the 'subjective' holiness of her members in this context. The whole of chapter V is evidence of this. But the functions of chapters IV and VI, too, can only be meaningful within the context of the whole decree if the necessity of this 'subjective' holiness is recognised. Hence the Church must be 'subjectively' at once 'holy' and sinful. But how and in what sense this is possible is a question which is not considered in any more precise detail.

[47] *loc. cit.*, p. 93.
[48] Accordingly the document speaks of the '*sanctitas Ecclesiae*' (cf. nos. 39, 42, 47, 48) and not just of the holiness of individual Christians; cf. also the expression '*sanctitas Populi Dei*' (no. 40).
[49] Cf. for the exegesis of this the bibliography cited in note 4 above.

It is stated that the Church on earth has a 'vera *sanctitas, licet imperfecta*' (no. 48). One could be led from this into thinking simply that the same is true of her holiness as is true of the holiness of the justified individual: he is truly holy through the grace of justification but his holiness is still in danger and has still to find its fulfilment and perfection.[50] This holinèss must still be 'actualised', as it is expressly put in no. 40. One could add that the decree furthermore explicitly presupposes that there are in the Church as a matter of fact such justified persons, even persons in a state of great perfection, as chapters V and VI presume and expressly state (cf. e.g. no. 42).

But by establishing that there are in the Church both sinners and just (even perhaps of great perfection), are the two statements really reconciled? The possibility and reality of the reconciliation of these two would become more apparent if one were to take into account that in Mary at least the earthly Church has already reached that '*perfectio*' by which she is 'without spot or wrinkle' (cf. no. 65). But a simultaneous assertion of these two propositions is clearly insufficient. No matter how correct, it would be an evasion in the face of the particular structure of our question. The solution would be too hasty. For the '*indefectibilitas*' of the holiness of the Church (no. 39) does not belong to the holiness of the individual (even with regard to his 'ontological' and subjectively still imperfect holiness).[51] Therefore this '*indefectibilitas*' of the Church's holiness has not yet been made intelligible.

But the very concept clearly signifies that the relationship of sin and holiness in the Church is not the merely external, dialectical one of the juxtaposition of sin and holiness (distributed among different members), but that the holiness of the Church has a precedence over her sinfulness, so that in the eyes of God the ultimately determining predicate of the Church is not her sinfulness but the holiness effected in her by God's eschatological action, the sanctification bestowed upon her by God in Christ which constantly triumphs over sin. For this reason it is impossible simply to transfer to the relationship between the sinfulness and holiness of the Church the relationship between sin and holiness as in a Catholic sense it can be said to exist in the justified individual whom one can also

---

[50] Cf. for the New Testament H. Küng, 'Rechtfertigung und Heiligung nach dem Neuen Testament' in M. Roesle and O. Cullmann, *Begegnung der Christen, Festschrift für Otto Karrer* (Frankfurt 1960), pp. 249–270.

[51] Cf. *DS* 1541, 1544, 1573, etc.

call *'simul justus et peccator'*.[52] Nowhere is it more apparent that the essence of the Church is not merely the sum of her individual members. But it is precisely at this point that the decisive problem is situated, for this proper 'essence' of the Church must not be allowed to give rise to a false 'hypostasisation' of the Church.

But the decree does not reflect on any of these exact distinctions. One can only refer to no. 48, where there is at least a point of departure for the solution of this more precise problem. Through Christ, his incarnation, his cross and his glorification, the eschatological situation is already present. *'Iam (ergo) fines saeculorum ad nos pervenerunt* (cf. 1 Co 10:11) *et renovatio mundi* irrevocabiliter *est* constituta *atque in* hoc *saeculo* reali *quodam modo anticipatur: etenim Ecclesia iam in terris* vera *sanctitate licet imperfecta insignitur'*. But this means in effect:[53] through Christ and his victory upon the cross there is given to redeemed humanity as a whole, and therefore above all to the Church, not only the *possibility* of salvation, but by his grace which is *in fact victorious* there is given and manifested the *realisation* of this possibility. Because the eschatological victory of Christ has brought it about and made it manifest that the *efficacious* (and not merely sufficient) grace of God and Christ is not only possible but is in fact given, and this to the end of time, the Church as a whole,[54] through this predestination of efficacious grace made visible in Christ, is preserved

[52] For *'simul iustus et peccator'* cf. the bibliography cited in note 22 above. For Luther cf. the critical work of W. Joest, 'Paulus und das lutherische Simul Iustus et Peccator' in *Kerygma und Dogma* I (1965), pp. 269–320; for a possible Catholic understanding of this formula cf. H. Küng, *Justification: the Doctrine of Karl Barth and a Catholic Reflection* (London 1965); H. U. von Balthasar, *Karl Barth: Darstellung und Deutung seiner Theologie* (Cologne 1962²), p. 378 *sqq.* (Cf. also the literature cited there by R. Grosche, A. Kirchgässner, H. Volk); cf. K. Rahner, 'Justified and Sinner at the Same Time' in this volume p. 218 *sqq.*

[53] To bring out this connection of subject-matter it would have been more appropriate to make use here (no. 48) of the expression 'indefectibilis *sanctitas*' (no. 39), for it is not just an imperfect though true holiness such as already existed, for example, under the Old Covenant which is the special characteristic of the Church's eschatological situation, but the indefectibility of this holiness (parallel to the charism of indefectibility in truth of the Church's witness as an institutional entity, which also did not exist in the Old Testament, which did not know or possess an 'infallible magisterium').

[54] Naturally nothing is stated thereby about the individual member of the Church as such. He can suffer the loss of grace and normally does not know whether he will persevere in grace (cf. *DS* 1534, 1540, 1541, 1563 *sq.*). Cf. a few remarks on this by K. Rahner, 'Justified and Sinner at the Same Time', above p. 218 *sqq.* Cf. note 52 above.

by God, antecedently to the actual behaviour of her members, from falling away from the grace and promises of God in any fundamental and essential way. Hence the Church is (even subjectively) 'indefectibiliter *sancta*'. For this reason the relationship of the Church as a whole to justice and sin is not the relationship of a neutral freedom or indifference to two possibilities which are, as it were 'objectively' (from her point of view), on the same level. She is as a whole, from the human point of view, one who is utterly incapable by her own power of performing any saving act or of reaching a state of justice,[55] who is therefore in this sense also sinful; and she is by God's prevenient, efficacious grace to which she has been absolutely predestined one who has been raised to true holiness, even though on earth this divinely bestowed holiness still has to grow. This predestination by God of efficacious grace for the Church as a whole has already superseded man's freedom, without destroying or damaging it, and this has been made manifest in Christ's victory: therefore for the Church, which after all has been brought into being by God and not by men, it is the predicate of holiness which is the decisive and determining factor as opposed to her sinfulness.

Yet the appellation 'the Church of sinners' has a profound meaning. Not only every individual in the Church must truthfully and humbly confess himself a sinner,[56] but also the Church, for she is the community of these sinners. As such a community of sinful men redeemed and organised by Christ (the fruit of salvation), she is also the instrument by means of which God effects the salvation of the individual (the means of salvation). She would not be the really existing people of God but a purely ideal entity, possessing an almost mythological character, if one were to think that the sinfulness of her members did not also determine herself. Only if the Church recognises herself to be the Church of sinners will she be permanently convinced[57] of the fact, and aware of the full

---

[55] Cf. *DS* 1541 *sqq.*, etc.

[56] Cf. *DS* 229, 230; 1537.

[57] Consciousness of the necessity for such constant renewal need no longer be rejected as suspect since the highest authority in the Church has himself made this element the matter of his concern: cf. the allocution of Paul VI '*ad Emmos Patres Cardinales, Exmos Praesules, Revmos Praelatos ceterosque Romanae Curiae Officiales*' in *AAS* LV (1963), pp. 793–800, e.g. '... *ma trova la Curia stessa all'avanguardia di quella perenna riforma, di cui la Chiesa stessa, in quanto istituzione umana e terrena, ha perpetuo bisogno*' (p. 797); cf. the talk about '*perenne rinnovamento*' (*ibid.*); cf. also Julius Cardinal Döpfner, *Die Reform als Wesenselement der Kirche* (Würzburg 1965).

force of the obligation it entails, that she has a constant need of being cleansed, that she must always strive to do penance and achieve inner reform (cf. no. 8). Otherwise all demands for reform will become merely presumptious prescriptions and inefficacious desires all of which, while they can perfect the legal system of an institution and develop a pastoral technique on the grand scale, are not in touch with real life, true faith, and the human Church. Once it is kept clearly in mind that the Church on earth is *always* the Church of sinners, then it becomes intelligible how and why she is the holy Church: namely by the grace of God, which alone does not permit the Church as a whole to fall away from God's grace and truth and so makes her indefectibly holy. This grace operates in the Church as such particularly where she actualises her whole essence *fully*, that is in the definitive witness to her faith and in the sacraments.[58]

Since ultimately this is always and in every individual case the work of efficacious, unmerited grace, and not at man's free disposal, that 'actualistic' element in the being and action of the Church which Protestant theology quite falsely finds wanting in Catholic ecclesiology is in fact present in a Catholic understanding of the Church. Even the most 'objective' and most 'institutional' element in the Church is only accomplished, and rightly accomplished from every point of view, under the grace of God. And if the Church is holy not only institutionally but also 'subjectively' and her holiness is a reality already present here and now, and not a mere juridical claim or an eschatological hope for future credit, then God gives this holiness to the Church *in so far as* he grants to her and her members the possibility and the reality of constantly fleeing from their sinful state to the mercy of God which alone makes holy.

[58] The official life of the Church and its functions in doctrine, cult, sacraments, government and ecclesiastical discipline need not necessarily possess without further qualification under all circumstances and in every condition the same quality of eschatological indefectibility which we must ascribe to the Church as a whole. For the meaning of this question, its answer and its consequences, cf. K. Rahner, 'The Church and the Parousia of Christ', below p. 295 *sqq.*, particularly the third section, p. 305 *sqq.* The ideas developed in that essay are also in other ways the basis of the present article and can serve to complete it and exclude misunderstanding of it.

The following bibliography only gives a selection of the secondary literature utilised in the above essay. It does not make any claim to be complete.

Balthasar, H. U. von, 'Casta Meretrix' in *Sponsa Verbi: Skizzen zur Theologie* II (Einsiedeln 1961), pp. 203–305.

Balthasar, H. U. von, *Augustinus: Das Antlitz der Kirche* (Einsiedeln 1955²).

Congar, Y. M.-J., *Vraie et fausse réforme dans l'église*, Unam Sanctam 20 (Paris 1950).

Congar, Y. M.-J., 'Comment l'église sainte doit se renouveler sans cesse?' in *Sainte Église*, Unam Sanctam 41 (Paris 1963), pp. 131–154.

Daniélou, J., *Sacramentum Futuri* (Paris 1950), p. 217 *sqq.*

Dobschütz, E., von, *Das Decretum Gelasianum in kritischem Text herausgegeben und untersucht*, Texte and Untersuchungen 38, 4 (Leipzig/Berlin 1912), p. 236 *sq.* (A history of patristic interpretation of Ep 5:27).

Grundmann, H., *Ketzergeschichte des Mittelalters, Die Kirche in ihrer Geschichte*, Band II, Lieferung G, Teil I (Göttingen 1963).

Holzmeister, U., 'Die Magdalenenfrage in der kirchlichen Überlieferung' in *ZKT* XLVI (1922), pp. 402–422, 556–584.

Hofmann, F., *Der Kirchenbegriff des hl. Augustinus in seinen Grundlagen und in seiner Entwicklung* (Munich 1933), p. 233 *sqq.*

Knox, R. A., *Enthusiasm* (Oxford 1950).

Küng, H., *Justification: the Doctrine of Karl Barth and a Catholic Reflection* (London 1965).

Küng, H., 'Rechtfertigung und Heiligung nach dem Neuen Testament' in M. Roesle and O. Cullmann, *Begegnung der Christen*, a *Festschrift* for Otto Karrer (Frankfurt a.M. 1960), pp. 249–270.

Küng, H., *The Council and Reunion* (London 1962), pp. 34–52.

Landgraf, A. M., *Dogmengeschichte der Frühscholastik* IV/2 (Regensburg 1956), pp. 48–99.

László, S., 'Sin in the Holy Church of God' in Y. Congar, H. Küng and D. O'Hanlon (Eds), *Council Speeches of Vatican II* (London & New York 1964), pp. 29–31.

Lubac, H., de, *Katholizismus als Gemeinschaft* (Einsiedeln/Köln 1943), p. 61 *sqq.*

Rahner, Hugo, *Die Kirche, Gottes Kraft in menschlicher Schwäche* (Freiburg 1957).

Rahner, Hugo, *Symbole der Kirche: die Ekklesiologie der Väter* (Salzburg 1964), p. 394 *sq.*

Rahner, Karl, 'The Church of Sinners' in this volume pp. 253–269

Rahner, Karl, 'Membership of the Church According to the Teaching of Pius XII's Encyclical "Mystici Corporis Christi"' in *Theological Investigations* II (London & Baltimore 1963), pp. 1–88.

Rahner, Karl, 'Forgotten Truths Concerning the Sacrament of Penance' in *Theological Investigations* II (London & Baltimore 1963), pp. 135–174.

Rahner, Karl, 'The Church of the Saints' in *Theological Investigations* III (London & Baltimore 1967), pp. 91–104.

Rahner, Karl, 'The Church and the Parousia of Christ' in this volume pp. 295–312.

Rahner, Karl, 'Justified and Sinner at the Same Time' in this volume pp. 218–230.

Ratzinger, J., *Volk und Haus Gottes in Augustins Lehre von der Kirche* (Munich 1954).

Riedlinger, H., *Die Makellosigkeit der Kirche in den lateinischen Hohelied-Kommentaren des Mittelalters* (Münster 1958).

Schlier, H., *Der Brief an die Epheser* (Düsseldorf 1957), p. 256 *sqq.*

Seybold, M., *Sozialtheologische Aspekte der Sünde bei Augustinus*, Studien zur Geschichte der katholischen Moraltheologie, XI (Regensburg 1964).

Teichtweier, G., *Die Sündenlehre des Origenes*, Studien zur Geschichte der katholischen Moraltheologie VII, (Regensburg 1958).

19

THE CHURCH AND THE PAROUSIA
OF CHRIST

WHILE the title chosen for this systematic paper is 'The Church and the Parousia of Christ', the word 'Parousia' can and must be understood as including all those events of the divinely effected consummation which in Catholic theology are customarily comprised in the phrase 'The Last Things', and not only that particular moment of them which we call the 'Second Coming of Christ'. This is justified not merely by the fact that it is scarcely possible to establish a special relationship of the Church, her nature and her existence, to the Second Coming of Christ as such in the narrower sense alone, but also by the fact that the reality of the Second Coming which can be expressed in dogmatic terms, in so far as it can and must be distinguished from its mode of expression, is scarcely separable from the Last Things as a whole, as long as these are thought of (as is naturally the case here) in their relationship to the fulfilment of the whole world's history and not merely to the fulfilment of the individual as such. For otherwise we could only say of the Parousia of Christ that it is nothing more than the completion of history (Christ's, humanity's, and the world's) in God, in so far as it is then evident to all (because all have reached their end in the finality of being saved or lost) that the reality of the crucified and risen Christ who 'comes again', in so far as all come before him, is the beginning of, and the continuing reason for, the irreversibility of the history of salvation, its central meaning and its climax.[1] Therefore in so far as we are here practically identifying the

[1] If on the one hand we consider what can be objective 'in itself' in a return of Christ and what must be imaginative representation of it in the biblical and traditional accounts (cf. K. Rahner, 'The Hermeneutics of Eschatological Assertions' in *Theological Investigations* IV (London & Baltimore 1966), pp. 323–346), and on the other hand do not forget that men's 'coming before' the glorified Christ by their own (personal and collective) completion is itself an act of God in Christ, then this

Parousia with the Last Things as the consummation of the whole history of humanity and of the world (so including the return of Christ, the resurrection of the body, the universal judgement, eternal life in the vision of God, damnation, the new Heaven and the new Earth as aspects of the final cosmic completion), we are also presupposing that the really basic Christian understanding of the history of salvation recognises in it a genuine temporal order, the real inclusion of the whole man (body, soul, and world) in salvation and a dialectical identity in difference in man as an individual person and as a member of human society. This leads us to conclude, however, that the Last Things, as truly still awaited, are to be understood as still lying in the future in a genuine, even 'worldly', temporal order. The question here is therefore that of the relationship of the Church to the Parousia and the completion of the history of salvation and of the world, understood in that sense. Hence also the theme of our whole consideration is not the Parousia of Christ, but the relationship of the Church to the Parousia. It must of course be admitted that not all aspects of this relationship are here considered. For example, the question of the proximity or remoteness of the Parousia can be understood to be as much a part of the question of the relationship of the Church to the Parousia as a part of the question of the Parousia in itself; but we do not treat of it here.

I

The Church is the community, called together by God's grace in Jesus Christ, of those who in hope and love believe in the Parousia of Christ as still to come. By this proposition we do not intend to imply, on the one hand, that the nature of the Church is thereby adequately determined, particularly since belief, while essentially *always* eschatological, can also make its appearance in forms in which it is not yet a faith fully expressed, immediately related to the incarnate Word, or put into the concrete form of a common profession, through which alone it is in the proper sense constitutive of the Church. On the other hand, this proposition is

---

statement can be accepted without hesitation. But it is important, because the second coming of Christ, if it is not to be understood mythologically, cannot be a renewed entry of Christ into our dimension of space and time as we now know it, but the elevation of this dimension into its glory. And that is exactly what this sentence is trying to say.

intended to express an essential element of the Church: this faith which hopefully awaits the return of Christ is not merely something which the Church teaches and mediates to individual men for their individual salvation, but is a constitutive element of the Church as such. The Church is after all not merely a means of salvation, an institution for salvation, but herself a fruit of salvation, a community of faith, and she is a means of salvation precisely in so far as she is also a community of faith. But this faith with its concrete profession in cult and social life is precisely faith in the Parousia, because belief in the one living God, in the incarnation of God, the self-communication of God to his creature in the forgiving and divinising grace of Christ, is essentially not belief in a perpetually valid, static truth and reality, but faith in the sense of acceptance, made possible by the action of God, of a saving *event* which is now already taking place but is not yet finished, so that it can be accepted by the believer as having happened only by his reaching forward in hope to its fulfilment. The Church would therefore understand herself falsely as a mere saving institution and only as a means of salvation, were she not to think of herself in her first and fundamental self-realisation and accept herself as the community of those who hope, those who are waiting, of pilgrims who still seek their own homeland, of those who understand and master their present in terms of the future.

If the Church is to understand herself as the fruit of salvation and as a community of faith in this sense, then she must always understand herself as still provisional, as still looking for her fulfilment, as overcoming herself, since indeed we call the fulfilment which she seeks no longer Church, but the kingdom of God. Inasmuch therefore as she recognises herself to be the intimation and sacrament of final salvation which is already present in her even if it is accessible only to the eyes of faith and hope, she ought never to misunderstand herself to the extent of thinking that her present form is the ultimate one, or that her historical dimension affects in the last analysis only the individual for whom she is the means of salvation, or that while her present form will one day pass away, namely at the Parousia, yet between Pentecost and Parousia it has no history.[2] If even the last alone were the case, then the Church as such

---

[2] This formal and abstract sentence does not convey much in its empty abstraction. We admit this. It would have to be materially filled out in a genuine theology of Church history. One would have to show from the Church's history, for example, that it can be no part of a Catholic understanding of the Church (and is in no way

would not primarily be the community of pilgrims in faith and hope, but merely a static, unchanging instrument of salvation which, being itself without history, would merely be applied to individuals and their salvation.

It is true that the Church has something which remains permanent throughout history, because she has a real essence which will be annulled not by history but by its abolition, and because she is the fulfilled sacrament of final salvation, at once hearing God's exhibitive word of grace and salvation as present and herself being this word, the two in mutual interdependence; but even this permanent and indestructible element she has in a really genuine historical form which changes, which must always be sought anew, which must be endured in its historical originality and contingence, and whose transformation, while always both aim and result of the action of men obedient to the Word of God, is yet never adequately calculable in advance.

Therefore the Church, if only she be rightly understood, is living always on the proclamation of her own provisional status and of her historically advancing elimination in the coming kingdom of God towards which she is expectantly travelling as a pilgrim, because God for his own part is coming to meet her in the Parousia and her own pilgrimage, too, is taking place in the power of Christ's coming. The essential nature of the Church consists in pilgrimage towards the promised future.

II

Yet the Church has a quite special relationship to the fulfilment of created reality and history and therefore to the Parousia of Christ, and one which is different from other created beings, because she is herself an eschatological reality; that is to say, the future fulfilment, notwithstanding its being still to come, is in her already a present event, so that she makes her pilgrimage in a certain sense in her end to her end and in her faith is

---

justified by ecclesiastical history) that the Church is becoming ever 'more perfect', that she 'unfolds' her essence and her faith always 'better', but that, if she has a history directed to the Parousia, she can also be seen and experienced dispassionately as the Church which grows old, for which every 'development' (which really takes place) signifies at the same time a symptom of old age, the danger of losing herself in details and matters of secondary importance or in a too self-reliant entrenchment in this aeon.

conscious of this her unique – in fact eschatological – situation in such a way that this element belongs also to the faith which is constitutive of her being.

1. In the first place, the Church is herself an eschatological entity in the sense that she is the Church of those graced by Christ's Holy Spirit and this bestowal of grace upon her members is of her very essence. For notwithstanding the uncertainty of salvation for the individual[3] and the fact that it is always in peril, and notwithstanding the Catholic doctrine that even sinners belong to the Church, the Church cannot be conceived as a purely external religious organisation. She is the Body of Christ precisely to the extent that her members are graced with Christ's Spirit, and this possession of the Spirit is one of the most essential constitutive elements of the Church. And so our understanding of the nature of the Church depends essentially on our understanding of what we call justification, sanctification, being anointed and sealed with the Holy Spirit, participation in the divine nature, indwelling of the Blessed Trinity, the New Creation. It will be readily understood that we cannot expound here in this connection the whole of Catholic doctrine on grace as supernatural, divinising and justifying (imparting pardon), bestowed upon man in Jesus Christ through faith, hope and charity and by baptism, or even further to clarify it from an apologetic point of view, although it is of course true that only this way could an adequate understanding of the essence of the Church in the Catholic sense and of her relationship to the Parousia be achieved. Here we intend to confine ourselves to saying at least a little about this, that as a consequence of the Catholic doctrine of justification the Church herself appears as an eschatological entity.

Sanctifying justification, *as* the supernatural self-communication of God to man which really takes place in the event of justification and is not merely promised as a future and still completely outstanding gift, is itself already in truth and reality the gift of eternal life, precisely that in which eternal life as the fulfilment of man and his history will consist: God himself, who in his grace has given himself into man's possession, for

---

[3] This is not the place to expound more precisely the teaching on the uncertainty of salvation for the individual (cf. *DS* 1541, 1566) and to reconcile it 'dialectically' with the '*firmissima spes*' which the Christian may and should also have. The only point here is that we should recognise that the situation of the individual and the situation of the Church as a whole (or the situation of all Christians understood distributively and the situation of all Christians understood collectively) are not the same.

this grace is in the last analysis nothing else than God communicating himself and making himself the principle and object of life for the spiritual creature. Christianity of course rejects the doctrine that from the beginning God's life is itself man's own fundamental being, so that he only has to come to himself in order to be with God, but Christianity, at least in the Catholic understanding of it, unmistakably teaches that God gives himself even now with his own, infinite glory into the possession of him who believes and loves; that he offers this his own life as source and object of a creature's life at all times to every man, even – in virtue of his universal salvific will – to sinners, though out of pure grace and love, so that man as he in fact exists inevitably meets in the history of his essential fulfilment the God of eternal life in Christ Jesus, provided that he does not by a deliberate fault deny his own being and its concrete history. And in so far as justifying grace is in the Catholic understanding of it not merely any kind of forgiveness of sin or justification or equipment for a positively moral act which pleases God, but in the last analysis God communicating himself in his whole inexpressible glory and fullness of life, so is this grace fundamentally an unsurpassable and therefore definitive and in this sense eschatological constitution of man. It is ultimately no merely creaturely condition of man on the basis of which and by means of which he seeks a coming constitution which still lies wholly in the future, which he might perhaps already foresee and long for in a purely mental way as something not yet existing. It is the arrival of his definitive future which precisely as already given bears his history in which he accepts and takes possession of this his future. However much the Catholic doctrine of the universal salvific will of God forces us to say with regard to all sinners that this movement in the end towards the end is possible to all men at least in principle by the grace which is offered to all men, the knowledge in faith and the acceptance of this eschatological situation of all men is itself again made possible and supported by the same grace.[4] To that extent it belongs itself to the eschatological situation of men and together

---

[4] In so far as the acceptance of grace in faith and love is itself not only the history of man's reaction to God's offer of grace but the history of grace as such, it is clear even from this that talking about the eschatological movement of history to the goal *in* the goal itself is quite compatible with a true being-in-the-future or with a true 'not-yet' of the goal. But the converse is also true: the being-still-to-come of the future does not nullify its pure presentiality. For the doctrine of grace, at least in the Catholic understanding of it, states that God is in his *self*-communication the principle of the movement to the goal which is *himself*.

with the offer of God's communication of himself to all men constitutes that eschatological reality in which the justification of the explicitly believing Christian and with it the inner reality of the Church herself consists. This eschatological, final and essentially unsurpassable bestowal of grace upon man by God's self-communication, which is explicitly grasped and proclaimed in Christian faith, is naturally to be understood as at once supernaturally divinising and justifying the sinner by forgiveness, and in this its unity it constitutes that eschatological gift by which the Church is what it is.

2. This eschatological, unsurpassable and irrevocable self-offer of the Blessed Trinity to mankind is not only fundamentally unsurpassable as the communication of God himself and not only irrevocable through the incarnation of the Word of God remaining eternally valid and through the resurrection of the Son, so that the Judgement too takes place precisely by reason of the unrepentant salvific will: this self-offer is also eschatological and thereby constitutive of the nature of the Church in so far as this self-offer produces by its own power (through the pre-defining power of grace) its acceptance in fact on the part of mankind and for its part guarantees this acceptance to be final and, as *victory* of God's love, irrevocable. The victorious self-communication of God, not only proffered but *accepted* in faith, hope and love by the power of grace, is itself as eschatological and victorious a part of the content of that faith by which the Church herself is constituted, confesses with praise the victory of God over the sin of the world, and thereby already here and now lends to this victory an historical and in a certain sense sacramental presence and accessibility in the world. The Church is constituted thereby as the community of those who believe and confess that God's grace as love which forgives and communicates God himself is really victorious in the world and that its victory in the free acceptance of that love by man is itself the work of God's self-communication in grace.

In so far as this faith confessing the eschatological victory of the grace of God is itself an element in this victory and not merely a polite answer on the part of man to an act of God which as such does not yet include this reaction of the creature but is synergistically added to it, the Church believes and confesses that this eschatological victory of God's communication of himself happens, even if not exclusively in her, yet precisely *also* in her and upon her. For the Church is the community whose faith proclaims this victory and this in such a way that the proclamation of the final and irrevocably initiated victory of God, and not merely the victory itself, can no longer disappear from the history of mankind. But if this proclamation of faith in the victory, as that faith made concrete in history, is itself invincible and an inner constitutive element of the victory itself and at the same time of the Church, then the Church must necessarily be one which confesses of herself in praise of God's grace that in her the acceptance of the divine self-communication, that is the justification of man, is indefectible and that her faith in it as the historical presence of this victory can never disappear. To this extent therefore the Church professes of herself an indefectibility of her holiness and faith. Whether, in what way, and under what conditions this indefectibility of the Church in love, hope and faith which derives from her ultimate nature is and must be also a characteristic trait of the institutional and of the official in her, is a question which cannot and need not be further considered at this point of our discussion, although it is to be suspected that only this new question would touch the real apologetic problem. The Church is therefore not merely that reality which moves in the end to the end, but at the same time and because of it that whose movement both signifies and proclaims the permanence of this movement in the end and by means of both these together represents that eschatological entity which waits upon the Parousia of the Lord as future by bearing in herself the Parousia of the Lord as present, so that present and future mutually bear one another out of the event of Christ which happened once and for all in the 'past' and remains eternally valid in the incarnation of the Word of God, the death and resurrection of Christ.

3. What we have said under I and II, 1–2, is simultaneously true and possible in so far as God's communication of himself to mankind is accepted and possessed by the Church through the power of grace in that particular way which must be described as faith, in distinction to unveiled contemplation, and as hope, as reaching out to what is still in the future, and thereby leads to the received grace of everlasting life the peculiar characteristic of hiddenness. The hiddenness of grace as the life of eternity already given here and now and the possession of this life as faith and hope in distinction to unhidden possession mutually condition one another and constitute in their unity the peculiar note of the eschatological situation of the Church. Yet they permit of being described in some way one after the other.

God's communication of himself to man is hidden to the extent that in the phase and situation of its free, historical acceptance by man's vital act it is not given to him as something with which he can be concerned in its own reality as the immediate object of his own spiritual self-realisation, that is by immediate vision and unmediated community, but as the principle (even though known by the word of faith) of his obedient intercourse with the objects of the world, personal and otherwise, which are distinct from God. The man of grace moves towards the goal precisely and only as far as this goal is itself the principle of his movement towards the goal. Faith and hope, therefore, although built upon God as their principle, are 'only' faith and hope, as distinct from the vision which possesses and enjoys immediately, and they give to God's communication of himself as received and accepted the characteristic of hiddenness to the extent that faith is always mediated by the categorial word of faith (*fides ex auditu*) and therefore does not permit man's absolute transcendental dependence on the life of the Blessed Trinity by its real communication of itself to be for him given in itself. Therefore hope, too, although it is borne by the hoped-for itself and only so can be hope, can represent the hoped-for to itself only in the categorial word about it. Movement in the end to the end becomes faith and hope through the objectification brought about in the world of what is already really possessed in faith and hope, and only because of this necessary categorial objectification in the world can the divine self-communication still be accepted by an historical, free decision of man. This for its part is demanded not only by the dignity of the free human person who is to be favoured with God's life and by the proper nature of the divine life which is to be communicated, which is personal free love and of itself calls for a similar answer, but also and above all by the ultimate structure of the divine economy of salvation, which is built upon that Christ who freely and in obedience became man precisely because in that way God can appear in the finite as what he really is and freely wants to be in our regard.[5]

By the hiddenness of the divine self-communication in grace which is already here and now the gift of eternal life, and by the particular character of the acceptance of this divine self-communication as an acceptance in faith and hope, the real eschatological presence of the future as final and irrevocable and as such definitively accepted is not suppressed but rather

[5] Cf. the author's 'Current Problems in Christology' in *Theological Investigations* I (London & Baltimore 1961), pp. 149–200; and 'On the Theology of the Incarnation' in *Theological Investigations* IV (London & Baltimore 1966), pp. 105–120.

confirmed. For faith and hope are not merely human attitudes towards something to come, and therefore only promised, but they are man's personal self-realisation, the ultimate and most necessary principle for whose being and actualisation is the grace of God itself. But this is not any kind of aid given to an act which would still be merely human and creaturely and rob the aid and the divine word of revelation of its power by making it subject to the *a priori* of human nature. The grace of faith and hope in the last analysis (leaving out of account creaturely and necessary effects of grace which can rightly in their turn be called grace) is God himself making it possible by his communication of himself to man for his act to remain truly human and yet to be the hearing and the uttering of the Word of God as such and not merely of the response to it within the horizon of mere finitude and merely human-spiritual transcendence; this self-communication of God as the reason for hope results in man's hope grasping not merely the *concept* of a future hoped-for object within the horizon of human desire but the hoped-for object itself.

In so far as faith and hope have what is believed and hoped for, namely the God of eternal life, as the inner principle of faith and hope and to that extent experience in the act of believing and hoping this *a priori* principle of faith and hope itself notwithstanding its necessary categorial mediation through the human word, and although it is not represented objectively in its own self, we must without hesitation speak of an experience of grace, of revelation, and of faith. In it the Church is not only in fact given the eschatological gift by which she is herself constituted but this is experienced. The Church is the community of those who already possess the eschatological gift which is God himself, who in full liberty really accept this possession, who confess in faith that this possession and its acceptance has been caused by the free action of God's love, and who hope for the unveiling of this possession by the power contained within it. She belongs therefore to the present time in so far as she is still moving towards the goal by faith and hope, that is in so far as she must still let the Parousia of Christ come upon her, and at the same time she belongs to eternity, as she moves towards her end in virtue of the future which has already arrived.

The Church's experience of herself as the community which possesses the eschatological good of salvation 'only' in faith and hope is naturally not only an experience of faith and hope to the extent that what is really believed and hoped is experienced through the mediation of human categorial objectivity in a way which is itself again merely abstract. This mediation is a concrete historical one and signifies for faith and hope real darkness, trouble, constancy in the face of always new and unforeseen situations, of contradiction on the part of unbelief, of despair, of a future Utopia conceived within the limits of this world. In brief, the concrete history of the Church is the means by which the transcendental experience in faith and hope of grace as the divine life itself is objectified and so becomes in the concrete the object of man's saving decision. And this history of the Church's experience is therefore at once a means and a temptation for faith and hope. If one were to deny to history a positive function as a means one would fundamentally be disputing that in her explicit confession of faith, which is after all part of the dimension of history, the Church is herself again a work of grace and not only a merely human reaction to a grace which remains meta-historical. If one were to deny in this history the character of temptation for faith (in theory or in practice), then the Church would be regarded fundamentally as the manifest presence of God in the world and faith and hope would become an evident possession of eternal life, which could at the most be hidden in some way by that human history which remains extrinsic to salvation and its possession and does not play any part in the history of salvation as such.

III

In this third section we would like at least briefly to touch upon a question which was left open in the previous section, namely the question what exactly is the relationship of the Church as institution and official ministry to the Church as eschatological entity. The eschatological character of the Church was after all developed from the concept of the Church as the fruit of salvation, not so much from the Church as means of salvation. Now these two aspects are essentially interdependent, even though they cannot be simply identified with one another. For the Church is at least in part the means of salvation precisely in so far as she is the believing and confessing community, constituted by the predetermining power of God's grace, of those who glory in the triumphant grace of God's divinising and forgiving self-communication to mankind and who with missionary zeal as 'God's co-workers' in the service of grace move men precisely through this confession of faith to accept divine grace. On this ground alone there can be no adequate distinction between the Church as the institutional means of salvation and the Church as the fruit of salvation.

But since there is an official ministry in the Church and this and its functions cannot be simply identified in a Donatist fashion with the Church as grace, the question of the relationship between the Church as institution and the Church as fruit of salvation, that is as the eschatological being-present of final salvation, is not yet answered by what was said above in the previous section about the Church as an eschatological entity. The distinctions which it is necessary to make between faith as officially proclaimed and faith as existentially accepted in a way conducive to salvation, between the valid sacramental sign and the sacrament as in fact effectively productive of grace, between the institutional and the charismatic structure of the Church, between the Church which as a whole is certain of salvation and preserved in faith and love by God's grace, predetermined to be effective, and the individual who notwithstanding his external membership of the Church can be a sinner and destined to perdition, these show that the official ministry and its functions in the Church in teaching, cult, sacrament, administration and ecclesiastical discipline, do not without further qualification possess in all cases and under all conditions the same quality of eschatological indefectibility which we must ascribe to the Church as a whole. If the Church's indefectibility in faith and love (in each case of course in its own way) belongs to the Church in so far as she is herself the fruit of salvation and it is from this that we must ultimately deduce theologically an indefectibility of her official ministry,[6] then it becomes evident from the distinction we have just indicated between the Church as means of salvation and the Church as community of salvation, that absolutely speaking one must also assume in the Catholic understanding an indefectibility of the official ministry in *all* its functions, although in each case in a specifically different way; but at the same time it is permissible to view this indefectibility in so far as it is predicated of the official ministry, the institution and thereby

---

[6] In saying this we are not denying that an ultimate indefectibility of the Church's official ministry can be derived from those texts of the New Testament which speak directly about the Church's office, of its mission and its function within the Church. But if the question is then asked *why* such an indefectibility belongs to this office in the New Covenant although no such indefectibility ever belonged to any office up to then in the history of salvation in spite of its being positively led and guided by God, even when that office was bestowed by God himself, then the only possible answer is that here it is a question of an office in a Church which is itself the *eschatological* fruit of salvation and as such (but only as such) cannot be other than indefectible.

of the historically tangible form of the Church, as a peripheral instance of the Church (which to be sure really occurs concretely and tangibly according to the Catholic understanding of the Church), instead of, as is usually done in Catholic theology, developing fully this indefectibility only in relation to the *teaching office* of the Church and then setting up that indefectibility as the normal case and interpreting other acts of the teaching office which are lacking in that indefectibility (which in the case of teaching is called infallibility) as peripheral instances.

Nevertheless, and this at the moment is the decisive fact, there is an indefectibility of the Church also in her institutional office and not merely of the Church as an eschatological community of salvation. Yet this indefectibility, as we may legitimately say within a Catholic understanding of the Church, has its *raison d'être* in the Church as community of salvation. For not only can the former in fact be deduced from the latter, as we intend to show immediately, but the limits of the indefectibility of office become thereby understandable, whereas they would remain incomprehensible if this indefectibility were conceived purely and exclusively as the formal equipment given to the Church's office by God's juridical commission. Finally, only in this way does it become comprehensible why the Church ascribes to herself in her office such an indefectibility which she denies to the office in the Old Testament Church which was also originally founded by God.

In the Catholic understanding of the matter, the indefectibility of the eschatological community of salvation also gives rise to an indefectibility of the office of the Church because this office (as a teaching and pastoral office) was founded by Christ as an authoritative factor within the Church on which the faith, cult and action of the Church depend and must depend, while the community of salvation would in its faith and life, at least in the tangible dimension of history, cease to be the historical presence and visible victory of Christ's grace either if it could in principle and essentially as a whole be torn apart from Christ, his truth and his love by its official ministry, or if in order to prevent this happening it had to revolt and separate itself in principle from the official ministry and its historical legitimation.

In this way, however, we already have as well an indication in principle of the limits of the indefectibility of this office in regard to its teaching, sanctifying and pastoral power: such an official act participates in the indefectibility of the community of salvation if and in so far as it would, were it not itself indefectible, in safeguarding the structure of the Church tear her away from Christ so that the Church as an historical phenomenon would cease to be the eschatologically indefectible community of salvation. But this would happen if the highest teaching and pastoral office of the Church were to make use of its highest teaching and pastoral authority over the whole Church with a force definitively binding upon all with the fullest obligation, and in doing so were to contradict the truth and the salvific will of Christ to such an extent that the acceptance and the following of such an act would place the universal Church as a whole in unambiguous contradiction to Christ, and so into absolute error as 'No' to his truth or as 'No' to his unifying and sanctifying love. The canonical determination and making precise of this principle which enables us to accept an official act of the Church as indefectible by faith in her and in her eschatological indefectibility, no longer falls within the framework of these considerations. But from the stated point of departure it is possible to recognise clearly the limits of this indefectibility of the Church in the various forms of official action. Where it is not a question of a definitively and irreversibly posited official act of the universal Church it does not necessarily and with the certitude of faith have in itself the prerogative of indefectibility of the Church. And in so far as the Church as still in a pilgrim-state, waiting, hoping, must also be the tempted and tried Church in order that her relationship to the realisation of salvation which is already given in her should be one of faith and of hope, in fact tempted by her pilgrim existence itself, the acts which do not possess this indefectibility necessarily and inevitably belong to her pilgrim existence in faith and hope.

From here we would really have to reflect more accurately than is usually the case in Catholic ecclesiology on the fact that these indefectible and defectible self-realisations of the Church, specifically those of her official ministry, make their appearance in the concrete existence of the Church and the Christian presence in a way which does not really permit the reflection which accompanies historical existence to make an *absolutely* clear-cut division between these two acts. Unfortunately it is impossible to discuss this point further here, much as it would undoubtedly contribute to a notable softening of polemical opposition between the Christian confessions. At least let us note that even according to the Catholic conception an 'infallible' definition, for example, of Pope or Council does not necessarily signify that this definition must be opportune from every point of view, that is that its content must be easily capable of assimilation by the mass of the faithful in the historical situation of that time or that it must be particularly conducive to the accomplishment of the act of faith as a unified whole. Nor does a definition as infallible necessarily rule out the possibility that the way in which it is in fact understood in a determinate historical situation may be charged in spite of every clarity and precision in its formulation with associated interpretations, imaginative categories, practical consequences, and so on, which do not in any way participate in the infallibility of the definition, which render its acceptance in faith more difficult or even perhaps impossible for certain hearers without any subjective fault on their part, and which can only in a later historical situation of the Church be clearly and explicitly distinguished from that which was really and properly meant in the definition. The clearest proclamation of the principles of moral theology as guide-lines for actuating love for God and our neighbour still leave the individual and the Church to a large extent in the dark as to *how* they should be applied in the concrete situation: what concrete profession the individual should take up (although this can determine his eternal salvation); how the dialectically opposed principles of mildness and severity in the bringing up of children, of zeal and tolerance in public life, and so on, should in the concrete be combined and at the same time be respected; what attitude the Church should concretely and practically take up to world-powers which are hostile to Christ; what is really right in evaluating A B C warfare. There are innumerable obscurities of this and a similar kind in the life of the Church and of the individual Christian. The *Quaestiones Disputatae* of moral theology are really not concerned with mere subtleties which have no practical significance. The theories of the 'moral systems' which have been devised to solve such obscurities also do not take us much further because these theories in their turn are obscure in themselves and in their application. One cannot even console oneself with the thought that these obscurities cannot compromise one's salvation as long as goodwill is there. For it could be the case that one could more easily and more clearly become aware of the fact that one does not perhaps possess this goodwill at all, if a bad will were not able so easily to hide behind theoretical obscurities.

All these small indications which are really self-evident are here intended only to draw attention to one fact: the doctrine of the indefectibility of the teaching and ruling office does not imply at all that the

Church and the individual Christian wander idly from one clear certitude to another. Despite this indefectibility, Church and Christian must laboriously make their pilgrimage through the obscurity of this aeon, and for both there ultimately remains only one thing: trust in the grace of God alone. The Catholic doctrine of the indefectibility of the official ministry and its acts in determinate circumstances does not therefore in any way imply that this area can be so circumscribed as to make it from every possible viewpoint utterly and clearly distinct from all that is defectible in the Church, that according to the Catholic understanding there is, so to speak, a piece of the Church which is clearly distinct from everything else as purely the divinely founded Church of sure salvation and of the absolutely unobscured truth and love of Christ.

IV

Our treatment of the subject of the Church and eschatology would be left incomplete if we did not also cast a glance at those this-worldly future hopes and Utopias which exist today in a way and with an urgency which was impossible in earlier ages. Obviously even in earlier times man was a being who could and had to fashion his life actively in freedom. But in earlier times, and particularly at the time of the origin of Christianity, the area of man's capacity springing from his inner nature of freely and actively fashioning his own being was so narrowly limited and so well within his range of vision, that its possibility for the future had in practice to be experienced as the more or less near present. Man could at that time have only an inner attitude of surrender or protest against a fate laid upon him in point of fact simply by nature: he could not really be the active, creative designer and planner of himself, the world he lived in, and so also of a more remote future. But this is something which he can do today. He does not just more or less accept Nature as his world, but he changes it and fashions it into that world which he has of his own accord determined to live in. Nature is no longer merely the given unalterable stage upon which he acts out his being, including the history of his salvation and damnation, but the mere material, the quarry, out of which he first constructs the scenery in the midst of which as expressing his own self-understanding he wants to live out his historical existence. The practical possibilities of such an active self-realisation in the active transformation of the human sphere of existence are today perhaps still very limited: but this future has begun, and there is an enormously increased area of the future which man anticipates in his planning.

Christianity must come to meet this really new experience of man's existence; it cannot be mastered immediately and adequately from the New Testament alone, for such an existential experience did not exist at that time to any notable extent. The Church as the eschatological community of salvation living in the faith and the hope of a future which is the gift of God himself and which is not designed and created by man, must come to terms with this new existential experience of modern man to whom is opened both for himself as an individual and for mankind as a whole a real and extensive future which can be foreseen, planned and realised. This will mean in the first place, that Christianity should recognise the fundamentally Christian roots of this situation of modern man and so accept it as being itself genuinely Christian. In point of fact this situation has a Christian origin, firstly because Christianity of its very essence conceives the totality of reality primarily as history and Nature as one element of this, and not *vice versa*; secondly, because Nature as truly created and thereby as *not* divine and the role of God as the personal partner of man signify that it is not a numinous Nature but the Word of God and man himself who are the real representatives of God in the world and that Nature is in reality that which man is to make subject to himself, because it is nothing else than the continuation of his bodiliness and therefore reaches its fulfilment in him and his history: it is not the other way about, man ultimately sharing the extra-human and infra-human destiny of Nature.

Once the Christian antecedents of man's new situation as *homo faber sui ipsius et mundi* are seen in spite of all the *hybris* and corruption which surrounded this new understanding of existence at its birth and still surrounds it today as it continues upon its both beneficial and harmful way, then Christianity must unhesitatingly recognise that future plans and future utopias within this world are not only from the Christian standpoint legitimate, but are the destiny which God's providence has assigned to man, in the carrying out and suffering of which alone can he live his Christian calling genuinely and completely today. Only on this condition can Christianity say to the man of today that his future, too, stands under the sign of creatureliness, of sin, of law, of death, of point-lessness and of redemption by Christ and that this future, too, is redeemed and sanctified and given its own proper meaning by the fact that it is already overtaken by the future of Christ come upon us and by the divine self-communication, and that therefore this future too, if it is to bring man his salvation, must happen in the *kairos* of Christ. But the Church must see (and live out) the fact that she is not the true and credible eschatological community of salvation by being the resentful, ineffectual and fearful host of those who deny themselves the greatness, the duty and the danger of this world of the future or who have taken up towards it an attitude which regards it exclusively as material, indifferent in itself, for the practice of Christian virtue, material without any of that original, worldly value which precisely as secular and worldly must be accepted by the Christian as a Christian without again sublimating its worldliness in a religious sense. What all this signifies more precisely in the concrete, how in this situation the different Christian professions each have their own specific tasks, opportunities and dangers of failure, cannot be considered any further here. But this will have to happen, if the Church's understanding of herself as the eschatological salvation-community to which God has given himself and which still waits for his kingdom, is today not to be misinterpreted by the Church herself and misunderstood by non-Christians.

B. THE BISHOP IN THE CHURCH

20

THE EPISCOPAL OFFICE

FOREWORD

A VIGOROUS attack has been made in an article[1] by D. T. Strotmann on many of the considerations contained in the following article of mine. Right at the beginning I would beg the reader to read Strotmann's article for himself and then to ask himself quite impartially whether I have always been correctly interpreted and whether I have really been convincingly refuted. For my part, suffice it to say here that I answer this question in the negative But I restrict myself to a few remarks without entering into all the questions exactly.

In my opinion, Strotmann over-estimates the *theological* significance of the ancient tradition and practice of the East, and at the same time I find him offering no arguments against my considerations apart from a reference to these. Anyone who comes to realise how little it is possible in any case to draw a theological argument for the sacramentality of Orders from the sources of revelation themselves will allow to Orders a much greater flexibility than Strotmann is able to bring himself to do. The *multiplicity* of bishops in the ancient Church is a consequence not of the '*jus divinum*' of revelation but quite simply of the social and political conditions of the time and does not therefore constitute any argument that it *must always* be so. The multiplicity of small dioceses, for example in Italy, does not produce damaging results only because Rome excessively curtails true episcopal liberty (p. 195). When one considers how difficult it is from the point of view of the history of revelation and of dogma to justify the division of Orders (into bishop, priest and deacon) as based

[1] 'Primauté et Céphalisation: À propos d'une étude du P. Karl Rahner' in *Irénicon* XXXVIII (1964), pp. 187–197.

on *'jus divinum'*, one sees the indispensability of the *fundamental* principle that the Church can 'divide' the *one* fullness of the power of Orders according to practical requirements without vitiating its sacramentality. But then not only is the ascription of sacramentality to the minor Orders in the Middle Ages no longer quite so absurd as Strotmann thinks (p. 190), but there arises the possibility of an historical formation of the different grades of Orders, so that there is nothing really astonishing – from a dogmatic point of view – in a certain lack of definition of the borderline between patriarch and simple bishop, the emphasis upon which calls forth the indignation of Strotmann (p. 193), but which can have practical consequences. – If I conclude that Pope John XXIII's measure of making all cardinals bishops be theologically meaningful, then being in the pope's company I am in good company even if my opinion is not approved of by Strotmann (p. 191), without my being able to see – and this is no less important – how Strotmann really justifies his opinion in this matter.

If Strotmann holds the idea of a 'personal diocese' to be absurd (p. 195, 197), the decree on the Oriental Churches (no. 4) of Vatican II does not seem to support him, because here the possibility is foreseen that 'the Ordinaries of the various individual Churches' can exist 'in the *same* territory'. These are then surely to all intents and purposes personal dioceses. Why then should other cases which occur to us be *a priori* impossible? If this kind of thing were quite impossible in principle, then strictly speaking an abbey like Chevetogne with a rite alien to the place where it is situated would also be impossible.

My reflections upon the meaning and form of the college of cardinals in no way aimed at putting them in the place of the *college of bishops*. What Strotmann says in this connection about my ideas is a complete misunderstanding. His own description of the essence of the episcopal office (p. 193), when measured against the statements of Vatican II, is only half the truth. The bishops are as *corpus* and *collegium* (with and under the pope) the one supreme bearer of the fullness of power in the Church; this is definitely a part of the essence of the episcopal office. But then today there necessarily arises the question whether and how this college can be represented and made effective by a smaller group. Such a smaller group would not down-grade the episcopate to a college of parish priests, as Strotmann seems to fear, any more than an assembly of patriarchs would turn the bishops subordinate to them into simple priests. After all, the question of a representation of this kind was raised by the Council and not just by me, and was accepted by the pope ('Senate of Bishops'). A plenary Council can today no longer effectively exercise the universal function of the episcopal college. Surely it is the case that the bearer of that episcopal and immediate jurisdiction over the whole Church and over each individual Church which dogma ascribes to the Roman primacy is chosen most meaningfully by a representation of the whole Church. But if *this* representation for *this* election cannot in practice be effectively brought about by a meeting of all the bishops of the Church, then the most meaningful alternative is for an electoral commission of the episcopal college (namely, the college of cardinals) to be entrusted with the election. The only condition is that the college of cardinals should be so constituted as really to embody such a representation of the whole episcopal college. Even now I cannot see what reasons motivate Strotmann's protest against this idea. We will have to wait and see how Paul VI will develop and reconstitute the college of cardinals. The indications of this further development which are to hand up to the present do not in any case absolutely contradict the kind of development we have here outlined.[2] At least there is no sign that in Rome the college of cardinals is regarded as an '*institution périmée*' (p. 191). Against this one could ask quite simply, who then is to elect the pope, if the college of cardinals is abolished?

[2] Since then Paul VI in his allocution at the beginning of the Fourth Session and in the *Motu proprio* which was published later has announced the formation of the 'synod of bishops'. In its present structure this synod of bishops is not identical with the existing college of cardinals. To that extent the remarks we have made above and in the following essay appear to be overtaken by events. But in reality we will have to wait and see what concrete constitution the two organs of the bishops' council assume, how the two consultative assemblies are co-ordinated and what relationship the *whole* 'synod' has *in reality* to the college of cardinals. A large percentage of the cardinals of today are certainly represented in one way or another in this synod of bishops. But what in the concrete the relationship between the college of cardinals and the synod of bishops is to be is not at all clear, at least for the more remote future. There are all sorts of possible lines of development and of evolution open. Besides, it would be disastrous if in the joyful exuberance of seeing the synod of bishops realised at long last the actual significance of the college of cardinals were to be underestimated. We need only remind ourselves that the college of cardinals is invested with the power of electing the pope and – at least for the present – will clearly continue to be. In this sense the author would like to think that even today, although under different conditions, his former reflections (certainly with changes of emphasis) are worthy of consideration. The whole question can really be taken up again only in a much larger context, but at present we are unable to make any very decisive comments, especially since the practical working of the synod of bishops (including its relationship with the reformed Curia) still lies before us.

Neither the three thousand bishops nor the parish priests of Rome appear to be practically fitted for the task. Who then? The possibility of participating in the election of the pope was for the patriarchs (at least for Maximos IV Saigh) a main reason for eventually entering the college of cardinals. At present four *Eastern* patriarchs are members of the college of cardinals, something which Strotmann previously rejected most vigorously (p. 191). I do not intend to go any further into this matter here and make capital for my thesis out of the fact that it was Maximos IV himself who eventually entered the college of cardinals. One would also have to discuss further the juridical alterations in the status of cardinal (precedence, titular church, and so on).[3]

If my simple question (it was no more than this) whether it is not possible to understand the primacy as being the supreme grade of the Sacrament of Orders is rejected by Strotmann as sheer nonsense (p. 189 *sq.*), I would like to ask again what is the transmission of the charism of infallibility in this office and the certain assurance from God, because of the indefectibility of the Church, of the divine grace of the office which is needed for its right exercise? Why is it impossible to understand this granting of such full power in the office as an '*opus operatum*'? If today it is the aim to bring jurisdiction and the episcopal power of Orders closer together (in this connection see Strotmann's remark on page 190, note 2), if we are again coming to emphasise relative ordination as the normal case of episcopal consecration, why should it be absurd to regard the relative consecration of the pope *for this* primatial See as a *specific* episcopal consecration (as its highest degree)? If the objection is made that today and for a long time past the pope is usually already a bishop before the papal election, then one could point to previous ages and their practice as a theological fundamental model for the answering of the question: one could say that the same problem appears whenever a bishop becomes a patriarch in another See and one must find a meaningful solution for this case; one could say that election and acceptance of the powers of the primacy can be regarded as a sacramental sign (in particular cases as a completion of the episcopal laying on of hands) just as much as the laying on of hands itself, particularly since everyone knows today that the possibility of the Church's determining for herself the form and matter of a sacramental rite is very far-reaching. There are other sacra-

[3] This is not the place for a discussion of the so-called Latin Patriarchates in the East and in the West.

ments (Matrimony, Penance) which consist in a juridical procedure and yet are sacraments. This question has never been asked before: we are not accustomed to it. But is this really a penetrating reason for rejecting it as a meaningless piece of scholastic hair-splitting? Considering the historical development of sacramental doctrine and of the papal primacy, this does not seem to me to be the case, because this history is certainly not concluded. Strotmann objects that the election to the papacy when accepted does not confer any 'character indelebilis'. I ask in response, does this involve the negation of a sacrament? What about the 'character indelebilis' of a bishop consecrated in a relative ordination for a particular Church, when he renounces definitively his Church and jurisdiction over it? Would it not be possible to see the case of the resignation of a pope from his office as being the same as that of such a bishop, so that it is by no means established that in the case of a papal election there is no such thing as a 'character indelebilis' rightly understood? Should we not be particularly careful in handling this indelible character from the point of view of Eastern theology? – Nor do I propose any 'nouveau genre d'évêques' (p. 195), but merely seek to find some theological meaning in an existing institution (that of titular bishops), precisely in order to have a principle for guarding against the *misuse* of this institution. I do not see that in doing this I am doing something senseless.

THE EPISCOPAL OFFICE

The question of the episcopate within the Church, of its collegial unity and its function in the Church as the supreme bearer of the fullness of power in union with the pope is one of the central questions of the Council now meeting. In accordance with the nature of a Council, with the kind of possibilities open to it for expressing itself and their limitations, the Council will be able to say very little expressly regarding this topic, though what it does say may be important and fundamental. It may be presumed that it will declare firstly, that there exists in the Church not merely an accidental, conceptual collectivity of many individual bishops, but a proper college as a collegial unit (a 'moral person'), that this collegially composed unit of the universal episcopate is part of the unalterable constitution of the Church (of 'divine' law, not of positive ecclesiastical and changeable law), that this college has its head in the Roman pope, who is not merely 'princeps inter pares' but possesses

(precisely as head of this college) the supreme powers accorded him by
Vatican I, and that therefore this college is a college and can act as such
only in union with the pope. Presumably the Council will declare secondly,
that the college, understood in this way, is the bearer of that supreme and
full power in the Church (the power of Orders and of jurisdiction in the
three 'offices' of teacher, priest and shepherd) which according to the will
of Christ and the nature of the Church belongs to her. We think that it
will declare thirdly, that not only does this college exercise its power in an
extraordinary way in an Ecumenical Council, but that it *can* exercise it also
outside a Council (subject to the conditions which derive from its very
nature, among which is of course the participation of the pope). Fourthly,
there will probably then be drawn from these dogmatic principles a few
– very modest – conclusions: that every bishop bears a responsibility
(even though no jurisdiction) towards the whole Church flowing from
the episcopal office itself, which must, for example, give rise to a duty of
helping the missions; and that conferences of bishops are a practical
consequence of this fraternal union of bishops.

Presumably nothing will be said about the more exact determination
of the relationship of the pope to the (rest of the) college, that is about the
question which in the context of the relation of Pope to Council was
expressly left open by the First Vatican Council and is even today a
matter of controversy, whether there are *two* inadequately distinct
subjects of the supreme power (pope and college) or only one, the second
theory in its turn being capable of being understood in several quite
different ways. The historical question remains open, *how* the present
subject of full power in the Church came to be developed from the 'constitution' of the primitive Apostolic Church, that is to say the question
of the *more precise* historical descent of the episcopal college from the
Apostolic college (and contained in this is the question of the manner in
which the ecclesiastical office, which in the last analysis is one, came to be
divided up into the office of bishop and the office of simple priest, and
hence of the precise delimitation of these two powers). The question
remains untouched, how more precisely the entry of the individual bishop
into the college is effected (we will come to speak of this question almost
immediately). The question is not discussed, what more precisely are the
modes of the extra-Conciliar yet collegial acts of the college, that is to say
what possibilities of initiative belong to the members of the college in
relation to their head, what kind of part the pope must play or can play

in it (explicit or tacit, canonically instituted or para-canonical), whether the so-called 'ordinary magisterium' of the college of bishops (together with the pope) which according to Catholic doctrine enjoys in determinate conditions the same infallibility as an *ex cathedra* decision of the pope is such a collegial act or not. (To us it seems self-evidently so.)

I

It is not our intention here to enter any further into the theological foundation of the doctrine proposed by the Council, or to take up any *direct* position regarding the questions mentioned above as remaining open which are connected with this doctrine. Rather we will attempt at our own risk and on our own responsibility to cast some glances from this doctrine upon a possible future practice. In so far as *for this purpose* it is necessary to form opinions on theologically controverted questions we must naturally venture to do this. In this connection it must of course not be overlooked that while practical possibilities of this kind can be aligned with such theological opinions as a point of departure, they cease to be merely possible if those opinions should be right. Positive legal enactments in the Church within the framework of the unalterable divine constitution of the Church can be justified in different ways, and they are not necessarily impossible or inopportune if a particular reason for them does not enjoy universal consent.

In all the considerations which follow this is not to be forgotten: the Church is an eschatological salvation-entity, which remains constantly enveloped by God's grace, and at the same time a visible society which is the historical presence of this salvation-entity in something like a sacramental way (that is, the permanent authentic presence of grace). With this is given the fact that her essential structure, in so far as it is *iuris divini*, participates in her indefectibility. It cannot therefore come about that essential elements of the constitution which the Church ought to have should become complete casualties or be completely ignored. It cannot therefore happen, for example, that the college of bishops *iure divino* under the Pope as head should at one stage simply be unknown as the bearer of supreme power in the Church or should be an element not producing any effect in the life of the Church. And with a little unprejudiced attention the reality and the effectiveness of such an entity can in fact be observed. All this in its turn does not exclude the possibility that much of this reality should exist and live para-canonically, if only because there does not really exist a written constitution of the Church. The code of canon law is not such, though it specifies elements of it. Moreover, the Church's consciousness of her constitution has a history exactly as her dogma and the understanding of her faith do. As it lives by her life carried on unreflectively, so it has in its development and its history also an influence on the concrete life of the Church. Moreover, the constantly changing external historical situation of the Church demands a continually new concretisation of the permanent essential structure of the Church to correspond to the conditions of the time, because the *real* essence of the Church (which is more than the idea of its essence) only exists in contingent, historical men and in their historically conditioned activity. It is therefore self-evident that the permanent essence of the Church, her divinely bestowed constitution, can be more or less clearly, purely and effectively in evidence in the historical image presented by the Church. In this sense, there is no doubt that the papal primacy of jurisdiction, for example, was not always 'there' as it is now. In consequence it is always perfectly legitimate to ask whether this or that element of the Church's constitution could not be brought out more clearly or be lived more intensely, whether accidents of historical development do not obscure such elements, whether the 'phenotype' (if we may use this expression) could not in constitutional practice (in written and unwritten constitutional law and life) correspond better to the 'genotype' of the Church in constitutional theory. That this is self-evident can be doubted only where the constitution of the Church is reduced to a written constitution, where without mystery or history it is identified with the paragraphs of a fixed enactment so that the only way of examining the constitutional life of the Church would be to ask whether in fact these paragraphs are being observed or not.

In this connection the following should be noted when evaluating the earliest development of constitutional doctrine and life in the transition from the Apostolic Church (the 'primitive Church' in the theological sense) to the Church of the second century ('Early Catholicism'). In the Church of this period a *development* might under certain conditions be possible and historically observed which, on the one hand, is really a determination specifying in history the originally given, manifold possibilities in the constitutional structure of the Church, and yet which on the other hand possesses and permanently retains the character of divine law for the Catholic understanding of the Church's constitution. For this it is only necessary that (a) it be understood that every historically unique entity, and therefore also the Church, has in many ways a 'one-way' history and consequently not every development and historical decision must be or can be subject to revision; (b) one can and may suppose (a supposition which can afterwards be demonstrated to be historically comprehensible and justified, even though perhaps not 'compelling') that a particular development was a decision made legitimately even if not simply necessarily and caused what was in itself open to manifold possibilities to be made meaningfully and inevitably concrete and specified in *one* direction; and (c) it can be taken as a fact that such a decision still belongs to the apostolic age, and therefore can be regarded theologically as part of the process of revelation itself and not merely as part of the handing on of that revelation 'which closed with the death of the last apostle'. For example, if at the end of the apostolic age the Church has as a matter of universal practice an episcopal constitution, because at the beginning of the period of 'Early Catholicism' it is everywhere historically in evidence, then it can be taken to be *'iuris divini'* *without* one's being compelled to take up the position that already in the writings of the New Testament it is so clearly formed, so unmistakably predominant over 'presbyteral' tendencies, that any other constitutional development would from the beginning have been totally *unthinkable*. This remark is not without importance here. As we have neither the duty nor the intention of establishing here the collegiality of the episcopal college theologically from the *loci theologici* of dogmatics and ecclesiastical law, that remark can serve to make understandable that the later, more clearly given constitutional structure of the Church which we presuppose in the following considerations is a good 'scriptural' one, and in what sense this is so. And moreover it is precisely the collegial, the 'presbyteral' (if the word be rightly understood) idea in the Church's constitution for which we are here considering practical concrete forms without endangering the 'monarchic' idea in the same constitution.

Our reflections take as their starting-point the question how exactly the co-option of a bishop into the college is related to his appointment as bishop, to the conferring of the office (by ordination and by the granting of jurisdiction or by the first alone). Do these two sides of the episcopal office (membership of the college and the granting of the office) *mutually* implicate one another in a relationship of interdependence, or is the

322   THE EPISCOPAL OFFICE

membership of the college a mere *consequence*, and to a certain extent a secondary one, of the individual episcopal office and its bestowal? The same question may be studied in an analogous case: is the pope supreme pastor of the Church simply and solely because he is Bishop of Rome, with which Roman episcopal office the supreme pastorate is connected (inseparably or – by a papal act – separably), or is he, at least from a really absolute point of view, logically 'simultaneously' or even logically 'first' head of the whole Church and elected *as such*, so that *together* with this or through it he is also Bishop of Rome? In a papal election is it the successor of St Peter who is elected, in so far as he is supreme pastor of the Church even in the last analysis independently of the Roman See, so that *indirectly* the Bishop of Rome is also determined because Peter had charge of the Roman community, or is the *primary* aim to elect 'only' the Bishop of Rome who becomes *by the fact* that he is Bishop of Rome also the occupant of the universal Petrine office, because this must exist in the Church and the Bishop of Rome as the successor of Peter the first of these Roman Bishops also acquires this supreme pastoral office? The practical consequences which this intricate and seemingly uninteresting question could give rise to (for the pope and, here particularly, for the *bishops*) will appear later. In answering these two questions, which are ultimately one and the same, we do not here defend an absolutely *one*-way material relationship of logical priority and posteriority between the two elements which are in fact present in each of the two offices (pope and bishop). For us it is sufficient to maintain a relationship of at least *reciprocal* dependence between the two elements, that is to refute the opinion that membership in the college, or the supreme pastoral office, is purely a further consequence of the other element (the episcopal individual office, usually territorially circumscribed; the local Roman episcopal office). We are saying, therefore, that it is *at least equally* legitimate to see the given situation in such a way that it can be formulated so: *because* someone is admitted (by Orders and canonical mission) into the college of bishops, he is a bishop. *Because* someone is elected as supreme pastor of the Church (and accepts *this*), he is Bishop of Rome. And not *only* the other way about. We are quite conscious of the fact that this so carefully formulated thesis may not possess the ultimate clarity of formal law and logic. But it seems to us well-founded (at least as a minimal theory) and is sufficient to enable us to catch those glimpses of the present or hoped-for future practice of the Church which we are striving for.

As a foundation for our thesis we must first point out the fact that the college of bishops is regarded in the whole of Christian tradition as the successor of the apostolic college. That the bishops are the successors of the apostles in their (inheritable) office is a doctrine of Catholic faith. If there exists an episcopal college and there existed an apostolic college, then we can and must say as a consequence of that doctrine of the faith that the *college* of bishops is as such the successor of the *college* of apostles. There is also no other way of explaining the fullness of power of a Council, since the individual bishop is not infallible but the Council is, and this supreme authority and doctrinal infallibility cannot be delegated to it by the pope, for then this *delegated* power would not be the highest authority in the Church, which however it is. Accordingly Salaverri, for example, qualifies as a Catholic dogma the thesis that the *college* of bishops (both within and without a Council) is the bearer of infallible teaching authority (under determinate conditions). The college as such succeeds the apostolic college and is *formally* its continued existence, and in it the bishop has *as* its member the highest power of any which he possesses. Now the apostolic college is not constituted – if the word may be forgiven – by *local* apostles. Its existence and authority is objectively prior to a possible assumption of an individual territorial function by the individual apostle, even if the legendary division of the world among the apostles should be true. And in the same way the Petrine office, at least at one stage in Peter himself and in his main function in the apostolic college, is not originally 'locally' specified. Neither Peter nor the apostolic college exercised in the proper sense the function of a 'local Bishop' of Jerusalem, which was always regarded as belonging to James. Hence if the college of bishops is formally as such the successor of the college of apostles, this characteristic too must be found in it. *As* a college it is not simply the union of *local* bishops as such, but a collegial governing board in the Church which cannot *as* such derive its authority from the locally limited authority of its members as local bishops. Of course it is a theological problem demanding an answer, why this successor-college consists of men who occupy (at least in the majority of cases and at the beginning exclusively) a localised and limited ecclesiastical position: from this one could of course penetrate further into the *difference* which also exists between the apostolic and episcopal colleges. But these questions which are not here in dispute must not be allowed to obscure our discernment of the fact that the college of bishops as such derives its existence and its right from a college which did not consist of men having a territorially circumscribed mission and authority, and that the college of bishops cannot in any case be formally made up of individual bishops *in so far* as they have territorially limited authority. The same is true of the Petrine office. The function of supreme pastor cannot be derived from the local function of Peter and his successors *as* bearers of these local duties and powers. Consciousness of this fundamental structure is also attested by that practice of the ancient Church whereby in the case of the election of a new local bishop not only the local community and their clergy took part, but also the neighbouring bishops, metropolitans and patriarchs. The election of the pope by the college of cardinals is at least formally an election by the suburbicarian bishops, or at any rate not simply by the representatives of the Roman community as such. Also the practice of an *international* college of cardinals, which today we take practically for granted, indicates that at least today it is formally and immediately not only a question of electing the Bishop of Rome as such, but of electing the supreme pastor of the whole Church. *For this reason* an ever stronger internationalisation of the college of cardinals has prevailed since the establishment of this method of election. The assignment of a Roman titular church to the cardinals who are not suburbicarian bishops only serves to make it clear that it was desired with this wider view of the meaning of the election not to lose consciousness of the fact that it was always at the same time *also* a matter of the appointment of the local Roman bishop.

On the basis of the indications we have given, we may now state the following: admittance to, and membership of, the college of bishops (or respectively appointment to the supreme pastorate *as* such) is one side of the episcopal (or respectively Petrine) office or its bestowal which is essential, of equal importance and immediately given with the respective office, which cannot be one-sidedly derived *from* the other side (local authority) or be viewed exclusively from the point of view of the latter. A bishop is bishop of a given locality because and *in so far* as he is a member of the episcopal college as the supreme governing body of the universal Church, although in saying this the justification for the converse view is not being disputed. Ordination and canonical mission *also* have as their *immediate* signification admission into this college which itself has no territorial character and whose authority over the whole Church is not achieved by the individual bishops piecing together their limited territorial authority and thereby covering the whole earth. At the same time it remains true and not without importance that they represent their particular Churches in the college and place their treasures at the disposal of the whole Church: their spiritual character, historical situation, vital power, the will to responsibility for the totality of the Church.

II

From the point that we have reached we must now strive to gain those glimpses which we are seeking of the outlook for the future in the practical order. We will attempt to indicate a few of these without troubling about any particular systematic order.

1. The College of Cardinals

If the college of bishops with the pope at their head possesses the supreme and fullest authority in the Church, it would seem in itself an obvious conclusion that it should be this body which elects its new head whenever it should become necessary. For the determining of the pope as the supreme pastor of the whole Church is *dogmatically*, if we are right, at least as important as the electing of the pope as the Bishop of Rome. And the first aspect is for all *practical* purposes today by contrast with the early centuries of the Church of so much greater significance than the second, that if it comes to a kind of 'conflict of authority' regarding the method of election this must without any doubt be given priority. Also such an election by the corporate body which represents the whole Church would today with its world-wide facilities for travel no longer be a practical impossibility in contrast with the first eighteen centuries of the Church. We already pointed out earlier that the historical development of the college of cardinals itself is the result of the implicit consciousness that here it is not merely a question of the election of the Bishop of Rome as such by the local Church of Rome, but of the election of a man in whom the whole Church can be and ought to be interested. Therefore from the viewpoint of purely systematic thought it would seem obvious that the representatives of the whole Church should elect its head. Even if it were to be said that those who worked most closely with the deceased pope form the best electoral body, one would have to add that those who work most closely with the pope with regard to the government of the whole Church are, from the theological point of view, precisely the bishops and not the heads of central ministries, who as such can have at the most only a delegated authority over the Church from the pope which is essentially limited, and is not that fullness of power which belongs to the college *iure divino*.

But now we must consider with all due respect the fact of the existence and history of the college of cardinals as an electoral board for the pope. And there is no need to close our eyes to the fact that while an election of the pope by the college of bishops is today technically possible, it would yet be from other points of view difficult to carry out. An election of this kind would surely be possible in practice only if the assembly of all the bishops were to set up in their turn some kind of electoral committee (at least as preparatory). And then we would be back again at some kind of college of cardinals. The thought that the episcopal college has from the point of view of constitutional theology the prior claim to be called to elect the pope would therefore be best vindicated *in practice* by bringing it about that the college of cardinals itself is so formed that it can be regarded as a practical representation of the college of bishops. (This does not of course necessarily mean that the college of cardinals in electing the pope should be bound to any kind of 'mandates' and that a cardinal would not be free and indeed obliged to cast his vote according to his own conscience.) As is shown by the practice of the Council, such a representative function of the college of cardinals in fact gradually arises para-canonically almost of itself: the cardinals here have greater rights to submit their *vota*, and their word has in point of fact greater weight in the aula than that of other bishops. And yet they are speaking here as members of the episcopal college. Even if it be said that it befits the function of a cardinal as a member of the highest government of the Church to be also a bishop even if he is not regarded as a member of a more restricted representation of the college of bishops as such, it could again be held against this that a cardinal is not as such a member of the *supreme* government of the Church at all, but an official of the Pope, while it is the Pope himself and under him the college of bishops who constitute the highest government of the Church, so that the admission of a cardinal into the college of bishops cannot rightly be made comprehensible from his real function as it exists or is conceived. If the cardinals are in fact all bishops, this is most easily understood if their college is conceived as a restricted representation of the college of bishops. The progressive internationalisation of the college of cardinals which has been steadily carried forward for the last half-century points in the same direction.

In addition there is the following circumstance: John XXIII has consecrated as bishops all cardinals of the Curia who were not already bishops. It is difficult to say what exactly was his intention in doing this beyond emphasising the dignity and significance of a cardinal. Nor can it be foreseen whether this practice will be maintained in future. One may also admit that this procedure at first struck one as strange: one almost had the impression that the highest degree of the hierarchy of Orders was being used in the manner of honours and titles for something like social and decorative purposes, that the title of an office was being bestowed upon someone without any thought of the exercise of that office, because as mere cardinals without being bishops they would not necessarily and *iure divino* have a seat and a vote in the Council like residential bishops. In the perspective which has now opened up to us the matter assumes quite a different aspect. It is, to begin with, utterly appropriate that a man of the importance of a cardinal should belong to the college of bishops, since this, being by its nature (at least equally as much as the sum of local bishops as such) the supreme collegial governing board of the Church, must consist not *only* of local bishops but must *also* appropriately include such members as contribute to the government of the universal Church as immediately as the local bishops. Such are the cardinals. It represents therefore an adjustment, simplification and clarification of the concrete structure of the Church if these men also really belong to the governing board of the Church established by divine law, if what they already are juridically and practically is also sacramentally consolidated. This can be a difficulty only so long as one holds in too indiscriminate a fashion that of itself and fundamentally the college of bishops can be made up *only* of local bishops by its nature. If one can overcome this prejudice and realise that everyone who in point of fact actually participates in the highest governing body of the Church should also have the sacramental authorisation and grace of state for it, then John XXIII's measure will appear to be objectively correct. But then the college of Cardinals becomes a kind of commission or committee of the college of bishops, to which is committed most appropriately from the viewpoint of the ultimate constitutional structure of the Church the election of the pope, and it becomes understandable why it is today and will remain for the future the best papal electoral body. The only proviso is that its composition should be such as really to constitute a representation of the whole episcopate. For this it is precisely *not* required, according to what we have just said, that it should be composed *exclusively* of archbishops and bishops of residential sees. It is quite appropriate that in it should also be represented authoritative men from the central administration of the Church (with their meaningfully bestowed episcopal rank.) However it could be concluded from the foregoing that if the college of cardinals is to be viewed like this, the dignity of cardinal cannot be used as a kind of reward to crown a career in the diplomatic or curial service of the Holy See, and that it could be limited to that period of time in which someone authoritatively participates in the direction of the Church.

2. *Titular Bishops*

If it follows from the nature of the college of bishops that from the very beginning there can be members of it who are not properly bishops ruling a particular place (or their co-adjutors with right of succession), then it is also in principle quite thinkable, on the basis of an explicit realisation of the Church's ultimate constitutional structure and not merely on that of the possibility of an 'absolute' conferring of sacramental Orders, that there should be bishops who do not administer a local diocese, that is titular bishops of various kinds. From our point of view a pre-condition for this possibility, which is not only absolutely possible but quite consonant with the fundamental constitution of the Church, must certainly be that these men should occupy an *office*, should fulfil a function in the Church which corresponds to the office of a bishop and thus makes it appear meaningful and appropriate that its bearer should also be a member of the supreme governing college of the Church. There are functions and offices of this kind in the Church. It is impossible to divide up the Church *exclusively* on a territorial basis (even leaving out of consideration her summit). The territorial principle is *one* important, natural and permanent structural principle in a Church consisting of men living in space and time. But it is not the *only* structural principle. Just as it is right and necessary (and of this we will have more to say) that there should be in the Church exempt Orders, personal parishes, and institutions which cut right across the territorial divisions of the Church or embrace several dioceses, so there are in the Church offices and functions of an institutional kind which do not lend themselves to normal territorial division and yet are materially of the same importance for the Church as the functions of a local bishop. A Catholic university of the stature of Louvain, for example, is at least equally as significant a 'member' of the Church as a small Italian rural diocese. It is therefore not at all meaningless or alien to the constitution of the Church if its rector is a bishop. And this remains true even though we fully realise that the majority of the episcopal college will consist even in the future of local bishops and rightly so, precisely because the majority of really significant collegiate members of the Church will continue in future to be territorially distinct dioceses. Following upon this, one might freely ask whether it would not be most appropriate from the standpoint of a clear and courageous theology of the constitution of the Church if the supreme and permanent heads of the great exempt Orders (or a great part of them) were to become bishops. After all, they take part in the Council with a right to vote (although this is a situation bound up with great distortions which are merely historical in origin[4]).

As a consequence a distinction in the theological meaningfulness of different sorts of auxiliary bishops might be brought to light. According to Catholic dogmatics, the practice of the Oriental Churches and certain special dispositions of the Latin Church, even a simple priest is sacramentally empowered (conditional upon the necessary habitual or express permission) to administer confirmation validly and licitly. In itself there is nothing fundamentally against the extension of this practice, particularly since the religious effect (sacramental, but also psychological) of the administration of this sacrament by a bishop is no greater than that of administration by a simple priest and the Western practice consumes a great deal of the bishop's time which could be better spent in other ways for the salvation of souls.[5] From this point of view it would be difficult to maintain that the function of an auxiliary bishop if restricted to administering confirmation bestows upon him an importance in the Church such as to make it necessary for him to be a member of the

[4] If one looks at the matter dispassionately, it is really quite nonsensical that the superior of a small monastic congregation should be a member of the Council, whereas a Franciscan provincial with ten times as many priests under him as many a diocesan bishop is not. Is the difference in the duration of the office (for life in the one case, for a limited period in the other) really a sufficient ground for this?

[5] The fact that on the occasion of such a 'confirmation round' other useful things are also done (visitation of the parish, and so on) does not in any way alter what we have said.

apostolic college of bishops and so to be a bishop. If therefore the office of a mere auxiliary bishop is relatively rare outside Central Europe, this is from the constitutional-theological standpoint absolutely right. On the other hand, an additional bishop[6] in a large diocese which for various reasons (for example if it comprises a big city) cannot perhaps be meaningfully divided can have so many duties and so great a significance for the whole Church even beyond his diocese that it is entirely justified that he should be considered for membership of the college of bishops (and therefore should rightly be a bishop), indeed more so than the bishop of a miniature diocese which could easily be merged with a neighbouring one. From the point of view of the theology of the Church's constitution auxiliary bishops of this sort, too, are rightly bishops. We have already indicated that the same thing can be said analogously for the same reasons of the bearers of significant and decisively important offices in the central administration of the Church. In that case too the conferring of episcopal rank can appear not only justified by the fundamental conception which we have expounded, but as positively commendable, even though the bearer is not already a cardinal. On the other hand, from the same point of view it must be said that an episcopal consecration and dignity is not a suitable means of honouring the occupants of second-rank curial or diplomatic posts, particularly if they have superiors with the rank of bishop or cardinal, or of giving them more authority *vis-à-vis* the residential bishops.

3. 'Relative' and 'Absolute' Ordination

We can presume as well known what is meant by this heading: in a relative ordination a bishop is consecrated for a determined Church as its local bishop; in an absolute ordination Orders are conferred without any such special relationship (and we are given a constant reminder that in itself relative ordination is the normal case by the practice of conferring a titular see '*in partibus infidelium*', for which purpose nearly two thousand names are held in readiness). This is not the place to rehearse the history of the slow appearance of absolute ordination alongside the older relative ordination which for a thousand years was defended as the only justified form, or to set out the reasons for and against this absolute ordination. But we may suppose that under the previous two points we have acquired enough illustrative material to permit of a further clarification of the

[6] In the Archdiocese of New York there are ten auxiliary bishops.

central question. If the college of bishops is one and has as such a function in the Church, and if episcopal ordination as such immediately admits to the college, then *theologically* there cannot be a purely 'absolute' ordination in any unqualified sense: in every ordination there is bestowed besides the sacramental power of Orders membership in the college of bishops, which is not merely the bearer of the power of Orders but inseparably also of pastoral power. Therefore every ordination is a participation in the power of the Church in every respect, even if with regard to the pastoral power such participation is in the first place through membership of the episcopal college as such. This accords with the fact that, quite apart from our particular point of view, the idea is gradually gaining ground that ordination itself does not confer any radical sacramentally grounded and formed faculty for the exercise of pastoral power, as is also evidenced by the liturgy of Orders in the different Churches. If, then, there is a relative ordination in a really *theological* sense whenever an episcopal participation in the universal power of the Church is granted together with the bestowal of a real office (and so, for example, also of the function of membership in the college), then there cannot be any absolute ordination in an unqualified sense. What is called in vulgar or *merely* canonical usage relative ordination is then a particular species of relative ordination namely that in which is conferred also the office of a local bishop. But this does not alter in any way the theological structure of the conferring of the office. In both cases the ordination 'relates' to, is 'relative' to, an office.

This conception naturally presupposes that titular bishops too belong to the college of bishops. There are no serious objections to this conception. An objection could only be justified if it was possible to show that only someone who has the power of jurisdiction in his own diocese could be a member of the supreme bearer of jurisdiction in the Church. But such a conception would presuppose the idea that the college of bishops becomes the bearer of this power by the individual bishops in some way adding together territorially and materially limited power of jurisdiction and *in this way* constituting the supreme bearer of the *full* power of jurisdiction. But this is impossible, as is demonstrated most clearly by an office which flows from this power, namely the infallible teaching office of this college (together with the pope): a mere summation of authentic but not infallible teaching offices in the individual bishops does not result in that teaching office which both in and out of a Council is indefectible. If one then wanted to say that this quality of indefectibility comes to the teaching office of the whole episcopate from the infallibility of the pope, then it would again be impossible to see why the pope can only permit a bishop to participate in this if he is also a residential bishop.

Nor can one object to these reflections by pointing out that while titular bishops can be and are members of the Council, they are not *necessarily* so, and this would have to be the case if they were members of the college. For even if it is granted that they are, it is still open to the positive law of the Church and of the disposition of the Holy See in determining more precisely the exact constitution of a Council for good reasons to *refrain* from calling individual members of the college of bishops to the Council, since this (as such *iuris humani*) being the representation of the college of bishops does not demand a physical completeness in the number of the assembled bishops and since there is no need to dispute that there is a certain difference in membership of the college as between local Ordinaries and certain kinds of titular bishops. The fact that titular bishops belong to the college of bishops can really not be doubted, neither on general principles nor precisely from the viewpoint that to be a bishop signifies *formaliter* to be a member of the college. This is true even if we emphasise that membership of a college admits of different degrees and modes so that a titular bishop does not have to be, nor is, a member of the episcopal college in precisely the same sense as a residential bishop.[7]

Added to this is the realisation that the ideal of relative ordination makes it desirable to have as subject of episcopal power and dignity someone whose *other* episcopal function (as distinct from his function as a member of the college) makes it precisely appropriate that he should be a member of the supreme governing body of the Church. Now we have sought to show that there are such functions which are not identical with the function of a local Ordinary, and that on the other hand titular bishops not infrequently exercise only such functions as do not make their

---

[7] Here we may briefly refer to the following: exactly as baptism constitutes a certain, although not a full, membership of the Church even if the baptised person is a heretic or a schismatic, so a valid episcopal consecration gives a certain, although not full, membership of the episcopal college, even if the consecrated person is a heretic or schismatic. This is especially so where the heresy or schism is only material and the absence of any '*affectus haereticalis aut schismaticus*' is sociologically obvious.

bearer appear objectively as a suitable member of the supreme governing body of the Church. A relative ordination, therefore, which would be desirable from every point of view, that is both theologically *and juridically*, would be one in which someone receives an office or in which someone's office is sacramentally consecrated which truly qualifies him to be a suitable member of the college of bishops. This office may then be of a local or non-local kind. A merely 'absolute' ordination (even if it is relative in the sense previously described) which would be wholly undesirable would be one which, apart from the membership of the college and the bare power of Orders, does not give anything and does not come upon or confer any function in its bearer which in its significance for the universal Church makes him 'homologous' with a local Ordinary.

4. The Essential Nature of the Diocese

If we listen to a recital of the statements of the Schoolmen on the nature of the diocese we will be given few illuminating insights: a diocese is a member-Church over which presides a bishop with a pastoral authority which is prescribed and precisely delimited (against pope and perhaps patriarch and metropolitan) by ecclesiastical law; a bishop on the other hand (if one abstracts from his power of Orders, which does not give any sign of being related in any immediately visible way to a circumscribed territory, and certainly not to its shape and size) is a man who governs a diocese with pastoral authority. There is thus a perfect circle in our understanding. But now that we are faced with the new and urgent question in practical law and pastoral theology of how large a diocese should in fact be and whether dioceses should be divided or amalgamated, we see that we can no longer be satisfied with such answers. On the other hand these practical questions which we have just mentioned cannot be answered simply 'in practice'. It is only when we know *what* a diocese is intended to be, what are really its functions and what are not (for example, because they can equally well be carried out by a dean, if necessary armed with the power to confirm; or because in all cases they can only be dealt with by a 'chief bishop', that is a metropolitan, a patriarch and their combinations, or a national or continental bishops' conference) that we can 'practically' ask *how* a diocese should be formed with regard to its size and institutions in order to enable it to carry out these functions. For example, someone who is of the opinion that a bishop must 'know' all his priests or be in a position to confirm all the members of his flock personally will form a different ideal image of the most desirable extent of a diocese than will someone who rejects a guide-line of this kind as romantic and paternalistic.

Now it is surely evident at the start that we can neither have an 'ideal' image of the diocese which is equally valid for all times, nor develop an imaginative 'model' of the diocese *for today* in such a way as to allow us to deduce from it, for example, a particular number of square miles or of inhabitants as its 'ideal' size. The first is impossible, because quite clearly a diocese in its concrete historical form is a consequence of many natural (geographic, racial, social, historical) conditions which are changeable. The second is impossible, because these differences can be found to exist even today at the same time. But setting out from the fundamental idea of these new reflections we can say something to make the 'idea' of the diocese more concrete than it is in the formal determination of the notion with which we began.

At this point, it is good once more to arouse our wonder at the fact that the supreme governing body of the Church which originally had its normal seat in *one* place – Jerusalem – is largely composed of men who are at the same time governors of a 'province' of the Church and so are 'scattered' throughout the world. In the case of other sociological entities this is seldom so: the 'Government', the 'Cabinet' of a country will scarcely ever be composed of the governors of the provinces of the country. Neither is our wonder in any way dissipated by the mere consideration that the Roman Pope represents in this governing body the unity of the Church while the bishops represent the plurality and multiplicity of the Church's members so that these members of the board must come from all parts of the world. For even though the bipolar structure of the supreme governing body (a head of the college who is personally capable of action and a synodal plurality of members) includes a representation of the whole Church, this is no reason why it should be in itself identical with the total number of the leaders of the local Churches. And yet this fact which is so far from being self-evident is the case. Again, this is not the place to draw consequences for the theological character of the college of bishops and the particular nature of its origin from the apostolic college from these observations of the difference between a supra-local apostolic college which exists in one place and an episcopal college composed of local bishops who are 'scattered'. (Clearly it is not the successor-college in the sense that the same permanent college as a moral person is merely made up of different physical persons: it is *one* college following upon *another* college.)

If we are to take full account of this surprising fact we will have to say that the members of the supreme governing body of the universal Church must be men governing such a notable part of the Church that it can rightly expect to be personally represented on that board. But this means conversely that a diocese must be such (in size, life, and character) that in it (precisely in its geographic, demographic, historical and religious make-up of that particular period) the totality of the Church is made to appear, that it can really be called a 'Church', that is, it can be characterised by the same theological concept (and not just that of a part, a province and so on, of the Church) as the universal Church herself, something which one could not say nor ought to say of a local parish. For the Church in contrast with every other society has the peculiar characteristic of being able to make her appearance *whole* on the spot. A State has in a particular place only *one* of its places: a city or a province which can never rightly be called by the same name as the whole State. But in the Church it is quite otherwise: she can be in one place as a whole and therefore the community of that place can rightly be called 'the Church'. The Church is 'there' on the spot, because her highest self-realisation which qualifies her as a whole and which cannot be thought of as any higher or more concentrated even in the totality of the Church can take place in a particular spot and not only in the territorial totality of the Church: the celebration of the Eucharist, where the Lord is truly present as Lord and sacrifice of the Church, and the proclamation of the efficacious Word of God in which the mighty deeds of God towards man are heralded in the event.

As a consequence one might be tempted to think that simply every local community about an altar and not only the diocese is already Church. It is a fact that this difficulty could scarcely be felt at all in ancient times because the average true and full community about an altar coincided with the community about a bishop. But it is precisely this view of the local community as a kind of actual presence of the whole Church which leads to the conclusion that only that local community is really completely 'Church', and so a diocese, in which the *whole* of the Church's realisation of her life can be representatively brought about, and not only the celebration of the Eucharist (Sacrament) and the proclamation of the

Word. This presence of the whole of the Church is of course not conceived in the sense that wheresoever there are 'genuine' dioceses the Church is really present *wholly* with her life, but in the sense (and this is a variable requirement according to place and time) that a proper diocese must also be to a sufficient extent the bearer of such functions as necessarily belong to the universal Church over and above the Eucharistic celebration and the proclamation of the Word. For only such a member-part of the Church can meaningfully claim that its leader should be a member of the supreme governing board of the Church.

In connection with the foregoing the following consideration should be kept in mind: the possibility of the Church as such coming to appear in some way as a whole at a particular point in space and time in the world depends to a large extent on the secular sociological conditions existing in that particular place at that particular time. For a diocese *today* to be able to be a diocese, that is a Church which really represents at least in some way *the* Church in all her dimensions, it requires pre-existing conditions of a sociological, economic, and cultural sort which are simply not possible in a very small diocese (we are always speaking of a diocese which is already developed or at least capable of being developed). Because the spiritual, cultural and social life of today is of such a particular kind, and therefore the organisation of the Church with her theological, spiritual and religious life must also as its analogue be of this kind, it can exist only in relatively widespread or highly populated areas. A 'village' cannot support the image of a developed and complete diocese. But the same is now true also of smaller areas which by contrast with earlier social frameworks are now no more than the villages of the present age. When today one reflects upon the diocese which corresponds to the present, one must keep in mind that the fundamental extension of the local community of today is no longer the town but the industrial zone. Just as there was a historical transition (of a gradual kind) from the village-culture to that of the town, so today we are experiencing a transition from the town-culture to a culture for whose local unit we do not even yet have a proper name, which for the moment we may call 'industrial zone'. These sociological developments ought not to be overlooked when one reflects upon the nature of a contemporary 'proper' diocese. Could one possibly conceive, for example, of the Ruhr having several dioceses? If not, and if such an industrial area is becoming more and more the normal type of human life, what are the consequences for the correct size of a diocese?

What we have so far said may still be only a vague indication of the fundamental-theological nature of a diocese: if we wanted to say anything immediately more precise, we would be led into the difficult question we do not intend to discuss here, in what sense the bishop and the diocese are '*iuris divini*', that is once more how and why the one office of the Church (given in and supported by a successor-college similar to the apostolic college in its unity of Peter's office and the 'Twelve') should be borne by a college organised on a *territorial* basis; and why, for example, (*de facto* or *de jure*?) the sum of patriarchs or metropolitans alone does not deserve consideration as such a successor-college, so that these alone would have to be called 'bishops' in the theological sense, whereas those we now call bishops would be merely a kind of 'archpriest' or 'dean'.[8] But even the still vague information what a bishop is (as member of the college) and what therefore he should be (in his particular office) already offers a criterion by which to measure dioceses as they exist in fact. If it is necessary for the diocese to be a real representation of the life of the universal Church (in its natural and supernatural character), then it is not excluded but rather implied that this kind of representation and therefore the form of the diocese is subject to historical change. The ancient bishopric of a

[8] If we consider the fact that on the one hand even a 'simple' priest can under certain conditions confirm, perhaps even ordain to the priesthood (cf. *DS* 1145 *sq.*), and that on the other hand a patriarch or metropolitan nearly always participates as a consecrator at a normal episcopal consecration, we see how difficult it is to say dogmatically just what a bishop is. Even if we maintain that *de facto* he is distinct from the simple priest '*ratione ordinis*', the question still remains open whether *this* distinction is itself *iuris divini* or not, precisely *how* it is to be explained (whether by the fact that a simple priest has the episcopal power of ordination restricted to the point of invalidity of the act, or by the fact that it is simply not there) and whether this distinction must have been the same at all times in the Church's history or whether the Church's intention regarding the two Orders could itself be subject to historical change. It is difficult to characterise the bishop on the basis of the power of jurisdiction because at least as a matter of fact his pastoral power is limited by that of the pope (and perhaps of other higher bishops) and because even those who are not bishops can have a share in this power which is capable of being divided and apportioned in the most diverse ways. And so it is really simplest and clearest to say that a bishop is a member of the supreme governing body of the Church and to determine *from this* what office he should fill and what powers he should be invested with in order that he might meaningfully be called a bishop, that is to say, that he might meaningfully and appropriately from the nature of things be co-opted into this supreme college.

locality and the contemporary (apart from Italy) bishopric of a province, for example, represent the change from the ancient *Polis*-State (which also exercised a great historical influence in the Hellenistic-Roman Empire) to the region-State. We cannot here go any further into the history of the form and function of a bishopric, a history which is complex and varies greatly in different continents. But if our fundamental line of thought is correct then certain consequences will follow which are of considerable practical importance for our time. A diocese, as it ought to be, should not be too small: it must really be able to support of itself the organs which belong to the Church as such (prescinding from her central government). And since the apparatus of the institutional in the life of the Church in today's world of technology and mass society necessarily becomes ever more complicated (pastoral institutes, training places for the most diverse forms of aid in the Church, finance, widely organised charitable works, and much more of the same kind), the objectively correct trend is tending to an increase rather than a decrease in the size of dioceses. If the city is becoming increasingly the normal domicile and usually there is only one diocese in the one city, then by force of circumstance the large diocese will become the normal type of diocese. And this is also theologically justified: the occupant of a miniature see of a few thousand souls, and this in regions where dioceses could easily be combined, has no meaningful claim to be a member of the supreme governing college of the universal Church.[9] This is particularly so in a period when the universal Church consists of four hundred millions and almost unavoidably has at the same time two to three thousand bishops whose number can after all not be multiplied indefinitely if – and one need only think of a Council and its technical problems – they are really still to constitute the supreme government of the universal Church. It is no use resisting a development towards relatively greater dioceses, hindering the fusion of small dioceses, or pleading for the division of dioceses on grounds which are of a rather romantic or paternalistic kind. The only consequence of such a procedure would be that what a real bishop must be if he is to be a member of the episcopal college would

---

[9] If it be objected that this is all very well, but such a one is still a consecrated bishop, then we need only remark that the question here is precisely this, *who should* be meaningfully consecrated a bishop as member of the college of the Church's universal government and under what conditions; the question is not whether someone once he has been consecrated is then rightly a member of that college.

practically even if not terminologically be found only in the case of higher bishops, patriarchs or metropolitans, or with the presidents of bishops' conferences, and he who is still called bishop but is no longer really fully such would in practice be no more than a dean with the power to administer confirmation. He would no longer be at the head of such institutions as make a territorial district into a 'Church'.

Wherever a diocese is incapable of supporting by itself a seminary corresponding to the demands of today, wherever the institutions demanded by the educational system, or charitable organisation, the influencing of public opinion, the management of mass media or of cultural life, cannot be supported by a diocese in such a manner that in some way they are representative of the whole Church, then in that place there does not exist a member-Church which can and should be led by a successor of the apostles such that over him he needs to have only the principle of the unity of the college, the successor of the apostolic college, for his normal activity. In other words, it would be a diocese more in name than in reality. If in order to be effective a genuine, large, living diocese of the kind we have envisaged really requires further intermediaries between its head and the individual local community, that is intermediate instances 'below', which may easily be the case, then these should be created, if those which already exist (deaneries, inter-parochial diocesan organisations, personal parishes like student communities, and so on) are insufficient; or those which exist should be allowed more powers in accordance with the principle of subsidiarity which also applies to the Church. But this is no reason for making the dioceses so small that their head must sink in the spiritual, sociological, and properly ecclesiastical sense to the level of a parish priest who administers confirmation and is able to ordain priests. His pastoral authority too must be capable of showing the stature and impressiveness of a successor of the apostles and a member of the total government of the Church. For this there is required not merely the existence of a formal pastoral authority, but it must also have an object, a field of activity, and a matter for its objectification which is worthy of its significance. What we have said is of course primarily intended to apply to a diocese which is fully constituted and not to one still in process of being built up, and naturally it must be filled out in the concrete in a very variable way according to times, regions and their cultural and social development.

5. *The Bishop and his Priests*

Here and there the anxious question has already been raised, whether a clearer prominence given to the mission and authority of the bishop who rules his diocese in the name of Christ and not as a mere official of the pope may not be accompanied by the danger of substituting for a centralised and – allegedly or really – autocratic régime from Rome a practical 'episcopalism' with an autocratic régime in the diocese. We, in our middle-European lands, will not feel ourselves bound to hold this danger to be very great or urgent. Our diaspora-situation does not favour such a danger: bishops and priests are too dependent on one another in the crisis of neo-paganism. If we prescind from quirks of character and temperamental outbreaks which can have a good or bad effect in *every* 'system' and in the latter case must be borne with patience and . . . humour, and which with virile and fraternal openness of priests before their bishop can always be sufficiently contained, our bishops are in no danger and under no suspicion of being or becoming autocrats. But this may be quite otherwise in other countries with a different historical and psychological conditioning. Perhaps an African bishop may involuntarily affect the attitude of a tribal chief, or there may be still preserved in one or another French bishop something like a piece of the mentality of the *ancien régime*. In any case, in order to avoid this danger it is at all times and in every place necessary that the theologically correct relationship between bishop and presbyterium should be kept vitally in the forefront of our consciousness.

Our approach permits us to clarify this relationship. We do not in any way maintain that the relationship of pope to episcopate is in our fundamental theology simply carried further down in the same sense as equally '*iuris divini*' and so can be simply transferred univocally and mechanically to the relationship of bishop to presbyterium. But at this point we can say two things. First, the fundamental-theological structure of the Church, in so far as it demands a bipolar unity of a monarchical and a collegial element inseparably related to one another (without on that account being a college of mere equals, as in the 'definition' of a college given by Ulpian), can surely also serve as a guide for the relationship of bishop and presbyterium. Second, if the principle of collegiality is applied to this relationship at least as a guide from the point of view here emphasised, then we must say the following. The priest enters by his priestly ordination into a college, the presbyterium, which is surely to be thought of as fundamentally *iure divino*[10] a college for the bishop. And in point of fact the New Testament and the primitive Church do not actually show any knowledge of the single priest but only of the presbyterium. The latter is even locally united with the bishop, it is not a subsequent collection of parish priests residing in places where there is no bishop, but precisely the college in the same place where the bishop is: he does not ordain a priest because he cannot be everywhere, but as a helper in his office where he actually is. He does not ordain an individual, but surrounds himself with a college. He does not act without the presbyterium. This does not mean that he is dependent upon his presbyterium juridically and in a way subject to legal action, but that he knows himself to be no lonely, autocratic monarch who could say, or would want to say: 'The diocese, *c'est moi*!'. One can unhesitatingly say that the 'synod' of the bishop with his presbyterium is just as old and original as the synod of bishops among themselves (even though it is not on that account constitutionally of the same kind). Perhaps today it may legitimately be the case on practical grounds that the function of the former episcopal presbyterium is carried out to a large extent (leaving aside the rare occasion of a diocesan synod, *CIC c.* 356–362) by the cathedral chapter and the other priest-members of an episcopal Curia, and perhaps in the concrete situation of today with the necessary big dioceses and the local separation of most priests from the episcopal seat it must be so. But if one looks at this episcopal Curia keeping in mind the bipolarity of bishop and presbyterium, one must say that the fundamental-theological structure of the Church is realised purely and clearly only if the episcopal Curia is chosen and constituted in such a way that it can be accepted to be really the representation of the presbyterium; that therefore a similar

[10] Although it has not been strictly defined, it is theologically certain that the threefold gradation of the Church's office (bishop – priest – deacon) is part of the unalterable, divine constitution of the Church. But if in stating this one were to think merely of priests as individuals, called into being simply to the extent that a bishop has need of help, then it would also be possible to conceive of a bishop deciding that he can do without such help and so eliminating the threefold gradation of the office at one fell swoop. To bring this about one need only think of the theoretical possibility of consecrating every parish priest a bishop and so making individual priestly assistants superfluous. Therefore if the 'second grade' of the priestly office is really to be *iuris divini*, it can only be thought of as the college for the bishop; strictly speaking, therefore, priests do not primarily take the place of the bishop where he cannot be himself, but support him as the presbyterium surrounding the bishop where he is.

relationship exists from a theological point of view as our previous reflections showed to be desirable between the college of cardinals and the episcopal college. This does not in any way mean that the episcopal Curia must be elected by the presbyterium 'from below' (or even as a kind of supervisory body over the bishop on behalf of the presbyterium). This is not the case with the college of cardinals and it would offend against the subordination of the presbyterium to the bishop. But this may well mean on fundamental-theological grounds (and not on merely pragmatic-psychological ones) that the bishop has the moral obligation to constitute his Curia in such a way that it is also the representation of his presbyterium which he himself after all has ordained as *his* presbyterium, as his council of 'Elders', even if the honouring of this moral obligation is not subject to a juridically laid down control by the presbyterium.

Only when the priest is seen as always the member of the presbyterium does it become quite understandable (particularly when one thinks of the practice of the early Church with her many small episcopal sees) why every head of a permanent, local altar-community of any size, that is above all every parish priest, is not a bishop. It becomes understandable why a diocese is a really theological entity, not merely an administrative organisation of many local communities, but a real, spiritual entity: the bishop does not ordain priests in order to send them *away* from him with their faculties, so that each may be a priest for himself, but he entrusts to the members of his presbyterium, which remains always his, particular local commitments and so remains the episcopal Father of his whole diocese. From this it will also be understandable that the local parish is indeed the normal and most common type of such a commission of the member of the presbyterium, but that members of the presbyterium can be called upon as representatives of the bishop for other kinds of altar-communities, if and in so far as such non-parochial, permanent altar communities (personal parishes, religious communities, and so on) remain meaningful. The 'territorial principle' is not the only constitutive principle. It is precisely when the individual priest is seen as a member of the presbyterium that a romantic parochialism is avoided which would make of the parish priest a little bishop (and tries to make him, for example, irremovable or untransferable in the same sense as the bishop). The dignity of the parish priest is not lessened but increased, if he is seen as a member of the episcopal presbyterium, as the representative here and now of the episcopal church. But the parish is not a diocese in miniature.

If it were regarded as such, it would properly have to become a diocese. But against this must be said everything that was set out above against miniature dioceses.

Finally, our approach makes it theologically comprehensible why up to the present the dividing-line between the sacramental powers of the bishop and those of the simple priest has not achieved perfect clarity in the Church's consciousness of her faith. One can only say with any certainty that a priest cannot consecrate a bishop. But it is not even certain whether he cannot under certain circumstances validly administer priestly Orders. It is certain that he can confirm. This is a curious situation. For since a simple priest is the bearer of all the jurisdictional authority of a bishop, it might in the abstract be held according to present-day theology that simple priests exercise alone all without any bishops the offices in the Church which are really necessary for her life, since one needs episcopal consecration only if one needs bishops. But these are not required if all their functions can equally well be carried out by the simple priest, in so far as these functions are necessary for the salvation of Christians. These speculative reflections are merely meant to show that the border-line *iuris divini* between priest and bishop is not so easy to draw as it is sometimes thought. But this is the point which becomes understandable if the bishop cannot really be thought of without his presbyterium and therefore if in certain circumstances a subordinate member of this unity of bishop and presbyterium (who is designated by sacramental Orders) can represent the bishop. In the ultimately decisive matter he does it in any case: in the celebration of the Eucharist. And this has always been and is today the most central function of the bishop (because here in this most intimate mystery of the Church she is made present most actually and most intensively): it is for this reason that Thomas Aquinas and all the great theologians would not admit any sacramentality of episcopal Orders as distinct from priestly Orders. This is again an indication of the point we are making: bishop and priest belong most closely together because the priest is not a smaller 'recapitulation' of the bishop, but a member of his presbyterium apart from which in the last analysis[11] he cannot be thought of; and *this* is the reason why his

---

[11] Even if we think of an individual consecrated bishop in abstraction without any priests of his own, he is still surrounded by priests through his necessary union with the whole college of bishops, since according to *DS* 1776 the universal episcopate can certainly not be without a presbyterium.

powers as representative of the head of the presbyterium are somewhat changeable and have not always been the same perhaps in the different periods of the Church's history in accordance with the possibly changing intention of the Church in raising men to the priesthood.[12]

6. *The Unity of Offices and Powers in the Church*

By this heading we do not mean the unity of the *bearers* of the offices and the powers, but that of the offices and powers themselves, certainly in so far as this unity can be seen from the unity of the episcopal college with and under (and also through[13]) the Pope and from the inseparable unity of the conferring of powers and the co-option into the college in the case of the bishop. It is of course obvious that these brief reflections from a particular standpoint can in no way claim to be a complete treatment of the subject indicated by the title 'Unity of Powers'.

We set out once more from the fundamental fact that the college of bishops with the pope at its head is the bearer of supreme and full authority in the Church. A society ('people of God', 'people of the Covenant', 'community' of Christ) which proclaims its unity as one of its most essential characteristics and which has *one* goal and *one* mission must also be necessarily one in its office, and this ultimately single authority and this ultimately single office pertains to the college of bishops, which is

---

[12] Theologically such a possibility must be taken seriously. Although a society's office may ultimately be one by reason of the unity of the society and of its aim and purpose, a partial participation in it is changeable of its very nature and as a consequence of historical situations without this involving any change in the nature of the one office. There is no reason to suppose that the same cannot be true of the Church. The nature of the one office which is *iuris divini* and its threefold gradation need not be affected by this. If, for example, the Church declared one day that no priest is capable of administering priestly ordination in any circumstance and under any condition whatever, this would not mean that this had always and at all times been so. Perhaps the case is somewhat similar when the question is asked whether an episcopal consecration even without a preceding priestly ordination is valid or not. After all, we have at least an analogous case with regard to the 'matter' of the Sacrament of Orders, where the Church has explicitly (*DS* 3861) left open the question whether this essential matter has at all times been the same. Presumably the Church can also determine the precise extent of the powers which she intends to confer through priestly ordination and by this means vary the distance between the simple priesthood and the episcopate, although her intention is on occasion very implicit. Such a consideration could perhaps diminish or eliminate altogether many a difficulty arising in these matters in the early periods of the Church's history.

[13] *DS* 3051.

thus actually characterised by the full possession of this one authority and this one office. In so far as in this one office and in the one authority upon which it is based we can and must distinguish, no matter for what reasons, offices and authorities of various kinds, these must therefore never be simply enumerated purely arithmetically but grasped in their unity, or developed from the one fundamental essence of the Church, from her unity and the unity of her mission and her goal.

We must now take note, to a certain extent empirically, of the fact that the supreme bearer of this one office, or alternatively that the members of the college which is this bearer, are constituted as such on the one hand by a sacramental consecration which gives them a power to sanctify (*potestas ordinis*), and on the other by the conferring of a pastoral power (*potestas iurisdictionis*) which is not yet given or need not be given by episcopal consecration (at least as 'absolute') at any rate as *wholly* at their free and actual disposal. And yet it follows from what we have just said that these two powers (and the offices which are built upon them and through which they are exercised) must have an inner unity and an ultimately indissoluble connection. If one wishes to see this, it is no use looking merely or in the first place at the individual bishop as such, but it is necessary to reflect on the college of bishops as such and their onto-logical and logical equality with or precedence over the single bishops or their merely consequent summation. For there is no difficulty in the case of the college of bishops in propounding the thesis that in it as *such* a separation of the two powers is quite impossible, without coming into conflict with the fact indicated above.[14] The Church cannot after all be thought of without bishops, that is without that power of Orders which involves the legitimate authority to celebrate the Eucharist and to hand on this authority (power of ordination). But neither can there be any Church without the pastoral power, without which the *one* life of the *visible* Church is not thinkable. Now it is surely unthinkable that these two powers which necessarily exist in the Church should be distributed between two completely and fundamentally different bearers. For apart from the question *how* one could even imagine this being carried out in practice, this is quite impossible for the reason that these two powers in-clude one another at least in part. The leader of the Eucharistic celebration

---

[14] Namely the fact that someone may have an 'episcopal' jurisdiction without being consecrated a bishop, or someone may be a consecrated bishop without – at least apparently – having the *potestas iurisdictionis*.

is after all not to be thought of as the mere agent of the consecration *ex opere operato*, but as the fully authorised leader of the celebration of the community with the right and the duty of admitting to the altar-community or excluding from it as the highest realisation of the unity of the visible Church. If he does this *because he* is the possessor of the *power of Orders*, he is already positing sacred *law*. If the exercise of the power of Orders of reconciling with God and the Church in the Sacrament of Penance were simply dependent on someone who does not himself possess this power as a matter of principle and in every case, then it would be no more than an abstract theoretical postulate and nothing in reality. The giver of the jurisdiction for confession would be the true possessor of the Church's power of reconciliation, since only by him would its exercise be made possible. This is further unthinkable for the reason that this power also essentially signifies the power to admit to the full Eucharistic community of the altar, which power must however by the very nature of the case be possessed by the leader of the community's celebration of the Last Supper. Therefore the power of Orders and pastoral power at least partially include one another; they are basically two elements of one and the same fundamental power, which is divided into two powers only in relatively secondary effects and applications, where each of them is not necessarily determined in the same way or by the same norms as the other. But if they hang together in such an inseparable way in their deepest root, then the bearer of this *completely* one power can only be he who *necessarily* possesses *both*. And this bearer is the college of bishops under and with the pope.

It follows from this that it is a duty of the pope to receive episcopal consecration, if he should be elected when he is not a bishop. For even though one might justify the prescription of canon 219 of the Code[15] in the considerations we are here concerned with by saying that as head of the college he already participates in a certain sense in the power of Orders of his college before he is himself consecrated a bishop and so participates in this power also personally as an individual and not merely as a member of the college, it is surely more than a demand of reasonableness or even of the look of the thing that the supreme head of the whole Church, in whose person inhéres the fullness of pastoral power, should also possess that power which in the last analysis cannot be separated from

---

[15] '*Romanus Pontifex, legitime electus, statim ab acceptata electione, obtinet, iure divino, plenam supremae iurisdictionis potestatem.*'

pastoral power in the Church or in the whole college, namely the power of Orders, with which is immediately given sacred law, and in which the latter in fact has its origin.[16]

[16] At this point we may ask in some surprise – if for once we may be permitted to say this out loud – why it is taken so much for granted that the act of transmitting the supreme pastoral power resident in the pope is not a grade of the Sacrament of Orders. It is clear that the *mode* of appointment to this office (without any laying-on of hands) is no absolute barrier to maintaining the opposite opinion: a sacrament (as may be seen in Penance and Matrimony) is not necessarily bound to a 'matter' which is distinct from the 'form' (the word which assures the grace). If it is said that papal election (with its acceptance) does not confer any higher 'power of Orders' but only constitutes '*ratione iurisdictionis*' a higher degree in the official hierarchy, we are entitled to ask the counter-question whether this answer is really as clear as it appears to be at first sight in view of the radical unity of the two powers, whether it was not with a formally similar argument that St Thomas and the medieval theologians disputed the sacramentality of episcopal consecration (that is, because it did not confer any new authoritative power – in this case in relation to the Body of Christ), whether it is *a priori* evident that the conferring of the power of an office can only then be sacramental, that is bound up with the *ex opere operato* bestowal of the grace of the office, when this official power is itself a commission to perform sacramental acts. If it be said that the idea that the election of a pope could be the highest grade of the Sacrament of Orders is quite unheard of up to now, we may point out that up to the Second Vatican Council it was also not absolutely certain that episcopal consecration is a grade of the Sacrament of Orders. One might continue by asking whether, arguing from the nature of the Church as the basic sacrament, it is not necessary to say that appointment to the highest and most decisive office in the Church is also God's absolute promise of the divine Pneuma for rightly fulfilling this office (no matter whether the man completely takes up this promise or not), and what is really the difference between such an absolute promise and an *opus operatum*. One could ask whether the radical unity of the two powers in the Church does not suggest that the gradation of each of the two powers is given in the same way on both sides. If it be objected that appointment to the papacy does not produce an 'indelible mark', the character which is part of the essence of the Sacrament of Orders, it could be pointed out that a pope can be released from his authority only by his own act of renunciation, something which is not so in the case of any other degree in the hierarchy of jurisdiction, and that by this fact alone his office is already assimilated to the permanent powers of Orders in the lower degrees of the hierarchy of Orders, especially since the bearers of all these degrees can in practice renounce every exercise of their powers; the difference which then still remains can be explained by the nature of the case, that is by the essence of the supreme office, which cannot be taken up again by someone once he has completely renounced its exercise. It must also be always kept in mind that the theological nature of the pope's office can only be rightly seen if he is regarded *also* as a bishop, because he is head of the episcopal college as a hierarchy of Orders, 'and that therefore his appointment as pope necessarily signifies a modification of the episcopal authoritative power which he has or must have. Why should this modification in fact not have a sacramental character?

This unity of powers in which is given the one essence and the one mission of the college of bishops is also a manifestation of the fact that law and the juridical order in the Church are an expression and an element of that grace which is preached in the gospel, and that they are an instrument of salvation and not the sting of sin only when they accompany grace and are redeemed by it, by that grace which is promised us efficaciously and without repentance in the Sacraments.

This unity of powers in one and the same bearer, in the one college of bishops, also brings home from the point of view of constitutional theology, even though it does not urge it in every individual case, the principle that wherever there is given an 'Ordinarius' with reference to pastoral power as a permanent office in a subject for life, then that subject should also be a bishop. This is not merely because (as we saw above) such a one can meaningfully be a member of the supreme governing body of the Church (as also *vice versa*), but also because the exercise of such pastoral power should be supported by that grace which first sanctifies power in the Church and makes it a means of sanctification, and seeing that it involves such decisive events of grace should also be made historically and ecclesiologically (socially) visible in the Sacrament. As we have said, this may not be urgent in the individual case, because even without such a sacramental foundation and consecration of the pastoral power in the individual he and his activity stand within the whole of the mystical Body of Christ and as a consequence (that is, of the Sacrament of Orders which is infallibly present in the Church) the activity of such an individual also has this grace assured to it. But careful consideration should be given to this reflection in the practice of the Church. The fundamental-theological structures of the Church would thus be brought to a clearer and purer concrete development.

The question why and how the radically single power of the Church, while remaining one in its root, even though possessing two constitutive elements, yet unfolds into two separate powers which then in their

---

Merely because we are not accustomed to see things in this way? But could we not see them in this way if we were once accustomed to seeing that the conferring of an office in the Church (as a whole) is of its nature a sacrament under the necessary conditions and with the corresponding intention on the part of the Church (to confer a definitive office) and that *therefore* and as a consequence of this the degrees of this office introduced by the Church (even it may be from apostolic times and irrevocably) are sacramental stages of the one office sacramentally conferred?

divided form no longer exhibit precisely the same characteristics, is a question which naturally does not concern us here. We only wish to add here the note, that it is certainly insufficient to characterise the one power (power of Orders) as incapable of being lost and the other (pastoral power) as capable of being lost. For in its first bearer, the college of bishops with the pope, the pastoral power, too, cannot be lost: the college as such cannot lose it, and it is also implicit in the doctrine of the ultimate indefectibility of the socially constituted Church as such and the necessity for the power of Orders *and* for pastoral power of a historically visible apostolic succession that the historically visible college of bishops with the pope can never (as it were, all of a sudden) cease to exist and be replaced by an absolutely new college which is brought into being, so to speak, by a '*generatio aequivoca*'. Certainly the fact that Catholic ecclesiology both regards it as self-evident that a pope should be *elected* and therefore does not receive his office (as in the case of the bishop) handed on by his predecessor, and is also able to reckon with the possibility of a pope as a heretic or schismatic losing his membership of the Church and thus his office, indicates that the office of pope, rightly understood, is also supported by the college of bishops: it is because the Church remains an hierarchically ordered one even at the death (whether understood physically or morally) of the pope and the office is therefore historically then still in existence, that the election of a new pope is possible. In such a situation the Church posits without the pope an ecclesiastico-juridical act of the highest importance, namely the election of a new pope, even though this act consists merely in indicating the person who is to receive from the Spirit his full authority as pope (admittedly only in *one* respect, since the episcopal consecration of the pope is not purely an event 'from above' and episcopal powers yet belong to the essence of the papacy), and even though the Church is obliged to the act of choosing a pope. So if ultimately the power of jurisdiction cannot be lost in the Church, in so far as it reposes in the college of bishops, the power of Orders is on the other hand in many ways capable of being lost, or rather it is at least capable of being 'bound' to the extent of invalidating an act (for example, a priest's power of absolution; his power of confirming which is surely radically conferred on him *sacramentally*), and there is still not complete clarity in sacramental theology on the question of how far it is possible for the Church (even if this power, for whatever reason, should not be unlimited) to withhold validity and not merely lawfulness from a determinate subject's act even of the power of Orders. One ought to study anew from this point of view the historical questions of the 're-ordinations' in ancient and early medieval times and of the invalidity of Anglican Orders: perhaps the situation is simply this, that *both* the positions adopted in these questions are 'in themselves' *possible* and the dispute, rightly seen, is really over whether the Church in making its decision *de facto* allowed or (from the beginning) denied any validity to a simoniacal Ordination (as an act). (Similarly with Anglican Orders.) From such reflections, too, it follows how close is the unity of the two powers in the Church. Yet this is not the place to pursue this question any further.

7. Exemption

The whole problematic area designated by this heading, too, cannot here be treated in all its depth and to its full extent. But our point of view permits us to attain to a very basic understanding of the real fundamental-theological side of the problem. The college of bishops with and under the pope is one, and it has as a college and in its head a unified function which is inter- or supra-territorial, which is not really the sum of the territorially limited functions of its individual members but is at least equal to them. From this fundamental idea it follows that someone can quite meaningfully be thought of as a member of this college who does not exercise at the same time any territorially determined pastoral function in the Church, provided only that his membership of the college be justified on other grounds, as, for example, in the case of a curial cardinal who is a 'titular bishop'.

Now there exist in the Church 'member-Churches' which on the one hand have every right to exist from the essence of the Church and yet are not simply a territorial 'province' of the Church, and on the other are of that importance for the whole Church and exercise that representative function for the Church as a whole which we demanded above for the constitutionally correct essence of a territorial diocese. In a word, there are 'personal dioceses', or at least there can be, indeed ought to be in certain circumstances. We do not mean by this that every 'personal diocese' which in fact exists (for example, the military Ordinariate of Colombia with twenty-four military chaplains) is from the fundamental-theological point of view such a 'personal diocese' which ought to exist. Just as juridically there exist miniature territorial dioceses which from the fundamental-theological point of view should not exist, the same can happen in the case of 'personal dioceses'. But it is quite possible for large divisions of the Church to exist as representative of the whole Church without coming into being simply by the territorial division of the earth as the one field of the Church. For while man's relationship to a place is a very important and primordial element of his existential condition, it is not the only one and not necessarily the most fundamental where it is a question of the effect which such existential elements have upon the mode of man's incorporation into the supernatural community of faith, cult and life which is the Church. Localisation is after all in the first place a profane and not specifically Christian and ecclesiastical datum. Its importance for the mode of membership in the Church is therefore to be proved and not assumed as self-evident, especially since no one can any longer say today that the *necessary* localisation of the *altar*-community is identical with the territoriality of the diocese (as was almost everywhere the case in practice in the first centuries of the Church). The principle of territoriality is a natural principle for the essence of a diocese, in most cases rightly applied, but not one which is always the only valid one. This is already the case with the parish, and it is fundamentally no different with the diocese.

When in the Church a group which has the characteristic of being representative of the whole Church is in being as a result of the natural presuppositions for such divisions or of some qualities specifically proper to the Church and is unable to live and develop its own being and life within the framework of a territorial diocese, then in principle it has the same function and the same right as a territorial diocese. For the most part it then also has, according to current law, an '*Ordinarius*'! So it does not take anything from the territorial diocese; its equally original right is not an exception from something which of itself belongs only to a territorial diocese.

The word 'exemption' is conditioned by history (because such personal dioceses arose in *most* cases chronologically later than the territorial diocese, the juridical recognition of their own legal status was thought of as an 'exception', as an 'exemption'), but the term is unfortunate and obscures the true state of affairs. That explanation of exemption as it exists in fact in the Church which relies upon the episcopal and direct jurisdiction of the pope over every bishop, every diocese, and every individual Christian, to which particular members of the Church therefore 'directly' subject themselves, is *alone* insufficient. It is true that this line of reasoning shows why such 'exempt' organs of the Church still have an episcopal head and therefore do not fall outside the framework of the hierarchy even if their immediate Ordinary is not a residential bishop. But, to begin with, the explanation of 'exemption' as an immediate subjection to the Holy See is unfortunate, since on the one hand the pope exercises an 'immediate' jurisdiction over every member of the Church and on the other even in the case of exemption the pope is not the immediate Ordinary. In the second place, this explanation presupposes what must itself be explained, namely that the pope can exercise his *always* immediate jurisdiction in *some* cases even by 'cutting out' the territorially structured jurisdiction of an immediate episcopal Ordinary which would otherwise be given, and that this is meaningful.

It is not our intention here to delineate in particular the more personally structured forms which, because they have a nature similar to a genuine diocese (unity, size, the capacity to represent the Church by their own spiritual-ecclesiastical make-up, and so on), also have the 'right' to exist (in the wider sense, in that they ought to exist from the point of view of constitutional theology) just as much as a diocese, that is to say, to be subject to their own Ordinary. But there are such member-Churches: they are quite thinkable from the constitutional-theological point of view and do in fact really exist. They do not really become 'detached' from a diocesan unit by 'exemption' in order to begin to exist, but the 'exemption' is only recognising from the point of view of constitutional law what already was the case from the point of view of constitutional theology: a part-Church whose principle of distinction from other parts is not territory. That these formations in the Church, while having an Ordinary, do not in most cases have an episcopal head does not alter the correctness of these reflections. Even apart from such 'exemptions', there are part-Churches which do not yet have a bishop (for example, apostolic prefectures) but tend to such a status. Besides, from the constitutional-theological point of view it would be best if under the necessary conditions such 'exempt' part-Churches did have a bishop as their superior.[17] But of this we have already spoken in a different connection. If such part

---

[17] It must not be forgotten that once life according to the evangelical counsels is ecclesiastically institutionalised in religious orders specially directed by the Church, it is no longer possible to say that this involvement in the hierarchy contradicts the spirit of the free charismatic life which religious life strives to be.

Churches, which do not strictly follow the territorial principle, rightly exist, then between them and the local dioceses (precisely as between these themselves) there is required a legally regulated co-operation, so that 'exemption' from the local bishop can never be absolute. Independence from and obligations towards the local diocese will naturally vary according to the nature of the subject-matter in question (the interior life, activities proper to an Order which are or are not exclusively those of a local bishop, normal pastoral concern with the members of a local diocese, and so on). The question could unhesitatingly be asked as a consequence whether those non-episcopal Ordinaries who have a seat in the Ecumenical Council or at least should have one *pari iure* should not also be meaningfully members of a corresponding conference of bishops.

From such considerations it is quite possible to pose the question in an ecumenical context, whether in promoting the unity of Christians we should not reckon more courageously and with less inhibition with the possibility that those forms of Christianity which have arisen in history and are still separated, once they are united with the Catholic Church under the necessary dogmatic and constitutional conditions, would be allowed to conserve to a large extent their previous independence and their own character in constitution, liturgy, theology, and so on, even if territorially they co-exist with Latin Churches. Such a thing may appear to the mere jurist and administrator impractical and difficult. But that is no reason for simply annihilating these part-Churches.

8. The Duties of the Bishop

Given that a bishop is '*aeque principaliter*' member of the college of bishops as he is pastor of his own diocese, it follows that he also has duties and responsibilities with regard to the whole Church. It is true that *in part* he attends to these precisely in so far as he participates *as* a member of the college in the strict sense in a proper collegial act of the college, and in so far as he leads his own diocese and strives to make it into a living member of the universal Church, which really contributes to the welfare of the whole Mystical Body. But because he is a member of the college, he has beyond this even as an individual a responsibility for the universal Church, a responsibility for the neighbouring dioceses, for the missions of the whole Church, and so on (although as an individual he naturally has no pastoral authority outside his own diocese). How such a co-responsibility can be given an institutional expression, for example by bishops' conferences, has already been discussed elsewhere. This responsibility of every bishop for the whole Church was clearly realised and expressed in the institutional life of the ancient Church, and this already at a time when there was as yet no written law for synods and similar institutional expressions of the responsibilities of the individual bishop towards the universal Church.

9. The Idea of the Patriarchate

If a bishop can only be bishop of his diocese in so far as he is at the same time a member of the college, then his unity and co-operation with other bishops is in principle not a matter for his own free judgement but something which flows essentially from the nature of his office. If there necessarily exists a college, then the union of a bishop with other bishops is not merely the union of all individual bishops with the pope. For while this is *one* constitutive element of the unity of the college, and its foundation, its guarantee and a criterion of its existence, it is not its only constitutive element. For the mere union of many with one does not yet turn the many into a college. A collegial unity of the kind we have in mind was realised in earlier times in the patriarchates:[18] a territory which formed a geographical, historical and ecclesiastical (missionary) unity, notwithstanding the fact that it consisted of several dioceses, became constitutionally one unit, or alternatively the single dioceses which originated as daughter Churches of the original unit were conserved in that unity.

From the point of view of constitutional law it can certainly be said that these patriarchates are only of human and ecclesiastical law. But as we indicated above already, we must distinguish two types of human law in the Church: firstly a human law which – even if motivated by objectively good motives – supervenes more or less as a pure addition on divine law, at best as a purely additional help for the carrying out of divine law, and secondly that human law which is no more than divine law made concrete in history. This latter is at times so much the case that it is difficult to say where exactly the boundary should be drawn between what remains divine in a law and what is its concrete historical realisation. This can be

---

[18] We are not concerned here with the difference between patriarch and metropolitan, which is determined by historical factors and is fluid in meaning, as long as we look beyond the words to their content. Everything we are saying here could equally well be put under the heading 'Chief Bishop' and 'Chief Diocese'.

seen in the dioceses themselves: each one is a concrete realisation of the episcopal principle in the Church, they could not all at the same time cease to exist, and yet no individual diocese can lay claim to divine law for its existence and its boundaries and the exact contents of its rights.

The old institution of the patriarchate, apart from the historical rights of the individual existing patriarchates, also belongs without any doubt so much to the second type of human law in the Church that it may even be questioned (if one attends to the reality and not to the nomenclature) whether a patriarchate is any less of divine law than a particular diocese or 'the' diocese, that is that organisation in the Church which in fact is designated by this term. One only has to think of the fact that, without altering the reality, one could in certain circumstances objectively and terminologically just as well say for 'patriarch': 'bishop of a large diocese', and for the bishops subject to him: 'auxiliary bishops with the rights of a vicar-general of the (chief) bishop', in order to see that the distribution of the labels 'divine law' and 'human law' between bishop and patriarch is not quite as self-evident as is usually assumed.

As soon as one has clear ideas about the collegiality of all bishops the unfavourable impression at first created by these relationships between different legal structures with fluid lines of demarcation disappears: after all one can participate in the one authority of the one college in different ways which can be determined in the concrete by the Church herself. What name is then given to the various bearers of the various ways in which this participation can be formulated is then almost merely a matter of regulating language – which should be done as accurately as possible. Rightly understood, one can say without any scruples that the real, fundamental-theological essence of the patriarchate belongs to the *ius divinum*[19] in the Church, because the collegiality of the bishops gives rise to the conclusion that they must realise a concrete and particular unity with one another at that time and in that place where a large part-Church embracing several dioceses grows up in the spheres of history, ecclesiastical tradition, sociology, and so on, or where such a unity already precedes the division into dioceses. Whether such a greater Church is called a patriarchate, a metropolitan union, or anything else, is a question of secondary importance. This is especially so because the dividing line

[19] Although we realise at the same time that this *ius divinum* must become concrete in determinate historical forms and will therefore rightly become concrete *differently* in different times and places.

between the duties and rights of a 'patriarch' on the one hand and those of the individual local bishops on the other have been fluid and can vary according to time and place. Where energetic and effective national conferences of bishops exist or are in process of formation, a 'patriarchate' is already materially there, provided that there also corresponds to the national (or continental) unity of such a union of bishops a greater Church which has historically, liturgically (or para-liturgically), theologically etc., its own proper character which enables it to fulfil within the whole Church a function which is proper to it (which does not mean that it must be legally exceptional).

If, however, it becomes clearly evident that patriarchates of this kind (in many respects newly fashioned) are already there or in process of formation in a para-canonical way, then these ought to be consciously promoted in such a way that their concrete form is a genuine realisation of their fundamental-theological essence. This involves above all a balanced relationship between the patriarch (no matter how he is designated: whether metropolitan, patriarch, president of the conference of bishops, cardinal,[20] or anything else) and the college of bishops belonging to this 'patriarchate'. The relationship need not be exactly the same as that which prevailed in the earlier historical patriarchates; much less is it necessarily that which prevails *iure divino* between pope and bishops. It is precisely because the unity of the episcopate is already guaranteed in the pope that the relationship between the members of a particular grouping of bishops can be more 'democratic'. But this again does not mean that it is desirable from the fundamental-theological

---

[20] If the constitution of the college of cardinals is such as we have sketched it above, in other words if the college of cardinals genuinely represents the whole episcopate (which does not necessarily mean that it must be made up *exclusively* of residential bishops), and if in many cases (not necessarily always and exclusively) cardinals and presidents of national bishops' conferences are accordingly one and the same, then 'cardinal' could quite possibly become the new title for that person who is from the point of view of constitutional theology all that is meant by a real patriarch. It would also be a start towards getting rid once and for all of the unfortunate problem of the relationship between patriarchs and cardinals. In such a development one ought not to worry about moving even further from the traditional number of seventy cardinals than John XXIII has already done. Of the forty-four bishops' conferences listed in the *Annuario Pontificio* many already have or are worthy of having a cardinal as their president. As a consequence, a college of cardinals should not be thought of in too small a way, since it cannot be thought of as composed merely of the presidents of bishops' conferences.

point of view for the 'patriarch' to have the patriarchal right simply of a *'primus inter pares'*. Since in fact he will not be such, it is much more intelligent to recognise this without scruple and make it a juridical fact and so provide a firm hope that the 'patriarch' will not unduly limit the independence and responsibility of the individual bishops but rather protect it, more so then if he exercises in a purely extra-canonical way a power which he in fact possesses even if juridically it does not exist at all.

10. A Consultative Board of Bishops around the Pope

It is well-known that Paul VI declared himself very willing to accede to any request that might be expressed by the Council for him to set up in Rome a consultative board of bishops from the whole world to support him in the government of the universal Church. About this possibility there are three remarks to be made from the standpoint of fundamental theology.

1. A board of this kind is of its nature a *consultative* board. For it cannot limit the supreme jurisdiction of the pope, since this is not dependent upon the co-operation of such a board. The pope *could* indeed, if he wanted, work together with this board in the manner of a Council. For – in the abstract – one could quite conceive this board as being the real and authorised representation of the universal episcopate, so that the pope could set up with it a real and permanent Ecumenical Council in miniature without making it necessary for this board to consist of very many members. For there have been Councils enough in which there were present a very small number of bishops and which are yet reckoned to be Ecumenical. Moreover, the ecumenicity of very many of the old councils was a very para-canonical matter, that is to say, it arose not so much from the nature of the gathering itself but from an express or tacit subsequent consent of the universal episcopate and of the pope. But as we have said, in the case of this board the intention appears not to go beyond a consultative body, and there is no need to go beyond it. Its significance can nevertheless be great.

2. It must not be overlooked that even *without* such a board there can be given, and was and is given, the fundamental-theological necessity of co-operation between the pope and the universal episcopate. The phrase *'ex sese'* in the definition of Vatican I[21] does indeed signify that the supreme

---

[21] '. . . *ideoque eiusmodi Romani Pontificis definitiones ex sese, non autem ex consensu Ecclesiae, irreformabiles esse'*: sess. IV, cap. 4; cf. *DS* 3074.

decision of the pope in matters of faith and ecclesiastical law cannot be subject to any legal control or confirmation on the part of another juridical instance, but it does not exclude but rather implies that in making such a decision the pope is acting *as* head and member of the Church and thereby (since this Church has necessarily by her very nature an episcopal structure) also as head of the college of bishops, that he is bound to the scriptures and the faith of *that* Church which has its authentic teaching authority in the universal episcopate, that he must proceed according to the norms of justice and love and must therefore respect the concrete form of the Church, her wishes and the movements of the Spirit within her.[22]

A really living and constant agreement between the pope and the universal episcopate is therefore normal and necessary for the pope in the whole accomplishment of his office: even though the fulfilment of this requirement is not subject to a legal check by the remaining bishops, as was taught by a false Gallicanism and Episcopalism which placed the Council above the pope. Such unity and co-operation has also in fact always been present – according to the possibilities and needs of particular times – in a sufficient (which does not necessarily mean ideal) way, even if to a large extent it was accomplished para-canonically. The bishops are directly or indirectly (through nuncios, and so on) in touch with the pope; the papal theologians are moved or influenced (consciously or unconsciously) by the theology of the whole Church – which in its turn is in contact with bishops: even if it wanted to, Rome could not possibly ward off the influence of the total life of the Church. Indeed it is the case in man's intellectual history as elsewhere that even a 'No' to a movement becomes in its turn subject to the law of that against which it is protesting. The Church and her Spirit have a thousand ways of influencing Rome, and perhaps those which are not legally defined and therefore cannot be deliberately checked are the most effective, even though there may be need of much patience until they have made their mark and become so much accepted in Rome that they are then sent out again as impulses from there.

While it is true, therefore, that the unity of pope and universal episco-

---

[22] So much is this true that the old canonists had no hesitation in reckoning with the possibility of the pope, if he does not act in this way and therefore becomes a schismatic (by *his* breaking away from the total organism of the Church) or even a heretic, ceasing to be a Catholic and therefore pope.

pate which from the fundamental-theological point of view is necessary does always exist (*quoad substantiam*), it can yet be greater or less, more quickly or more slowly effective, can in different periods evolve different means and modes of effectiveness, it can become more explicit and canonically more evident. And in this respect the planned board is theologically an important and useful arrangement. It does away even 'optically' with the false impression that the vital flow of the Church is exclusively from head to members, that the supreme, officially organised centre of the Church is always the only place where her Spirit is permitted to launch his new charismatic impulses. It makes it easier to take account of the present day. For today it is practically impossible to guarantee that the head of a large community (or company) with a multiplicity of interests in extremely complicated situations should be 'kept fully informed' in any other way than by a team of leaders, a brains trust, and so on, even though the head himself alone has the last word. To imagine that a well-educated, well-intentioned man of great personal 'experience' can today still be sufficiently informed without any further trouble, and that in any case he has no need of any institutionalised sources of information, is an antiquated paternalism which has nothing to do with the rightful freedom and independence of a supreme head. A consultative board around the pope of the suggested kind drawn from the universal episcopate is a good constitutional concrete expression of the theological unity of pope and universal episcopate in the government of the Church. Then one also sees where the responsibility for such information lies; national bias in the observation of the reality about which information is sought can more easily be avoided; the information can be gathered more quickly and more regularly. Naturally this board must be rightly structured and organised if it is to fulfil its tasks. Its task is after all to be a means of overcoming the fortuitousness and the subjective contingency of the experience of individuals (the pope and the Roman Curia), and this would not happen if a number of bishops were merely to meet together from time to time in Rome for an 'informative exchange of ideas'. All-round and comprehensive information demands here as in other spheres of high politics today, organs of assembly, examination and correct assessment of events, movements and the appearance of new ideas.

3. The standpoint from which we have been contemplating this consultative board makes it clear that it need not be *only* non-Roman members of the universal episcopate who belong to it. If we set out from

the fundamental-theological recognition that the universal episcopate does not have to consist merely of diocesan bishops but that it can meaningfully have other members too, and that for example really leading men of the Roman central government under the pope would from the fundamental-theological point of view meaningfully be members of the supreme episcopal governing board of the Church, then this also applies to a kind of 'committee' of the college of bishops. If the rector of a university which is in some way representative of Catholic learning is rightly a bishop, he could in certain circumstances also rightly be a member of this consultative board. And this is all the more true of episcopal members of the Roman Curia. While it is inevitable but meaningful that with the existence of such a board the Roman Congregations must appear more than heretofore mere administrative rather than legislative organs of the pope, at the same time if the insight we have just called attention to is respected, even more clearly will the impression be avoided that the Roman Congregations with their experience of legal deliberation are themselves to be excluded whenever the episcopal consultative board is engaged upon such legal deliberations and the establishing of laws, that is to say exercises a legislative function.

21

PASTORAL-THEOLOGICAL OBSERVATIONS ON EPISCOPACY IN THE TEACHING OF VATICAN II

THERE can be no doubt that the Dogmatic Constitution on the Church is the most significant achievement of Vatican II as far as the immediately tangible results of the Council are concerned. Within this Constitution itself the teaching on episcopacy is the most important section. It would not be true to say that everything else in the Dogmatic Constitution is only the framework and ornament of this; it may even happen that only at some later date will the full significance of something else in the document become apparent to the Church and to the world, for example what it says about the possibility of salvation for all men, even those outside the Church. But the very lengthiness and sharpness of conciliar debate over this section on the bishops demonstrate that the Council itself saw in this its greatest achievement.

Conciliar teaching on this matter has a great pastoral-theological importance both in itself and in its consequences which are pointed out by the Dogmatic Constitution itself. In what follows we wish to make some remarks about this. Within the limitations of a brief essay we may be permitted to omit from our consideration those parts of the chapter on the hierarchy which treat either of the pope or of the particular functions of each individual bishop as such (as priest, teacher, and shepherd of his diocese) which are already well known and realised in practice, or directly of the individual priest or deacon.

To begin with, the teaching on the episcopal office in this document may be summarised as briefly as possible. Jesus Christ gave to his Church a hierarchical constitution, that is he established offices with a sacred authority (as service) whose bearers are in the first place the bishops as successors of Christ's apostles under the pope, who is the visible foundation and principle of the unity of the episcopate (no. 18). According to

361

the will of Christ, the apostles, chosen as the leaders of the Church, already formed a college (no. 19). Their successors are '*ex divina institutione*' the bishops with and under the pope (no. 20). In their episcopal consecration by the laying-on of hands, which is a true Sacrament, they receive all their offices, even though the teaching and pastoral offices can be exercised only in the unity of the Church (no. 21). The bishops form a true college in the same way as the apostles formed a college as ordained by Christ. This college possesses its authority only in union with the Roman pontiff and under his leadership, in accordance with the supreme authority ascribed to him by Vatican I. But in forming such a college all the bishops are the bearers of full and supreme power in the Church. This power can be exercised by the college of bishops both in a conciliar way (in an Ecumenical Council) and in an extra-conciliar way, provided only that a collegial act takes place in co-operation with the pope. One becomes a member of this college by sacramental consecration as a bishop and union with the head and members of the college (no. 22). Hence the individual bishop as an individual is not only the leader of his own diocese, endowed with sovereign authority, but as a member of the college has also by Christ's institution and command a responsibility (not jurisdiction) and a duty towards the whole Church, for the unity of her faith and life and for her mission. The unity of the college and of its function is displayed and made effective in the practical order by wider ecclesiastical units (patriarchates, etc.) and today also in bishops' conferences (no. 23), although these are determined by historical circumstances.

What then is the significance of this conciliar document on episcopacy from the standpoint of pastoral theology? First of all, although practice, which is the difficulty, has yet fully to implement theory, this doctrine represents a clear rejection of the idea implicit in the practice of recent years and so prevalent under the surface among many of the laity and the clergy, that a bishop is nothing more than a subordinate official of the pope. The bishop rules his flock by his *own* (not delegated) ordinary power in the name of *Christ* and not that of the pope (no. 27); this does not detract from his obligation to lead his flock in unity with and under the authority of the supreme power in the Church. To the bishop is *fully* committed the pastoral office in its normal form ('*habitualis et cotidiana cura*') (no. 27). He cannot therefore consider himself to be the mere recipient and executor of commands received from higher quarters. He has an independent duty and responsibility which he cannot simply shirk. He would therefore not be fulfilling his office fully, if he regarded himself as the mere executive organ of universal ecclesiastical laws or of initiatives emanating from Rome. Whether alone or in union with his neighbours in regional bishops' conferences he must strive to recognise for himself the scope of his tasks and the right moment for acting: *he* must make decisions, develop initiatives, discover solutions, which are not the mere application of universal norms provided by ecclesiastical law and pastoral theology. Only in this way can his diocese and the fulfilment of his duty contribute to the good of the 'whole body' of the Church (no. 23), for this Church is not a homogeneous mass but an organic structure which possesses a real variety of members and *by means of it* '*universalitas*' (nos. 13, 22, 23).

The conciliar declaration that the sacramental Ordination of the bishop confers all three offices (of teacher, priest and shepherd) will cause the canonists many a headache. For it is not too easy to reconcile this with the doctrine for so long traditional that there are two fundamental powers (sacramental and pastoral power: *potestas ordinis* and *potestas iurisdictionis*), the latter of which is not transmitted by Ordination (considered in this case as absolute) but by a canonical mission. This is not the place to deal with this question; but the fact that the Council finds a *sacramental* and therefore *pneumatic* basis for the transmission of *every* office is of incalculable significance for juridical practice in the Church. Justice and love, law and fraternity, charisma and institution cannot be simply identified even in the future, because for man, a pluralistic being in spite of his pneumatic unity, they are not the same, and it is precisely the distinction which serves the unity. But the very fact that the law is rooted in the *Pneuma* makes it unmistakably clear that in the Church the law is no worldly law but a law which is holy and sustained by the Spirit, the embodiment of grace, and that it is put into effect and applied in accordance with the will of Christ only when its application is inspired and sustained by this Spirit: the spirit of humility, of the will to serve, of fraternity, of respect for every person and his conscience, of self-criticism, of the will of those in authority to be open to advice and new experience, of the '*affectus collegialis*' which the bishop too must cultivate towards his priests, of the will to co-operate with them and regard them as his friends (cf. nos. 27, 28). Canon law must be sustained and inspired by the *Pneuma* of Christ, for only then can it really be called the law of Christ's Church.

The Council says that the one, whole office which is sacramentally conferred on the bishop (in its threefold direction) is legitimately divided in the Church '*vario gradu, variis subiectis*' (priests, deacons) (no. 28). Although this does not set out to solve the problem encountered in the history of dogma whether Christ himself expressly willed the three levels of the one sacrament of Orders or whether this is the result of a legitimate decision of the apostolic Church, it does indicate the dogmatic basis for an outlook and attitude which are important from the pastoral point of view. The almost incalculable multiplicity of offices, functions, authorities and institutions which exist in the hierarchical Church and which often have an almost secular air, evidently determined by merely external circumstances, and which are reflected very inaccurately in the three stages of Orders, must all be seen and lived as rooted in pneumatic unity in the sacrament of the episcopal and priestly office. Every office in the Church must be understood spiritually, as the making concrete of the sacramental mystery of Orders, and where this is no longer seriously possible it should be entrusted to lay people who can carry it out just as well or even better.

As the conciliar teaching on episcopacy clearly indicates (no. 23), the institution of patriarchates, ecclesiastical provinces and episcopal conferences is an application (even if formally of human law) of the collegial structure of the Church, an application which is determined by historical circumstance. The subject of bishops' conferences is too wide and important for us to be able to do justice to it here. Besides, we must wait to see what will be the juridical development of this institution after the Council. One can only hope that the *collegialis affectus* will here be given a '*concreta applicatio*' (no. 23), that is to say, that the bishops' conferences achieve that juridical form and acquire that spirit which the pastoral situation of the different countries and continents renders necessary, if we are really to have Churches in those countries and continents which are capable of acting on their own and do not depend exclusively on Rome and its nuncios for representation, leadership and united responsibility. In the long run it will inevitably happen that in particular cases an individual bishop will be legally bound by the decision of a bishops' conference. It will also be the task of such bishops' conferences to administer those interdiocesan organisations and institutions (charitable organisations, film institutes, etc.) which in this day and age are pastorally indispensable. The same applies to the re-drawing of diocesan and provincial boundaries: it is essential that the bishops' conferences fully share in this work.

A further practical conclusion of human law may be drawn from the collegiality of the bishops with one another and with the pope as head of the college: the need for the pope to be supported in the government of the universal Church by representatives of the *bishops of the whole Church*. This is, of course, not intended to lead to the establishment of a permanent Council, for this co-operation does not involve a collegial act of the whole episcopate. Nor is this support already sufficiently given by the episcopal character of many of the officials of the papal Curia. It should be genuinely a matter of representatives of the bishops of the world. Hence it would also not do for the bishops in question to reside permanently in Rome, otherwise they will only become Roman curial officials or agents for bishops or bishops' conferences without any initiative or responsibility of their own. This does not exclude the possibility that the bishops could be additional members of Roman official bodies without, presumably, permanently residing in Rome. From the nature of the case, they would have to be episcopal representatives of bishops' conferences, chosen by these conferences, meeting at regular intervals in Rome and there constituting an advisory body to the pope, which would thus be superior to the executive of the curial offices since it would be immediately attached to the pope as the bearer of legislative power in the Church. If the episcopal advisory board which the Council desires were erected in this fashion, a quite considerable piece of that curial reform which Paul VI at the beginning of his pontificate declared himself to favour, and which the Council too wished to see, would thereby already be accomplished.

Although the Constitution on the Church does not contain any express indication regarding the proper size of a diocese, it does provide the objective basis for deciding this difficult question. A diocese is ruled by a member of the supreme governing body of the universal Church and not by some subordinate official of this government. The universal Church is also the *corpus Ecclesiarum*. This yields as the supreme *positive principle* for the *extensiveness* of a diocese, that the essence of the Church must be clearly allowed to appear in it; and as the *negative principle* for the limitation of a diocese, that the bishop must still be able really to fulfil his office in its regard. If at present or in the future a diocese is not in a condition to represent and make actual in some way the life and fulfilment of the whole Church in all its different dimensions, it is not in the full sense a 'Church' and is not suited for government by a member of the supreme governing board of the Church. The concrete application of this principle naturally depends on many demographic, social, psychological, economic, geographical and historical factors, but none of this detracts from its great pastoral-theological significance. There is no doubt that the resolute application of this principle must lead to the amalgamation of many miniature dioceses. But this is not to deny that the negative principle set out above, which is likewise a consequence of the nature of episcopacy, also demands the division of dioceses which are too large.

When we reflect upon the teaching of the Council on episcopacy we feel constrained to face a problem which is partly dogmatic and partly pastoral-theological. It is not easy to formulate this problem. We could perhaps call it the problem of the relationship and the tension between the *theoretical* and the *real* structures of the Church. We must explain what we mean by this. In the Constitution on the Church the bishop appears (leaving aside the pope for the moment) as *the* pastor of his Church without further qualification: in *him* is to be found the fullness of all sacred authority, *he* preaches, *he* teaches, *he* sanctifies and *he* guides the Church's people entrusted to him. The whole official action of the Church in the transmission of truth and grace is concentrated in him. And at this point the objection might be raised that this description is surely very unrealistic: in reality the bishop is surely a kind of higher administrative official, watching over and co-ordinating the real and essential work of the Church, while this latter, the real care of souls, the *Kerygma*, the word of grace in the sacraments, the witness to Christ before the 'World', is in reality (in so far as it has an official character) carried out by the priests in the parish. One could object that the description of the episcopal office in this Constitution has an *a priori* and unrealistic character and does not describe basically and adequately what the Church really is in actual fact. (We might briefly note here that we are in this matter touching upon a problem which is also ecumenical and theologically controversial: the Lutheran theology of the Church views the official activity of the Church as primarily to be found in the actual preaching of the gospel in the concrete community by the pastor and therefore can only recognise the 'bishop' as the necessary 'superintendent' of this life of the concrete community.) It is of course possible to answer these objections by saying that the Council's teaching recognises and recounts at length the importance of the individual parochial priest as a helper of the bishop, as a real priest and leader of the concrete community (especially the altar-community). One could add that the Council underlines the essence of the concrete community (the altar-community, the local community, the parish) as a true 'Church', in which *the* Church is realised and made present to the world, in a way in which it has never appeared before in any doctrinal document; a doctrine whose pastoral-theological consequences can hardly even be foreseen as yet, because in reality the foundation has here been laid for a *theology* of the parish and not merely for its juridical position. But theologically and pastorally all this does not really meet the difficulty or solve the problem which we have in mind. For this one would have to develop further the theology of the local altar-community as the manifestation and actualisation of the Church as such at a particular point in space and time, and make it vital and fruitful in the life of the individual community. One might say that as long as the local community does not recognise itself with an existential faith in thought and deed to be the Church to which can truly be applied everything that the Council proclaims of the glory and mystery belonging to *the* Church, as long as the individual community feels itself to be no more than the smallest administrative unit by means of which the *universal Church* (alone) effects the salvation of the individual, it has not yet truly understood itself. Here there are tasks before us which are pastorally of the greatest importance for the life of the individual communities and for the full and correct structuring of this life, without which the episcopal Church too is not what it ought to be.

In order to overcome this difficulty, that is in order to understand thoroughly and theologically the relationship of tension between the episcopal Church and the local Church, it is necessary to reflect further upon this relationship. In the ancient Church there was no problem: every real local Church was an episcopal Church. In medieval and modern times in the West the problem could not be properly formulated either: the local community did not feel itself to be the Church, and there was therefore no problem in regarding its institutions as institutions of human law which can be set up at will as appears necessary. But if the local community is the Church, its concrete form while being changeable and determined by historical circumstance is the concrete form of the *essence* of the Church, in which must be manifested '*iure divino*' what the Church is, so that the Christian can truly experience *here* what is really meant by 'the Church': the sacramental presence of the divinising and forgiving grace of God in the unity of men in love. If the empirically real structure of the Church in the local community is really present and capable of being experienced, the episcopal nature of the Church's essential structure which lies as it were at a deeper level in the organism of the Church will become accessible to the religious experience of the Christian and will no longer give the impression of being an abstract theory which has little contact with the concrete life of the Church.[1]

[1] For a deeper theological discussion of the above reflections, apart from the other contributions to the topic in this volume, cf. K. Rahner and J. Ratzinger, *The Episcopate and the Primacy*, Quaestiones Disputatae 4 (Freiburg/Edinburgh-London 1962); K. Rahner, 'Zur Theologie der Pfarrei' in H. Rahner, *Die Pfarre* (Freiburg i. B. 1956), pp. 27–36; K. Rahner, 'Reflection on the Concept of "Ius Divinum" in Catholic Thought' in *Theological Investigations* V (London & Baltimore 1966), pp. 219–243; cf. also 'Dogmatische Fragen des Konzils' in *Oberrheinisches Pastoralblatt* LXIV (1963), pp. 234–250.

22

ON BISHOPS' CONFERENCES

THE question of the nature and significance of bishops' conferences, of the position which they ought to occupy and which has still to be assigned to them in the common law of the Church, is one which has been newly posed by the Council.[1] At the very beginning of the Council it was already evident that conferences of bishops possess in practice a greater significance than has been accorded them in law. We saw it in the first general assembly of the Italian hierarchy known to history (in Rome on the 15 October 1962). We saw it in the formation of a pan-african bishops' conference which joined together nine separate conferences of bishops already in existence or in process of formation: this became one of the most dynamic and the best organised of all the bishops' conferences which came into being during the first session of the Council. The selection of Council Fathers to serve on the different conciliar commissions was made largely on the basis of the suggestions put forward by the various national bishops' conferences. Already in the first session of the Council there was a growing tendency for single bishops in the Council to speak on occasion no longer in their own name only, but to be permitted and encouraged to appear as the spokesmen of particular groups of bishops, which meant in practice of bishops' conferences. It may be assumed that this development will be carried further during the second session on the practical grounds of better organising the agenda, that is to say in order to speed up the debate and make it more searching. But what is most important of all is that in the very schemata of the Council's decrees there appears to be a marked desire to accord to large episcopal conferences (national and perhaps even supra-national) a much more secure canonical status and to entrust to them duties and responsibilities which up to now have never been possessed by any

[1] Cf. Piet Fransen, 'Die Bischofskonferenz – Kornproblem des Konzils', *Orientierung* XXVII (1963), pp. 119–123, esp. p. 122 *sq*.

individual bishop, or even by any provincial or plenary (national) Council, but only by the Holy See. In this way there would be created again a real intermediate legal instance between the Apostolic See and the individual bishop, something like the older patriarchal and metropolitan unions which today exist only in name, but in a new form. It is of course quite likely that the actual regulation in common law of the nature, duties and competence of bishops' conferences will only come about in an exact form with the new codification of canon law which can only happen after the Council, although it is quite possible that the Council itself will lay down fundamental norms for such episcopal conferences. But it will be absolutely necessary for this codification to be vigorously pursued, as the preparations already made to this end do indeed promise.[2] It might be objected that before the end of the Council a purely personal consideration of bishops' conferences is somewhat premature. But even in the Council and in the official consultations after the Council for the reform of canon law this question will need a great deal of intellectual co-operation from individual theologians, canonists and experts in the pastoral and administrative practice of the Church, and· it is so important for an understanding of the nature of the Church in general that perhaps it is permissible and helpful to set down a few thoughts on the matter even now. In a short essay like this the question can of course be treated only in a fragmentary way. It is moreover noteworthy how sparse is the literature on it.[3]

[2] Cf. *AAS* LV (1963), p. 363. The members of the Commission for the Revision of the Code include, for example, the two German cardinals Bea and Döpfner.

[3] One could, for example, compare the commentaries on *c*. 292 of *CIC*: cf. e.g. E. Eichmann and Klaus Mörsdorf, *Lehrbuch des Kirchenrechts* ([9]1959), I, 393; M. Conte, A. Coronata, *Institutiones Iuris Canonici* I (Turin 1928), 427 *sqq*.; H. Jone, *Commentarium in Codicem Iuris Canonici* I (Paderborn 1950), 257; A. Toso, *Ad codicem iuris canonici commentaria minora*, Lib. II De personis, Tom. I (Rome 1922), 111 *sqq*.; E. Regatillo, *Institutiones Iuris Canonici* I[5] (Santander 1956), 322 *sq*. (A typical comment may be read here: '*Aliae conferentiae . . . In Germania omnes episcopi Borussiae quotannis ad sepulcrum S. Bonifatii, Fuldae. Hae vi iuridica carent.*' This therefore seemed to the noted canonist the most important thing about such bishops' conferences.) For the history of episcopal conferences cf. H. E. Feine, *Kirchliche Rechtsgeschichte* I[3] (Weimar 1955), 577, 591, 614; W. M. Plöchl, *Geschichte des Kirchenrechts* III.1 (Vienna 1959), 212–216. Further reading: *LTK* II[1] (Freiburg 1931), 377 *sq*.[2]; II (Freiburg 1958), 506 '*sq*.; *RGG* III[2], 1804; *DDC* I (Paris 1935), 1175 *sq*.; N. Hilling, *AKKR* XCIII (1913), 265–268 (Leo XIII and the bishops' conferences); H. Storz, *Staat und Kirche in Deutschland im Lichte der Würzburger Bischofsdenkschrift von 1848* (Bonn 1934); J. Rommerskirchen, 393–407; C. Wolfs

There can be no question here of recounting the pre-history and the history of bishops' conferences. Their pre-history would consist of the story of the origin, constitution, government and effectiveness of those major units of the Church which join together several territorial dioceses and which, as regards the Church's government, stand between the individual diocese with its bishop and the universal government of the whole Church by the pope. This pre-history would therefore be practically identical with the history of metropolitan unions and patriarchates, with the significance and effectiveness of metropolitans, patriarchs, primates, and with the effectiveness of provincial synods, plenary and national Councils. All these canonical entities still exist in some form in the current law of the Church, in so far as there still exist metropolitan unions with a certain, though extraordinarily limited, range of duties, and provision is made for plenary and provincial Councils in canon law, the latter being supposed to meet in principle at least every twenty years.[4] Also they still have some practical effect in so far as right up to the present provincial, plenary and national synods are in fact held in many parts of the world. And they are the antecedents of present and future bishops' conferences in so far as they have united several dioceses in common juridical and pastoral action and this not merely for that part of the Church which was so united, but directly or indirectly have been of importance beyond this for the universal Church. With a view to the question we are discussing we wish to make only two remarks about all these different stages of the antecedents of bishops' conferences: in the first place, it is noteworthy that these juridical structures already existed and were put into effect in synods before the universal primacy of jurisdiction of the Bishop of Rome became practically evident to any notable

gruber, 'Die Konferenzen der Bischöfe Österreichs', *ThPQ* LVIII (1905), 241–266; Ph. Maroto, 'Circa le Conferenze Episcopali in Italia', *Apollinaris* V (1932), 277–280; Fr. Houtart, 'Les formes modernes de la Collégialité Episcopale' in J. Congar and P. D. Dupuy, *L'Episcopat et l'Église universelle* (Paris 1962), 497–535; J. Faupin, *La Mission de France* (Tournai 1960), 16–18 (French bishops' conferences only since 1919); Regional bishops' conferences in Africa: *Stimmen der Zeit* CLXXII (1962/3), 142 *sq.*; A. Simon, *Réunions des évêques de Belgique 1830–1867: Procès-verbaux*, Centre interuniversitaire d' histoire contemporaine, Cahier 10 (Louvain-Paris 1960); V.-L. Chaigneau, *L'organisation de l'Église catholique en France* (Paris 1956); *Informations catholiques internationales*, 15 April 1957, no. 46, 15–22.
4 *CIC* c. 271–291.

extent, in fact even before the first Ecumenical Council at Nicaea. This fact certainly should serve to call our attention to the necessity and importance of such major assemblies of the Church existing between the individual dioceses and the supreme government of the Church, the pope and the Ecumenical Council. In the second place, ever since the Middle Ages the importance of these entities within the Church has been constantly reduced in the West by a long and complicated process, and this process is practically identical with the historical development of the papal primacy of immediate jurisdiction over the whole Church and over every single diocese, which for the Western Church reached its highest point ever in Vatican I, the legal structure of the code of canon law based upon it and the administrative practice of the Holy See in accordance with it. The fact of this process of decline in the importance of the major ecclesiastical units in the West standing between individual dioceses and the Roman See, at least under a juridical aspect, undoubtedly poses the question whether this process is really terminated or whether tendencies and energies are not making themselves felt in dogma and the concrete situation of the Church's life which, while not simply leading back to the ancient forms of these major units, do impel us forward to new structures similar to the old, which will fulfil in the present and in the future the former duties of these major units in a new form, for example in the form of bishops' conferences.

The real history of bishops' conferences began one hundred and thirty years ago.[5] Already in 1830 the Belgian bishops gathered together at least once a year in the archiepiscopal palace at Mechelen. After a small episcopal conference in Cologne, 10–13 May 1848, the German and Austrian bishops at the invitation of Archbishop Geissel of Cologne met in Würzburg in 1848 in thirty-six sessions from 23 October to 16 November

---

[5] Examples from the second half of the nineteenth century are still accessible in *Collectio Lacensis* III, 7. 853, 1203, 1057; V, 931 (s'Hertogenbosch 1868), 941–946 (Cologne 1848), 946–958 (Geissel's plan for a German bishops' conference), 959–1143 (the bishops' conference at Würzburg), 1144–1161 (Cologne 1849), 1161 (Cologne 1850), 1162–1189 (Freising 1850), 1189–1200 (Bamberg 1864), 1201–1204 (Passau 1864), 1203–1216 (Freiburg 1851), 1215–1220 (Fulda 1869: the first Pastoral Letter of the Fulda bishops' conference), 1317–1324 (Salzburg 1848), 1313–1332 (Görz 1848), 1331–1394 (Vienna 1849: first Pastoral Letter of the whole Austrian hierarchy), 1393–1398 (Vienna 1868), 1397–1408 (Prague 1868); VI, 699–726 (Milan 1849), 727–738 (Milan 1850), 739–772 (Spoleto 1849), 773–810 (Loreto 1850), etc. (In the same volume there are the acts of the bishops' conferences at Pisa, in Sicily, at Siena, at Milan in 1850).

for voluntary synodal discussions and occupied themselves especially with the relationship between Church and State. (They strove during the course of this for a strengthening of the metropolitan unions and expressed a desire for a national synod, without however pursuing Döllinger's plan for a German National Church with a primate[6] at its head.) There followed in 1850 a first bishops' conference of the Bavarian episcopate in Freising. Since 1869 the bishops' conference of Fulda is a gathering which takes place regularly once a year, but in addition to this there are conferences of Bavarian, West German, and latterly also of East German bishops. In the course of the past century the practice of episcopal conferences as assemblies of bishops from a more or less extensive territory has gradually spread throughout the whole Church. This was a development already encouraged by Leo XIII,[7] who, for example, gave to the bishops' conferences of Austria-Hungary and of South America something in the nature of statutes.[8] This development also had a certain outcome in canon 292, § 1 of *CIC*,[9] in so far as this prescribes that the bishops of an ecclesiastical province (therefore of a metropolitan union) should meet together at least every five years for pastoral-theological consultation.[10] Yet these prescriptions do not do justice to the proper nature of a bishops' conference as demanded by the real situation, since a metropolitan union usually covers too small a territory and includes too few bishops to act as a basis for giving the bishops' conferences their real importance. Therefore in practice the real bishops' conferences cover a much greater territory. It is noteworthy that there are such episcopal conferences also in missionary lands.[11] Almost everywhere today, in fact, they are already replacing the plenary and provincial synods.[12] Yet the bishops' conferences are not, at

---

[6] Cf. H. Becher, *Der deutsche Primas* (Kolmar 1940), 224–281.

[7] Cf. N. Hilling in *AKKR* XCIII (1913), 265–268. Pius X in his time praised such annual '*congressus*', yet he urged the holding of provincial synods (*Coll. Lac.* V, 1200). Cf. also *Acta Pii IX*, pars I, vol. III, 674.

[8] Cf. *AKKR* LXXX (1900), 381–383 (Austria), 766 *sq.* (South America).

[9] It is interesting to note that Gasparri cites no sources for this canon. Cf. also for the Eastern Church, I Opera *c.* 351 (*AAS* XLIX [1957], 538).

[10] In the questionnaire for the use of metropolitans and bishops making their reports to Rome there is also a question on the holding of bishops' conferences: *AAS* II (1910), 20; X (1918), 488.

[11] Cf. J. Rommerskirchen (note 3 above). The astonishing effectiveness of the African bishops' conference at the Second Vatican Council is a matter of common knowledge.

[12] A list of bishops' conferences today: *Annuario Pontificio* 1963, 796–801.

least up to the present, merely a modern and useful form of plenary and provincial synod; they differ from them juridically especially in two ways: firstly, plenary and provincial synods are the bearers of their own superior authority and are therefore capable of passing laws within the framework of the Church's common law which bind the individual bishop and the individual diocese who fall within the competence of the synod even when the bishop in question has voted against these laws in the course of it. By contrast, in the conference of bishops existing up to the present only those agreements can be reached from a legal point of view which bind the individual bishop and his diocese by his own consent, which therefore become law and then only diocesan law by this consent alone. Secondly, plenary Councils (synods of bishops uniting several metropolitan unions) can only be held with the previous consent of the pope and under the presidency of his legate; the decisions of a plenary or provincial council can only be promulgated and enter into force after being previously confirmed by the Roman See (through the Congregation of the Council). On the other hand, free discussions by individual bishops with one another at bishops' conferences are effective without any participation by the Roman See, as long as they remain within the limits of that jurisdiction within which every bishop can arrive at decisions without any special express permission from Rome in virtue of his '*potestas ordinaria*' which makes him more than a mere official of Rome. (This is not to forget the fact that the central government of the Church in accordance with canon 250, § 4 of *CIC* has in certain cases reserved to itself the ratification of the decisions of bishops' conferences.[13]) In addition, the episcopal conferences are not bound by the prescriptions of *CIC c.* 281–291 concerning the methods of convocation and procedure of plenary and provincial synods, and are in this way much more easily able to accommodate themselves to the circumstances of the place, the needs of the time, and the nature of the matter under discussion, and so are also technically easier to organise. Yet it is true that up to the present they have no real canonical existence; the holding of them is at present subject to no regulation in common law,[14] their competence is not clearly

---

[13] Cf. e.g. *AAS* XXIV (1932), p. 242.

[14] With regard to more recent declarations of the Holy See on the question of bishops' conferences, cf. also *AAS* III (1911), p. 264 (Bavarian bishops' conferences); *AAS* XI (1919), pp. 72–74, 175–177 (the division of Italy into eighteen '*regioni*' for bishops' conferences); *AAS* XI (1919), pp. 171–174 (American bishops' con-

defined and up to now it cannot in any case exceed that of the individual bishops. Above all, we are faced with the question whether their character as a voluntary agreement of individual bishops is sufficient for the needs of today.

DOGMATIC CONSIDERATIONS

Before we attempt to set about making some observations about the problem of bishops' conferences as it arises from the Church's situation today, we must first set out some dogmatic considerations intended to clarify the position of bishops' conferences in the Church from the point of view of a dogmatic ecclesiology.

Just as according to the gospel Peter and the remaining apostles by the institution of Christ formed an apostolic college as a real, single entity of sacred right, so also the Roman pope as the successor of Peter and the bishops as the successors of the apostles are closely bound together. The college of bishops, which succeeds the apostolic college in its doctrinal and pastoral power and in which the apostolic college possesses its historical continuation, forms with the Bishop of Rome as its head the one, undivided subject of full and supreme official power in and for the universal Church; as a college made up of *many* members it represents the legitimate diversity of the members of God's people, and as a *united* college under *one* head the unity of the same people of God. This united college of bishops as the bearer of full and supreme power in the Church can exercise the supreme power of the doctrinal and pastoral office not only in a solemn and extraordinary way in an Ecumenical Council, but it is also capable of a collegial act of this kind outside a Council, so that one can see such a collegial act of the college of bishops under and with the Bishop of Rome, for example, in the 'ordinary magisterium' wherever it

---

ferences); *AAS* XV (1923), p. 108 (Australian bishops' conferences); XV (1923), p. 339 *sq.* (Portuguese bishops' conferences); XXIV (1932), p. 242 *sq.* (the annual meeting of bishops' conferences, submission of their resolutions to the Congregation of the Council); XLV (1953), p. 247 (bishops' conference for the Philippines); XLVII (1955), p. 461 (approbation of the statutes of the Canadian bishops' conference); XLVII (1955), pp. 539–544 (letter to Cardinal Piazza, president of the Latin American bishops' conference); L (1958), p. 224 *sq.* (approval of the '*Estatutos de la Conferencia Episcopal de Colombia*'; unfortunately these statutes are not given here); L (1958), pp. 997–1005 (the pope's allocution to the Latin American bishops' conference in Rome).

possesses an infallible authority.[15] With regard to his power as teacher and pastor the individual bishop is bishop of his particular diocese, but over and beyond this he has a certain function in the universal Church in so far as he is a member of the one episcopal college and in it shares responsibility for the act of the college as a whole. It is of the very essence of the episcopate that the individual bishop belongs to this college. This fact gives rise to further duties, rights and obligations on the part of the individual bishop even as an individual in regard to the universal Church. He has a relationship to it, and while he has it as a member of the college, for that very reason he has it as an individual. It is true that he has no real jurisdictional power except in relationship to his own diocese. But this does not mean that he has no duties, rights and obligations towards the universal Church. In the first place he represents the whole Church in its unity before his own diocese, his own Church, in which the whole Church is made present in the dimensions of space and time. As a member of the episcopal college which is the supreme governing body of the universal Church he also has an official duty towards the whole Church. All bishops must defend and promote the unity of faith and discipline of the universal Church and must educate the faithful to a love of the whole mystical Body of Christ, above all of those members who are poor, suffering and enduring persecution for the sake of justice. They must promote each and every kind of saving activity which is proper to the whole Church, particularly the propagation of the faith among the heathen. Moreover it is clear that the effective pastoral care which they bestow upon their own flock is of benefit to the whole mystical Body of Christ, which, as St Basil says, is the corporate unity of many Churches.[16] Pope Celestine[17] already emphasised in the presence of the Fathers of the Council of Ephesus that the anxious duty of proclaiming the gospel to the whole world lies equally upon the whole college of episcopal pastors as upon the pope.

This fundamental relationship which every individual bishop as such has to the whole Church and to all its members (though precisely because he is a member of the college of bishops) allows us to recognise the proper

[15] Cf. K. Rahner and J. Ratzinger, *The Episcopate and the Primacy* (Freiburg/Edinburgh-London 1963), p. 92 *sqq.*

[16] St Basil, *In Is. 15*, 296 (*PG* XXX, 637); cf. St Gregory the Great, *Mor.* 4, 7, 12 (*PL* LXXV, 643).

[17] E. Schwartz, *Act. Conc. Oec.* I, 2 (Berlin 1925/6), 23.

dogmatic ecclesiological foundations for the bishops' conference. Such conferences of bishops do not rest merely upon the practical necessity of co-operation between individual bishops, particularly if their dioceses are adjacent. While a bishop as an individual is incapable of exercising any jurisdictional power over another diocese, it is on the other hand not the case that in such a conference he is no more than a counsellor quite freely and arbitrarily selected as such merely because bishops are 'professional colleagues'. Antecedent to their meeting together in a bishops' conference and independently of any mutual request for advice and help, every bishop bears a responsibility for the whole Church and therefore for all those members of the Church which we call dioceses. And since this universal responsibility of the individual bishop as an individual cannot be allowed to remain a merely abstract and formal requirement but must be embodied in a concrete and visible way, just as the general love for mankind becomes in God's grace love for our 'neighbour', so the responsibility of the individual bishop for the universal Church is naturally expressed in the concrete by a shared concern for the kingdom of God and the salvation of souls in the 'neighbour' dioceses and in the whole of the actual natural and supernatural surroundings in which the bishop and his own diocese are situated but which at the same time extend beyond it.

In this case, then, the notion of the bishops' conference springs from the very nature of the Church. Certainly it is of 'human law' and certainly did not always exist in the Church in the sense in which it is intended and practised today; it is still seeking its concrete legal form; this depends on many circumstances determined by the times. Yet the bishops' conference is a possible and today perhaps even an absolutely necessary expression of an essential element of the Church. It is based on the one hand on the fact (which up to this point in our reflections we have perhaps not emphasised sufficiently) that the plurality of independent members of the Church (called dioceses) belongs to the immutable essential structure of the Church and that therefore the dioceses do not merely represent sub-divisions, demanded by practical considerations, of a united ecclesiastical monarchy which is fully homogeneous or should be as homogeneous as possible. But once this is clear and once we take into consideration the fact that an individual diocese too is in its extent, manner of administration, etc., largely dependent upon natural and historical conditions, then it also becomes clear that larger parts of the Church which are composed of several dioceses but have much in common in their natural conditions and in their historical origin within the Church form genuine major structures of the Church as such and can therefore supply a real theologically significant basis for patriarchates, metropolitan unions, bishops' conferences, and so on. For this reason 'intermediate instances' of this kind between the individual dioceses and the power of the primacy are not entities to be established or abolished simply at whim for mere convenience of administration. Rather they are seeking in a positive, canonical statute of human law a concrete form of their essence which is antecedent to this its legal expression. On the other hand, that essential element of the Church on which the idea of a bishops' conference is based includes the right and duty on the part of the individual bishops to shoulder their share of the burden of care for the universal Church and so for the members of the Church next to them, from which our reflections on the dogmatic foundation of bishops' conferences set out.

Only one further remark needs to be made regarding this dogmatic foundation for the bishops' conference, even though the groundwork of this remark cannot here be more precisely laid. It is true that the organisation of the Church into dioceses, the 'monarchic' government of such a diocese and therefore the difference between bishop and simple priest are *iuris divini*. Yet theologically and from the viewpoint of the history of the Church's structures it is surely quite legitimate to hold that this necessary subdivision of the Church into individual 'Churches' (not merely into provinces of the one Church) as demanded by the *ius divinum* is not necessarily and inevitably made concrete in the plurality of those Churches which *today* we call dioceses. If we proceed from the principle, which dogmatically is surely above suspicion, that the Church by using her *own* judgement can divide the sovereign and sacramental fullness of power given her by Christ, that she has also in different times and places divided it differently, then the conclusion surely becomes more difficult to avoid that we must not absolutely restrict our search for the plurality and collegiality (*iuris divini*) of the Church's power of government and its bearers rigidly to what' today we call bishop and bishopric in simple opposition to patriarchates, metropolitan unions, and so on. Fundamentally, it is too simple and schematically biased a distinction, which does not fully respect the possibilities we have indicated for the concrete Church in determining her constitution, if one regards the dioceses as divisions of the Church which are *iuris divini* and other major divisions between the dioceses and the universal Church as merely of human law. In these greater divisions of the Church falling between the diocese and the universal Church, too, an essential structure of the Church *iuris divini* can be put into effect and made concrete, even though in a historically determined form.[18]

BISHOPS' CONFERENCES

In the following section of our reflections we wish to make a few remarks about the legal status, competence and structure of the bishops' conference, not as it already exists today but as it ought to exist. In a question of this kind we are naturally concerned with many matters of mere opinion on which it is possible to hold different views and which can be solved in the practical order only by the free legislation of ecclesiastical authority itself.

The Bishops' conferences which have existed and been seen in practice up to the present do not of themselves signify a college which is more than the sum of the bishops taking part in it. In contrast with plenary or provincial councils, episcopal conferences up to the present have no authority of their own, they are not a legislative organ of a part of the Church. Leaving aside at this stage the question which we will have to deal with later, *when* and to what extent a bishops' conference should be able to aquire the right to legislate for its part of the Church in a way binding the individual bishop, in principle one can hold that the bishops'

---

[18] The resolute will of the Uniate Churches of the Near East to preserve and extend their patriarchal institution cannot therefore be decried as an obstinate clinging to outmoded structures of the Church. The same essential reasons which determine the territorial division of the Church into dioceses are effective to produce larger territorial divisions. We must also keep in mind that the ultimate theological nature of a diocese cannot be determined from the nature of the bishop. For the question is precisely why this determinate piece of territory must be given a leader who possesses the fullness of the power of Orders and an ordinary power of jurisdiction while other (larger or smaller) territories must not. But once it is clear that the nature of a diocese must be viewed as based upon the unity of a particular area of natural and supernatural life, then it becomes quite understandable that even greater natural and historical areas (which in our case correspond to particular conferences of bishops) are not simply arbitrary divisions introduced by the central administration which can abstain from introducing them if it thinks that it can manage without such 'divisions'.

conferences of the future should be collegial bearers of superior authority and legislative power for their part of the Church, that they should therefore acquire a status corresponding to that of the present plenary or provincial councils. The importance of bishops' conferences has grown greatly, as the history of the last hundred years and also the Second Vatican Council have demonstrated. The bishops' conferences fulfil today, and will no doubt increasingly fulfil in the future, functions which on the one hand cannot be carried out by the individual bishop and the individual dioceses, but which on the other hand should not be transferred to the supreme government of the universal Church, in accordance with the principle of subsidiarity which equally applies to the Church.[19] But if such an intermediate instance between the pope and the bishops is necessary, then it must be granted a legal status. This status is not granted by *CIC* c. 292, since the bishops' conference there envisaged is only the conference which corresponds to the provincial council and therefore comprises only the bishops of a single metropolitan union, and this, at least as a general principle, is today too small to support a bishops' conference of a kind which as a genuine intermediate instance between Rome and the individual dioceses could fulfil those functions which today and in the near future will increasingly devolve upon bishops' conferences. Moreover the bishops' conference of *c.* 292 does not have its own superior authority. But as such it is not really a genuine intermediate instance, for its prescriptions derive their real effective force either from the pope alone or from the individual bishop as such, and this does not suffice to constitute a true intermediate instance. For this reason it would also not contribute to giving a bishops' conference the nature and powers of a true intermediate instance with its own initiative and responsibility, if its decrees were to receive their binding force only through the approbation of Rome, so that, from the viewpoint of the bishops' conference, such decrees would really be nothing else than proposals made to the central administration in Rome. Since it is self-evident that bishops whether individually or in common can make such proposals, it does not require the organisation of bishops' conferences to enable them to do it. A real intermediate instance is given only where it is recognised as possessing its own sovereign power and so the right of making its own independent decisions. Just as such a power residing in the individual bishop does not detract from the meaning of the papal primacy of power and its organs, so

[19] Cf. e.g. Pius XII, *AAS* XLIX (1957), p. 927.

ON BISHOPS' CONFERENCES   381

it cannot be said that a bishops' conference does, if it is capable of enforcing decisions without their needing specific papal approbation. This is not to deny in any way that ordinary and immediate papal jurisdiction extends to the bishops' conferences just as it does to the individual bishop. Moreover the duty of reporting regularly to Rome which is laid upon the bishops will naturally apply also to the bishops' conferences. Hence is is highly desirable that the new code of canon law soon to be drawn up should make the setting up of such bishops' conferences which are in principle also the bearers of their own sovereign authority juridically possible, by analogy with the patriarchates and metropolitan unions of the Eastern Church.

As regards the extent of the bishops' conference, that is regarding the question as to which bishops should be collegially joined together in one and the same bishops' conference, it must be said that today and in the near future the first and most important bishops' conference will be that which unites all the bishops of one and the same State. Bishops' conferences based upon an ecclesiastical province are now out of date. If we leave aside the question, which is after all secondary, as to what is the situation of a bishops' conference or of bishops' conferences in a State which is itself a federal State, where the principle of parallelism between bishops' conference and State must be sub-distinguished according to whether the single federated States within such a State are still genuine, independent entities or mere administrative circumscriptions of a single State with the honorific title of 'Federal State' or '*Land*', we must say that today the most pressingly important form of bishops' conference is the college of bishops of one and the same State, that is the *national* bishops' conference. The individual State is today a force which influences and penetrates every sphere of human life. So much does it impress itself upon all spheres of life in accordance with its own particular historical and political character that the Church must necessarily have a representation parallel to it, and precisely a representation of the Church of this particular country (and not merely of the Holy See and the universal Church as such, which may be represented in this State by a nuncio, who cannot, however, in the nature of the case be regarded simply as the representative of the Church of this country itself). Leaving out of consideration the tendency to create supranational entities like UNO, NATO, EEC etc., and the tendency to transfer certain of the sovereign rights of individual States to these supranational instances, the States of today are more than ever before the managers and representatives of the life of the human community and even to a large extent of the individual. Social, cultural and political circumstances in the different parts of a modern State which roughly correspond to individual dioceses have become very much alike. The conditions underlying the most important political and pastoral decisions of the Church in the different dioceses of one and the same country are therefore to a large extent the same throughout that country. When the different dioceses come to make these important decisions they all find in practice that their negotiating partner is one and the same State. Hence it is self-evident that the national conference must be the basic type of bishops' conference today and in the near future. If within a single nation (either because it is a modern State of giant proportions, like Brazil for example, or because for historical reasons there is a vast number of dioceses within the territory of one single nation) a bishops' conference of this kind would convoke such an immense number of bishops that the capacity for quick and clear action could be greatly impaired, such a circumstance is no evidence against the principle that the fundamental type of bishops' conference today is the national one. In cases of this kind the capacity for quick and efficient action on the part of a national bishops' conference could be guaranteed by other means, whether by courageously reducing the excessive number of diminutive dioceses, as for example in Italy, or by establishing a practical procedure which safeguards the capacity for effective action on the part of the national bishops' conference (perhaps by providing that only the metropolitans of a country need appear at its ordinary assembly).

Nor does it speak against the fundamental principle that national episcopal conferences are the norm, if in certain missionary territories and States of smaller dimensions which are still in the process of being built up and are still seeking their national identity it is possibly the case, or even in actual fact the case, that an inter-State bishops' conference, which unites together the bishops of several such States, can be more urgently needed and will then be a better expression in this part of the world of the theological meaning of such conferences than a national conference would be. The principle we have laid down does after all proceed upon the assumption of a culturally, socially and above all historically developed State of a certain size with a genuine social and political character of its own which allows it to be an independent partner in the community of peoples.

This fundamental principle regarding the extensiveness of a national bishops' conference does not in any way exclude but rather implies, at least in this day and age, that beyond the national bishops' conferences, there may also be supranational bishops' conferences, and indeed that in certain circumstances there must be such. It was, for example, no mere chance that during the first session of the Second Vatican Council such supranational groupings of bishops came into being almost of themselves. It was not a question here of a pressure-group tactic, characteristic of power-politics, aiming to achieve momentarily urgent goals, but rather of the grouping which naturally takes place of itself even outside the Council whenever Middle and West European, African, or South American bishops find themselves together even if rather informally. Today supranational political, cultural, and social spheres of interest are being formed which even from the point of view of ecclesiastical politics and pastoral practice manifest a certain unity, so it can be quite meaningful, sometimes quite necessary, to organise a supranational bishops' conference geared to dealing with them, since these greater spheres of interest are in their turn such that neither the individual bishop nor the central government of the Church is immediately competent in their regard. One only has to think, for example, of the adaptation of the liturgy to the spirit and culture of the African continent, or of the pastoral problems that will ensue if the old Europe increasingly grows together economically, socially and culturally into a unity transcending individual States. It will easily be seen that the same reasons which demand national bishops' conferences can also beyond this demand supranational bishops' conferences. And we have not yet touched the question whether a canonical determination of the influence of the larger sections of the one Church upon the central administration of the Church in Rome could not itself demand such supranational major organisations and therefore supranational bishops' conferences. If, for example, we wish to conceive a consultative representation of the universal Church at the Holy See and its particular 'ministries' in such a way that there would be proportional representation and yet the number of representatives could not on practical grounds be too great, we necessarily come to the conception of major ecclesiastical spheres of common interest (e.g. Middle and West Europe, Latin America, North America, Latin Europe, Near East, etc.) which, if only to determine who are to be the aforesaid representatives in Rome, would have to organise corresponding supranational bishops' conferences. Perhaps one could call them, even if with a certain terminological inexactitude, *continental* bishops' conferences.[20]

A further question regarding the bishops' conference of the future concerns the matter and extent of its duties and competence. Leo XIII already in his time drew up a very extensive agenda for the Austrian bishops' conferences.[21] The range of duties of a national bishops' conference arises of itself from its nature and composition. To begin with, among its responsibilities will naturally be that range of duties which, while belonging to the individual bishop who is its member in virtue of his office and his ordinary jurisdiction, cannot in practice be fulfilled by him without the agreement and co-operation of the other bishops in the same country. Within the limits of these duties a bishops' conference, at least if it succeeds in achieving the free agreement of all its members, is the bearer and wielder of its own duties and rights[22] (even though the result will represent only diocesan law as long as a bishops' conference does not as a college possess its own sovereign authority or chooses in a given case not to exercise it). Not only properly pastoral questions committed to the individual bishops are comprised in the conference's duties. These include also the duty of representing before the State the particular Church which is brought together in the national bishops' conference. This can be deduced of itself from what we have said, and historically, too, it has been the occasion for the formation of such bishops' conferences. Its tasks also extend to fulfilling the role of chief supervisor to those ecclesiastical organisations and institutions which are themselves of an interdiocesan kind (although this may vary in degree according to the particular nature of the institution in question). For modern social development has brought it about that in the ecclesiastical sphere, too, societies and institutions have had to be created extending as single entities over several dioceses (and yet which are not 'exempt' like certain religious orders). One need only think, for example, of the

---

[20] The first such continental bishops' conference was held at Rio de Janeiro in 1955 from 25 July to 4 August as the Latin American bishops' conference. Cf. also *AAS* XLVII (1955), pp. 539–544: Pius XII, '*Ad Ecclesiam Christi*'; *Conferencia general del Episcopado Latino-Americano* (Rome 1956).

[21] *AKKR* LXXX (1920), p. 382 *sq.*; similarly for Latin America, *AKKR* LXXX (1920), p. 766 *sq.*

[22] 'It is quite clear that what is discussed and decided at a bishops' conference has no need of being submitted also to the Apostolic See': J. B. Sägmüller, *Lehrbuch des katholischen Kirchenrechtes* I, 4 (Freiburg 1934), p. 613, note 4.

German Caritas Organisation, of the many organisations with a central administration covering the whole territory of the Federal Republic, of the national branches of papal works of charity, and so on. So long as a bishops' conference is not the bearer of sovereign authority these inter-diocesan institutions have on the side of the hierarchy nothing really corresponding to them of the same status from the formal legal point of view. From a pastoral standpoint, a bishop must encourage and promote such an inter-diocesan organisation within his diocese; from the legal standpoint he is not really equal to it. Only by friendly agreement can their relationship be regulated at the moment, as long as the bishop does not wish to have recourse to the extreme means of forbidding such an organisation in his territory altogether. This fact, too, clearly leads us to the need for a bishops' conference, and moreover one with its own authority, in order that a legally equal partner should stand over against these inder-diocesan organisations. This does not necessarily mean that all these inter-diocesan organisations would have to be mere organs of the bishops' conference without any autonomy of their own, irrespective of their particular nature. The more precise determination of their relationship to a bishops' conference depends assuredly also on their *own* proper nature and the degree of their 'ecclesiality', which varies considerably between the various institutions.

If the exposition of the duties of individual bishops in the doctrinal section is correct, it follows as a consequence that such a bishops' conference, simply as the assembly of several bishops, has of itself duties also towards the central government of the Church and towards the universal Church. For these duties and tasks fall upon the individual bishop already, and so all the more do they fall upon a bishops' conference without there being required for this in principle any special authorisation from the pope. After all, the individual bishop is not a mere recipient of orders or executive of the supreme, central authority in the Church: on the contrary, as a bearer of ordinary jurisdiction by divine law and as a member of the college of bishops he also has the mission, right and duty to maintain an active attitude over against the papal central government, even if such a duty, in the face of the universal primacy of jurisdiction of the Roman pope (and this even regarding the individual bishop), is not susceptible of a strictly juridical codification, one which would allow a claim to be laid before a higher instance to ensure that these rights and duties are respected by the Roman central government. An active influence of this kind from the individual diocese upon the central government has always in fact been present. Naturally every bishop has the right to have recourse to the highest authority in the Church with petitions, submissions, information, proposals, complaints, etc., and he does so almost of necessity, because the reports required of him are in the concrete not merely something like the rendering of accounts by a provincial official before the central government but inevitably also represent quite justifiably an influencing of the supreme government of the Church. If, then, the individual bishop is not the mere executive arm of the supreme central leadership of the Church but also, even if in a completely para-canonical way, actively shares in the universal government[23] of the Church (although this participation by the individual as such does not possess a properly sovereign character), this is all the more true of a conference of bishops. Moreover, it would be quite likely that in the case of the bishops' conference such assistance in government would be laid down in the positive, human law of the Church. (For example, in the filling of episcopal sees its assistance may be prescribed, or it may be granted the right to be heard before decisions are made by the Roman Congregations.)

Among the duties of a bishops' conference which derive simply from the nature and the mission of the episcopal office itself there is after all also that of playing a part in meeting the needs and problems of other parts of the Church. Of its nature, for example, a bishops' conference must assume an obligation for the propagation of the faith throughout the world. When campaigns like '*Misereor*' for the developing countries or '*Adveniat*' for Latin America are supported by a bishops' conference, this corresponds precisely to the theological nature of such a conference.

Regarding the range of its tasks, ultimately we must surely consider the fact that it is in principle possible and in many cases perhaps also desirable that the Holy See should transfer to such a bishops' conference the competence over certain matters which do not immediately follow from its particular nature but which can be habitually delegated to it by the Holy See as a participation in its own responsibilities of divine or

---

[23] We have already referred above to the 'ordinary magisterium' of the whole episcopate, through which the individual bishop is in fact the teacher not only of his own diocese, although his authority to teach with respect to his diocese is of a different kind in sacred law from his participation in the ordinary teaching office of the college of bishops with respect to the universal Church.

positive human law. While hitherto, for example, the Holy See has reserved to itself each and every regulation of the official liturgy of the Western Church, it would be quite possible and desirable that certain responsibilities in this field, at least within previously defined limits (for example, the regulation of the more precise proportions to be observed between the Latin and the vernacular liturgy) should be committed to such national or continental bishops' conferences. With respect to this sector of possible duties conferred upon a bishops' conference there then arises the question whether each particular actualisation of this sort of competence by a bishops' conference should then again be made dependent for its validity upon a special act of approbation by Rome or not, a question arising from the Pope's general right of supervision over all that goes on in the Church, based upon his primacy of jurisdiction. The answer to this question will largely depend, from the material point of view, on the particular kind of powers in question and cannot therefore be answered in the same way for all cases. However, basing ourselves upon the principle of subsidiarity and the necessity for a bishops' conference to be a genuine intermediate instance between the individual diocese and the papal primacy, we may say that as great an independence and autonomy as possible is desirable for such bishops' conferences even in their relationship with Rome.

In conclusion we may attempt a final consideration concerning the inner structure of such a bishops' conference. Such a college must naturally have a president. It is taken for granted that this president is not the nuncio or apostolic delegate to the country in question. Where there already exists in a particular country a traditional primate (beyond the mere title) this primate will quite naturally be the president of the national bishops' conference. Where there is no such primate it will be scarcely necessary in this day and age to confer such a title on the president of a national bishops' conference. It will rather be quite natural for the senior cardinal or metropolitan to be the president. Such a bishops' conference, because it will have permanent commitments, will also form commissions assigned to the different spheres of interest (education, press, State relations, charitable organisation, etc.), and it will have a permanent office (secretariat) and a public relations service corresponding to the size of the bishops' conference and the range of its concerns[24].

[24] Cf. in connection with this e.g. in Houtart (note 3 above) the account given of the commissions (or departments) of bishops' conferences (pp. 505–506) in the

In this connection we must finally touch briefly upon the most delicate question of all, namely *how* the decisions of a bishops' conference are to be reached. Since all bishops' conferences up to the present have been free meetings without any proper authority of their own between individual bishops, their decisions have been based upon the free agreement of all the bishops and have bound each bishop legally only by his own consent. To be sure there are many bishops who feel that this system of a merely fraternal discussion should be maintained even in the future. They fear that otherwise, if one may put it this way, they will find in addition to the pope in Rome another Lord and Master nearer at hand who brings with him the danger that the bishop is no longer the Master and Father in his own diocese but has become the subordinate executive of this intermediate instance, and in this case it does not make much difference whether this new Lord and Master is the majority of the conference or perhaps in practice its president or the primate of the country. On the other hand, it must be recognised quite simply that the bishops' conference is an urgent necessity because in the sociological and pastoral conditions of today a quick, secure and efficient intermediate instance is necessary. And at least in the case of many countries it may be doubted whether today or in the near future a bishops' conference can fulfil its functions as we have conceived them, if its decisions remain in all cases dependent upon the agreement and the goodwill of each and every individual bishop.[25] The question therefore arises whether the bishops' conference of the future must not be legally recognised as possessing a superior authority, enabling it to make a decision binding upon all its members even if the complete unanimity of all its members is unobtainable. Perhaps a possible solution to the problem would be to strike a middle path between these two systems of decision-making (of a free agreement or a majority decision binding upon all) by assigning from the beginning certain areas of its work to the one method of arriving at a decision and others to the other. Another middle path would be found, for example, by

[25] In Brazil it has happened even in recent times that individual bishops have openly protested against the decisions of a commission appointed by a bishops' conference and have rejected it as having no competence.

various countries, of the permanent secretariats of bishops' conferences (pp. 506–508), of CELAM (the council of the Latin American bishops in Bogotà) (pp. 516–519, 522–532). Concerning the establishment of the French bishops' conference cf. *Herder-Korrespondenz* XVI (1961/2), pp. 447–450.

laying it down in the constitution of such a national bishops' conference that a majority decision of the conference binds all members only whenever the majority is two-thirds or more of all those present, and that in other cases the individual bishop remains free to decide on objective grounds whether he will accede to the majority decision or not.

In conclusion we may add two remarks. The foregoing considerations refer to the abstract and formal nature of a bishops' conference, to its formal juridical structure. The real importance of such a conference can only be clearly seen if one turns one's eyes to the urgent concrete pastoral needs and problems facing the Church in this day and age. If as a result of this the need for bishops' conferences is demonstrated, it will also become much clearer what their nature must be and why they are an urgent necessity, something being urged by the development of the constitutional law of the Church. The second remark is this: what has been said here is a purely private reflection, and not even that of an expert in the question; therefore its value is no more than the value of the reasons advanced in its favour.

C. THE INDIVIDUAL AND THE CHURCH

23

ANONYMOUS CHRISTIANS

IT is almost two thousand years since the Church received her commission to preach the message of Christ to all nations unto the ends
of the earth. In principle we have reached those ends of the earth:
the limits of our world have been marked out. Yet what position does
the message of Christ occupy in it?

In the ancient cultures of Asia it has never been able to gain a foothold,
and in the West where it became one of the historical roots it is still
steadily losing in importance and influence. The Christian faith is widely
interpreted as one possible form of religious explanation of man's existence,
alongside of which others are to be ranged either by an equal right or
even as showing greater promise. Religion itself appears to many as only
one of many forms of man's understanding of himself, which should be
allowed to have its say or which should be combated as harmful.

This is the situation in which the believing Christian finds himself, and
he is forced to recognise that the future will only bring this picture into
sharper relief,[1] that the saying about the little flock will become still more
true in spite of all the Church's pastoral and missionary efforts.

The Christian is convinced that in order to achieve salvation man must
believe in God, and not merely in God but in Christ; that this faith is not
merely a positive commandment from which one could be dispensed
under certain conditions; that membership of the one true Church does
not constitute a merely extrinsic condition from which it would be
appropriate for someone to be freed by the mere fact that he does not and
cannot know about it and its necessity. On the contrary, this faith is in

[1] Cf. K. Rahner, 'The Teaching of Vatican II on the Church and the Future Reality
of Christian Life' in *The Christian of the Future* (Freiburg/London 1967), pp. 77-101.

itself necessary and therefore demanded absolutely, not merely as a commandment but as the only possible means, not as a condition alone but as an unavoidable way of access, for man's salvation is nothing less than the fulfilment and definitive coming to maturity of precisely *this* beginning, for which therefore nothing else can substitute. – In this sense there really is no salvation outside the Church, as the old theological formula has it. But can the Christian believe even for a moment that the overwhelming mass of his brothers, not only those before the appearance of Christ right back to the most distant past (whose horizons are being constantly extended by palaeontology) but also those of the present and of the future before us, are unquestionably and in principle excluded from the fulfilment of their lives and condemned to eternal meaninglessness? He must reject any such suggestion, and his faith is itself in agreement with his doing so. For the scriptures tell him expressly that God wants everyone to be saved (1 Tm 2:4); the covenant of peace which God made with Noah after the flood has never been abrogated: on the contrary, the Son of God himself has sealed it with the incontestable authority of his self-sacrificing love embracing all men.

But when we have to keep in mind both principles together, namely the necessity of Christian faith and the universal salvific will of God's love and omnipotence, we can only reconcile them by saying that somehow all men must be capable of being members of the Church; and this capacity must not be understood merely in the sense of an abstract and purely logical possibility, but as a real and historically concrete one. – But this means in its turn that there must be degrees of membership of the Church, not only in ascending order from being baptised, through the acceptance of the fullness of the Christian faith and the recognition of the visible head of the Church, to the living community of the Eucharist, indeed to the realisation of holiness, but also in descending order from the explicitness of baptism into a non-official and anonymous Christianity which can and should yet be called Christianity in a meaningful sense, even though it itself cannot and would not describe itself as such. If it be true that the man who is the object of the Church's missionary endeavour is or can be already prior to it a man who is on the way towards his salvation and finds it in certain circumstances without being reached by the Church's preaching, and if it be true at the same time that the salvation which he achieves is the salvation of Christ, because there is no other, then it must be possible to be not only an anonymous 'theist', but also an anonymous *Christian*, and this (since the Church of Christ is not a purely interior reality) not in any merely intangible inner way, but also with a *certain* making visible and tangible of the anonymous relationship. – How is a relationship of this kind to be conceived?

It cannot be simply given already by the mere fact of being human. The attempt to account for the grace of redemption and nearness to God in such a way would merely negate it *as* grace. Grace, as the free self-communication of God to his creature, does presuppose the creature, and this in such possession of its being and its capacities that it can stand in and on itself and bear witness to the glory of that almighty creative power and goodness which was able to say of its works that they were good. At the same time such a creature must be given the possibility of hearing and accepting as beyond itself the incalculable new turning of God towards it in his revelation. That is to say, it must be, to begin with, a being of unlimited openness for the limitless being of God, therefore that being we call spirit. Spirit signifies that immaterial being prior to and going beyond every individual thing that can be known and grasped, that openness which is always already opened by the creative call of infinite mystery which is and must be the ultimate and the first, the all-inclusive and the fathomless ground of all that can be grasped, of all that is real and all that is possible. In order to know something of this mystery which we call God there is also required some knowledge of his superiority over the world and of his personality, knowledge therefore of the fact that the fathomlessness of this ground is that of a freedom which man has to thank for his own awakening and of which he knows at the same time that it has not yet opened itself utterly and bound itself completely by this its first still open call. Awakened by its creative word, he now awaits more profound communication. Does the divine liberty banish him into the distance of its silence or has it given him these ears that he may now hear for the first time its real word?

Man therefore is not only *capable* of hearing a possible word from his hidden God, but in the sense we have explained is also positively expecting it, little as he has the least right to demand it. Every denial of this fact of his being ordered to the unsurpassably Absolute would implicitly merely affirm it once more, for it too would speak with the claim of absolute truth, would be subject to the demand of an indisputable good, would derive its force from the desire for a final and definitive meaning.

Now, how does this tendency towards God, which is on occasion quite implicit and incoherent and yet always completely permeates man's being and existence, include a reference to the incarnate God, to Jesus Christ? – Much as the fact of Christ is the freest and in this sense (although only in this sense) the most contingent fact of reality, it is equally the most decisive and important and moreover the fact which has the most obvious relevance to man. If one takes it seriously that God has become man, then – it must be said – man is that which happens when God expresses and divests himself. Man is accordingly in the most basic definition that which God becomes if he sets out to show himself in the region of the extra-divine.[2] And conversely, formulating it from the point of view of man: man is he who realises himself when he gives himself away into the incomprehensible mystery of God. Seen in this way, the incarnation of God is the uniquely supreme case of the actualisation of man's nature in general.

It is true that before Christ no philosopher ever recognised in man's self-interpretation these depths of the human reality, but as a historical being man is one who in the concrete comes to be and to know what he is only in the unfolding of his history. Now that his thinking is illuminated by the light of the revelation which has in fact been made in the historically accomplished reality of Christ, he can recognise this unapproachable height as that perfection of his own being which can be effected by God, not in order that in a rationalistic fashion man may have it under his control but in order that he may more fully recognise the fact that he is ordained to this mystery. Bestowal of grace and incarnation as the two basic modes of God's self-communication can therefore be conceived as the most radical modes of man's spiritual being, beyond his powers to compel and yet precisely as such eminently fulfilling the transcendence of his being.

The believer will then also grasp that this absolute eminence is not an optional adjunct to his reality; that it is not given to him as the juridical and external demand of God's will for him, but that this self-communication by God offered to all and fulfilled in the highest way in Christ rather constitutes the goal of all creation and – since God's word and will *effect* what they say – that, even before he freely takes up an attitude to it, it stamps and determines man's nature and lends it a character which we may call a 'supernatural existential'. A refusal of this offer would therefore

[2] Cf. the more detailed reasoning given in our essay, 'On the Theology of the Incarnation' in *Theological Investigations* IV (London & Baltimore 1966), pp. 105–120.

not leave man in a state of pure unimpaired nature, but would bring him into contradiction with himself even in the sphere of his own being. This means positively that man in experiencing his transcendence, his limitless openness – no matter how implicit and incomprehensible it always is – also already experiences the offer of grace – not necessarily expressly *as* grace, as a distinctly supernatural calling, but experiences the reality of its content. But this means that the express revelation of the word in Christ is not something which comes to us from without as entirely strange, but only the explicitation of what we already are by grace and what we experience at least incoherently in the limitlessness of our transcendence. The expressly Christian revelation becomes the explicit statement of the revelation of grace which man always experiences implicitly in the depths of his being.

If man accepts the revelation, he posits by that fact the act of supernatural faith. But he also already accepts this revelation whenever he really accepts *himself completely*, for it already speaks *in* him. Prior to the explicitness of official ecclesiastical faith this acceptance can be present in an implicit form whereby a person undertakes and lives the duty of each day in the quiet sincerity of patience, in devotion to his material duties and the demands made upon him by the persons under his care. What he is then taking upon himself is therefore not merely his basic relationship with the silent mystery of the Creator-God. Accordingly, no matter how he wants to understand and express this in his own reflective self-understanding, he is becoming thereby not merely an anonymous 'theist', but rather takes upon himself in that Yes to himself the grace of the mystery which has radically approached us. 'God has given himself to man in direct proximity': perhaps the essence of Christianity can be reduced to this formula.

In the acceptance of himself man is accepting Christ as the absolute perfection and guarantee of his own anonymous movement towards God by grace, and the acceptance of this belief is again not an act of man alone but the work of God's grace which is the grace of Christ, and this means in its turn the grace of his Church which is only the continuation of the mystery of Christ, his permanent visible presence in our history.

It is true that it would be wrong to go so far as to declare every man, whether he accepts the grace or not, an 'anonymous Christian'. Anyone who in his basic decision were really to deny and to reject his being ordered to God, who were to place himself decisively in opposition to his own concrete being, should not be designated a 'theist', even an anonymous 'theist'; only someone who gives – even if it be ever so confusedly – the glory to *God* should be thus designated. Therefore no matter what a man states in his conceptual, theoretical and religious reflection, anyone who does not say in his *heart*, 'there is no God' (like the 'fool' in the psalm) but testifies to him by the radical acceptance of his being, is a believer. But if in this way he believes in deed and in truth in the holy mystery of God, if he does not suppress this truth but leaves it free play, then the grace of this truth by which he allows himself to be led is always already the grace of the Father in his Son. And anyone who has let himself be taken hold of by this grace can be called with every right an 'anonymous Christian'.

This name implicitly signifies that this fundamental actuation of a man, like all actuations, cannot and does not want to stop in its anonymous state but strives towards an explicit expression, towards its full name. An unfavourable historical environment may impose limitations on the explicitness of this expression so that this actuation may not exceed the explicit appearance of a loving humaneness, but it will not act against this tendency whenever a new and higher stage of explicitness is presented to it right up to the ultimate perfection of a consciously accepted profession of Church membership. Here alone does this belief find not merely its greatest support and source of confidence but also its proper reality and that peace which St Augustine likened to repose in being: peace and repose which do not mean stagnation and flight but the capacity of casting oneself all the more resolutely into the inexorable will of the mystery of God, since now, as St Paul says, one knows whom one believes and to whom one fearlessly submits in radical trust.

To anyone who thinks that he cannot or dare not believe (perhaps because he fails to appreciate to what an immeasurable experience of relentless love the acceptance of its human nearness can call us – from a great distance, as though its mystery and its sublimity might thereby be destroyed), or to anyone who is quite certain that he does not believe, these reflections may mean very little, and they are not in the first place directed to him, although they could make even him attentive to the voice inside him. What is said about the 'anonymous Christian' would therefore be completely misunderstood if it were thought that it represents merely a last desperate attempt in a world where Christian faith is fast disappearing to 'rescue' in its ultimate significance all that is good and human for the Church – against every freedom of the spirit. But the Christian who finds himself in a diaspora situation[3] which is becoming increasingly acute, the believer who finds his faith and his hope sorely tried at the sight of his unbelieving brothers,[4] can derive from it comfort and the strength of objectivity. Knowledge about the anonymous Christian does not in any way dispense him from caring and troubling about those who do not yet know the one necessary truth in its explicit affirmation in the gospel message. But this knowledge will keep him from panic and will give him the strength to practice that patience which – according to the Lord's saying – brings salvation to life, his own as much as that of his brother.

Our topic with all its urgency cannot be avoided or dismissed as unimportant either by a theology of grace and of the Church which has a true understanding of itself, or by an honest pastoral theology which looks at our times dispassionately. The exact word may not have any importance, but the matter we are contemplating is undeniably of central importance for the relations of the contemporary Christian to the world around him. *Theologically* we should not make any mistake in assigning its proper 'place' to the doctrine of 'anonymous Christianity': this is not a hermeneutic *principle* critically to *reduce* the whole corpus of traditional theology and dogmatics (in the same way as an existentialist interpretation or the theses of the Anglican Bishop Robinson) and thereby to make Christianity in this form more acceptable; from a dogmatic point of view, this doctrine is perhaps even a *peripheral* phenomenon whose necessity, lawfulness and correctness derive from many other individual data of ecclesiastical teaching or are at least demanded by them.[5] As again this dogmatic-theoretical position, a theology which proceeds in a more historical-existential-practical way can certainly assign to these statements about 'anonymous Christianity' a more central position,[6] yet without coming into conflict with other fundamental dogmatic certainties. It

---

[3] Cf. also K. Rahner, 'Der Christ und seine Umwelt', *Stimmen der Zeit* XC (1965), pp. 481–489.

[4] Cf. K. Rahner, *Im Heute glauben*, Theol. Meditationen 9 (Einsiedeln 1965).

[5] This difference from Bultmann's demythologisation is perhaps too little stressed in the otherwise good article by H. Ott, 'Existentiale Interpretation und anonyme Christlichkeit' in *Zeit und Geschichte: Festgabe R. Bultmann* edited by E. Dinkler (Tübingen 1964), pp. 367–379.

[6] Cf. in a wider context K. Rahner, *Handbuch der Pastoraltheologie* II (Freiburg 1966), Kap. VII, §3, §4 no. 6, etc.

would be quite foolish to think that this talk about 'anonymous Christianity' must lessen the importance of mission, preaching, the Word of God, baptising, and so on.[7] Anyone who wants to interpret our remarks about anonymous Christianity in this way, has not merely fundamentally misunderstood them, but has not read our exposition of them with sufficient attention.[8] I think that only two things are necessary in order to understand correctly what is intended by this phrase: some really thorough *thinking* about various fundamental data of the traditional theology of the Schools, data which often are left lying together in sterile proximity, and at the same time an unbiased contemplation of the *real* situation of mankind, of Christianity and of the Church today.[9]

What is meant by this thesis of the anonymous Christian is actually also taught materially in the Constitution on the Church of Vatican II (no. 16). According to this document those who have not yet received the gospel and this *without any fault* of their own (and this possibility is clearly presupposed as a real one) are given the possibility of eternal salvation ('*aeterna salus*', which can only be understood of supernatural salvation). The only condition is, from the point of view of *God*, '*gratiae influxus*' (or '*divina gratia*' as it is also called), and from the point of view of *man*, '*Deum sincero corde quaerere eiusque voluntatem per conscientiae dictamen agnitam operibus adimplere*'. This fulfilment of the duty of conscience is explicitly supposed as possible also in the case of those '*qui sine culpa ad expressam agnitionem Dei nondum pervenerunt*'. That an inculpable atheism of this kind can last a long time whether individually or collectively is not stated, but not excluded either. Since this atheism is seen only in opposition to '*expressa agnitio Dei*', there is a clear indication that beneath such an atheism there may very well lie an unreflected, merely existentially actualised theism (precisely by a radical obedience to the dictates of conscience). But an incoherent theism of this kind can in

---

[7] Cf. e.g. L. Elders, 'Die Taufe der Weltreligionen. Bemerkungen zu einer Theorie Karl Rahners' in *Theologie und Glaube* LV (1965), pp. 124–131.

[8] Let me refer the reader merely to *Theological Investigations* V (London & Baltimore 1966), p. 131 *sq*. Regarding the dispute with L. Elders let me draw attention to the account by F. Ricken, '"Ecclesia ... universale salutis sacramentum": Theologische Erwägungen zur Lehre der Dogmatischen Konstitution "De Ecclesia" über die Kirchenzugehörigkeit', *Scholastik* XL (1965), pp. 352–388, esp. pp. 382–385 (note 147).

[9] For a further presentation cf. the abundant documentation given by Kl. Riesenhuber, 'Der anonyme Christ, nach Karl Rahner' *ZKT* LXXXVI (1964), pp. 286–303.

certain circumstances surely last a long time, without it becoming at any time during this period impossible to say any longer '*aeternam salutem consequi possunt*'. In its statements the Constitution on the Church is in no way implying that here in these cases salvation is achieved as it were in a substitute fashion by means of a purely natural morality. This would indeed contradict scripture and the magisterium.[10] It is also excluded by the words of the Constitution itself: salvation is reached '*non sine divina gratia*', '*sub influxu gratiae*'.

There is no justification for regarding this grace as being supernatural in a merely ontic, pre-conscious sense, such as would be required for the positing of any moral act which, as far as consciousness was concerned, was purely natural. Rather must we conceive this grace as more than merely ontic, as also entering consciousness and therefore as engendering true faith in the theological sense, even though this is not yet reflective.[11] The lesser interpretation is also excluded by a remark in the same Council's decree on the Missions (no. 7), in which it is explicitly said that God 'in the unknown ways' of his grace can give the *faith* without which there is no salvation even to those who have not yet heard the preaching of the gospel. Although in the face of this theological optimism of the Council regarding salvation it remains the task of theology to show why the necessity of the gospel, of the Church and the sacraments are not thereby devalued, it is quite impossible to doubt that what is *meant* by the 'anonymous Christian' (the name itself is unimportant) is compatible with the Council's teaching, indeed is explicitly stated by it. Neither is this the place to demonstrate that such a theory in no way cripples the missionary impulse of the Church but rather puts before it the person to whom it addresses itself in his true hopeful condition so that it can approach him with confidence.

[10] Cf. *DS* 3867 *sqq.*

[11] These two sentences are an amplification of the original German text made in the light of explanations furnished by the author himself. [Translator's note.]

LIST OF SOURCES[1]

1 THE MAN OF TODAY AND RELIGION

The first version of this was published under the title 'Der Unternehmer und die Religion' in a publication of the consortium E. V. Bonn (Bonn 1962), pp. 26–42 (the lecture given on 26 October 1962). A revised version was given in a lecture in the German Library in Rome and published after renewed revision and expansion in *Der Seelsorger* XXXV (1965), pp. 18–30.

2 A SMALL QUESTION REGARDING THE CONTEMPORARY PLURALISM IN THE INTELLECTUAL SITUATION OF CATHOLICS AND THE CHURCH

First published in *Stimmen der Zeit* XC (1965), pp. 191–199.

3 REFLECTIONS ON DIALOGUE WITHIN A PLURALISTIC SOCIETY

The speech of thanks at the celebration in connection with the bestowal of the Reuchlin Prize by the town of Pforzheim on 26 June 1965. The speech was printed in a revised form by the authorities of Pforzheim as a booklet under the same title. Cf. also *Stimmen der Zeit* XC (1965), pp. 321–330.

4 IDEOLOGY AND CHRISTIANITY

A talk to Catholic students of the University of Erlangen on 15 July 1964, published in *Concilium* I (1965), pp. 475–483 (German edition). [This has appeared in another translation in the English edition of *Concilium* Vol. 6, No. 1 (June 1965), pp. 23–31.]

---

1 We obviously cannot list here the numerous reprints in German or any of the translations which have appeared, apart from a few cases where there is some special justification for doing so.

5 MARXIST UTOPIA AND THE CHRISTIAN FUTURE OF MAN

A talk given on 1 May 1965 in Salzburg at a meeting of the *Paulus-Gesellschaft* on the theme 'Christianity and Marxism'. First published in *Orientierung* XXIX (1965), pp. 107–110 (No. 9 of 15 May).

6 PHILOSOPHY AND THEOLOGY

A talk given at a symposium on 'The Significance of European Culture for Universal History' in Salzburg 27–29 September 1961. The text printed here follows a tape-recording which was slightly edited. First published in *Kairos* IV (1962), pp. 162–169.

7 A SMALL FRAGMENT 'ON THE COLLECTIVE FINDING OF TRUTH'

Contribution to a *Festschrift* in honour of Helmut Kuhn, *Epimeleia: Die Sorge der Philosophie um den Menschen*, published by Franz Wiedmann (Munich 1964), pp. 61–67.

8 SCRIPTURE AND THEOLOGY

An article printed in *Handbuch theologischer Grundbegriffe* edited by H. Fries (Munich 1963), Vol. II, pp. 517–525.

9 SCRIPTURE AND TRADITION

Lecture given at a meeting of the Catholic Academy in Bavaria on 10 February 1963 in Munich. Published in *Wort und Wahrheit* XVIII (1963), pp. 269–279, and in *Das Zweite Vatikanische Konzil*, No. 24 in the series 'Studien und Berichte der Katholischen Akademie in Bayern' edited by K. Forster (Würzburg 1963), pp. 71–91.

10 REFLECTIONS ON THE CONTEMPORARY INTELLECTUAL FORMATION OF FUTURE PRIESTS

Published in *Stimmen der Zeit* XC (1964/5), pp. 173–193. That essay has been reproduced here without alteration; but cf. the amplification provided in note 1.

11 THE SECRET OF LIFE

Lecture given at a meeting of the Catholic Academy of the archdiocese of Freiburg i. Br. on 23 May 1965 at Mannheim. The text has been revised and is published here for the first time.

12   THE UNITY OF SPIRIT AND MATTER IN THE CHRISTIAN
     UNDERSTANDING OF FAITH

A paper given at the Pentecost congress of lay theologians at Münster-
Gievenbeck, Haus Mariengrund, 4–8 June 1963, and also given as a
lecture on 27 April 1963 in Salzburg. Published together with the paper
'Das Selbstverständnis der Theologie vor dem Anspruch der Natur-
wissenschaft' in a special issue of the periodical *Religionsunterricht an
höheren Schulen* (Patmos-Verlag, Düsseldorf 1963). The author has in
certain parts of this paper taken over formulations from his *Hominisation:
The Evolutionary Origin of Man as a Theological Problem*, Quaestiones
Disputatae No. 13 (Freiburg and London 1965).

13   THEOLOGY OF FREEDOM

A lecture given on 30 November 1964 at the one hundred and seventy-
fifth anniversary celebration of Georgetown University within the framework of the 'Patrick F. Healy Conference on "Freedom and Man"'. The
text given here has been revised and considerably expanded.

14   GUILT – RESPONSIBILITY – PUNISHMENT WITHIN THE
     VIEW OF CATHOLIC THEOLOGY

A contribution to the cycle of lectures at the University of Zürich in
the winter term 1962/3 given on 17 January 1963. Published in the
symposium *Schuld – Verantwortung – Strafe im Lichte der Theologie,
Jurisprudenz, Soziologie, Medizin und Philosophie*, edited by Prof. E. R.
Frey (Zürich 1964), pp. 151–172.

15   JUSTIFIED AND SINNER AT THE SAME TIME

Published in *Geist und Leben* XXXVI (1963), pp. 434–443.

16   REFLECTIONS ON THE UNITY OF THE LOVE OF NEIGHBOUR
     AND THE LOVE OF GOD

Theological draft of a lecture given at the general meeting of the
Katholische Fürsorgeverein für Mädchen, Frauen und Kinder on 11 May
1965 in Cologne. Published in *Geist und Leben* XXXVIII (1965), pp.
168–185.

17 THE CHURCH OF SINNERS

First published in *Stimmen der Zeit* LXXII (1947), pp. 163–177, afterwards separately under the same title (Freiburg i. Br. 1948 and Vienna 1948).

18 THE SINFUL CHURCH IN THE DECREES OF VATICAN II

The main part of this essay originates in a study written by the author for the collective work *L'Église de Vatican II*, edited by P. Guillaume Baraúna, O.F.M., and published in seven languages. The text given here is one which has been expanded by incorporating considerations relating to *De Oecumenismo* and by amplifying the exegetical and dogmatic-historical part.

19 THE CHURCH AND THE PAROUSIA OF CHRIST

Lecture given at the united meeting. of the Protestant and Catholic ecumenical working-groups in April 1963. Published in *Catholica* XVII (1963), pp. 113–128.

20 THE EPISCOPAL OFFICE

Published in *Stimmen der Zeit* LXXXIX (1963/4), pp. 161–195, and in W. Stählin, J. H. Lerche, E. Fincke, L. Klein and K. Rahner, *Das Amt der Einheit: Grundlegendes zur Theologie des Bischofsamtes* (Stuttgart 1964), pp. 245–311. The foreword which has here been prefixed to the article was specially written for the present volume.

21 PASTORAL-THEOLOGICAL OBSERVATIONS ON EPISCOPACY IN THE TEACHING OF VATICAN II

Published in *Concilium* I (1965), pp. 170–174 (German edition). [This has appeared in another translation in the English edition of *Concilium* Vol. 3, No. 1 (March 1965), pp. 10–14.]

22 ON BISHOPS' CONFERENCES

Published in *Stimmen der Zeit* LXXXVIII (1962/3), pp. 267–283.

23 ANONYMOUS CHRISTIANS

This essay was originally a broadcast review of the book by A. Röper, *Die anonymen Christen* (Mainz 1963) which was put on the air in the summer of 1964 by *Westdeutscher Rundfunk* and has never before been published. In preparing it for publication here any references to its original context have been removed and some additional matter has been incorporated which tries to take account of certain objections.

Index

INDEX OF PERSONS

SUBJECT INDEX

Angels:
  as mundane and cosmic beings 151,
    158 *sq*., 172
Art:
  meaning lost when limited to signifi-
    cance for business 3
Atheism:
  made possible by characteristics of
    knowledge of God 79 *sqq*.
  inculpable type seen as unreflected,
    merely existentially actualised
    theism 397 *sq*.

Baptism:
  importance not lessened by talk of
    'anonymous Christianity' 397
Bible, cf. Scripture

Cardinal:
  College of Cardinals 325 *sqq*.
Christianity:
  involves development in man towards
    dominion of nature 9 *sqq*., 17 *sqq*.
  reasons for alleged stigma as negative
    ideology 45 *sqq*.
  not an ideology and thus not to be
    rejected on that score 47 *sqq*., 55*sq*.
  and transcendental experience of man
    50 *sqq*.
  essentially a history 52 *sqq*.
  'anonymous' element 54 *sqq*., 78 *sq*.,
    101, 238 *sq*., 390 *sqq*.
  necessity of tolerance 56 *sq*.
  necessity of guarding against danger
    of misunderstanding self as ideology
    57 *sqq*.
  as religion of future 60 *sq*., 300 *sqq*.,
    311 *sqq*.
  as religion of absolute future 61 *sqq*.

absence of utopian ideas about future
  in this world 80 *sqq*., 310 *sqq*.
inestimable significance towards
  movement for genuine and meaningful earthly goals 82 *sqq*.
permanence and this precisely as
  institutional religion 83 *sqq*.
as event in which God in his grace acts
  on us 99 *sqq*.
and significance of formula for
  existence itself 109 *sq*.
as the teaching about life as such 152
thesis of 'anonymous Christian' in
  Vatican II 397 *sq*.
Church:
  very much in a state of becoming
    when related to sanctified but not
    sacralised world 19 *sqq*.
  contemporary pluralism in intellectual
    situation of Catholics and the Church
    21 *sqq*.
  significance of catch-word 'dialogue'
    only appearing in present-day
    official pronouncements 34 *sqq*.
  as assembly of salvation and sacra-
    ment 53
  permanent religion of Christianity
    will always remain but concrete
    form of socio-ecclesiological struc-
    ture cannot be predicted 67
  as what is handed on 102 *sq*.
  as pilgrim 253 *sqq*., 281 *sqq*.
  of sinners 253 *sqq*., 270
  sinners in Church as article of faith
    256 *sqq*., 270 *sqq*.
  as sinful yet holy 259 *sqq*., 271 *sqq*.,
    281 *sqq*.
  attitude of sinful man to the holy
    Church of sinners 265 *sqq*.